The Official Guide to Corel PHOTO-PAINT™ 6 for Windows 95

About the Author...

David Huss is a graphics and desktop publishing consultant for several Fortune 100 companies and a regular speaker at Corel seminars. He is the author of *PHOTO-PAINT 5 Unleashed* and Corel Corporation's user manual for Corel PHOTO-PAINT™ 5 Plus.

The Official Guide to Corel PHOTO-PAINT™ 6 for Windows 95

David Huss

Osborne **McGraw-Hill**

Berkeley   New York   St. Louis   San Francisco
Auckland   Bogotá   Hamburg   London
Madrid   Mexico City   Milan   Montreal
New Delhi   Panama City   Paris   São Paulo
Singapore   Sydney   Tokyo   Toronto

Osborne **McGraw-Hill**
2600 Tenth Street
Berkeley, California 94710
U.S.A.

For information on translations or book distributors outside the U.S.A., or to arrange bulk purchase discounts for sales promotions, premiums, or fundraisers, please contact Osborne **McGraw-Hill** at the above address.

The Official Guide to Corel PHOTO-PAINT™ 6 for Windows 95

1234567890 DOC 99876

ISBN 0-07-882207-6

Executive Editor: Scott Rogers
Editorial Assistant: Daniela Dell'Orco
Project Editor: Claire Splan
Copy Editor: Gary Morris
Proofreader: Pat Mannion
Technical Editor: Jennifer Campbell
Computer Designer: Jani Beckwith
Cover Designer: Ted Mader Associates
Color Insert: Mason Fong
Quality Control Specialist: Joe Scuderi

**This book is dedicated to
Mr. Bill Clayton— a great man and a good friend.**

CONTENTS AT A GLANCE

CONTENTS

The Official Guide to Corel PHOTO-PAINT™ 6 represents another in a series of books dedicated to the users of Corel software. This series gives users the ability to understand the depth of the software product they have purchased. The author, along with staff at Corel, has spent many hours working on the accuracy and scope of this book.

This publication will provide an in-depth overview of Corel PHOTO-PAINT 6. New users, as well as those who have purchased upgrades, will find significant value in these pages. The step-by-step tutorials will help improve your ability to make excellent use of Corel PHOTO-PAINT. The publication will also reveal tips and tricks which have been developed over several versions of the software by the most experienced users.

The "Official Guide to Corel" products series represents a giant step in the ability of Corel to disseminate information to our users through the help of Osborne/McGraw-Hill and the fine authors involved in the series. Congratulations to the team at Osborne who have created an excellent book.

Dr. Michael C.J. Cowpland
President & CEO
Corel Corporation

FOREWORD

No book of any size can be created without the help of a lot of people and this one is no exception. Writing a book about Corel PHOTO-PAINT is made even more challenging by the fact that it is a constantly evolving product—it is always being improved. My hat goes off first to Jennifer Campbell, the technical editor who made sure the program details in the book were correct (she also edits my articles for *Corel Magazine*). If it wasn't for her tireless efforts, there would be many areas of the book that wouldn't exactly match the product. Another trooper in the technical arena is Doug Chaoyn who works for Corel in Ottawa. His job was to field all of the "what does this do?" questions. I would also like to thank the Corel Quality Assurance team who went over the text with a fine-tooth comb and rooted out technical inaccuracies. They also tried to remove my lame jokes—without success (sorry fellows, better luck next time).

I would be remiss if I did not also thank Michael Bellefeuille for his supervision of the project. He was a great help. (Is it just me or is this starting to sound like an acceptance speech for the Academy Awards?) No thanks would be complete without acknowledging Dr. Michael Cowpland, whose vision created Corel. I also wish to thank Ide Ide who has done such a incredible job of technically directing the Corel products for the past few years. Lastly, thanks to Lucian Mustatea of Corel, who answered endless questions, complaints, and generally too long phone calls during the Corel PHOTO-PAINT 5 and Corel PHOTO-PAINT 5 Plus days.

The folks at Osborne/McGraw-Hill have done a Herculean task of converting my original manuscript into this book. Claire Splan has done something just short of magic in somehow deciphering all of the screen shots and putting them in the right order, as well as translating my fragments into complete sentences. She still, however, needs some work on her understanding of techno-gibberish. For example, she couldn't figure out the meaning of the following sentence: "It is therefore the Color Adjust filter with the Slider in past to the maximum with the preceding pixelation that it was done." (By the way, if you can understand it, get some therapy—quickly.) Thanks to Scott Rogers, my Acquisitions Editor, and Mason Fong, who did the layout for the wonderful color insert. Daniela Dell'Orco, who was my main contact at Osborne/McGraw-Hill, was a trooper and fun to work with.

ACKNOWLEDGMENTS

Enough already. I am sure I have missed someone who was of immense help in making this book, so this is the thank you to the unnamed contributors (it's like the Tomb of the Unknown Solider except there isn't a solider standing guard and all that neat stuff).

Hey! You need to read this part! This introduction is like the README file for this book. Writing a book about Corel PHOTO-PAINT is like shooting at a moving target. After I had completed most of the book, the stand-alone version of the product was released. The big surprise was that almost all of the 1,000 photographs included with the stand-alone package were different from the ones that shipped with the CorelDRAW 6 suite. Since some of these photographs are used in the step-by-step procedures, we needed to come up with a way to make these available to those who bought the standalone version. The solution is to make the missing pictures available through CorelNET. The address is **http:\\www.corelnet.com**. You can also get them from the Osborne/McGraw-Hill web site. The address is **http:\\www.osborne.com**. If you find a photograph that needs to be included in the web page, please let us now.

I hope you enjoy this book. Corel PHOTO-PAINT is a powerful tool, but it is fun to use as well. You can leave comments, complaints, and suggestions at my Internet address (**dhuss@prismnet.com**) or contact me on CompuServe (76575,241). I will try to answer questions as time allows but no promises. Corel PHOTO-PAINT questions only—any questions about raises, marriages, etc. should be directed to a psychic hot-line. I try and get to the PHOTO-PAINT page of CorelNET at least several times a week. I would love to see any work you are doing with Corel PHOTO-PAINT. Since I write articles every month in *Corel Magazine*, you might get your work included.

INTRODUCTION

Introducing Corel
PHOTO-PAINT 6

1

Y ou are about to begin an incredible journey into the world of photo-editing and digital wizardry. Is it me or does that last sentence sound like the preview for a new movie? This world of photo-editing was once the exclusive domain of multi-million dollar computer systems and dedicated graphic artists.

With Corel PHOTO-PAINT 6, you will quickly correct and produce images that can make your desktop projects dazzle. Photo-editing programs have traditionally been labor intensive. They required many hours of tedious effort in order to manipulate images (removing trees, adding people, changing sky color, etc.). Corel PHOTO-PAINT 6 greatly simplifies this time-consuming process. Just as CorelDRAW enables you to achieve professional computer graphic effects with little effort, Corel PHOTO-PAINT 6 will allow you to reach that same professional level in the manipulation of photographs, paintings, and other bitmap images. The bottom line is that Corel PHOTO-PAINT 6 is fun to work with, period. The fact that you can quickly produce professional results is a bonus. Next, Dave's genuine history of Corel PHOTO-PAINT.

A Brief History of Corel PHOTO-PAINT

Corel PHOTO-PAINT began its life as a software product called Photofinish, created by Zsoft. It was introduced as Corel PHOTO-PAINT 3 in May 1992. It was then, at best, an interesting bitmap editing package that was very similar to Microsoft PAINT, which Zsoft also wrote.

When Corel PHOTO-PAINT 4 was released in May 1993, there were many improvements, and only a small amount of the original Zsoft program remained in it. Corel PHOTO-PAINT 4 had limitations in the size of the image files it could handle, and the absence of several other key features prevented it from being a first-class product. In fact, it resembled Microsoft PAINT on steroids.

Corel PHOTO-PAINT 5, which Corel originally released in May 1994, showed marked improvement. There were many changes still in progress when the product had to ship. Those changes appeared when the maintenance release (E2) was shipped in September. Corel PHOTO-PAINT 5 began to draw serious attention from the graphics community with its support of objects and layers and other features.

With the current release, Corel PHOTO-PAINT 6 entered the world of 32-bit applications, offering a very robust set of photo-editing tools coupled with the power of a 32-bit architecture. If all this talk about 32-bit power is confusing, then—to borrow some terms from *Star Trek*—think of 32-bit power as warp drive and 16-bit as impulse power.

Corel PHOTO-PAINT 6 has changed substantially from the Corel PHOTO-PAINT 5 release. Keyboard assignments, drop-down lists, filter names, mask and object methodology, and dialog boxes have all been modified to improve the product. Throughout the book I have placed notes like this to alert Corel PHOTO-PAINT 5 users of specific changes.

Before We Get Started

One of the things that makes Corel PHOTO-PAINT such a powerful package is that there are so many combinations of tools and functions available. Of course, one of the things that make Corel PHOTO-PAINT confusing to a new user is that there are so many combinations of tools and functions available. If you are new to photo-editing programs, I have included a section in this book to help you understand the sometimes confusing world of bitmap images. If you are an experienced Photoshop user, I have tried to associate Corel names with their equivalent Adobe Photoshop names wherever appropriate.

If you have worked with Corel PHOTO-PAINT 5, you may be overwhelmed with the changes that have been made for release 6. Truth is, when I first opened the beta version in early 1995, I wondered if I would ever get used to the new changes. Remember that we beta testers did not have documentation, or help files for that matter. The Corel PHOTO-PAINT interface has changed, but not radically from version 5. The exciting news is in the program itself. But I am getting ahead of myself. First, let me formally introduce to you Corel PHOTO-PAINT 6.

The Envelope, Please

Corel PHOTO-PAINT 6 is foremost a photo- or image-editing program. It is in the same league as Adobe Photoshop, but it costs hundreds of dollars less. As a photo-editing program, it offers all of the features one should expect from a professional photo-editing package, and in several areas you will be able to do more with Corel PHOTO-PAINT 6 than with its main competitor. In case you are wondering why I mention Adobe Photoshop, it is because before Corel PHOTO-PAINT came along, Adobe Photoshop was the unchallenged leader in digital photo-editing. Corel is, not so quietly, trying to change that.

One of the more useful tasks you can perform with Corel PHOTO-PAINT 6 is to take a poorly composed, overexposed, scratchy photograph and make it look as if the photographer did a great job. Only you and Corel PHOTO-PAINT 6 will know the truth. People today tend to get excited about all of the breathtaking, surrealistic effects they can achieve with photo-editing packages such as Corel PHOTO-PAINT 6. In truth, I get excited, too. But it is the everyday work of making the images in our documents look as professional as possible, with the least amount of effort, that makes Corel PHOTO-PAINT 6 such an important addition to your desktop publishing library.

Changing Reality (Virtually)

With Corel PHOTO-PAINT 6 and this book, you will learn how easy it is to add people or objects to existing images. You can change a photograph's background that is a drab and dull into a beautiful, sunny sky as shown in Figure 1-1. More importantly, you will find it even easier to remove unwanted objects, like scratches, stains, or old boyfriends, which I have shown in Figure 1-2. You will even be able to change the way people look. I recently did a brochure for our church. The photo of one of the pastors had been taken several months and over 20 pounds ago. No problem with Corel PHOTO-PAINT 6. I took off those excess pounds in less than an hour—which is more than the pastor or the diet industry can say.

Altering people's appearance (removing blemishes, changing hair color, and so on) has been done by professionals for a long time. I knew a guy who was one of the kings of the airbrush (back in the pre-digital days), who was greatly appreciated by more than one playmate-of-the-month. Now, like my friend, you will be able to change the way people look. The only difference is that Corel PHOTO-PAINT 6 doesn't require an airbrush, long hours, or years of experience.

a

With Corel
PHOTO-
PAINT 6
we can
quickly
change an
uninteresting
photograph
into a
visually
appealing
one

b

FIGURE 1-1

What else can you do with Corel PHOTO-PAINT 6? We have been talking up until now about changing existing images, but you can also create original images. If you're not an artist, do not feel excluded from this discussion. Just as with CorelDRAW you are able to take clip art and assemble it to make exciting images, you can do the same with Corel PHOTO-PAINT 6. Corel has provided an assortment of objects that can be placed together to make a composite image. Using the Corel PHOTO-PAINT filters and its powerful editing tools, you will quickly learn to create all kinds of original images, logos, and what-have-yous (and still maintain your

a

Breaking up
may be hard
to do, as the
song goes,
but
removing
people from
photographs
is simple
with Corel
PHOTO-
PAINT 6

b

■ FIGURE 1-2

I'm-not-an-artist standing). In Figure 1-3 I have created a postcard by placing several floating objects on an existing photograph.

What's New in Corel PHOTO-PAINT 6?

The following is a list of the important features in Corel PHOTO-PAINT 6.

▶ **32-Bit Power**—Being a WIN'95 application has made Corel PHOTO-PAINT 6 nearly three times faster than Corel PHOTO-PAINT 5. This speed improvement is especially evident in some of the built-in filters that used to take forever to finish their work on large images.

This lovely scene is actually composed of several objects placed together on a background

◼ **FIGURE 1-3**

▶ **Unlimited File Size**—This is easily the biggest improvement for those using the product professionally. Corel PHOTO-PAINT 5 image file size was restricted to a 16MB image file. If the image was larger than 16MB, it was necessary to load it as a partial file. Corel PHOTO-PAINT 6 can load any size of image file without the need to load as a partial file.

▶ **Unlimited Undo Capability**—What more can I say? You are no longer limited to one of the real restrictions of programs of this nature, that of being able to only Undo the last command.

▶ **New Filters**—Many new filters have been added to the already robust set of filters that were part of Corel PHOTO-PAINT 5. There is a filter to automatically remove scratches and imperfections in a photograph, another that adds lens flare, lighting effects, and more.

▶ **Improved Mask Capabilities**—With Corel PHOTO-PAINT 6 you will experience a much larger selection of mask options. You can now feather masks, make them grow and shrink, or add borders to them. You can take objects and convert them to masks or convert objects to masks. There is even a command that will automatically remove those little pieces of masks that sometimes remained when using a Magic Wand mask tool on a multicolored background. If you worked with Corel PHOTO-PAINT 5, you will find the new selection of masks will dramatically increase your ability to control effects and image selections.

► **Improved Text Editing and Handling**—With Corel PHOTO-PAINT 5, you enter text directly on the image and the text becomes an object. With Corel PHOTO-PAINT 6, when text is placed on an image, the text becomes an object but still retains its text attributes and can be edited later.

► **Support for 16-Bit Plug-In Filters**—Many of the more popular plug-in filters have not been converted to operate in the 32-bit environment. Corel PHOTO-PAINT 6 can work with most existing 16-bit plug-in filters as well as utilize the power of the new 32-bit filters as they become available. The plug-in filter concept was introduced by Adobe with Photoshop. Today, many third-party developers make products that can tap directly into the powerful Corel PHOTO-PAINT program to produce effects such as making a photograph look like a charcoal sketch. Corel PHOTO-PAINT already comes with an impressive set of built-in filters, while support of the plug-in standard means that you can purchase third-party filters such as Adobe Gallery Effects, Andromeda Series, or Kai Power Tools and achieve even more varied graphic effects.

► **Improvement of Object Handling**—The Layers/Objects Roll-up of Corel PHOTO-PAINT 5 has been completely redesigned. The new interface offers improved control of objects in an image. A favorite feature of mine is the new ability to protect a layer without the necessity of hiding it from view. If you have not worked with objects in Corel PHOTO-PAINT 5, you might not appreciate this feature. If you are unfamiliar with the term *objects,* don't be concerned. It will be explained in due time. Just believe me when I say that in Corel PHOTO-PAINT 6 it is even easier to selectively control effects with the new Object roll-up.

This is only a partial list of the improvements that have been made to Corel PHOTO-PAINT 6. I hope you are excited about some of the things that you will be able to do with this program. But before we run, we must learn to walk. The next chapter begins that walk with a tour of Corel PHOTO-PAINT 6.

A Tour of Corel
PHOTO-PAINT 6

2

I know you want to get going as soon as possible. Many readers tend to skip a book's introduction and basic chapters such as this one. Because it is a WIN'95 application, Corel PHOTO-PAINT 6 is really twice new: in addition to the changes in Corel PHOTO-PAINT, you need to learn how a new operating system works. Throughout the book I will be including tips on using WIN'95. You see, in the evenings I work for Microsoft answering technical questions about WIN'95. About 20,000 people call every day and believe it or not most of the calls are not to tell Bill Gates how much they like their new operating system. Of course some of the questions are quite delightful such as "I have a three-button mouse and I was told to click the RIGHT mouse button. Which of the three buttons is the RIGHT one (to choose)?"

There is a lot of useful information in this chapter, so I urge you to look through it. If you are a first time user of Corel PHOTO-PAINT, I recommend that you familiarize yourself with (don't memorize) the terms and concepts described in this chapter before you begin to use the program. Time invested in this chapter will pay off in later chapters.

Elements of the Corel PHOTO-PAINT Screen

Figure 2-1 shows the Corel PHOTO-PAINT 6 main screen. Yours may look quite different depending on how your screen is configured. The following are the key elements that compose the Corel PHOTO-PAINT screen.

Color Palette

This is a new feature to Corel PHOTO-PAINT 6. The onscreen color palette is used to select the Paint (foreground/color used by the brushes), Paper (background), and Fill colors. These three terms are used throughout Corel PHOTO-PAINT so you should try to remember them. To choose a Paint color, that is, to change the color of a brush, click a color on the palette with the left mouse button. To choose a Fill color,

Control   Title   Menu   Rulers   Minimize button   Roll-up Roll-up
menu   bar   grid
                              Maximize button   Toolbars

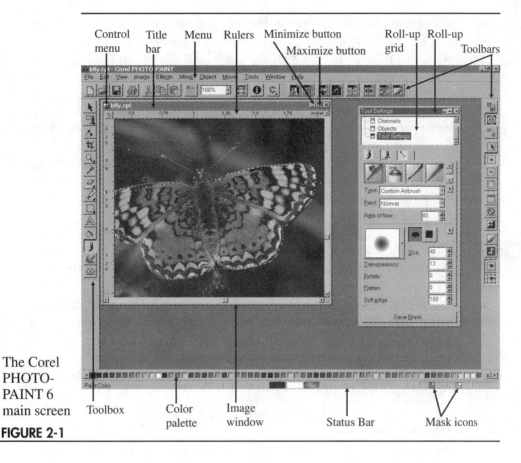

The Corel
PHOTO-
PAINT 6
main screen   Toolbox   Color   Image   Mask icons
                           palette   window   Status Bar

FIGURE 2-1

click with the right mouse button. Selecting the Paper color requires you to hold down the CTRL key and click the left mouse button.

IP: *If you don't enjoy memorizing mouse button/keyboard combinations, click and hold the right mouse button over the desired color. After two seconds a pop-up menu appears allowing you to set the Paint, Paper, or Fill to that color.*

Clicking the up arrow scroll button on the right side of the palette expands the palette so that up to four rows of color temporarily appear on screen. Selecting a color returns the onscreen palette to its default viewing setting of a single row. To scroll through the colors one at a time, click either the left or right scroll button on the onscreen palette with the left mouse button. Clicking the scroll button with the right mouse button replaces the current row of color with another.

This onscreen palette can be moved anywhere on the screen by clicking on the border around the palette and dragging it to a new location on the screen. By placing it on the screen you convert it into a floating palette with a title bar. Dragging the palette into any of the four sides of the Corel PHOTO-PAINT window docks the palette at that point making it part of the Corel PHOTO-PAINT window border.

To change the colors displayed on the onscreen palette, select Color Palette from the View menu and select another color model from the drop-down list that appears with a large list of color models. If you don't know what all of them mean, don't be concerned. We'll learn more about them later. Choose None from the drop-down list if you want to turn off the onscreen palette.

 IP: *If your screen is getting cramped for space, temporarily turning off the onscreen palette is one way to give you a little more working room.*

One last thing… If you are using the Custom Colors only palette, you can change the order in which colors appear in the onscreen palette. This is actually quite useful when you are working on a project involving a specific group of colors. You can drag the desired colors into one area rather than scrolling around the palette to select them. To move the color, click and drag the color well (officially, each color square is called a *well*) to its new location.

Control Menu

With WIN'95 the Control Menu went from an uninteresting square to an icon. Located on the left side of the Title bar, it still does most of the same things it did in Windows: display commands to restore (if file is minimized), move, resize, minimize, maximize, and close windows. The control menu for an image also provides image information.

Menu Bar

Press any menu heading in this bar in order to access dialog boxes, submenus, and commands. Access is also available by depressing the ALT key followed by the highlighted or underlined letter in the command.

Title Bar

Displays the application title or the image title (image filename). While it's nice to know the title the important thing about the title bar is the background. The

2

background color of the title bar indicates whether an image window is selected, which is important when you have several image files open and want to know which one you are about to apply an effect to.

Minimize Button

Click the application's Minimize button to shrink Corel PHOTO-PAINT to an icon. Click the image window's Minimize button to shrink the active image to an icon. Shrinking the image area to an icon does not reduce the amount of system memory that is consumed by the image. The advantage of doing so is that it speeds up image redrawing on the screen, which is handy if you have a sluggish graphics card.

Maximize Button

Click the application's Maximize button to enlarge the Corel PHOTO-PAINT window. Click the image window's Maximize button to enlarge the image window. When a window is at maximum size, the Maximum button becomes a Restore button (the icon is two overlapping rectangles). Click the Restore button to restore a window to its previous size.

Roll-Ups

Roll-ups are used to streamline operations using commands that are repetitively accessed. Roll-ups are opened through the Roll-ups command in the View menu on the menu bar, through keyboard combinations, or through the Roll-up toolbar if it is open.

Roll-up	Keyboard Combination
Channels	CTRL-F9
Color	CTRL-F2
Color Mask	CTRL-F5
Navigator	CTRL-F6
Nibs	CTRL-F11
Objects	CTRL-F7
Recorder	CTRL-F3
Tool Settings	CTRL-F8

A roll-up provides access to controls for choosing and applying fills, outlines, text attributes, and other options. Roll-up windows contain many of the controls found in dialog boxes: command buttons, text boxes, drop-down list boxes, and so on. But unlike most dialog boxes, the window stays open after you apply the selected options. This lets you make adjustments and experiment with different options without having to continually reopen a dialog box.

When you are not using a roll-up, you can roll it up through its control menu (right-click on the title bar), leaving just the title bar visible. When you begin to accumulate a lot of roll-ups all over your screen, you can select Arrange All from the control menu, and they will all roll-up and go into the corner nice and tidy.

A Quick Tour of the New, Improved Roll-Up

A number of changes occurred to the basic structure of the roll-up in Corel PHOTO-PAINT 6. To provide a way to manage the ever-increasing number of roll-ups, you can now group several roll-ups together. Figure 2-2 shows the three

Grouping allows each of these three roll-ups to be quickly accessed

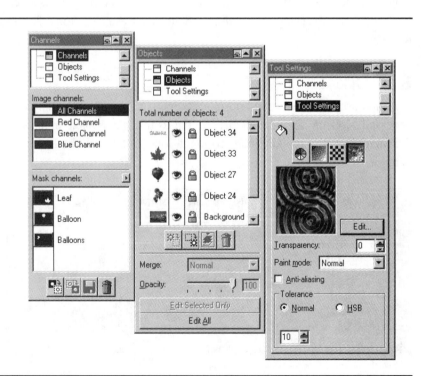

FIGURE 2-2

views of a grouped roll-up that contains three separate roll-ups. Clicking on the name in the upper part of the roll-up instantly changes the roll-up that is displayed.

How to Group a Roll-Up

By holding down the CTRL key and dragging one roll-up onto the title bar of another, the two combine into a roll-up group. In the roll-up group only one roll-up can be active at a time. Grouping the roll-ups allows multiple roll-ups to be contained in a single roll-up box (Figure 2-2), thereby saving precious display area for the image you are working on.

Roll-Up Operations

In the upper-right corner, there are three controls: the Auto-close button, up/down arrows, and an X.

- ► **To keep a roll-up open or make it close**: Click the Thumbtack icon. If the thumbtack is in the up position, the roll-up will close automatically after the action is chosen; if it is in the down position, the roll-up will "stick" or stay open.

IP: *The Auto Close button does just what it says. If enabled, it will close the roll-up as soon as you click anywhere else on the screen. This can be alarming if you unknowingly enabled it. The result is that your roll-up keeps closing and you don't know why. Maybe that won't happen to you, but it drove me crazy during beta testing. Just remember to disable it when you are not using it.*

- ► **To roll a roll-up up or down:** Click the up or down arrow in the title bar, or double-click the roll-up's title bar.

- ► **To close a roll-up:** Click the X button in the top-right corner, or enable the Auto Close button and click anywhere on the screen.

- ► **To move a roll-up:** Click the title bar with the left mouse button and drag it to the desired position.

- ► **To get help from a roll-up:** Click the right mouse button on the roll-up and choose Help from the drop-down list that pops up. The cursor will change to a question mark. Click on the area of the roll-up where you require additional information. A context-sensitive help screen will open.

- ► **To arrange roll-ups:** Don't laugh; this is a handy feature that most people do not use. Click the right mouse button on the roll-up's title bar and choose Arrange All. All of the roll-ups will roll up and move to the top corners of the main screen.

▶ **Defining custom roll-up configurations:** This feature allows you to control what side of the screen each roll-up appears on when it is opened, how the roll-ups are arranged on startup, and the renaming of your roll-up groups. Like many features in WIN'95, there is more than one way to open the Roll-Up configuration dialog box.

 OTE: *Corel PHOTO-PAINT must have an image file open for the Roll-Up configuration to be available.*

▶ **To open the Roll-up configuration from the Tools menu:** You can either select Customize… and select the Roll-Up tab, or choose Roll-Up Groups… and select Roll-Up Customization. Either way will take you to the Roll-Up tab of the Customize dialog box as shown in Figure 2-3.

▶ **To change the alignment of the roll-ups:** Just select the roll-ups in the Customize dialog box and click the appropriate Move button. You will note that in my roll-up shown in Figure 2-3, all of the roll-ups are on the right. I assume that is because the software detected I am a Republican.

▶ **To change the name of a roll-up group:** Click on the default name of the new group (that is, NewGroup1) once and then click a second time. This will allow you to rename the group name.

IP: *Many people double-click filenames in an attempt to rename them. The result of double-clicking the name is, in many cases, to launch the application. Click the name twice s-l-o-w-l-y and you will be in filename edit mode.*

The Start-Up Settings

The Start-up Settings give you three options for what the roll-ups do the next time you launch Corel PHOTO-PAINT.

▶ **Save On Exit:** All changes to roll-ups remain in effect.

▶ **No Roll-ups:** All roll-ups are closed.

▶ **All Roll-ups Arranged:** All roll-ups are rolled up/arranged.

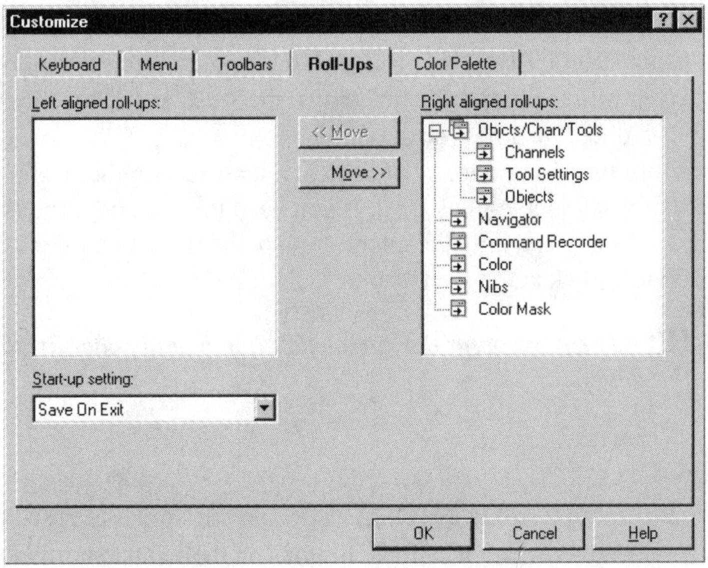

The Customize dialog box provides complete control over the operation and appearance of Corel PHOTO-PAINT 6.

■ **FIGURE 2-3**

Rulers

Select **Rulers** from the View command in the menu bar or the keyboard combination CTRL-R.

Rulers are important in Corel PHOTO-PAINT because they provide the only visual indicator as to how big an image actually is. We will explore why this happens later in the book. For now, be aware that it is possible for a photograph to completely fill the screen and be smaller than a postage stamp when you print it. That is why rulers are important.

The rulers' units of measure are selected using the Options command in the Tool menu. On the Options dialog box, select the General tab and choose one of the units of measure from the drop-down list. The selected units of measure are used for both the horizontal and vertical ruler. I recommend using inches as the unit of measure in North America (and Hawaii too).

The ruler normally uses the edge of the image window as its zero point. This is important to remember if you should make the image window larger than the image. To change the zero point of the image, click and drag the zero point to the new desired position.

Repositioning the Rulers

New in Corel PHOTO-PAINT 6 is the ability to place the rulers anywhere on the image. To reposition either ruler, hold down the SHIFT key, click the ruler you want to move, and drag it to a new position.

To return either the horizontal or vertical ruler to its previous position, hold down the SHIFT key and double-click on it. If you need to move both rulers at once, hold down the SHIFT key and drag the intersection point of the two rulers. To return both at once, double-click at the intersection.

 IP: *The position of the cursor on an image appears as dashed lines on the rulers.*

Toolbars

Toolbars are new to Corel PHOTO-PAINT 6 and are similar to the ribbon bar found in many other Windows applications. Buttons on the toolbars provide quick access to commonly used commands. All of the functions available on the toolbars can also be accessed through the menu bar. The appearance of the Ribbon Bar and the number of buttons are dependent upon tool selection.

In Corel PHOTO-PAINT 5 there is a single ribbon bar; with Corel PHOTO-PAINT 6, it has returned and brought its entire family. There are now 11 toolbars in all (counting the Toolbox), which I have shown in Figure 2-4. As you can see, opening and floating them all at the same time doesn't leave any room for the image you need to work on. The good news is that only a few of them need to be open at any given moment. Right-clicking on the Toolbox brings up a menu where you can select or deselect from the list of 11.

Image window

This is the image-display window. The zoom factor of each image window is controlled independently by the Zoom command in View or by the Zoom control in the Ribbon Bar. The default setting of Zoom—100 percent—is set in the Preferences section of the Special menu. If you have a good graphic board in your system, choose Best Fit.

IP: *When you choose a zoom factor that is less or greater than 100 percent, the image may have a poor appearance. This is a result of the way the image is displayed in Corel PHOTO-PAINT and does not reflect the actual image quality.*

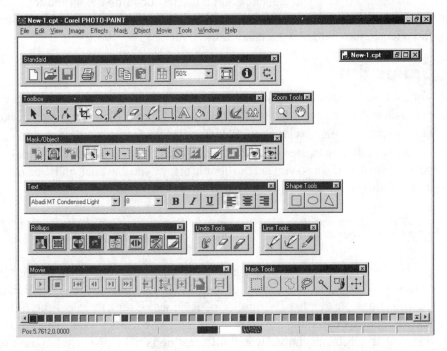

All the
toolbars
displayed

FIGURE 2-4

Toolbox/Flyouts

This contains all of the tools used for image editing. Many of the buttons in the
Toolbox have flyouts to allow access to additional related tools. Most flyouts are
identical to a toolbar. For example, look at the flyout shown below and compare it
to the Mask Tools toolbar shown in Figure 2-4.

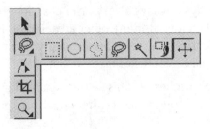

Availability of a flyout is indicated by a tiny black arrow in the lower right-hand
corner of the button.

To open a flyout, you can click and hold the cursor on the button for more than a second or click directly on the black arrow. Clicking on any tool in the flyout places the selected tool button at the head of the flyout.

Status Bar

The Status Bar contains a wealth of information. Unfortunately, it used to be either confusing or so remotely located that it was at times difficult to remember to look at it. That has changed with Corel PHOTO-PAINT 6.

By default, it is located at the bottom of the screen, below the color palette. By positioning the cursor so you get the double arrow, you can click and drag the border of the Status Bar to make it display two lines of information.

You can also move the Status Bar to the top of the screen. Right-clicking the Status Bar opens a large selection of options for configuring the Status Bar. One of the selections on this list is Number of Regions. Use it to select the number of horizontal areas the Status Bar is divided into. Then, when you select Show from the same list, you can choose which information is to be displayed in each region.

Be aware that if you have the Large Status Bar selected, you can place two items in each region, one on top and the other on the bottom. You can also place multiple copies of displays in the Status Bar; for example, you could have the time and date in each of the regions.

The Options available when you select Show are:

► **Mouse Coordinates:** This option displays the cursor position when the cursor is in an image window. When the cursor is over the Toolbox, the Status Bar always displays a very brief description of the tool or command. When it is over any other area, it retains the last information displayed. The trick to using it is to actually find the information in what looks like a Wall Street ticker tape of data.

► **Small Color Swatches:** This setting, enabled by default, displays currently selected foreground (Paint) color, background (Paper) color, and

Fill color, respectively. The fill-color rectangle also shows a representation of the type of fill that is selected, e.g., Fountain, Uniform, and so on.

▶ **State Icons:**   This is used to display the Mask, Color Mask, and Partial File indicators.

▶ **None, Time and Date, Keyboard States:**   These should be self-explanatory.

Window Border, Window Corner

Click and drag a horizontal or vertical border or corner to resize the window.

Scroll Arrow

When the image is larger than the current window size, the scroll arrows appear. Clicking the up or down arrow provides movement (panning) of the image in the window. The Hand tool in the Toolbox provides a much quicker way to perform the function of the scroll arrows.

Mask Icons

The mask icons are displayed in the lower right-hand corner of the main screen. The two mask icons shown are the Mask icon and the Color Mask icon. These icons are more important than you might imagine. You will sometimes try to apply an effect or use a brush stroke and nothing will happen. More often than not, the cause will be that you have a mask somewhere in the image that is preventing whatever it is   that you are trying to do. Make a habit of looking for the Mask icon when things don't work as planned.

The Standard Toolbar

The first seven buttons of the Standard Toolbar are common Windows functions. The last button with the Corel logo on it is the Application Launcher. The remaining buttons of the Standard Toolbar will be discussed in greater detail as we learn when to use them. Table 2-1 shows each of the Standard Toolbar buttons and describes their functions.

Button	Name	Function
	New	Activates the Create A New Image dialog box for creating new image files.
	Open	Activates the Open An Image dialog box to open existing files.
	Save	Saves the currently selected image. This button is grayed-out (unavailable) until the selected image has been modified.
	Print	Opens the Print dialog box to allow printing of the selected image.
	Cut	Cuts (removes) the defined (masked) area and copies it to the clipboard.
	Copy	Copies a defined (masked) area to the clipboard.
	Paste as Object	Pastes (copies) the image in the clipboard into the selected image as an object. (Note: Unlike the Paste *command*, which gives you a choice of pasting as an object or as a new document, the Paste as Object *button* does not give you a choice.)
	Select Partial Area	Used when you have a partial file. Partial files and this button are explained in the chapter on opening files.
50%	Zoom Level	Displays and controls the zoom level of the currently selected image.
	Maximize Work Area	Clicking this button makes the title and menu bar disappear from the screen. Clicking the button again restores them.

Standard Toolbar buttons and functions

TABLE 2-1

| Standard Toolbar buttons and functions *(continued)* | Image Information | Provides information about the currently selected image, that is, name, color, format, size, and so on. |
| | Application Launcher | Used to launch other Corel applications without leaving Corel PHOTO-PAINT. |

TABLE 2-1

Setting Up Your System (or "Do You Have What It Takes?")

This is more than just a cute title. Corel PHOTO-PAINT 6 requires some substantial systems resources in order to work properly. To make sure that you have sufficient system resources, it is necessary to spend a little time understanding what is "under the hood" with the system you already have. (Good news for you techno-wizards: If you already know everything about hardware, go directly to the next section.)

Hardware Considerations

The minimum requirement to run Corel PHOTO-PAINT 6 is that you must have WIN'95 installed and running. The minimum hardware necessary to run WIN'95 is not insignificant and for photo-editing, it is not enough. Let's look at realistic values to work with this program.

RAM

While it is possible to run WIN'95 on 4MB of RAM (lots of luck), the minimum amount of RAM that you should be using is 8MB (even that's tight). If you can afford it, you should be running with 16MB of RAM installed. I am running with 32MB of RAM while working on this book. The performance increase you will realize with additional RAM installed greatly outweighs the dollar/benefit increase you will see with almost any other hardware purchase.

CPU

I would recommend a 486 DX-33 MHz as the minimum system CPU for running Corel PHOTO-PAINT 6. A Pentium (P5) 120 MHz (or, by the time this book is in print, you may be one of the fortunate few to get one of the new P6 CPUs) is even better. As a side note, I understand that the P6 goes really fast. How fast? You can actually finish your photo-editing before you start. Now that's fast!

Hard Disk

At least 300MB. If that figure gave you a start, take a look at your local super computer center. You should have at least 50 to 100MB of free disk space. In the early part of 1995, 1.2GB drives were selling for $350 or less! Bitmap images take up a lot of space. So does WIN'95, for that matter. If you are going to be working on a lot of images and not archiving them off to tape or floppies all of the time, then get yourself a drive large enough to handle the load.

Digital Image
Fundamentals

3

A s the field of digital imagery expands, many people are getting deeply involved with computer graphics with little or no background on the subject. While there are many books about graphics on the shelves today, most of them assume that you know the terminology and the technical material that serves as the foundation of computer graphics. The end result is frustration for the user. This chapter will try and help you fill in some of the gaps you might have in your graphics background.

Corel PHOTO-PAINT works with bitmapped images. Even if a vector-based (non-bitmap) file is loaded into Corel PHOTO-PAINT, it is converted (rasterized) to a bitmap when it is loaded. To work effectively with bitmap images, it is necessary to understand why they act differently than the object-based images in CorelDRAW. Let us begin by defining our terms.

Basic Computer Graphics Terminology

Before we dive into computer terms and acronyms, there is something you must first understand: There are many terms in the computer industry that are nonstandard, colloquial, or just plain dumb. This has led to one of my theorems regarding computer terminology: *The only thing that is universally accepted in the computer industry is that nothing is universally accepted in the computer industry.*

I don't expect the Nobel prize for that one, but it goes a long way toward explaining why there are so many different terms to describe the same thing in the computer industry. I am also a strong believer in using the terminology in common use, rather than the "technically correct" term. When it comes to communicating ideas, the popular term is more important. In this book, I will always try to use the commonly used term (even if it isn't accurate) as well as the technically correct term. Here are the terms we need to know something about.

Pixels

These are not little elflike creatures that fly through the forest at twilight. The term "pixel" is short for PIcture ELement. Bitmap images are composed of pixels. They are the individual squares that make up an image on a computer screen or on hard copy. One way to understand pixels is to think of a wall mural created with mosaic tiles. When you get close to a mural made of mosaic tiles, it looks like someone had a bad Lego day. This is because you are so close you are looking at individual tiles. But step away a few feet from the mosaic, and the individual tiles begin to lose their definition and visually merge. The tiles have not changed their size or number, yet the further back you move, the better the image looks. Pixels in bitmaps work much the same way. I have created a sample image, shown in Figure 3-1, to illustrate how pixels make up an image. The area surrounded by the white rectangle on the left has been zoomed in to 1000 percent and displayed on the right. It shows that as you zoom in on an image, the individual pixels begin to stand out more and the image they produce becomes less and less evident. Returning to our mosaic tile analogy, there are, of course, major differences between pixels and mosaic tiles. Pixels come in a greater selection of decorator colors (more than 16.7 million, to be exact), and pixels don't weigh as much as tiles. However, tiles and pixels operate in the same way to produce an image.

Image Size and Resolution

The terms *image size* and *resolution* represent two of the more elusive concepts of digital imaging. An image's *size* describes the physical dimensions of the image. Image size is measured in pixels. The reason for using pixels is that the size of an

The pixel composition of the image becomes evident at a zoom factor of 1000%

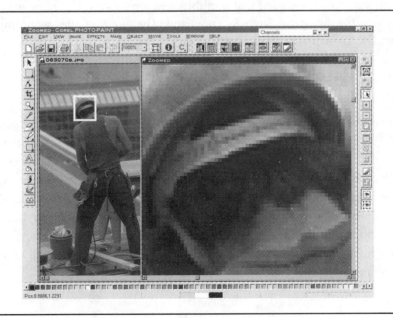

FIGURE 3-1

image in pixels is fixed. So when I speak of an image being 1200 x 600 pixels, I know approximately how big the image is. If I use a system other than pixels—say, inches—the size of the image is dependent on the resolution of the image. If I receive an image that is described as being 3 x 1.5 inches, I must ask, "At what resolution?"

So What Is Resolution?

Resolution is the density of pixels-per-inch (ppi) that make up an image, and it is measured in dots-per-inch (dpi). It is a measure of the amount of space between each pixel.

Let's assume we have an image 300 pixels wide and 300 pixels high. The size of the image is described as being 300 x 300 pixels. So how big will the image be when I import it into CorelDRAW? Trick question! There is not enough information to determine the size. This is where resolution comes in. If the resolution of this image is set to 300 pixels per inch, then the image dimensions are 1 x 1 inches when imported into CorelDRAW. If the resolution is doubled (set to 600 dpi), the image would be half the size or .5 x .5 inches. If the resolution is reduced by half (150 dpi), the image size doubles to 2 x 2 inches. It is an inverse relationship, which means that if one value increases, the other decreases. The physical size of an image is most accurately expressed as the length (in pixels) of each side. Resolution tells you how many pixels are contained in each unit of measure. In Figure 3-2, I have taken a photograph and resampled it at four different resolutions. Each one was saved as a different file, using the Save As command. Then all four files were imported into CorelDRAW, with the results shown below.

Image Resolution, or ... Hey! Why Is My Corel PHOTO-PAINT Image So Tiny?

If you have been working with Corel PHOTO-PAINT, you may have opened a Corel PHOTO-PAINT file in CorelDRAW and wondered why an image that fills your screen is only one inch wide when you print it. If you have always worked in vector-based programs such as CorelDRAW (which is resolution-independent), you never had to know this before. Don't get discouraged; it isn't as difficult to understand as it may first appear. This is because you probably had the image resolution set to 300 dpi or greater. Look at Figure 3-2 again to see what a difference changing the resolution can make. Now that you have been formally introduced to image resolution, let's move on to screen resolution.

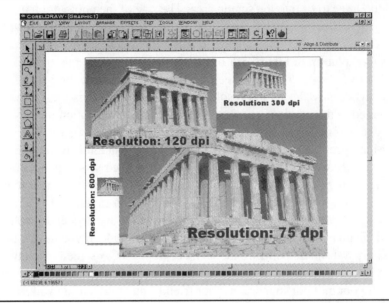

An identical
photograph
saved at
four
different
resolutions
and then
imported
into
CorelDRAW

FIGURE 3-2

Screen Resolution

No matter what resolution you are using, Corel PHOTO-PAINT displays each pixel onscreen according to the zoom ratio. For example, if the zoom ratio is 1:1 (which is displayed in Corel PHOTO-PAINT as a percentage of 100 percent), each image pixel takes up a single screen pixel. This is why the size of the image remains unchanged regardless of the image resolution. The display's zoom setting has no effect on the actual image. If you are a little fuzzy on monitors and pixels, read on. If you know them cold, skip ahead.

When you bought your monitor and/or display card, you may have been bewildered by such terms as 640 x 480, 800 x 600, and so on. These figures refer to the number of screen pixels that the monitor can display horizontally and vertically. For example, let's say you have a plain vanilla VGA monitor. The standard resolution for this monitor is 640 pixels wide by 480 pixels high (640 x 480). In Figure 3-3, I have loaded a file that is 729 pixels wide x 491 pixels high. The image at 100% zoom is too large to fit into the screen of Corel PHOTO-PAINT. Figure 3-4 shows the same photograph with the screen resolution changed to 800 x 600 (also called Super VGA). Notice that the image appears smaller than in the previous figure, but it is still too large to fit into the screen area. The size of the photograph hasn't changed, but the screen resolution has. In Figure 3-4, the screen was 640 pixels wide. In Figure 3-5, the screen is 800 pixels wide, making the image smaller by comparison. The screen resolution in Figure 3-5 has again been changed, this time to 1024 x 768. Now all of the photo can be seen on the screen. Again, the photograph remains unchanged, only the screen resolution has increased. It is the same principle we discussed in the previous paragraph. As the screen resolution increases, the image size decreases proportionally.

Many people have been surprised to discover that after spending a lot of money to get a high-resolution monitor and display card, their screen images only appeared smaller rather than sharper. Now that you know the secret of the screen resolution game, have your friends buy you lunch and you can explain it to them, too.

With all of the exciting ads for high-resolution displays and graphics adapters, it is difficult not to get caught up in the fever to upgrade. If you have a 14- or 15-inch monitor, you should be using the VGA or Super VGA screen resolution setting on your graphics card. If you go for a higher resolution on a 14- or 15-inch display, even if your monitor supports it, your friends may start calling you Blinky, because you will be squinting all of the time to read the screen. Also, be cautious about recommendations from the retail clerk/computer expert at your computer super-discount center. Remember that last week your "computer expert" might have

A photograph is viewed at a screen resolution of 640 x 480 pixels and it cannot fit into the screen

FIGURE 3-3

The same photograph is viewed on a monitor set to 800 x 600 pixels (Super VGA). The image size hasn't changed, but the screen resolution has increased

FIGURE 3-4

The screen resolution was increased to 1024 x 768 and the image now fits the screen

FIGURE 3-5

been bagging groceries at the local supermarket and may know less about computers than you do.

Resolution: the Name Game

If this were a perfect world, image resolution would be the same as printer resolution (which is also measured in dpi). Then if we were printing to a 600 dpi printer in our perfect world, we would be using a 600 dpi resolution image. Each image pixel would occupy one printer dot. However, it is not a perfect world, and when we talk about printer resolution, we should really be talking about *line frequency*. What? Nobody advertises or talks about their printer in terms of line frequency. And why not? Because, in this hyper-advertised computer marketplace bigger is better (except for price). So what sounds like a better printer? A 600 dpi printer or a 153 lpi (lines-per-inch) printer? The 153 lpi printer would have a resolution of around 1200 dpi. The names and numbers are everything in selling a product. Another story.

I live in Texas and the number one selling beer in this state is a Lite beer. What if the brewing company decided to change its name to diet beer (which is what it is)? I guarantee you, they wouldn't be able to give the stuff away. People who loved it wouldn't touch it because of the name. The point is that if HP advertised their 600 dpi laser printer as an 83 lpi printer, they would lose lots of sales.

This resolution specification hype also adds general confusion to the scanner market as well. If you are printing grayscale on a 600-800 dpi printer, your image should use an image resolution of 120-150 dpi. If you are printing a color image to the same printer, an image resolution of 80-140 dpi will work well.

Color

Color is everywhere. Even black and white is color (really). Color has the greatest and most immediate effect on the viewer of any factor in graphic design. Psychologists confirm that color has an enormous capacity for getting our attention. To use color effectively, we must understand it, both technically and aesthetically. It is a vast undertaking. However, in this chapter we will learn the minimum necessary to get the job done.

Color Depth

Every pixel of a Corel PHOTO-PAINT image has information associated with it that defines its color. The amount of information stored with each pixel is referred to as its color depth, which some call data types. The more information that is stored with

Color Depth	Type of Image	Color(s) Available
1-Bit	Black-and-White	2 colors
8-Bit	Grayscale	256 shades of gray
4-Bit	Color	16 colors
8-Bit	Color	256 colors
16-Bit	Color	65,000 colors
24-Bit	Color, also called true color and RGB color	16.7 million colors
32-Bit	Color, also called CMYK	16.7 million colors

Color depth for the various image types

TABLE 3-1

each bit, the greater the number of colors that can be represented. Fortunately, the information can only come in certain sizes, as shown in Table 3-1.

All image-file formats have some restrictions regarding the color depth that each can accommodate, so it becomes necessary to know what color depth you are working with in order to recognize what kinds of colors and other tools you may use with it.

If color depth is new to you, you may be wondering, Why do we have all of these different color depths? Why not make all of the images 24 bit and be done with it? There are many reasons for the different sizes. One of the major factors that restricts color depth is file size. The greater the number of bits associated with each pixel, the greater the file size. If an image took 20KB as a black-and-white (1-bit) image, it will take more than 480KB as a true-color image. If an 8 x 10 color photograph is scanned in at 600 dpi (don't ever do it!) and at a color depth of 24-bit, the resulting 64MB+ file will probably not even fit in your system. Not to mention that every operation with this image will be measured in hours instead of seconds. There are many other factors that also come into play. Why have a true color (24-bit) image if the output device is a low-end ink-jet printer? The scanner may only support 8-bit color (which is not uncommon). Let's take a closer look at the various color depth types that are being used in the industry today.

Black-and-White Images

This term "black and white" has caused some confusion in the past because old movies and television shows are referred to as being in black and white. They are actually grayscale, not black and white. Don't try to educate anyone on this subject.

Just remember that the old *Andy Griffith* and *Dick Van Dyke* shows are really in grayscale, not black-and-white.

Real black-and-white images are as simple as they get. One bit of information is used per pixel to define its color. Because it has only one bit, it can only show one of two states, either black or white. The little pixel is either turned on or it is turned off. It doesn't get any simpler than this.

Black-and-white images are more common than you would imagine. There is a lot that can be done with them. This kind of image is sometimes referred to as line art. It is possible to see black-and-white (1-bit) for grayscale-looking photographs. I used a scanner for several years that was a 1-bit scanner. It approximated the grayscale look by dithering. Such output can be acceptable. The drawback occurs if you must resize a dithered image; if so, you will experience moiré patterns, which look like a TV set with bad reception.

Grayscale Images

These are images using eight bits of information for each pixel, producing 256 shades of gray. The shades range from white (0) to black (255). Grayscale is used for many other things besides "black-and-white" photos. Corel PHOTO-PAINT uses grayscale images for transparency masks, color masks, and color information in several color models.

4-Bit and 8-Bit Color

This is also referred to as *indexed color.* The software creates a reference palette to which all of the colors used in the image are assigned. An 8-bit color image can only have one of a possible 256 combinations of color assigned to each pixel. Now, the software doesn't start in the upper-left corner and take the first 256 colors it runs into as its palette. (You would have some seriously strange images if it did.) Instead, the software looks at the entire color range of the image and selects 256 of the most common colors. Next, it assigns each of the colors in the image to one of those 256 that is the closest to the original color. An exception to this is called the Uniform palette, which takes 256 colors across the entire spectrum. Images that have a narrow color range look fine in 8-bit color, but color photographs with a wide range of color suffer somewhat by the color reduction unless you convert them in Corel PHOTO-PAINT using the correct palette and dithering.

You won't see many 4-bit (16-color) images anymore. Having said that, most of the color wallpaper patterns that come with Windows 3.x are 4-bit color images. Today, 8-bit (256-color) images are all over the place. Almost every color image you download from CompuServe or on the Internet is an 8-bit (256-color) image. In fact, the graphic format created by CompuServe, GIF, can only support 8-bit color or grayscale.

16-Bit Color (64K Color)

This color reminds me of EGA. There was a brief time when CGA wasn't enough. There is nothing worse than seeing a graphic computer game in CGA, and so EGA came next. It offered more colors and slightly better resolution than CGA. EGA was quickly replaced by VGA. In a way, 16-bit color (65K color) is like that. It came when 24-bit color was just too expensive and 8-bit (256-color) wasn't enough. Most of the higher-performance cards are now moving toward 24-bit color.

Using 16 bits to define the color depth provides approximately 65,000 colors. This is enough for almost any color image. I have seen the images in 16-bit and 24-bit side-by-side, and it is almost impossible to tell them apart. All things being equal, most of the photo-editing public could work with 65K color from now until the Second Coming and never tell any difference. What are the advantages of 16-bit color? Lower-cost graphics cards, and faster performance because you are moving one-third fewer bits. With the cost of 24-bit color cards so low these days, 16-bit color cards are probably no longer being manufactured.

24-Bit (True Color)

True-color images may use up to 16.7 million colors. They are so closely associated with the RGB color model that they are sometimes referred to as RGB 24-bit. (We talk about color models later in this chapter.) RGB stands for Red-Green-Blue. Your monitor makes all of its colors by a combination of these three colors. Your eye perceives color the same way: red, green, blue. The three colors that make up the RGB models each have eight bits assigned to them, allowing for 256 possible shades of each color. Each color gun in the color monitor can display 256 possible shades of its color. The mixing together of three sets of 256 combinations produces a possible 16.7 million color combinations. While true color doesn't display every possible color in all of creation, it gets pretty close. It is the model of choice for the desktop computer artist.

32-Bit Color

Look back at Table 3-1. Do you notice anything unusual about 32-bit color? Although the color depth increased by 25 percent, the numbers of colors remained the same. Why is that?

There are two answers, because there are two types of color depth that involve 32 bits. The first is more commonly seen on the Mac side of the world. When they say something is 32-bit, they are referring to a 24-bit RGB model with an additional 8-bit channel called an *alpha channel.* Apple reserved the alpha channel, but it has never specified a purpose for this data. Alpha channel is used by some applications to pass on additional grayscale mask information.

The other 32-bit type of color image expresses a CMYK (Cyan-Magenta-Yellow-blacK) model. (We will discuss the color models in more detail later in this chapter.) In case you didn't know, human eyes and computer monitors work according to RGB color models. Color output devices (printers) cannot use RGB information to produce accurate color output and must use CMYK information. It still covers a total palette of 16.7 million colors. With the release of Corel PHOTO-PAINT 5, the CMYK 32-bit color model is supported.

n **OTE:** *Most of the graphic processors are advertising that they offer 32-bit, 64-bit, and now 128-bit graphic processor boards. This has nothing to do with color depth. It is a reference to the width of the data path. Theoretically, the wider the data path, the greater the amount of color data that can be moved, and therefore the faster the screens are redrawn.*

Color Models

I knew I wasn't going to like high school physics the first day of class. We were asked to calculate the direction we would have to steer a rowboat up a fast-moving river in order to get to a pine tree on the other side. My answer was to row toward the pine tree. I got half credit. I mention this because, if you were looking for a detailed discussion on color models, you won't find it here. We are going to learn about some of the rules that govern the color models, but it is going to be simple and I think you will find it interesting.

One of the first things they taught me in that physics class I didn't like was that color is made up of components that, when combined in varying percentages, create other distinct and separate colors. You also learned this in elementary school when the teacher had you take the blue poster paint and mix it with the yellow paint to make green. Mixing pigments on a palette is simple. Mixing colors on a computer is not. The rules that govern the mixing of computer colors change, depending on the color model being used.

Color models represent different ways to define color. Let us briefly review some of the color models we have already discussed and introduce a few new ones. Later we will deal with a few of them in more detail.

RGB (Red-Green-Blue) is the color model the relates to transmitted light as the source of color. CMYK (Cyan-Magenta-Yellow-blacK) is a printer's model, based on inks and dyes. Some of the other ones out there are HSB (Hue-Saturation-Brightness) and HSL (Hue-Saturation-Lightness). Hue is unique in the color models in that it ranges across the entire spectrum of available colors. Another color model that is slowly gaining some acceptance is the LAB model (also called CIE), which was designed as an international standard for color. At this point, remember my theorem about nothing being universally accepted in the computer industry.

Each color model represents a different viewpoint on the same subject. Each offers advantages and disadvantages. For the casual Corel PHOTO-PAINT user, knowing how to get what you need out of RGB and HSB will more than satisfy your requirements. If you must accurately get from the screen to the printed page, you must get more deeply involved in CMYK.

You can work on the same image in different color models, although you can only have one color model active at any time. Color models are three-dimensional, as you will see when we look at the Color roll-up in Corel PHOTO-PAINT 6. The *color depth* of your image will determine what tools and techniques you will be able to use with them and on them. The *color model* that you are using determines how Corel PHOTO-PAINT will create the color that you will be applying to your image. Both color depth and color models can be changed in Corel PHOTO-PAINT.

RGB Versus CMYK

In our daily conversation, we describe colors inaccurately. If you doubt that, go to the auto parts store and try to get touch-up paint for your car. I did this once with a Chevy I owned. I thought its color was tan. Silly me. It was either golden fawn or hazy dawn, according to the color samples. It wasn't until I retrieved the eight-digit number off of the door panel that I learned my car's exterior color was golden fawn. Was golden fawn an accurate description of the color? No. It was just a name assigned to that specific color. I still referred to my Chevy as tan-colored because the parking valet wouldn't have been able to find a golden fawn Chevy.

Color specificity is commonplace with high-dollar accounts. The client will often specify what the corporate colors must look like. That is what they want and that is what they will get, without exception. I have personally seen tens of thousands of dollars spent to correct a color deviation caused by someone missing the correct color number by a single digit in a four-color ad for a national publication. Yet if I showed you the two ads side by side, I doubt that you could find the color that was altered.

So why do colors on the screen look different from the printed output? To understand, we must return to the dreaded high school physics class.

Color is created by the reflection or absorption of various wavelengths of light. When I look at the blue plastic diskette sitting on my desk, I see the blue because all of the other colors except blue are absorbed by the pigment in the plastic. The blue color was not absorbed but rather reflected, and it found its way into my eye. If I pull out an older 5.25-inch floppy diskette, it is black. If all of the colors are absorbed and none reflected, then it appears to be black. Moving on, we take a prism and shine sunlight through it. What do we get? A rainbow. Why? Because white light (sunlight, in this case) is made up of all the colors in the universe.

So, all of the colors mixed together should produce black. After all, all of the color pigments will absorb all of the color and reflect nothing, resulting in black. Try it if you like, but it won't work. You will end up with a color something akin to Mississippi swamp mud, but not black. To understand why, we need to look at the first two theories of color. These are called the *additive theory* and the *subtractive theory*. In spite of their names, these are not mathematical mazes, but they are important to understanding why the color on a computer monitor and the printed page can be quite different.

Additive theory tells us that when Red-Green-Blue are added together, the result is white. The absence of any color is black. This was shown in the example of the prism. Subtractive theory tells us that when Cyan-Magenta-Yellow are added together, the result is, theoretically, black. The absence of color is white. In reality, CMY together produce only a close approximation of black (the Mississippi swamp mud color), which is why printers use blacK (K) and all production color printing uses the four-color (CMYK) model.

Both theories are correct—yet they contradict each other. How can both be right? Because the additive theory applies to transmitted light (such as your monitor or TV) and the subtractive theory applies to reflected light (the printed page).

All of the color images you see on a monitor are controlled by the rules of additive color. When you send the image you have been viewing on your monitor to a color printer, the colors on the page are governed by the rules of subtractive color.

Another example of the two is a color photograph and a color slide. The color slide always looks different than the photograph. (I avoided the temptation to say it looks "better.") The color slide displays transmitted light, and the photograph uses reflected light. All of this leads to the following: *Flip Wilson was wrong! What you see* on the display (transmitted light) *is never exactly what you get* on the page (reflected light).

There are additional obstacles to matching colors. The design and age of a monitor will affect the colors it displays. Its colors will even be slightly different between the time the display is first turned on and several hours later, after it has heated up. The lighting in the room also affects how the colors on the display appear. Two identical displays made by the same manufacturer displaying the same color bars can vary significantly. An image made in an RGB model will not translate perfectly to a CMYK image. Printer's inks do not precisely follow the rules of subtractive color.

What is a person to do? Not so long ago, the only solution was a lot of educated guessing, cursing, and praying for an image to successfully run the gauntlet from the scanner, through the display, and out of the printer. Now things are much better, thanks largely to two separate systems that are included in Corel PHOTO-PAINT 6. They are *color-correction systems* and *color-management systems*. Let me briefly summarize the differences between them.

A color-correction system is used to correct the parameters of individual color devices (display, printer, scanner, and so on) to compensate for any minor deficiencies in the color response of the unit. I say "minor" because there are limits as to how much correction can be applied.

A color-management system works with the entire system to produce uniform transition between different color devices and color models to produce uniform results.

Image File Formats

For some, the question will be, "What is an image file format?" The answer is: An image format defines a way of storing an image and any related information along with it in a way that other programs can recognize and use. Each format has its own unique form, called a *file structure,* of saving the image pixels and other related file information such as resolution and color-depth information. Each format is unique and is generally identified by its three-letter file extension. For example, the three-letter extension "CPT" on a filename identifies the file format as a Corel PHOTO-PAINT file. This extension is important because many programs use the three-character extension to identify the type of file import filter to select. If the wrong extension or a unique extension is used, it will be difficult, if not impossible to import the image.

Corel PHOTO-PAINT 6 has several new formats. The ability to read and write alpha channel information in several different formats increases the flexibility of the product. Also new in Corel PHOTO-PAINT 6 is the ability to open, edit, and save animation files.

Each image file format has its own advantages and limitations as well. Some formats cannot store more than 256 colors, some cannot be compressed, and others produce enormous files. Corel PHOTO-PAINT gives you a large assortment of file formats to choose from when you save a file. If you are not familiar with the choices, this blessing of a wide assortment can become confusing. In this section we will try to take some of the mystery out of these formats with strange-sounding names.

Because there are dozens of file formats, it would be confusing to try to cover them all. Instead, we will look at the major ones supported by Corel PHOTO-PAINT and discuss their strengths and limitations. Corel PHOTO-PAINT is aware of the color depth of the image you are attempting to save and changes the drop-down list of available file-format choices automatically. For example, if you have a 32-bit color image, the drop-down list will be reduced from the normal selection to only the four file format choices that support 32-bit color.

CPT

This is a native format of Corel PHOTO-PAINT. CPT is the best format for your originals. Saving in a CPT format retains all of the associated transparency masks and objects. Saving in any other image format results in the merging of all objects in the image. The only limitation to this format is portability. To my knowledge, there are no non-Corel Windows applications that can recognize a CPT file.

Windows Bitmap (.BMP, .DIB)

BMP (Windows Bitmap) is the native image format for Microsoft Paint, which is included with every copy of Microsoft Windows. It is widely supported by nearly every Windows program. Corel PHOTO-PAINT supports BMP images up to 24-bit color (16.7 million colors).

GIF (.GIF)

CompuServe licensed GIF (Graphics Interchange Format) a long time ago as a means of compressing images for use over their extensive online network. Actually, they bought the rights to use it from another company. GIF has become a very popular format, especially now that everyone is jumping on the Internet. As a way to send pictures over phone lines, it can't be beat. It has a major limitation of supporting only 8-bit (256-color) images. Corel PHOTO-PAINT does not offer an option to compress images saved as GIF files.

New to Corel PHOTO-PAINT is the ability to save GIF files in 89a and 87a format. These formats provide the capability to save a file with transparency and interlacing options, which is becoming increasingly important for creating Web graphics for use on the Internet. The four options are detailed as follows.

89A   The 89a (enhanced) format enables interlacing and transparency options.

87A   The 87a (normal) format is for standard GIF file export (or when and where 89a Enhanced is not supportable).

INTERLACED IMAGE   The Interlaced image is used to speed up the drawing of an image onscreen later. This is accomplished by redrawing the image in stages, from low to high resolution, providing an impression of the image before it is completely redrawn. This is advantageous when an image is mistakenly selected; the redrawing process can be halted before the image is fully redrawn.

TRANSPARENT COLOR   The Transparent color option is used to choose what color from the image (represented by index values in the color palette on the dialog box) becomes transparent. This is useful in creating nonrectangular bitmaps. The color selected is masked in the image. Use this option to create unusual effects.

Paintbrush (.PCX)

PCX is one of the original file formats, created by Z-Soft for PC Paintbrush back when Noah was working on the ark. It is unquestionably one of the most popular image-file formats around, mainly because PC Paintbrush is the oldest painting program for the IBM PC. Corel PHOTO-PAINT supports PCX images up to 24-bit color. The only concern with using PCX images involves importing them into older applications. Because the PCX format has been around so long, there are many versions of PCX import filters around. It is possible, even likely, to find an older application that imports PCX files but cannot read the file exported by Corel PHOTO-PAINT.

EPS

EPS stands for Encapsulated PostScript. PostScript is a page description language used by imagesetters and laser printers. This format is a favorite of your friendly neighborhood service bureau. Many people do not think about using the EPS format when working with Paint's bitmap images. This is because this format is associated with vector-based drawings like CorelDRAW. Actually, EPS does work with bitmap images... for a price. By that I mean a bitmap image saved in the EPS format will be roughly three times as large as the same file saved in the TIF format. So why use EPS? There is a marvelous feature unique to this format: the ability to have the image borders match irregular objects.

PICT

I should discuss this format because Corel PHOTO-PAINT can import it. Apple developed PICT as the primary format for Macintosh graphics. Like PostScript, it is a page description language. This format has been troublesome for importing images into either Corel, Pagemaker, or others. The rule with this format is simple. If the image you are using is in PICT format, you have no choice but to import it as a PICT file and hope for the best. If you are saving an image so that it can be used on a Macintosh, use JPEG or TIF. They are both excellent formats for the Mac and are much more reliable than PICT.

TARGA (.TGA, .TVA)

This format was originally created for TARGA display boards. If you haven't seen this image format before, it is probably because it is used by a small segment of the professional market that works with high-end color and video. In Corel PHOTO-PAINT, this file format supports up to 24-bit color. TARGA does not support 32-bit color (CMYK). TARGA format supports 32-bit images; it is 24-bit color with an 8-bit alpha channel, which can be used to retrieve mask information by Corel PHOTO-PAINT 6. Corel PHOTO-PAINT 5 cannot read the alpha channel information in TARGA file format. Many people believe that the TARGA format is technically superior to any other on the marketplace. Others feel it is only good for multimedia support because it is a narrow niche format that is not widely used. With the growth of the 3D market, it is becoming a popular format for all of the information that a 3D image requires.

TIFF (Tagged Image File Format, .TIF)

TIFF is probably the most popular full-color bitmapped format around, supported by every PC and Macintosh paint program I have ever seen. TIFF is clearly the image format of choice. It is used as a default setting for every scanning program on the marketplace today.

You may have heard that there are many different versions of TIFF, which can conceivably cause some compatibility problems when moving images between programs. To date, the only problems we have experienced with TIFF involved saving images as 24-bit color TIFF files and trying to read them on an application that doesn't offer 24-bit color support.

Corel PHOTO-PAINT supports all color-depth settings in TIFF format, including 32-bit color (CMYK). However, don't save your images in 32-bit color unless it is specifically requested. Because 32-bit color (CMYK) is very new, you may end up with a TIFF file that many older applications cannot read. Remember that 32-bit (CMYK) TIFF contains the same color information as 24-bit color TIFF.

Scitex CT Bitmap (.SCT, .CT)

High-end commercial printers use Scitex computers to generate color separations of images and other documents. Corel PHOTO-PAINT can open images digitized with Scitex scanners and save the edited images to the Scitex CT (Continuous Tone) format. Because there are several restrictions regarding the transfer of images from the PC to a Scitex drive, you will probably want to consult with the person using the Scitex printer before saving to the CT format. It is possible that a TIFF or JPEG format is preferred. Scitex is only available when the image is in 32-bit color (CMYK).

JPEG/LEAD Compression Formats (.JPG, .JFF, .JTF)

JPEG stands for the Joint Photographic Experts Group, which created the format. JPEG is the most efficient compression format available on the market today. It has quickly become a standard for saving large 24-bit color images by compressing them into very small files. LEAD has attracted a large following as a compression scheme that offers great image compression while experiencing less of the image deterioration associated with JPEG compression. Both compression formats cause some image deterioration every time the image file is saved. So, when using one of these formats, save your original in CPT or other lossless formats such as TIFF. Also, with JPEG, use the highest-quality image setting to keep the amount of image deterioration to a minimum.

Corel PHOTO-PAINT offers both compression formats, with many selections possible in each. You can save files in either of the JPEG or LEAD bitmap formats. Images compressed using the JPEG export dialog box can be exchanged between a wide variety of platforms and applications. Images compressed using the LEAD compression may have problems being uncompressed if the destination computer does not support LEAD compression. This can cause some confusion since they both have .JPG extensions. The JPEG format provides you with superior compression techniques. However, with extra compression comes a loss in file information.

How Suite It Is...

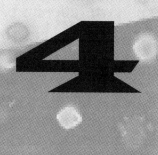

4

The Corel suite of applications is a powerful collection of programs. As a result, some of the best sources for images for Corel PHOTO-PAINT are the other Corel applications. Corel PHOTO-PAINT and CorelDRAW have had a strong relationship since the release of the version 5.0 in 1994. Corel PHOTO-PAINT imports CorelDRAW CDR files as well as other industry-standard vector files, which means you no longer are required to export your CorelDRAW files into bitmap format. Furthermore, Corel PHOTO-PAINT can export with clipping paths. The term *clipping path* refers to the border that surrounds an object as opposed to the rectangular border that surrounds an image. In Figure 4-1, the apple on the left was imported as a Corel PHOTO-PAINT file. The apple on the right was masked and saved in a manner that preserved its clipping path. Notice there is no white rectangle behind it.

By using clipping paths, we can import irregularly shaped objects from Corel PHOTO-PAINT to CorelDRAW.

FIGURE 4-1

The addition of clipping paths gives increased flexibility with bitmaps in programs like CorelDRAW and Corel VENTURA and non-Corel programs like PageMaker and Quark.

This chapter explores the powerful relationship between Corel PHOTO-PAINT and other Corel applications. We will look at the best ways to import files created in CorelDRAW into Corel PHOTO-PAINT, and techniques for saving images in Corel PHOTO-PAINT so that they will be the correct size and shape when brought into CorelDRAW. At times you might find the material a little intimidating.

IP: *I have tried to cover all of the material about this subject in this chapter. If you don't understand a section, don't concern yourself with it. Skip it and refer back to it when you need the details.*

While Corel PHOTO-PAINT's capabilities have increased dramatically, CorelDRAW and Corel VENTURA are still much better suited for layout, type manipulation, and text placement. Avoid falling into the one-program-does-all mentality. You will learn that combining each program's strengths achieves the best results. Many of the people that I talk with everyday are trying to do everything in Corel PHOTO-PAINT. I have two words for those of you who are doing that: *STOP IT!!!* As an example, in Figure 4-2 I imported the photograph that was masked in Corel PHOTO-PAINT (which removed the background) into CorelDRAW. The text was created in CorelDRAW because it provides control of the leading (space between the lines of text). In Figure 4-3, the photograph was created in Corel PHOTO-PAINT and the text was added in CorelDRAW.

When to Use Corel PHOTO-PAINT

Just because this is a book on Corel PHOTO-PAINT doesn't mean that I think everything should be done in Corel PHOTO-PAINT. In fact, the opposite is true. Get into the practice of deciding which program(s) to use on a project *before* you begin. For example, you may want to use Corel PHOTO-PAINT to enhance bitmap images and then bring them back into CorelDRAW for adding text. An exception to this rule is if you need to apply special effects to the text. Many times you will find I recommend that paragraph style text be placed in another application. The reason for placing text in CorelDRAW is that the resulting output text will be much sharper. When text is created in Corel PHOTO-PAINT, the text is a bitmap image that is resolution-dependent. In other words, the text is no longer text but a bitmap picture of the text. It is fixed to the same resolution of the image it is placed in. This means

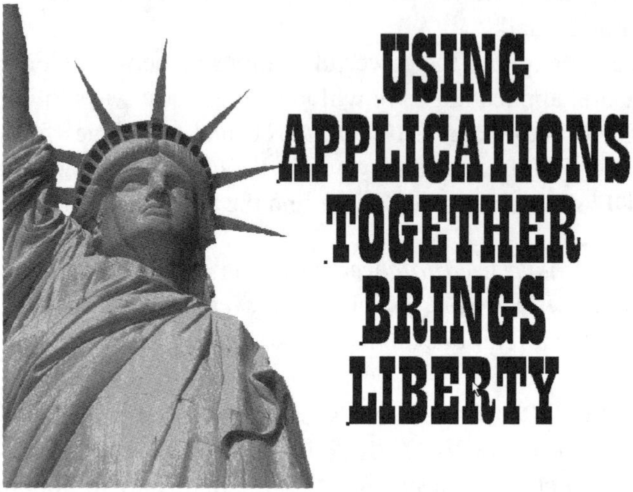
USING
APPLICATIONS
TOGETHER
BRINGS
LIBERTY

Importing a photograph into CorelDRAW allows users the flexibility of CorelDRAW's powerful text control features

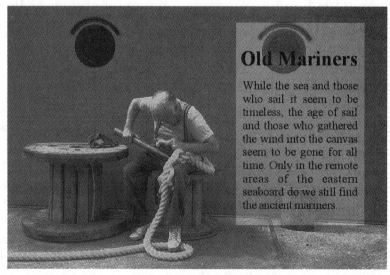

FIGURE 4-2

Old Mariners
While the sea and those who sail it seem to be timeless, the age of sail and those who gathered the wind into the canvas seem to be gone for all time. Only in the remote areas of the eastern seaboard do we still find the ancient mariners...

CorelDRAW and Corel PHOTO-PAINT are used together to achieve the best results

FIGURE 4-3

that text placed in Corel PHOTO-PAINT will be at the resolution of the image. If it is 300 dpi (dots per inch), then the text will be a bitmap image that is 300 dpi regardless of whether it is printed to a 300 dpi laser printer or a 2450 dpi imagesetter.

Text in a program like CorelDRAW is resolution-independent. Any text that is placed in CorelDRAW remains as text. At printing time, CorelDRAW sends the font information to the output device, allowing it to be printed at the maximum resolution of the device. If it is output to a 2450 dpi imagesetter, then the resolution of the text will be 2450 dpi. The result is sharper text. If you are fuzzy about resolution, it is thoroughly explored in Chapter 9.

In some cases, the printing of a bitmap image is easier to control (lay out) with CorelDRAW than it is with Corel PHOTO-PAINT. This is because Corel PHOTO-PAINT sees a page as one single bitmap image. In CorelDRAW, the bitmap image is seen as an object on the page, making it easier to control placement of the image than in Corel PHOTO-PAINT.

The Many Paths Between Corel PHOTO-PAINT and CorelDRAW

Before we begin demonstrating all of the neat tricks and effects, we must cover some basic concepts about transferring images between these two programs. It is a highly advertised fact that the entire Corel line of products, beginning with CorelDRAW 4, supports OLE 2.0 (Object Linking and Embedding). Corel PHOTO-PAINT 6 and CorelDRAW 6 now both support in-place editing. OLE is a powerful interapplication program that is routinely demonstrated by dragging an image from one application and dropping it into another. This is great, right? Well, sort of. The drag-and-drop method works. The only reservation is that the image quality isn't as good with this method as it is with others. OLE is given a lot of hype by Microsoft and the press. On paper, OLE looks great; in practice, it carries a lot of overhead.

In-place editing means that when you place a Corel PHOTO-PAINT image into a word processing application like Microsoft Word, you can right-click the image and Corel PHOTO-PAINT will open up within Word. For the average user this isn't a big issue. Because of the resources needed for photo-editing in Corel PHOTO-PAINT, I cannot recommend using OLE's in-place editing unless you have a really powerful system and even then, I am not sure what the great advantage would be. I guess this means I will get a lump of coal in my stocking from Santa Bill Gates this Christmas. Enough said about OLE.

So, what is the best way to get an image from CorelDRAW to Corel PHOTO-PAINT? Glad you asked.

Getting from CorelDRAW to Corel PHOTO-PAINT

There are four different ways to transfer images between CorelDRAW and Corel PHOTO-PAINT. The first—and quickest—is drag-and-drop (which we just mentioned). The second is to copy the image to the Windows clipboard and then paste it into Corel PHOTO-PAINT. The third is the traditional approach that was used until the introduction of Corel PHOTO-PAINT 5. This method involved an image being exported as a bitmap file from CorelDRAW and imported into Corel PHOTO-PAINT. The fourth—and probably best—way to transfer images between the two programs is to save the images in the native Corel CDR file format and then open the CDR file with Corel PHOTO-PAINT.

Each method offers advantages and disadvantages. Let's look at the rules for each one and explore the options and limitations for each method. To save a lot of explanation further down the page, here are a few concepts that are common to all four methods.

Rasterization and Dithering

When we go from CorelDRAW to Corel PHOTO-PAINT (or any other bitmap application), it is necessary to convert the vector (or line) format into bitmap (or paint) format. This process is called *rasterization*. How the rasterization is accomplished determines how faithfully the image we import into Corel PHOTO-PAINT is reproduced.

When a color in the original image cannot be produced precisely (either because of display or color mode limitations), the computer does its best to make an approximation of the color through a process called *dithering*. With dithering the computer changes the colors of adjacent pixels so that to the viewer they approximate the desired color. Dithering is accomplished by mathematically averaging the color values of adjacent pixels. The use of dithering can also affect the process of getting from CorelDRAW to Corel PHOTO-PAINT.

That's enough boring stuff for now. Let's look at our first method: drag-and-drop.

The Drag-and-Drop Method

The drag-and-drop method is limited to screen resolution if there isn't an existing image that is open. Screen resolution for a standard VGA monitor is 96 pixels per inch. However, images that are dragged between Corel applications are at a resolution of 72 dpi. If you drag a CorelDRAW object into a 300 dpi image, its resolution will be 300 dpi. It is not resolution that restricts the quality of the drag-and-drop method. The noticeable loss in image quality results when fountain fills and color blends are rasterized. Regardless of the resolution, fountain fills and blends are dithered. Generally, restrictions that apply to drag-and-drop apply to inter-application clipboard operations.

4

When to Use Drag-and-Drop

One of the big advantages of using the drag-and-drop method is the speed at which it operates. Without going into the technical details of how rasterization is accomplished with drag-and-drop, let's simply say that it is not the best choice for importing images that have fountain fills or other images that have a large number of colors, like color photographs.

So what good is drag-and-drop? Multimedia applications are, by design, generally limited to screen resolution, making them an ideal candidate. Drag-and-drop is an excellent way to import items with solid or no colors, such as symbols, or items with a limited number of diagonal lines. (Diagonal lines are a particular obstacle to any form of rasterization.)

Using Drag-and-Drop

If you do decide that drag-and-drop is the best choice for your project, you should follow these guidelines:

- ► Both applications must be open. This means that neither one can be reduced to a little icon in the Task Bar.

- ► Corel PHOTO-PAINT does not need to have an image area open. If an existing image is not open, a new image will be created.

- ► To drag an image from CorelDRAW, you must click on it and drag it into the Corel PHOTO-PAINT application. When the cursor is over the Corel PHOTO-PAINT application, the icon will turn into an arrow-rectangle icon.

IP: *When dragging an image into Corel PHOTO-PAINT, be patient. It sometimes takes longer than you might expect for the cursor to change into the arrow-rectangle icon. As Radar would say in M*A*S*H: "Wait for it."*

► When you let go of the left mouse button, two things happen:

   ► The image is rasterized and placed into Corel PHOTO-PAINT. If there was not an existing image file open, the object is rasterized at 72 dpi. If there is an existing image, it is rasterized at the resolution of the image.

   ► The image in CorelDRAW disappears. To restore the image that was dragged kicking and screaming out of CorelDRAW, just click anywhere in the CorelDRAW window (which makes it active again) and select Undo Delete from the Edit Menu or click the CTRL-Z key.

IP: To prevent an object from being deleted in CorelDRAW when it is dragged into another application, hold down the CTRL key when you click and drag and a copy of the object will be dragged into the other application.

The Down Side of Drag-And-Drop

I have included some examples of what you can expect when using the drag-and-drop method of moving images from CorelDRAW into Corel PHOTO-PAINT.

Figure 4-4 shows an image that was loaded in CorelDRAW from the Symbol library. I used a solid black fill. Next, using the drag-and-drop technique, I dragged it into Corel PHOTO-PAINT. Figure 4-5 shows a comparison between the original CorelDRAW symbol and the rasterized version of the same symbol. Don't panic. It isn't as bad as the figure makes it look. If it were viewed on the screen, I doubt you would notice the difference. When it is printed on a high resolution device, you would notice the difference.

Next, we will look at the same symbol except it will have a fountain fill instead of the 100% black fill. On the left is the original; on the right is the same image at the same zoom level after it was dragged into Corel PHOTO-PAINT. Notice that the image fill that was dragged into Corel PHOTO-PAINT is of poorer quality than the original in CorelDRAW. That is because the image in CorelDRAW is at a screen resolution of 72 dpi. It was originally brought into Corel PHOTO-PAINT at 300 dpi, resulting

A symbol in
CorelDRAW
with 100%
black fill

FIGURE 4-4

Now the
original
symbol
(top-left) is
placed
alongside
the resulting
symbol
(bottom-
right) after
it was
rasterized
using drag-
and-drop

FIGURE 4-5

in a smaller image. To correct for this reduction caused by resolution change, it was resampled in Corel PHOTO-PAINT so that both images appear to be the same size. You will learn how to use the Resample command in Chapters 5 and 6.

In Figure 4-6, the resampled image was saved as a CPT file and imported into CorelDRAW where the images are displayed next to each other. The original (in

The original (upper-left) is placed alongside the rasterized version made when it was dragged into Corel PHOTO-PAINT. Remember that the edges look bad because the image was viewed at zoom level greater than 100%

FIGURE 4-6

case you can't figure it out) is the one in the upper left. What doesn't show on the screen shot but does show when it is output on a printer are the moiré patterns that may result from this type of rasterization.

Exporting CorelDRAW Files as Bitmaps

Yes, you can still export CorelDRAW images as bitmap files for use in other Corel and non-Corel applications using the following method:

1. When you have the drawing the way that you want it in CorelDRAW, as a safety precaution save it as a CDR file using the Save command in the File menu.

2. Select the Export command in the File menu. You will be presented with a series of choices in the CorelDRAW Export... dialog box, shown here. It operates just the same as the Save dialog box for images. It fact, it is the same dialog box with a different title.

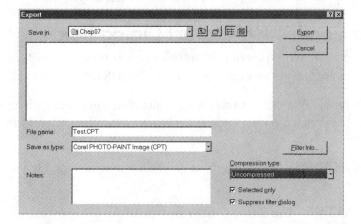

3. Select the options you need. You should generally check the Selected Only box when exporting images to Corel PHOTO-PAINT. The Selected Only feature will only export the object you have selected in CorelDRAW.

4. Select a file format. You should consider using the Corel PHOTO-PAINT format (CPT) if you are going to be opening it with Corel PHOTO-PAINT. If you are going to use the exported bitmap in another document, I would recommend using TIF, BMP, or PCX format, as they are the most widely used. For use of the exported images in applications

other than Corel PHOTO-PAINT, Corel has provided recommendations for selection of file formats, based on the type of printer you are using. Generally, if you have a PostScript printer and the program you are exporting to supports PostScript, use the EPS format. Otherwise, use the format shown in Table 4-1. For placement in other graphic applications, follow the recommendations in Table 4-2.

5. Click the Export button and another dialog box opens. You have a large selection of commands to choose from in this dialog box. The commands are explained in the next section. Not all of the options are available; it depends on the type of bitmap file that is selected. Make your selections and then click the OK button.

Converting an image to a bitmap, especially a large one, can take a significant amount of time. Don't be surprised if it takes several minutes to complete. My next book will be called *101 Neat Games to Play with Your Hourglass*. Once the file has been converted, you may open it with Corel PHOTO-PAINT or place it as a bitmap in any application that supports placement of bitmap graphics.

The CorelDRAW Export Dialog Box

The CorelDRAW Export function provides a vast variety of file formats, both vector and bitmap, that the user can convert the CorelDRAW files into.

FILE NAME Proposes a name for the export file. Either accept it, or type your own. The file extension corresponds to the Export file format selected from the Save As Type box.

DRIVE/FOLDERS Select the drive and folder in which the file you want to export is stored.

SAVE AS TYPE Use this to choose the type of file to export.

Program	PostScript Printers	Non-PostScript Printers
Word for Windows	EPS	WMF
Delrina Perform	GEM	GEM
PageMaker	EPS	WMF or TIF
Corel VENTURA	EPS	CMX
WordPerfect	EPS	WPG

File format recommendations for bitmap files based on output device

TABLE 4-1

Program	Recommended Format
Adobe Illustrator	AI
Arts & Letters	WMF, EPS (using Decipher)
AutoCAD	DXF
GEM Artline	GEM
Macintosh-based vector programs	Macintosh PICT, AI
Micrografx Designer	CGM
PC Paintbrush	PCX

File format recommendations for graphic applications

■ **TABLE 4-2**

4

NOTES   Allows you to include comments with the file. Great way to figure out what you had in mind when you originally saved the file. It is only available if the file format selection in the Save As Type box supports file notes.

COMPRESSION TYPE   Select from a large assortment of compression types. Computer files are often stored in a compressed format to save space on your hard disk. There are several compression techniques that can be used, depending on the original file format. Generally, the more compressed a file is, the slower it is to read from and/or write to.

ABOUT COMPRESSION   Compression can be lossless or lossy. Lossless compression has been around for some time. It retains all the original data through the compression and decompression processes. Lossless compression is recommended with images that need to be reopened at a later date. Lossy compression, on the other hand, loses some of the original data, but depending on your requirements, this loss may not make a difference in the final result of your work. Lossy compression can compress your original files to a much greater extent than lossless compression, and so it may be desired when disk space is at a premium or you need to send your image over an online service.

Pack-Bits, RLE, LZW, and CCITT are lossless compression techniques. JPEG is a lossy technique and is used mainly to compress 24-bit color continuous-tone images. The information that is discarded during compression does not seriously affect the image quality, but it must be remembered that each time the file is opened and saved using lossy compression, more data is lost and the image suffers.

SUPPRESS FILTER DIALOG   Checking this box prevents the program from asking you questions regarding lossy compression options. It only has an effect if you select a lossy file compression like JPEG.

FILTER INFO... Clicking this button brings up a screen that informs the user what version of filter is being used. This is only needed when you are talking with technical support or the TV cable is out and you are really bored.

EXPORT Begins the process of exporting the file opening the CorelDRAW Bitmap Export dialog box.

The CorelDRAW Bitmap Export Dialog Box

Use the Bitmap Export dialog box, shown here, to specify how you want to export files in any of the bitmap export formats, such as PCX, TIFF, TGA, GIF, Windows BMP, OS/2 BMP, SCITEX CT, and third-party filters.

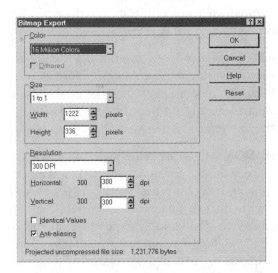

COLOR This option exports your drawing as shades of gray or color. Choose the number of shades of gray or color you want in the exported file from the list box. The greater the number of colors, the larger the exported file. Table 4-3 lists the available choices and the color depth of each choice.

Not all levels of color or grayscale are supported by all bitmap formats. If you have chosen a bitmap format that does not support a gray or color format, the option will not appear in the list box. For example, SCITEX CT is only exportable in 16 million color, 24-bit format.

Colors	Color Depth
Black-and-white	1 bit
16 shades of gray	4 bits
256 shades of gray	8 bits
16 colors	4 bits
256 colors	8 bits
16 million colors	24 bits

Available color choices and their color depth

TABLE 4-3

4

DITHERED   This option dithers the colors and gray shades in the exported file. Dithering may produce better results when exporting fewer colors than the original image. If the image contains fountain fills or color blends, dithering can cause obvious banding in the exported bitmap. Here are some guidelines to help you decide whether to dither the bitmap:

▶ If you are exporting 16 or 256 colors or grays, use dithering.

▶ If you intend to scale the bitmap in another application, dithering is not recommended.

SIZE   This option specifies the dimensions of the exported bitmap. Choose one of the preset sizes from the list box or choose Custom and type the dimensions in the Width and Height boxes.

By default, the size of the image in CorelDRAW is used. Smaller bitmaps (with lower resolution) or larger bitmaps (with higher resolution) can be created by scaling the image up or down in CorelDRAW prior to exporting.

n **OTE:**   *If you choose one of the preset sizes from the list box, the dimensions you choose may not be proportional to the bitmap's original aspect ratio. The exported bitmap will distort unless you place an empty border around your bitmap with the same ratio as the preset. For example, create a rectangle around your image 6.4 x 4.8 inches if you are exporting at 640 x 480. Then assign No Fill and No Outline to the rectangle. Now the aspect ratio of the image will be maintained when you export.*

RESOLUTION   This option specifies the resolution (in dots per inch) for bitmaps exported at a size of 1 to 1. Choose one of the preset resolutions from the list box, or choose Custom and type the resolution in the DPI box.

OTE: *As resolution increases, so does the size of the export file and the time required to print the image.*

IDENTICAL VALUES   When this check box is enabled, any values entered in either the horizontal or vertical value box are automatically reflected in the other box. Use this to keep the resolution uniform. There are applications where small differences in resolution allow the bitmap to fit a specific size without visible distortion.

ANTI-ALIAS   This check box, when enabled, uses a process that produces smoother bitmap rasterization. There is a small increase in the amount of time this feature takes. It is on by default and it is strongly recommend that you keep it enabled.

RESET   This option returns to the settings in effect when you opened the dialog box.

PROJECTED UNCOMPRESSED FILE SIZE   This option shows the estimated size of the exported file before compression. Compressed files will be smaller than the value displayed.

The Best Way ... Finally

No, I didn't get lost. The best way to bring an image from CorelDRAW into Corel PHOTO-PAINT is to save the file as a CDR file. To keep the file size from becoming ridiculously large, select the objects that are to be imported into Corel PHOTO-PAINT. Use the Save As... command and check the Selected Only option when saving the file. This way, only the CorelDRAW image and not a lot of white paper is converted into a bitmap.

Using Corel PHOTO-PAINT, open the CDR file. When a non-bitmap file is opened, Corel PHOTO-PAINT will automatically display the Import Into Bitmap dialog box. This dialog box is identical to the CorelDRAW Bitmap Export dialog box described in the previous section—except for the title.

So What's the Difference?

It would seem that it doesn't matter which way you do it. After all, the bitmap conversion engine in Corel does both the exporting from CorelDRAW and the importing for Corel PHOTO-PAINT. I can't explain it, but the results achieved by importing a CDR image with Corel PHOTO-PAINT at times appear superior to those achieved when the image is exported from CorelDRAW. Go figure.

Image File
Management

5

The first thing you may notice when you launch Corel PHOTO-PAINT is that, unlike CorelDRAW, there isn't a blank page, there is only an empty workspace. If you tried to do something in that empty space, you quickly discovered that nothing worked. To start using Corel PHOTO-PAINT (or any bitmap application), you must either open an existing image file or create a new one. Creating an image file with vector-based programs such as CorelDRAW involves very few decisions. You are asked to select paper size (letter or legal) and orientation (portrait or landscape), and little else. With Corel PHOTO-PAINT, there are many options available when you create a new file. That is why I have dedicated an entire chapter to this subject.

While there is nothing more exciting than jumping right into a new program and producing fantastic results, it only happens in the training videos. Invest some time in this chapter learning the basics, and you will save yourself hours of wasted effort later. In this chapter, you will learn how to create a new image and open an existing one, and manipulate and save the image.

Creating a New Image

1. Choose New from the File menu, opening the Create a New Image dialog box, shown here.

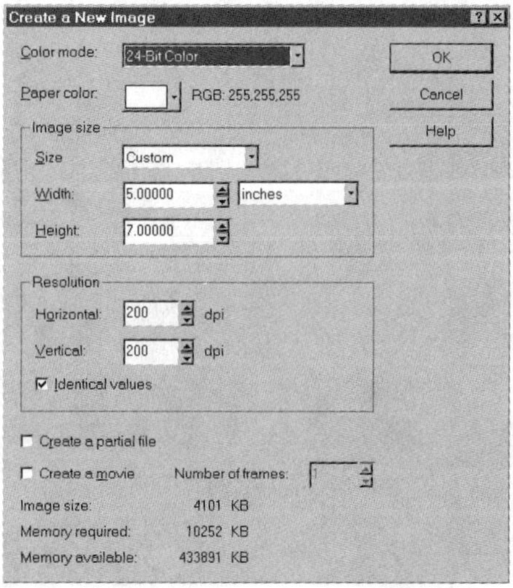

2. Select the Color Mode for the new image. A drop-down list of available selections can be accessed by clicking the down arrow. If you are unsure of the Color Modes, you may read about them in the Color Depth section in Chapter 3. The choices available are as follows:

▶ Black-and-white

▶ Grayscale

▶ 16 color (also known as 4-bit)

▶ 256 color (also known as 8-bit)

▶ 24-bit color (also known as 16.7 million color, or true color)

▶ 32-bit CMYK

IP: *Select a color mode that matches your requirements. For example, selecting 32-bit color when the final output only supports grayscale results in a file that is very large, difficult to manage (larger files slow down program operation), and a nightmare to transport to another system (at a service bureau) for output. It is like a man building a boat in his basement and then finding there is no way to get it out.*

3. Choose Paper Color. The currently selected color is displayed in the small preview area. Clicking the preview area or down arrow opens a color palette, allowing additional color selections. The colors that are available are dependent on the Color Model that is selected. Displayed to the right of the preview window is the numerical value of the selected color. The numerical system that is used is dependent on the Color Mode selection. For critical applications, you may specify a color model and its numerical equivalent by clicking on the color preview window and choosing the Others button at the bottom of the palette.

OTE: *The color palette that appears when you click on the paper color will always be the same, regardless of the color mode selected. This can be confusing if you pick Black-and-White or Grayscale and are presented with a color palette when the Preview button is clicked. The color mode that is finally displayed is correct even though the palette does not always correctly reflect it. For example, if Grayscale is selected, clicking on one of the colors returns a gray value in the preview that is displayed numerically. Clicking on the Others button opens a*

Select Color dialog box set to the Grayscale model. While this is inconvenient, it happens because Corel PHOTO-PAINT shares many modules with other Corel applications and technically there wasn't a good method to bring up a grayscale palette.

Paint and Paper ...
A Matter of Semantics

What Corel PHOTO-PAINT calls Paper color is referred to as Background color by everyone else on the planet. I understand the paper analogy, and it is appropriate; however, it is difficult to change common industry names this late in the game. To reduce confusion remember the following:

Paper color = Background color
Paint color = Foreground color

4. Select Size from the drop-down list. If you choose Custom, enter values for Width and Height. Values can be entered by typing or by clicking on the up/down arrows. Units of measure can be selected from a drop-down list that appears when the down arrow is clicked. The units of measure that appear are determined by the Options settings in the Tools menu. The default setting for Corel PHOTO-PAINT 6 is inches. When choosing values for image size, be aware that the larger the image, the larger the resulting file size. As you change the Width and Height values, the Image Size and Memory Required values at the bottom of the dialog box change, reflecting any changes in file size.

 IP: *Keep the size of your image small when you are experimenting with filters or effects. Everything operates faster, and when you are satisfied with the result, you can make the image the desired size and then apply the effects.*

5. Select Resolution: Enter the values or click on the arrows. If the Identical Values check box is checked, any value entered in one field will be automatically reflected in the other. Don't think that all images need to be 300 dpi. Here are some general guidelines about setting Resolution:

▶ Keep the Identical Values check box checked unless you have a specific requirement for nonidentical resolutions.

▶ For 24-bit or 32-bit color: Keep your resolution below 200 dpi.

▶ For black-and-white (but not grayscale): Use the maximum resolution of the output device.

▶ For grayscale: Keep the resolution at or below 150 dpi if the final output device is a laser printer (even if it's a 600/720 dpi printer).

If the values entered in steps 4 or 5 cause the Memory Required value to exceed the Memory Available displayed in the lower part of the dialog box, Corel PHOTO-PAINT will display a box warning that the file will be created as a partial file. This feature enables you to create files in partial segments that would normally be too large for your system. (This feature is discussed in greater detail in the section of this chapter called "Opening an Existing Image.")

Create as a Partial File

You also have an option to create a new image file as a Partial File. Originally the Partial File was created primarily to provide a work-around for files larger than 16MB. With the ability of Corel PHOTO-PAINT 6 to handle almost any size file, the value of this feature is limited to making posters. Very large posters, billboards maybe. To use it, check the Create a Partial File check box, which will open the Partial File dialog box after the OK button is clicked. The operation of this dialog box is discussed in the "Opening an Existing Image" section of this chapter.

Create as a Movie

This check box, if selected, allows you to create individual frames for an AVI movie file. Once it is checked, you can choose how many frames you require in the movie.

 OTE: *Corel PHOTO-PAINT 6 no longer has the 16MB image file size limit. So if the new image will be larger than 16MB, Corel PHOTO-PAINT will no longer automatically need to load it as a partial file. Applause, please.*

As the values for the image are being entered, the projected Image Size, Memory Required, and the amount of Memory Available are continually updated and displayed at the bottom section of the dialog box. This provides an interactive method to see what effect the changes made to the image values have on the final size of the new image.

Click OK or press ENTER. A new image window will appear. All new images are automatically named by Corel PHOTO-PAINT with the title "NEW-*x*.CPT", where *x* is a number assigned by PAINT. For example, the first new image you create after opening Corel PHOTO-PAINT will be NEW-1.CPT, the second NEW-2.CPT, and so on. This internal image counter resets each time Corel PHOTO-PAINT is closed, so that the first New File when Corel PHOTO-PAINT is reopened will always be NEW-1.CPT.

In case you are concerned about having to go through this every time you open a new file, I have good news. The Create a New Image dialog box retains the last setting you entered. I have found that once you have settings that are comfortable for your system and your needs, creating a new file rarely involves changing those settings.

Create a New File From Clipboard

New to Corel PHOTO-PAINT 6 is the New From Clipboard command, which is found in the File menu under the New File Creation command. This command, when selected, makes a new image with the contents of the clipboard. The color mode of the image is determined by the color mode of the contents of the Window clipboard. For example, if the contents of the clipboard are in 256 color, the image that is created with this command will be 256 color as well. This command is only available when the clipboard contains something.

 IP: *Make sure that you know what is in your clipboard before using the New From Clipboard command. I had a few paragraphs of text in my clipboard when I tested the command and it created a 35MB file.*

Opening an Existing Image

A majority of the work you do with Corel PHOTO-PAINT will involve opening image files that already exist. There are many options available when you open a file, so we will try to explore as many of them as possible. The following paragraphs contain detailed information about those options.

Click the Open File button on the Toolbar or choose Open from the File menu. The Open An Image dialog box appears, as shown here. This dialog box is fairly straightforward in its functions. Above the File Name section is a list of the files that are available in the selected folder. Highlighting any filename in this area will cause the filename to appear in the File Name box. The location of the files is selected in the Look in: box. Below the File Name section is the file filter selector called Files of Type. By selecting the type of file you want to open (e.g., Paintbrush *.PCX), only the files with that extension will be shown in the filename selection area. It may not seem like much, but when you are only looking for a particular file format, using the Files of Type selection filter can really speed things up.

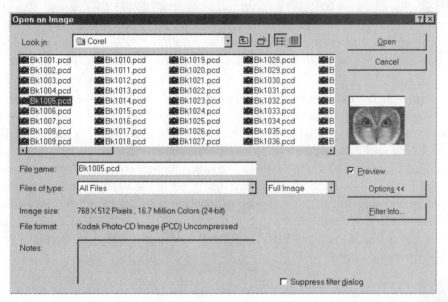

Click the Preview check box. Because a picture is worth a thousand words, Corel PHOTO-PAINT enables you to preview files before they are opened. On the far right side of the Open an Image window is the preview area. When Preview mode is selected by clicking on the Preview check box, a thumbnail of the currently selected image file appears. When Preview mode is not selected, there is a large X in the area. Preview is not available for vector files that do not have a bitmap header (a thumbnail image) associated with them. An example would be a Windows Metafile *.WMF file.

IP: *The Preview feature provides a quick way to look through file images. By using the arrow keys to move the highlight bar through the list of files, each file's image automatically appears in the preview area. If you want to preview a large number of files, I recommend using Multimedia Manager or some other browser program.*

Click the arrow in the Files of Type box. A lengthy filter selection drop-down list will appear. Selecting a specific type of image file allows only files with that extension to be viewed in the File Name section. This makes it easier to find files in a folder containing hundreds of files.

 OTE: *With Corel PHOTO-PAINT, you can load vector files (such as those in CorelDRAW) as well as traditional bitmap files. Vector files are converted to bitmaps (rasterized) as they are loaded. Rasterization is controlled by a separate dialog box. Selecting All Files *.* displays the names of all files in a directory (even files that cannot be opened by Corel PHOTO-PAINT).*

There are a few more features in the Open an Image Window that we need to explore.

Notice the selection box to the right of the Files of Type box. Clicking its down arrow reveals a drop-down list containing four methods for opening an image file. The default setting is Full Image. With Full Image selected, the entire graphic file is loaded into Corel PHOTO-PAINT. The other choices are Crop, Resample, and Partial Load. All of these methods are described in the section on "Options for Opening Existing Images." Click OK to load the selected image file into Corel PHOTO-PAINT. As you open an image, you will see the bar graph on the right side of the Status Bar of the Corel PHOTO-PAINT window showing the progress of your image file being loaded.

OTE: *If the image you have selected is a Photo CD image, an additional dialog box will open.*

When the image has been loaded, the standard Toolbar changes to reflect the options now available. Several buttons changed their appearance, indicating they are available for use. The Save button is not available because there have not been any changes made to the image. The image just loaded is an exact copy of the original; there is nothing to save. If you need to save the image at this point, you can do so by using the Save As feature in the File menu.

That's all that is required to open an image file. Additional options when loading standard image files and Photo CD files are explored in the next section.

Options for Opening Existing Images

Corel PHOTO-PAINT offers three additional ways to open image files other than the Full Image method just described. They are Crop, Resample, and Partial Load.

Each method is available through the drop-down list next to the Files of Type list box in the Open An Image dialog box.

 OTE: *When using any of the options for loading an image with a Photo CD, the Photo CD dialog box will open after the Open An Image dialog box. After you have made your selections in that dialog box, the Option dialog box opens.*

IP: *When you select one of the three options for opening an image file, it will remain set to that option until you change it back to Full Image or close Corel PHOTO-PAINT.*

Opening a Cropped Image

Selecting Crop in the Open Image dialog box and clicking Open brings up the Crop Image dialog box, shown here.

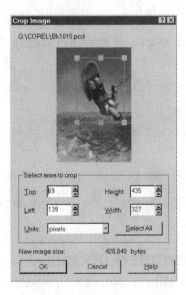

The Crop feature allows you to load only the part of the image that is required. The cropping is permanent, creating a new, smaller image. However, the original image is not altered. Although image cropping can be done within Corel PHOTO-PAINT, it is sometimes more efficient to use the Crop function to only load the part of the image file that is required. This is especially true with very large image files. In the preceding example, the Corel Professional Photo CD image was great, but we only needed the man on the water ski. We could have loaded the entire image (1.167MB) and cropped it, but it made more sense to only load the portion of the file that we needed. The bounding box was resized and moved, so most of the image was excluded when it was opened. The result is that we got only what we wanted, in a file of just 428KB, which loads faster and is easier to work with.

Crop Image Dialog Box Options

Following are the options available in the Crop Image dialog box.

PREVIEW WINDOW   Displays the entire image with a bounding box. Move the nodes on the bounding box to crop the image. Clicking and dragging anywhere inside the bounding box produces a hand cursor. Use the hand cursor to move the bounding box to a specific area of the image.

UNITS   Choose the units of measurement from a drop-down list.

TOP   Enter a number or use the scroll arrows to position the top of the cropped area.

LEFT   Enter a number or use the scroll arrows to position the left side of the cropped area.

WIDTH   Enter a number or use the scroll arrows to select the width of the cropped area (the right side moves).

HEIGHT   Enter a number or use the scroll arrows to select the height of the cropped area (the bottom edge moves).

SELECT ALL   Resets the bounding box to the edges of the image.

NEW IMAGE SIZE   Displays the file size of the cropped image based on the current size of the bounding box.

Opening a Resampled Image

Resampling may be a new term to some of you. Resampling resizes the image to a smaller size and/or a different resolution, thus creating a new file from the resampled image. The word "new" is important here, because when you resample an image, the original remains unchanged and a copy of the image, at the new size/resolution, is created. Using dialog box commands, you can reduce the width and height of the image either by size or percentage or change the resolution.

Selecting Resample in the Open Image dialog box and clicking the Open button opens the Resample Image dialog box, shown here.

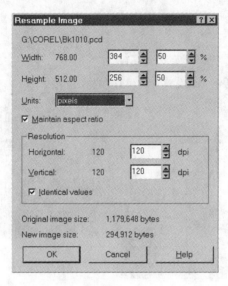

Figure 5-1 shows an image that has been resampled by 50 percent placed adjacent to the original image.

Resample Dialog Box Options (For Opening an Image Only)

The options in the Resample dialog box are fairly straightforward. The only part that may confuse some users is that the image being opened can only be resampled to a smaller size and cannot be made larger.

Corel PHOTO-PAINT also provides a Resample command for images that have already been opened. It uses a different dialog box and can be used to increase as well as decrease the image size.

UNITS   Choose a unit of measurement from the drop-down list box.

WIDTH/HEIGHT   Enter a number or use the scroll arrows to choose a size (entered in units of measure) or enter a percentage in the % box. The dimensions of the image remain proportional to the original. Any value entered in one box will cause the other box to change proportionally.

HORIZONTAL/VERTICAL   Enter a resolution. Resolution is measured in dots per inch (dpi).

By
resampling
on opening
we can
make
images
smaller than
the original
size.

FIGURE 5-1

IDENTICAL VALUES   If checked, any value entered will cause the other box to change to the same value.

ORIGINAL IMAGE SIZE   Displays the size of the original image.

NEW IMAGE SIZE   Displays the size of the resampled version based on the values entered in the dialog box.

IP: *When resampling an image, it is recommended that the Identical Values check box be left checked unless you have a specific requirement for mixed image resolution. Do not select a resolution that is greater than your final output device requires.*

Opening a Partial Load

When an image file size is larger than your system resources can handle, Corel PHOTO-PAINT provides partial-area loading. A partial area is a selected section of an image that is displayed as a separate image. You can open any of the partial areas from the same image. This enables you to work on separate areas of an image, without the system demands of opening the entire image. You can save a partial area as a new image. Partial areas are opened automatically by Corel PHOTO-PAINT if you have an image that is too large for your system to open. The Partial Area dialog box allows you to determine how many areas the image is to be divided into and to select the area that you want opened.

By working on selected image areas, you will be able to work on any size file regardless of existing system memory limitations. Lastly, Partial Area can be used to load parts of an image for purposes of special effects.

Open the Partial Area dialog box by selecting Partial Load in the Open An Image dialog box. When you click the Open button, the Partial Area dialog box opens, as shown here.

Figure 5-2 shows the partial area of an image after it is loaded. Notice the Select Partial Area button in the Toolbar is active.

Partial Area Dialog Box Options

Following are the options available in the Partial Area dialog box.

PREVIEW   This window displays the entire image with the grid. The grid square that is blinking is the one that will be loaded. Clicking on a grid square selects it for loading.

GRID SIZE   This is a drop-down list box with the following preset options:

2 x 2: Two rows and two columns
3 x 3: Three rows and three columns
4 x 4: Four rows and four columns

8 x 8: Eight rows and eight columns

Custom: Use the nodes on the grid lines to move the grid.

EDIT GRID CHECK BOX   Check this to edit the grid. If you choose "Custom Size", it is automatically checked. When the cursor is on the nodes of the grid lines, it changes to arrows, enabling you to resize the grid. At each intersection of the grid is a control handle. Moving the corner handle resizes the grid proportionally. The side handles move the grid either horizontally or vertically without maintaining proportion. When the cursor changes to the hand cursor, you can move the entire grid around the preview window and the Grid Size box displays the word "Custom Size."

PARTIAL IMAGE SIZE   Displays the expected file size of the partial area.

Moving Between Partial Images

After a partial image has been opened, the Select Partial Area button becomes activated in the ribbon bar. Clicking on this button saves the partial area image back into the original file and opens the Partial Area dialog box again. The changes made

The Partial Area button is only active when using the partial load feature.

FIGURE 5-2

to the partial image are reflected in the preview window. With the exception of some filters, all effects applied to a partial area are applied to the entire image.

Saving a Partial Area

There are two ways to save a partial-area file after it has been opened. The normal way is to save the image by using the standard File Save command in the File menu. This will cause the partial area you are working on to be merged back into the original file and saved as a complete image. The other method is to select Save Partial Area As from the File menu. This command allows you to save the partial area of an image that is currently open as a separate image with a different name. Remember, always save a partial-area file with the Save rather than the Save As command. You have been warned.

Opening a Photo CD Image

If the image you select in the Open An Image dialog box is a Photo CD image (*.PCD), the Photo CD Options dialog box opens when you select the OK button, as shown in Figure 5-3. Photo CD images are images from 35mm film negatives or slides that have been converted to digital format and stored on a compact disc (CD). Corel PHOTO-PAINT provides full import capability for Photo CD format.

 OTE: *Because CD-ROM drives operate at a slower data rate than ordinary disk drives, it may take noticeably longer for the preview image to appear from a CD than if it were loaded off of a hard disk drive.*

Photo CD Dialog Box Options

The following options in the Photo CD dialog box allow you to specify resolution and colors and apply image enhancement.

SIZE   In Corel PHOTO-PAINT 5 this box is called resolution. This is the name Kodak gives for the size of the image. It is a misleading term, because the settings have nothing to do with resolution. All of the images have the same resolution. When you import a Photo CD (*.PCD) file, a dialog box will appear prompting you to choose the desired file size, in pixels, from a drop-down list. Because the image sizes are defined by Kodak and based on photographs, the sizes have photographic names. The choices are as follows:

Wallet   (128 x 192)
Snapshot   (256 x 384)
Standard   (512 x 768)
Large   (1024 x 1536)
Poster   (2048 x 3072)

COLORS   Color selection is another drop-down list. You are presented with three different options regarding the color depth of the images. If you need to have the image in grayscale, import it as 256-color and then convert it to grayscale in Corel PHOTO-PAINT. The following color-depth options are available:

16.7 million (24-bit)
256 colors (8-bit)
256 grayscale

IMAGE SIZE   The Image Size indicator will update to reflect the choices you have made regarding resolution and color. I always load Standard in 24-bit color, which is approximately 1.167MB.

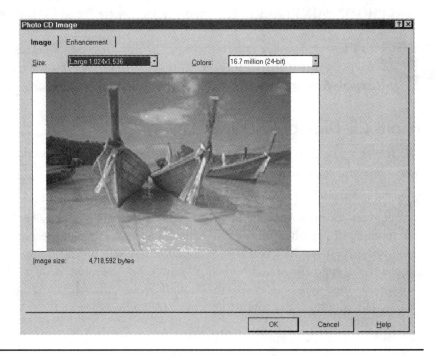

The Photo CD Options dialog box opens when a Photo CD image is opened.

FIGURE 5-3

ENHANCEMENT This tab, when selected, causes an image correction page to open before the image is opened. This page offers two different color correction systems. The Kodak Color Correction system and the Gamut-CD. The Gamut-CD system is a semi-automatic color-correction system that makes some of the not-so-great Photo CDs on the market look much better. Image Enhancement corrects the color of the image before you import it into Corel PHOTO-PAINT. The Kodak system is a manual system. The correction applied at this stage of the process is superior to any correction that might be applied in Corel PHOTO-PAINT. So, where can you learn how to use this wonderful color correction system?

PREVIEW Click Preview to see a thumbnail representation of the CD image.

NOTE: *Larger file sizes require large amounts of system memory, take longer to load and to apply effects, and require more disk space for storage. Therefore, always try to pick a resolution and color depth that is sufficient for your application.*

Loading a Photo CD Without Image Enhancement

Choose the PCD file to be loaded. Select the resolution and color of the Photo CD image and click the OK button. After the file loads, Corel PHOTO-PAINT issues a warning that the Photo CD is a read-only file that cannot be modified. I am still hoping that Corel will offer a preference setting allowing those of us who are sick of seeing this warning to disable it. When you load a lot of Photo CD images, you get a little tired of the message box that continually states the obvious.

Using the Checkpoint Command

The Checkpoint command provides a way to quickly save an interim, temporary copy of the currently selected image. At a Corel seminar in San Antonio, I talked with another Corel author about using the Checkpoint command. "I used it," he said, "and nothing happened." I was never clear what he expected it to do, but as far as he was concerned, the command didn't work.

To use the Checkpoint command, open the Edit menu and select Checkpoint. The progress bar will indicate the progress of the checkpoint file creation. That's all there is to it. It appears that nothing has happened. In fact, you have created a temporary copy of the image. When you open the Edit menu again, the command Restore to Checkpoint is now available. The Checkpoint file will remain as long as the image file it is associated with is open. When the image file is closed, the Checkpoint file is deleted.

 OTE: *The file that Checkpoint creates is a Corel PHOTO-PAINT file with a *.TMP extension. This is good to remember in case your system locks up and you must reboot out of Windows. To recover this file, you must first locate it, which is no easy task, since it could be in one of several directories. (Check the system TEMP directory, the TEMP directory used by Corel that you defined during installation, and then anywhere else.) Then, rename it with a *.CPT extension before restarting Corel. The reason for doing it before restarting Corel is that the Checkpoint file is automatically deleted whenever an image file is closed. When Corel starts up, it does housekeeping and looks for any stray *.TMP files left open (which would happen in a system lockup), and then promptly erases them.*

To use Checkpoint, choose Checkpoint in the Edit menu. To return to the image saved using Checkpoint, open the Edit menu and select Restore to Checkpoint. It doesn't get any easier than this. Only one checkpoint file can be maintained for an image. Subsequent applications of the Checkpoint command replace the previous Checkpoint file. If you have multiple images open, you can store a Checkpoint file for each one.

Revert to Last Saved

Similar in operation to the Restore to Checkpoint command, the Revert to Last Saved command, located in the File Menu, restores the image to the last saved version. Not very exciting, but it provides a quick way to return the image to the way it was the last time it was saved.

The Fundamentals of
Digital Manipulation

6

Now that you understand how to manage image files, the next step is to learn how to manipulate them once they have been opened. Don't worry when I say we are going to "manipulate"; we are not going to take advantage of innocent little bits. We will learn how to take images and make them the correct size for use in other programs.

Manipulating the Image by Resizing

Resizing an image is a common practice in word processing and page layout programs. There is more to resizing than first you might imagine.

Why You Shouldn't Resize or Crop an Image in Other Applications

Many page layout programs like Corel VENTURA, Pagemaker, and Quark offer graphic cropping and resizing as part of the program. They are usually fine for very minor image adjustments, but for any significant changes, you should open the files in Corel PHOTO-PAINT and make the changes there. There are several reasons for doing so, as follows:

► If you crop a large image file in a word processing or page layout program, the file size remains unchanged. Even if you use only 5 percent of a 16MB image file, the entire file remains as part of the document file. Large document files create problems with lengthy print times and difficulty in transport to a service bureau. If you crop that same 16MB file in Corel PHOTO-PAINT, it becomes an 800KB file.

► Resizing bitmap files in these applications can cause image distortion, which often shows up as unwanted moiré patterns over the entire image.

This chapter illustrates the different ways to change the size of an image once it has been loaded into Corel PHOTO-PAINT. Most of the commands are found in the Image menu. Commands in the Image menu affect the entire image and cannot be applied to a portion of the image.

How to Display Information About an Image

Corel PHOTO-PAINT gives the current size and resolution of an image, along with other data, at the bottom of the Image menu, which displays information about a selected image file. For a more complete picture, select Info from the Image menu located on the menu bar.

Another way to see the Image Info window is to click on the Corel PHOTO-PAINT icon in the upper-left corner of the window of the image and select Info from the drop-down menu.

Please note that the Image Info window is not a dialog box. Information is displayed but it cannot be edited. Once opened, the Image Info window must be closed by clicking the OK button before any other actions occur.

Image-File Information (Bigger is Not Better)

The Image Info window provides the following information:

Name:	Filename of the selected image file
Width:	Displays width in the units of measure selected by choosing Options in the Tools menu in the General page

Height:	Displays height in the units of measure selected by choosing Options in the Tools menu in the General page
X dpi:	Resolution (horizontal) in dots-per-inch
Y dpi:	Resolution (vertical) in dots-per-inch
Size in Memory:	Size of the uncompressed file
Original File Size:	Size of file after it is saved
Format:	Type of image file format, i.e., grayscale, 256 color, 24-bit color, etc.
Subformat:	Displays compression information
Type:	Color Mode of Image, e.g., grayscale
Objects:	Displays number of objects in an image (Corel PHOTO-PAINT format only)
Status:	Indicates if any changes have been made to the image since it was opened

You will find yourself using the Info command more than you may expect. Generally I use it to check the size of my image file before I save it.

Resizing the Image Window

Although this is not directly related to image resizing, it is essential for working with images. To resize the Image window, move the cursor over the corner or sides of the Image window until the cursor becomes a double-headed arrow. Click and drag the Image window until it is the desired size. The image remains unchanged and a gray border appears around the original image. It is very helpful to increase the image area size when working on an image close to the edge. When you are working with various Corel PHOTO-PAINT tools near the edge of the image, the program reacts when the cursor touches the Image window's border. Increasing the view area prevents the cursor from changing into a double-headed arrow any time the edge is approached.

 IP: *For a quick resize of the display size of the image to see it better, grab the corner of the window and drag it until it is the size you desire, then depress the Zoom to Fit (F4) key.*

Changing the Size of an Image

Images are rarely provided to you in the exact size that is required for your project. In the old days, when we needed to change the size of an image, we made a PMT (photo-mechanical transfer) of the image, which could then be reduced or enlarged. Fortunately, Corel PHOTO-PAINT provides several much simpler ways to change both the size and the surrounding working area of an image. There are several ways to change the size of an image. They include *resampling* and *cropping* and their variations.

Resizing Methods	Description
Resampling	This command makes the image larger or smaller by adding or subtracting pixels. It can also change the resolution of the image, which affects the printed size without adding or subtracting pixels.
Crop Tool	New to Corel PHOTO-PAINT 6, this tool acts like a traditional cropping tool. It allows you to define a specific area of an image and remove all of the area outside the defined area. In Corel PHOTO-PAINT 5, we did the same thing with a rectangle mask tool.
Changing paper size	This handy command uses a combination of resampling and cropping. The Paper Size command increases overall image size by increasing the size of the base image. It is as if you were to put a larger sheet of paper under the original. It can also be used to crop the image.

Resolution: the Key to Resampling

To use resampling, you need to know how it works. Before you can understand how resampling works, you need to understand some fundamentals of bitmap images. Before that we need to explore the "Big Bang" theory (just kidding!). If you learn how this part works, you will amaze your friends at user group meetings, because very few people understand this stuff.

Unlike images in CorelDRAW, which are composed of vectors, Corel PHOTO-PAINT files are bitmap images composed of millions of tiny picture elements called *pixels*. In Figure 6-1, I have enlarged part of a photograph of a flower by zooming in at 900 percent so you can see the pixels that compose that portion of the picture. Bet you didn't know pixels were square!

The spacing between pixels is called *resolution*. It is correctly measured in pixels-per-inch (ppi), although dots-per-inch (dpi) is the more common term.

Resolution is one of the most misunderstood terms in desktop publishing. This is because its meaning changes depending on what you are talking about. When you say the resolution of a laser printer is 600 dpi, you are referring to something completely different from the resolution of an image or a monitor.

Resolution in Corel PHOTO-PAINT 6 (or any other bitmap editing program) refers to the distance between pixels. So what does it matter how close the pixels are to each other? Good question. Pixel spacing (resolution) in a bitmap image affects how large the image will appear when it is printed and the amount of detail the image possesses.

A detail of the flower zoomed to 900 percent to show the individual pixels that make up the photograph. Photograph courtesy of Vivid Details

FIGURE 6-1

If the resolution of the 600 x 300 pixel image is set at 300 dpi, when it is imported into CorelDRAW it will be displayed in an area two inches wide and one inch high. That is because 600 pixels spaced at 300 dpi will take two inches to accommodate all of the pixels horizontally. If the resolution is changed to 150 dpi, the space between the pixels doubles. The image would now be four inches wide and two inches in height. To demonstrate this relationship, look at Figure 6-2. The photograph of the flower in the picture was saved in Corel PHOTO-PAINT at three different resolutions, and each one was imported into CorelDRAW. The file size (number of pixels it contains) of each of the three images is identical, but the dimensions are different because the resolution is different.

Rule: As resolution decreases, the dimensions of the image increase.

900 dpi

600 dpi

300 dpi

Same
photograph
shown at
different
resolutions

FIGURE 6-2

More Is Not Always Better

Many of you have been told that as the resolution of an image increases, so does the detail (quality) of the picture. This is true—but only for one type of image file. When working with black-and-white clip art (also called line art), you need the highest resolution possible. This is because all of the pixels in the image are either black or white. There is no gray area to provide transition. For this reason, it is important to have the pixels packed together as closely as possible (highest resolution) when working with line art images. This prevents those nasty jaggies that appear on lines that are not horizontal or vertical.

As the number of shades in an image increases (either grayscale or color), the need for high resolution decreases. This is because the eye is tricked by the gradual transitions between the pixels created by varying shades of gray or color. Look at the rose in the previous example again. How much difference do you see between the three pictures? When this photo was printed on a 600 dpi laser printer, all of the images appeared identical.

Rule: As the number of shades/colors in an image increases, the resolution may decrease (within reason) without serious loss of image quality.

Rule of Resolution

Every book printed on the subject of resolution always has this wonderful rule: For the image to look the best it can, it should possess a resolution that is not greater than twice the screen frequency of the final output device. Clear as mud? Usually those same books go on to list various settings for half-million dollar imagesetters. Meanwhile, there you sit with a 300 dpi laser printer wondering what its "screen frequency" is.

For the record, screen frequency is measured in lines-per-inch (lpi); some laser printers list them in halftone-cells-per-inch. For some reason, they never put screen frequency numbers in the printer manuals, so I have included Table 6-1 to help you. These are not absolute numbers but general guidelines for setting image resolution for grayscale and color images.

School is over! You now know more than the average desktop publisher. Let's apply our new-found knowledge and learn about the Resample command.

The Resample Command

The resolution and the dimensions of an image in Corel PHOTO-PAINT can be changed using the Resample command. One of the best aspects of the Resample

A listing of common desktop printers and recommended resolution settings for grayscale and color images

Output Device	Screen Frequency	Ideal Resolution	Acceptable Resolution
300 dpi laser printer	60 lpi	120 dpi	60-80 dpi
600 dpi laser printer	85-100 lpi	200 dpi	150 dpi
600-720 dpi color ink-jet printer	80-110 lpi	250 dpi	100-120 dpi
Imagesetter	150-300 lpi	300-600 dpi	200 dpi

TABLE 6-1

command is that it can change the size of an image without the need for you to grab the old calculator to work out the math.

Resampling should not be confused with the scaling features of CorelDRAW or other DTP programs like Pagemaker and Quark. These applications stretch or compress the bitmap images, often resulting in serious distortion. Resampling actually re-creates the image, adding or subtracting pixels as required. Figure 6-3 shows the effects of resampling a bitmap image. The original sample in the upper-left corner was resampled at 200, 400, and then 600 percent. Don't let the quality of this image keep you from resampling. The fill pattern is a worst case scenario—few shades and lots of diagonals.

— 100%

— 200%

— 400%

A graphic example of the effects of resampling

— 600%

FIGURE 6-3

IP: *Be aware that adding or subtracting pixels from an image decreases the quality of an image. Having said that, resampling is still the best way to change the size of an existing image.*

Two Approaches to Resampling and Their Results

Resampling an image with Corel PHOTO-PAINT 6 falls into two general categories: fixed and variable resolution. Each method changes the image size, and each has its own advantages and disadvantages.

Fixed Resolution Resampling

With this method, the resolution of the image remains unchanged, while the dimensions are either increased or decreased. Wait! Didn't I just explain that if the dimensions increased, the resolution had to decrease? I did. Because the resolution is fixed, Corel PHOTO-PAINT must either add or subtract pixels from the image to make it fit the new dimensions entered. When the space between the pixels increases, Corel PHOTO-PAINT creates more pixels to keep the resolution constant. When you resample, Corel PHOTO-PAINT goes through the entire image comparing pairs of adjacent pixels and creating pixels that represent the average tonal value. I told you that so you would know why your computer seems to take so long to resample an image.

Conversely, when the dimensions of the image decrease, Corel PHOTO-PAINT subtracts pixels from the image. This sounds ideal, doesn't it? Actually, you always lose some detail when you resample an image, regardless of the whether you add or subtract pixels. There is no magic here. The greater the amount of resampling, the greater the amount of image degradation introduced.

If the Maintain Aspect box in the Resample dialog box is checked, any change made to one dimension will automatically change the other. By disabling Maintain Aspect, it is possible to change one value without causing the other to change. Whenever you change the aspect ratio of an image, you introduce distortion. The distortion will be noticeable if the values entered vary too greatly from the original aspect ratio.

Another consideration when using the fixed resolution method is the increase in file size. Table 6-2 shows how quickly file sizes increase when a photo-CD (300 dpi) file is increased in size using fixed resolution resampling.

Before we go any further, let's resample an image using fixed resolution. To do the following exercise, you will need the 069091B.JPG file. It is located in the \IMAGES\PHOTOS\COASTS folder on CorelDRAW CD-ROM Disk #3.

How files increase in size geometrically when resampled at fixed resolutions	100%	200%	300%	400%
	1.01MB	4.03MB	9.82MB	17.23MB

TABLE 6-2

Using the Resample Command (Fixed Resolution) to Change the Size of an Image

In this exercise we will change the size of a photograph to fit in a brochure.

1. Open the file \Photos\Images\Coasts\069091B.JPG on Corel Disk #3 by selecting Open in the File menu and using the dialog box to locate and open the image file. When the file opens, it will not fit on most screens, so locate the Zoom window on the Ribbon Bar, click its down arrow, and select 50% from the drop-down list. If you bought PHOTO-PAINT 6 and not CorelDRAW 6 you do not have this file so I recommend looking at the illustrations here.

2. So that we can see the changes in size more accurately, open the Rulers by either selecting Rulers from the View menu or pressing CTRL-R. Please note the rulers measure in decimal units.

3. Select the Resample command in the Image menu. This opens the Resample dialog box.

4. The image has a width of a fraction over four inches. For this exercise it needs to be five inches wide. If it is not already highlighted, double-click the cursor in the Width box to select the current value and enter **5.0.** Because Maintain Aspect is checked, the height is recalculated immediately. Notice that the file size increased by about 500KB. The percentage of increase is also displayed. To the left of the Width and Height value boxes, the original size of the image is displayed.

5. Click the OK button. It will take some time to resample the image depending on the size of the file, how powerful your system is, and the amount of the increase. The results of the resampling can be seen in the Info screen shown in Figure 6-4. Click the Info button in the toolbar to confirm the new image size.

6. Save the file as RESAMPLE.CPT using the Save As command in the File menu, and close the file using the Close command in the File menu.

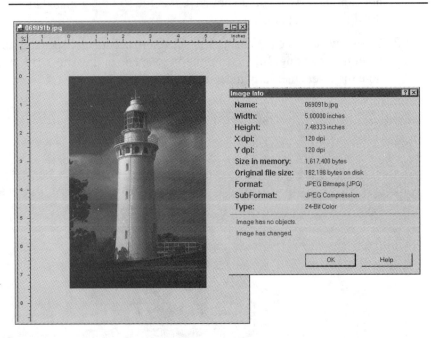

The Image Info screen confirms that resampling has changed the size of the image

FIGURE 6-4

Variable Resolution Resampling

The other resampling method is the one I generally use (when I must use one). Variable resolution resampling is accomplished by clicking the button labeled Maintain Original Size. By forcing Corel PHOTO-PAINT to keep the file size (number of pixels) unchanged, the resolution is changed to fit the newly requested image size. You can safely allow the resolution to be reduced to 150 dpi for grayscale and 100-120 dpi for color images.

The advantages of this method are that the file size remains the same and the operation is instantaneous. The reason it happens so quickly is that the image is not physically altered. Only information in the file header is changed. The resolution information is maintained in the header of bitmap image files. When Corel PHOTO-PAINT changes the resolution of an image, it only needs to change two sets of numbers in the file. The disadvantage to this method is the loss of image detail that results from the lower resolution. In most cases, if you keep the resolution at the recommended levels in Table 6-1, you should be able to resize the image without any noticeable loss of image detail.

6

IP: *When resampling by changing resolution, you cannot see any physical change in the displayed image while in Corel PHOTO-PAINT. This is because the program maps each pixel of the image to a pixel on the display regardless of the resolution setting. To see the effect, you must save the image and view it.*

Using the Resample Command (Variable Resolution) to Change the Size of an Image

1. Open the file 069091B.JPG again.

2. Select the Resample command in the Image menu and open the Resample dialog box.

3. Click the Maintain Original Size button. Notice that the percentage value boxes became gray, indicating that they are no longer available in this mode. Ensure the Maintain Aspect button is also enabled.

4. Enter a value of **5.0** in the Width box and click the cursor in any other value box. The values change to reflect the new size. Notice the file size remained the same and the Resolution changed to 99 dpi.

5. Click the OK button. A few points to note. First, the resampling was instantaneous. As previously mentioned, this is because the action only changed some control data in the image file and it did not change add or subtract pixels in the image. Second, the physical size of the displayed image does not appear to have changed unless we look at the rulers.

In Figure 6-5, both resampled images are shown side by side in Corel PHOTO-PAINT. Both are set to 50 percent zoom. The image on the right that was resampled using fixed resolution is physically larger on the display. This is because there are more pixels in it than in the image that was resampled using variable resolution on the left. The important point here is that both images will be the same size when they are printed.

Figure 6-6 shows the same two images after they were imported into CorelDRAW. Even though one of them contains more pixels, the pixels in the larger photograph are spaced closer together (higher resolution), making both photographs the same size.

The results of two different methods of resampling in Corel PHOTO-PAINT

FIGURE 6-5

The same two resampled photographs imported into CorelDRAW

FIGURE 6-6

Resample Dialog Box Options

Here is a list of the Resample dialog box controls and what they do. Not very interesting reading, but handy information when you need it.

UNITS   Choose a unit of measurement from the drop-down list box.

WIDTH/HEIGHT   Enter a number or use the scroll arrows to choose a size (entered in units of measure), or enter a percentage in the % box. The dimensions of the image remain proportional to the original. Any value entered in one box will cause the other box to change proportionally if the Maintain Aspect check box is checked.

HORIZONTAL/VERTICAL   Enter a resolution value or let Corel PHOTO-PAINT select a value for you. Resolution is measured in dots-per-inch (dpi).

PROCESS   Selects the process to convert. Choices are Anti-alias and Stretch/Truncate.

ANTI-ALIAS   This is the best selection. It creates a smoother image by removing jagged edges from the original. This is done by averaging or interpolating pixels. It takes longer to process, but it is worth it.

STRETCH/TRUNCATE   Only use this if you have a very slow system or you need rough approximations. It creates a rough image by stretching duplicated pixels and eliminating overlapped pixels. This process is very fast and the results less than great.

MAINTAIN ASPECT RATIO   When this is checked, the dimension/resolution values of the image remain proportional to the original. If you enable Maintain Aspect Ratio, values in the Width/ Height and Resolution boxes remain proportional to the original values. For example, if you increase the height by 50 percent, the width will be increased by 50 percent. The same is true of the Horizontal and Vertical resolutions. They remain equal, regardless of the values entered.

MAINTAIN ORIGINAL SIZE   When selected, this keeps the file size the same as the original, regardless of the values of resolution or Width/Height selected. This option is used to resample the image by changing the resolution. Changes in resolution are not reflected on the display, only when printed.

ORIGINAL IMAGE SIZE   Displays the size of the original image.

NEW IMAGE SIZE   Displays the calculated size of the resampled version based on the values entered in the dialog box.

RESET   Returns all the values in the dialog box to the values of the original image when the Resample dialog box was opened.

Resample on Open

The Resample option that is available when an image is opened is identical to the Resample command with one exception. The Resample command can increase or decrease the image size, while the Resample on Open option can only be used to decrease image size.

Additional Notes on Using Resample

Always use anti-aliasing when resampling an image unless time and/or system resources are critically short. Stretch/Truncate should be used when you need to see a quick sample of how the resampled size will fit. When changing resolution, remember that resolution settings that are greater than the final output device can support will result in large image files that require extra printing time without improvement in output quality. Changes to the resolution do not affect the appearance of the image displayed in Corel PHOTO-PAINT because each image pixel is mapped to the display screen.

Cropping an Image

Cropping involves the removal of part of an image either to change its size or to enhance the composition of the subject matter. Cropping in Corel PHOTO-PAINT 5 was done with either a Mask tool or the Paper Size command. Over the last year, many people asked Corel to provide a crop tool. Guess what? They did! The Crop tool is in the Toolbox located just under the Mask tool.

Using the Crop Tool

There are several ways to crop an image. In Chapter 5 we discussed cropping an image when opening it. The Crop tool offers several different ways to select what is cropped and what is not. The choices are:

▶ Crop to Selection

▶ Crop to Mask

▶ Crop to Border Color

Crop to Selection

After you select the Crop tool, you draw a rectangular bounding box that surrounds the subject and excludes the area you wish to crop. You can move the rectangle or size it using the handles that surround the box. Double-clicking the rectangle crops the image to the shape of the rectangle.

Instead of double-clicking the left mouse, you may click the right mouse button and the available options for the Crop tool appear. The Crop to Mask option is grayed out (not available) if there are no masks in the image. Selecting Crop to Selection crops the image.

Crop to Mask

This option operates like Crop to Selection except that it crops to a mask rather than to a rectangle created by the Crop tool. To crop an area, surround it with a mask. Select the Crop tool and right-click inside of the mask. Choose Crop to Mask.

Regardless of the type of mask you place on the image—circle, trapezoid, and so on—the Crop to Mask feature will calculate a rectangular area that will fit all of the points on the mask you have used. The final result will be a rectangular image. Figure 6-7a shows the original photograph with a circle mask on it; Figure 6-7b shows the resulting crop. Notice that the photograph was only cropped to the edges of the mask.

Crop to Border Color

The Crop to Border command removes borders of a particular color from an image. An example would be the ugly black border that seems to surround so many of the photo-CDs. The idea is to select the color of the border and click the button, and the black border disappears. In theory, that is the way it is supposed to work. The problem with the command has nothing to do with Corel PHOTO-PAINT. It is that nearly all borders are irregular, and since all crops must be rectangular, the result is that pieces of the original border do not get cropped.

The operation of the Crop to Border command is a two-step process. After you select the Crop tool, you right-click on the image to be cropped and select Crop to Border from the pop-up menu. This opens the Crop Border Color dialog box.

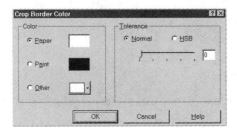

It is from the Crop Border Color dialog box that you select the color that will be used as the border color to be removed. The Crop Border Color dialog box lets you crop out the paper color, paint color, or a custom color you select from an image. The sensitivity of the cropping is controlled using the Tolerance sliders, which crop color based on similarities between adjacent pixels. These sliders control just how many shades of colors will be included in the cropping action.

A word of warning here. If the tolerance is set to zero, there is a chance that when you use the command nothing will happen. Let me explain. Let's say you have a black border surrounding a photo-CD image. You choose Paint (foreground) color, since the border is black (the default color for Paint is black). The Tolerance is set to zero, meaning that only the Paint color will be selected. Nothing changes after you execute the command. What happened? Because the Tolerance was set to zero,

a) Original
photograph
with circle
mask. b)
The result
of cropping
to mask

FIGURE 6-7

only an exact match of the Paint color would be cropped. While the black on the border looked black, it was only a close approximation. As you go through the book, you will learn about shading and numerical color values. To crop to the color, you can increase the Tolerance (a setting between 5-10 will suffice). Don't go crazy and set the Tolerance to a large value of 200. When the Tolerance value gets large enough, it reaches a threshold that I call the avalanche point. When it is set this high, almost all colors in the image are included in the border color.

For border colors that are not black or white, I recommend you use the Eyedropper tool to select the color from the image to be cropped. Your chances of finding the right color in a standard palette are very slim. When using the Eyedropper tool to get a color match, remember that most border colors are not uniform and you will still need to increase the Tolerance if you are going to include the entire border. Corel PHOTO-PAINT offers you two Tolerance modes to choose from, Normal and HSB. Stay with Normal and don't worry about the HSB for the Crop to Border command.

Using the Paper Size Command

The second command in the Image menu is used to increase or decrease the size of the image area by creating a new image area in the specified size and placing the original image within it. It is called Paper Size because Corel refers to the background as paper. This command takes the original image and places it *unchanged* on larger or smaller paper (background). The new image (Paper) color is determined by Corel PHOTO-PAINT's Paper Color setting. If the paper size is decreased to a size smaller than the original image, the image is cropped. If the paper size is larger than the original image, it is placed on a paper based on the Placement selection made in the dialog box.

Paper Size Dialog Box Options

The Paper Size dialog box provides the following options:

WIDTH/HEIGHT   Enter a value for the width and height of the paper.

UNITS   Determines the units of measurement for width and height. The options are inches, millimeters, picas/points, points, centimeters, pixels, and ciceros/didots.

MAINTAIN ASPECT RATIO   If Maintain Aspect Ratio is checked, the width and height values maintain their proportion to one another.

PLACEMENT   Determines the placement of the image on the paper. The drop-down list box has the following options: Top Left, Top Center, Top Right, Center Left, Centered, Center Right, Bottom Left, Bottom Center, Bottom Right, and Custom. If you choose Custom, use the hand cursor in the Preview window to move the image to the correct location.

PREVIEW WINDOW   Displays the position of the image based on the values entered in the dialog box. The cursor changes to the Hand cursor if placed over the Preview window. The image can be moved with the Hand cursor to the desired position on the paper. If the image is moved with the Hand cursor, the placement is automatically Custom.

Making a Postcard with the Paper Size Command

You will find that the Paper Size command can do quite a few tasks in Corel PHOTO-PAINT. In this exercise we will create a postcard using the Paper Size command. Initially, we will use Paper Size to crop the image and then use it to add white space to make the postcard. This exercise requires the file 046076B, which can found in folder \IMAGE\PHOTOS\COASTS on the Corel Disk #3. If you bought Corel PHOTO-PAINT 6 and not CorelDRAW 6 I am sorry to say you do not have this photograph. You can download it from the World Wide Web as described in the Introduction of this book.

1. Open the file using the File Open command in the File menu. Select a Zoom level of 50% from the Ribbon Bar.

2. Choose the Paper Size command in the Image menu. When the Paper Size dialog box opens, click on the Maintain Aspect box to disable it.

3. Our first use of the Paper Size command is to crop the photo to remove the mountains and the sky. Double-click the Height value box to highlight the current value. Enter a new height of **4.0** inches. Since the new height is much smaller than the original, the image will be cropped. The Preview window will not change until you click the next area.

4. Click the Placement arrow and choose Bottom Center from the list. The Preview window will change to show the new placement. By choosing Bottom Center, we are placing the original photo at the bottom and the center of the new paper size. Click the OK button and it will take Corel PHOTO-PAINT a few moments to create the new image, as shown in Figure 6-8.

 IP: *As a reminder for users of Corel PHOTO-PAINT 5, the Paper Size command no longer creates a duplicate image. Rather, it creates the new image and deletes the original.*

5. Open the Paper Size dialog box again. This time we will use it to extend our postcard to the right. As before, disable Maintain Aspect. Double-click the Width box to highlight it and enter a new value of 8 inches. Because this is much wider than the original, Corel PHOTO-PAINT will add to the existing image. In the Placement area, select Center Left. Click the OK button. You have finished your first postcard. Congratulations!

The Paper
Size dialog
box
provides
many
ways to
change the
background
of an image

FIGURE 6-8

I have added some text to show you some things that can be done with our postcard. You will learn how to create the drop shadows I created on the postcard in Chapter 16.

Tips on Changing Paper Size

The Paper Size command can be used to precisely crop an image by changing the paper size to the desired value and selecting centered placement. By moving the image with the cursor, it is possible to place the image at the exact desired position on the new paper size. Paper Size provides a method of placing an image on a larger background. You can make borders around an existing image. Try using Paper Size several times on the same image with complementary colors to make a quick border.

Changing the Orientation of an Image

7

Just as images don't always come in the proper size, they also don't always come in the desired orientation. When you are laying out a newsletter, for instance, it seems that when you get the images you want, they are inevitably facing the wrong direction. You usually want them facing inward if they are on the outside edge, and facing outward if they are on the inside edge. (I knew you knew that; I just thought I would throw it in.) Corel PHOTO-PAINT offers a collection of commands to allow the image to be reoriented quickly and easily.

The Duplicate Command

This command is new to Corel PHOTO-PAINT 6. In Corel PHOTO-PAINT 5 all of the commands in the Image menu produce changed copies of the image while leaving the original intact. Since many people complained that this produced many unnecessary copies of the image cluttering up the main screen, Corel changed the commands so they did not produce duplicates.

The Duplicate command produces a new file that is a copy of the original image. When you select Duplicate in the Image menu, a dialog box opens. You have two decisions to make. First, you enter a name for the duplicate file or accept the name generated by Corel PHOTO-PAINT. Second, you must decide whether to use Merge Objects with Background. If you don't know what objects are, don't be concerned; they are explored later in the book. For now, objects are bitmap images that float on top of the picture. The Merge Objects with Background option gives you the choice of making the duplicate image with all of the objects as they are in the original or with all of the objects merged into the background. Once they are merged, they are no longer objects.

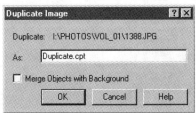

The Duplicate command becomes important when you must produce several copies of a file to create an effect, as we will soon see.

FOR *COREL* **PHOTO-PAINT 5** USERS

There is a Duplicate command in Corel PHOTO-PAINT 5 as well. It is located in the Window menu. That Duplicate command does not make a new file; it produces only a temporary copy of a file. Any changes made to it are reflected on the original. Each file made with the Duplicate command in Corel PHOTO-PAINT 6 is a separate file and has no relation to the file it was duplicated from.

The Image Flip and Rotate Commands

Many users in their headlong rush to get to the fancy effects ignore the Image Flip and Rotate commands. These commands are more useful than you might think.

7

The Flip Command

This command is pretty much self-explanatory. Accessed through the Image menu, it makes either a vertical or horizontal mirrored copy of the original image. To use the Flip command, select Flip from the Image menu. A flyout appears, showing the two choices: Horizontally and Vertically. Clicking on either of these executes the command, producing a copy of the image with the selected effect.

Now, if these commands seem pointless to you, you are not using your imagination. Remember, the best tool in Corel PHOTO-PAINT is located between your ears. I created an example to show you what I mean.

Making the Southwest image in Figure 7-1 began with a single cactus. Using the Duplicate command, a second copy of the entire image was made. The Flip Horizontal command was used to make the cactus a mirror copy of the original. The Paper Size command was used to double the width of the original. The original was copied to the clipboard and pasted as an object into the duplicate. The text and shadows were created with the Text tool.

This image shows what can be created using the Flip command in the Image menu

FIGURE 7-1

The Rotate Command

Rotate offers the ability to rotate the entire image. Again, this may not seem like much, but there are many things you can do with this little command.

Let's say you are laying out a sports magazine. You have a story about the playoffs that needs a graphic to introduce it. Everybody uses the picture of the arena packed with screaming fans and sweaty players. You want something different. You find what you want in a stock photo. The problem is it is a vertical photo and you wanted something to cover several columns. No problem with the Rotate command.

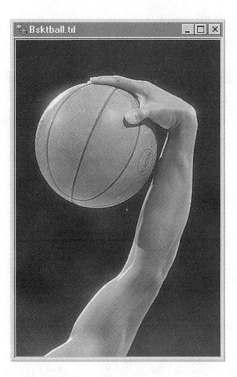

The original photo from the PhotoDisc library is great but it's not wide enough to cover several columns.

Choosing the Rotate command from the Image menu, you can select 90 degrees clockwise.

By using the Rotation command and a little imagination, you can create excellent banners for magazines, brochures, and so on.

Rotating an Image

To rotate an image, choose Rotate in the Image menu. A flyout appears with the available choices. Selecting Custom from the drop-down list opens the Custom Rotate dialog box.

The Custom Rotate Dialog Box

The Custom Rotate dialog box enables you to rotate the current image by a specified amount. A new image is created from the results of the rotation. The variables are as follows:

DEGREES Enter the amount of the rotation in whole numbers, not decimal numbers. Warning: the dialog box accepts decimal numbers without giving any indication that it isn't using them.

DIRECTION This option determines the direction of rotation. Click the Clockwise or Counterclockwise radio button.

MAINTAIN ORIGINAL IMAGE SIZE When this check box is selected, the image height and width dimensions are fixed. The rotated image is cropped at the image boundaries. If this is left unselected, the dimensions of the image are automatically calculated (adjusted) to fit the edges of the rotated image. The images on the following three pages demonstrate the several uses of rotated images.

ANTI-ALIASING When enabled, this check box reduces "jaggies" on rotated images.

The following sequence shows a variety of effects that can be achieved using the Custom Rotation dialog box.

1. This is the original image before any effects are applied.

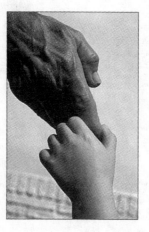

2. Here the image is rotated 30 degrees with Maintain Original Image Size unselected. Notice that the overall size of the image is increased to accommodate the rotated image.

7

3. By masking the white areas, I was able to paste several other photos on the rotated image to produce a collage. Masking techniques will be explored in Chapter 10.

4. Here the original image is rotated with the Maintain Original Image Size feature selected. Notice the cropping of the corners at the points where the rotated image went outside the original border.

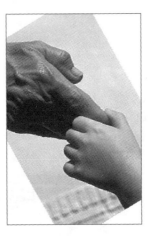

5. In this version, masking made it possible to apply Noise to the background and then apply the Airbrush tool to create the appearance of shadows.

Working with Custom Rotation

If the original image has objects, they will all become visible in the rotated copy. They will not be merged. This includes the hidden objects. (If you are bewildered by those last few sentences, it will become clearer when you get to the chapter on objects.)

Image Conversion

Corel PHOTO-PAINT does not have an export command like the one found in CorelDRAW. It can, however, convert images in two ways: by saving files in a wide variety of different formats (.EPS, .TIF, etc.), and by converting open images to different color modes (256-color, grayscale, etc.) using the Convert To command in the Image menu.

Converting color images to grayscale can save enormous amounts of disk space when producing graphics that will be printed in grayscale. Converting a 24-bit color image to grayscale reduces the image file to one-third of its original size. For example, if the original 24-bit color image is 1.1MB, converting it to grayscale will result in a file size of approximately 250-300KB.

Another use of this feature is viewing color images for pages that will be printed in grayscale. This book is an example of that type of work. All of the examples that are shown were originally color. I have learned that it is very important to convert the images to grayscale so I can see what they will look like when they appear in the book. Often, in my previous book, I would find an excellent example to show an effect or technique only to discover that the effect did not show up when printed in grayscale.

To Convert an Image

To convert an image, select Convert To in the Image menu. A drop-down list opens with the following choices.

Black and White (1-bit)

This option converts the image to black and white (not to be confused with grayscale). This selection opens another drop-down list with the following choices:

LINE ART Produces an image containing only black and white pixels. A pixel is assigned either a black or a white value, depending on the grayscale value assigned to the pixel (1-256) and the threshold level setting in the Options box. There are no intermediate steps between the two extremes. No halftone is applied to the image.

ORDERED Controls the appearance of images with pixel depths greater than those of the display device. Dithering is performed at a faster rate than error diffusion by approximating pixel values using fixed dot patterns.

ERROR DIFFUSION Controls the appearance of images with pixel depths greater than those of the display device. Provides the best results by calculating the value of each pixel using 256 shades of gray and spreading the calculation over several pixels.

HALF TONE Produces a continuous tone image such as a black-and-white photograph using dots of various sizes. On laser printers that cannot print different-sized dots, the halftone is produced by printing different numbers of dots in a given area.

16 Color (4-bit)

This option converts the image to 16 colors.

Grayscale (8-bit)

This option converts the image to grayscale.

Duotone

This is new in Corel PHOTO-PAINT 6. This converts a grayscale image into a duotone image.

256 Color (8-bit)

This option opens the Convert to 256 Colors dialog box. Converts the image to 256 colors. (See additional discussion later in this chapter.)

RGB Color (24-bit)

This option converts the image to 24-bit color (also called True-Color or 16.7 million color). It uses eight bits of data for each of the three channels of Red, Green, and Blue (RGB).

CMYK Color (32-bit)

This option converts the image to 32-bit color. This is a 24-bit color image that is separated into four channels: Cyan, Magenta, Yellow, and Black (CMYK), which is the standard separation for four-color printing.

Duotones

New to Corel PHOTO-PAINT 6 is the ability to create duotones, tritones, and quadtones. These are grayscale images printed using different colored inks, with each ink covering and reinforcing a particular range of the original grayscale image. The original purpose of duotones was to compensate for the fact that printing inks had a limited dynamic range when printing halftone images. When inks other than black or gray are used, duotones create incredible effects. The operation of this new function is discussed further in Chapter 26.

Using the Convert To Command

Choose the desired format to which the image is to be converted. The current format of the selected image is grayed out. With a 256-color image, for example, only the Duotone option is grayed out. Different 256-color options are valid choices. The selection of a format begins the conversion process. Remember that this process no longer creates a copy of the image being converted as it does in Corel PHOTO-PAINT 5. If you convert an image from 24-bit color to grayscale, the original will be converted. If you do not want to change the original, then use the Save As command in the File menu to save the file under a new name before you convert it.

IP: *Use the Convert To command when experimenting with different file formats. When I was making the screenshots for this book, I frequently converted images to grayscale to see what they would look like when printed. You can use the Undo command to revert to the original and try another color combination.*

Understanding Color Reduction

Before discussing the Convert To 256 Color dialog box, we must understand some more basics of color images. When we reduce a color image from a palette of 16.7 million colors (24-bit) to a palette of 256 possible colors, something has to give. It is much like putting 16.7 million pounds of flour in a 256-pound sack. Conversion is accomplished by using a color table. All 256 Color graphic images contain information about how color is supposed to be mapped in a feature called a *color table*. This produces a 256-color image that is indexed to the color table. This type of file is also referred to as an indexed color file.

In a Super VGA World, Why Convert Images to 256 Colors?

The answer is the Internet. The explosive growth of online services demands 256 colors. If you don't do a good job converting your image from 24-bit to 256 color, it can look terrible. Believe it or not, you can use some of the 256-color images in color publications and have them look as good as (or at least very close to) 24-bit quality.

IP: *Don't be too quick to dismiss the 256-color option because of previous bad experiences with a 256-color palette. Corel uses a proprietary 256-color palette that produces color that can be very close to 24-bit color but without the system overhead. (Image files in 256-color mode are two-thirds smaller than 24-bit files.)*

The Convert to 256 Colors Dialog Box

This dialog box is opened by the selection of 256 Color (8-bit) in the Convert To section of the Image menu. It allows you to choose the type of dithering and the palette type.

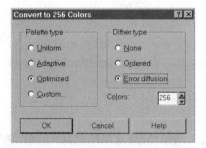

Four buttons determine the palette type that is used to convert the image. The options are Uniform, Adaptive, Optimized, and Custom.

UNIFORM PALETTE   When we convert an image to 256 color using a Uniform palette with no dithering (we will discuss dithering in a moment), colors lose their smooth transitions, resulting in a posterized effect. Corel PHOTO-PAINT allows us to look at the palette that was created using the Color Table command in the Image menu. The Uniform palette spreads out the colors across the entire spectrum, regardless of the color content of the image. With the Uniform Palette, there are usually colors in the palette that don't exist in the image. Because it includes the entire spectrum in the palette regardless of the image content, Uniform is rarely a good choice for palette selection. A new feature of this dialog box is the ability to convert to a number of colors other than 256. Using the Colors setting allows the user to define the exact number of colors to convert an image to.

Adaptive Palette

This palette is an improvement over the Uniform palette. It takes longer to process but the results are well worth the extra time. This method takes the overall range of hues (colors) and approximates the necessary palette to accommodate the greatest range of colors in the 256-color palette.

Optimized Palette

This is the best of all the palettes. It is a proprietary method that produces a palette that is as close to the original color as possible. It doesn't take much longer to process than does the Adaptive palette, but the results are noticeably superior on most images. There is still some image degradation, but it is very slight. There is a visual difference between the color palettes produced by the Adaptive and the Optimized, although the appearance of the palette is of little consequence.

Custom Palette

The Custom Palette allows you to pick all of the colors in the image. I cannot think of a single reason, other than for special effects, that you would ever want to use this option. The computer can do a far better job of creating a palette than any of us could ever hope to accomplish.

Dithering, or ... What Do You Do with the Leftover Colors?

When we convert an image that has many thousands of colors down to 256 colors, we are sometimes forced to practice a little visual sleight of hand to make the loss of color less apparent. We do it through dithering. *Dithering* is the placement of adjacent pixels in a bitmap image to create a value that the human eye sees as a color that does not really exist. Yes, it is eye trickery, plain and simple. If the color doesn't exist, then Paint creates a combination of adjacent colors to give an approximation of the missing color.

Three buttons determine the type of dithering performed when the image is converted. The choices are None, Ordered, and Error Diffusion.

None

The default is that no dithering is performed. This is the best choice if the image looks good without it. The colors in the image are limited to the 256 colors in the palette.

Ordered

Ordered dithering is performed at a faster rate, but the result is less attractive. It is also known as *pattern* dithering. Each pixel that is not in the available 256-color spectrum is evaluated and two palette colors are applied to the two adjacent pixels to give the appearance of the missing color. For example, if the missing color is green, one pixel would be made yellow and the other blue. Together in close proximity, they would appear to be green. Of the two dithering options, this is the least desirable. The Ordered option is only available for Uniform palette.

Error Diffusion

This provides the best results, but is slower to process. It is the best of the two types of dithering. Error diffusion changes a color pixel whose value falls outside of the 256-color palette into an adjacent pixel's color. That pixel in turn replaces another pixel's color and this continues until the last pixel is determined to be close enough to one of the colors in the palette. This type of dithering produces the softest transitions between the areas of color that would normally have harsh lines of color separation.

Tonal Enhancements, or . . . Making Bad Photos Look Good

8

This chapter is about using some of the basic Corel PHOTO-PAINT tools to fix photographs so they will look more professional when they are printed. The tonal enhancements discussed in this chapter will be the basic ones that apply to the entire image, not just portions of it. It is not about adding or removing body parts, people, or objects like trees. It is about the basic procedures you must do before the fancy stuff. It includes adjusting contrast, found in Color Adjust|Brightness-Contrast-Intensity; applying sharpening using Sharpen|Unsharp mask; equalizing using Color Adjust|Equalize; and correcting image tonal balance with Color Adjust|Gamma. While much of the work that desktop publishers do is restricted to grayscale (mainly due to the cost of color printing), we will discuss enhancing both color and grayscale images.

The Color Adjust Filters

Many of the filters we will be using are grouped under Color Adjust in the Effects menu. Only four of the filters work only with color as indicated below, so don't let the term "Color Adjust" confuse you. Following is a list of the Color Adjustment filters. (Filters marked with an * are not available if the selected image is not color.)

- ► Brightness-Contrast-Intensity
- ► Color Balance*
- ► Desaturate*
- ► Equalize
- ► Gamma
- ► Hue/Saturation/Lightness*
- ► Level Threshold
- ► Replace Colors*
- ► Tone Map

Brightness and Contrast, or . . . The First Shall Be Last

This is the most familiar filter to many users because most monitors have adjustments for brightness and contrast. In practical, day-to-day use, it has limited application. I have started this portion of the chapter with it because it will serve as a point of comparison as we learn how the other filters work. Even though Intensity is part of the filter group, I am limiting this initial discussion to the concept of Brightness and Contrast.

Brightness and Contrast represent one of the most basic tonal controls in any bitmap editing program. It has been said that every image that you work with could benefit from a slight increase (about 10 percent) in both brightness and contrast. While such an increase can sometimes give dull, flat pictures a little more pizzazz, it is not always the best choice.

An Introduction to Brightness and Contrast

You will always find Brightness and Contrast controls together in photo-editing programs. Tradition? No, their actions are complementary (although the controls work independently). You will probably never adjust brightness without making an adjustment to contrast, or vice versa. This is because if you increase brightness, it has a tendency to wash out both shadows and highlights of the image. To counter the "washout effect," you need to increase contrast. If you decrease brightness, darkness increases. (I know this stuff. I used to watch Mr. Wizard.) When darkness increases, contrast must also be decreased or all of the details of the image will look like a close-up of the La Brea Tar Pits in Los Angeles at midnight.

If the photograph that you are working with is too dark due to improper exposure or poor lighting conditions, Brightness and Contrast might be able to salvage what would be an unusable picture.

 IP: *Accept the fact that there will be some pictures that you can't fix. Filters have their limitations.*

Pitfalls of Contrast and Brightness

Be careful not to develop a disease I call Contrastus-Maximus-Vulgarus. This is a disorder suffered by newer Corel PHOTO-PAINT users when they first discover the

Contrast tool. Too much contrast makes the picture look grainy. The deceiving part of this disease is that many times, too much contrast will look good on the monitor, but the printed result will be disappointing. Another recommendation when you are working with scanned images is to make as many initial corrections as possible at the time you scan the image into the system.

Your first step before applying any enhancements is to study the photograph to determine what needs to be corrected. If the image is high contrast, meaning it has lots of dark areas and bright white areas (the result of being shot with a flash or on a bright sunny day, for example), it can create problems. This is because detail in the dark areas is lost, yet increasing the overall brightness causes detail to be washed out in the white areas. I am getting ahead of myself, so let's begin by looking at the "original" tonal enhancement tool, Brightness-Contrast-Intensity.

The Brightness-Contrast-Intensity Dialog Box

Nearly all of the filter dialog boxes are identical in their operation. All of the controls will be explained in this section. Each time the dialog box is referenced after this, only the controls that are unique to the filter will be discussed.

The dialog box as shown below consists of two viewing windows arranged in a Before and After format. The window on the left shows a thumbnail of the original image (Before). The window on the right is a preview window that displays the results of the filter action based on the current settings (After). More importantly, the subjects shown in both windows are my children Jonathan and Grace.

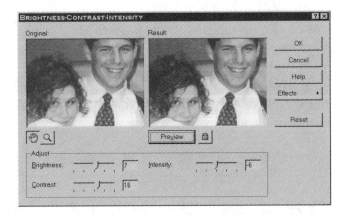

THE ZOOM BUTTON The Zoom button, when selected, changes the cursor to a magnifying glass when it is placed over the original window. Clicking the left mouse button on the image zooms it in. Clicking the right mouse button on the image zooms it out. The Results window on the right changes automatically to match the existing image window.

THE HAND BUTTON   The Hand button, when selected, causes the cursor to change to a hand when placed over the Results window. By clicking the left mouse button, you can drag the image in the window to position it as desired. The Preview window changes automatically to match the existing image window. The Hand button acts like the Zoom button if you click on the Original window and do not drag it. So, what is the purpose of the Zoom button? It is one of the great Corel PHOTO-PAINT mysteries.

THE PREVIEW BUTTON   The Preview button, when depressed, causes the selected filter to be previewed in the Results window. The Auto-Preview function automatically occurs two seconds after any use of the hand or zoom function in the left (before) window. If enabled, Auto-Preview occurs when any change is made to the settings in the dialog box.

THE AUTO-PREVIEW ENABLE/DISABLE BUTTON   This is the button with the lock on it to the right of the Preview button. If it is depressed, Auto-Preview is enabled. If it is not depressed, then the Preview button must be clicked to see the results of changed settings. The Results window will still automatically preview if there is a change in zoom or position in the Original window.

THE EFFECTS BUTTON   The Effects button, when depressed, gives you access to other filters without the need to use the Cancel button and open the Effects menu again.

THE RESET BUTTON   The Reset button, when depressed, returns all of the settings for the filter to their default values, and it updates the Results window to match zoom and position of the Original window.

THE HELP BUTTON   When the Help Button is depressed, a context-sensitive help file appears. It opens the help file that specifically deals with the currently selected filter.

WHAT'S THIS?   This is not a button, but rather an extension of the WIN'95 architecture. If you click the right mouse button on any control in any of the filter dialog boxes, a small "What's This?" message appears near the control. Click on the message with the left mouse button and an explanation of the individual control appears. If there is no help topic assigned to the particular control, you will be advised that one is not available.

Brightness-Contrast-Intensity

The descriptions of the controls unique to the Brightness-Contrast-Intensity filter follow:

BRIGHTNESS SLIDER The Brightness slider controls the brightness of the image. The slider operates on a percentage scale with a range of –100 percent through +100 percent. A negative setting makes the image darker; a positive setting makes it brighter.

CONTRAST SLIDER The Contrast slider controls the increase or decrease of contrast in an image. The slider operates on a percentage scale with a range of –100 percent through +100 percent. A negative setting decreases the contrast; a positive setting increases it.

INTENSITY SLIDER The Intensity slider controls the intensity of an image. The slider operates on a percentage scale with a range of –100 percent through +100 percent. A negative setting decreases the intensity of the picture; a positive setting increases it.

NOTES ABOUT THE PREVIEW WINDOWS The following bulleted items give you a summary of the features of the Preview windows that apply to all of the filter dialog boxes. These features include:

- ▶ Showing a thumbnail of the entire image if there are no masks present.
- ▶ Only displaying the masked area of an image if a mask is present.
- ▶ If the mask is complex (made of several parts), showing nonmasked areas as well.
- ▶ Not displaying any objects in the image that are locked.

What Brightness-Contrast-Intensity Filters Do and What They Do Not Do

If you are new to photo-editing, these may be the filters that seem the most familiar to you. As a result, you may have unreasonable expectations of what they can and cannot do. In this section we look at what we can reasonably expect from these filters.

Brightness

You can use the Brightness filter to either increase or decrease the brightness of an image. This capability allows you to make changes to a color image without affecting the overall color (hue) of the picture. Brightness is the only component in the color model that has nothing to do with a color value (Brightness can also be used with a grayscale image). Brightness can destroy an image when it is increased or decreased too much. When mismanaged, this component can wipe out a subject's detail and shading, or turn a lovely sunset into a faded blob.

The Brightness filter expresses values as a percentage. The extremes are –100 percent (solid black) and +100 percent (white). Brightness affects every pixel equally. Logically, the best way to lighten a dark picture is to apply Brightness. Or is it? When Brightness is applied, the darker areas are lightened, and as a result, more detail can be seen in the shadow areas. That's the good news. Now for the bad news. Most of the detail in the light areas disappears. Therefore, Brightness is not a magic cure-all for dark pictures. In fact, most photo-editing professionals do not use this feature very much.

Contrast

Contrast works by *adjusting the difference in the degree of shading between pixels,* causing pixels that are separated by a small difference in shading to be separated by an even greater amount of difference. When taken to an extreme, the contrast on a color image can be increased to a point where no other features can be distinguished. On a grayscale photograph, you can end up with an effect called *posterization,* where all of the shades of gray are polarized to just black or white. Always remember that the goal with Contrast is to enhance, not distort the image.

USING THE CONTRAST FILTER EFFECTIVELY   The Contrast filter expresses values as a percentage. The extremes are –100 percent (no contrast; image is solid gray) and +100 percent (extreme contrast; image is too dark, almost black). An application of positive Contrast appears to produce a much sharper picture, but detail has been lost.

Remember that Contrast only affects adjacent pixels of differing shade. Use the Contrast filter to change the distinction between the light and dark areas of an image.

Intensity

Intensity affects (brightens) the light areas of an image without washing out the darker ones. Intensity acts like a combination of both Brightness and Contrast. It isn't, but it has the effect of the two. Intensity increases the brightness of the lighter pixels and applies less brightness to the darker midtones and dark pixels. The result is that the image is supposed to look brighter without being washed out. The Intensity slider expresses values as a percentage. The extremes are –100 percent (zero intensity; the image is black) and +100 percent (the image does look bad on the screen and tends to print grainy). Intensity mainly affects lighter pixels, making them brighter.

Before You Give Up on These Filters

I have painted a pretty bleak picture of all the things that cannot be done with these three filters. They are not without some merit. In Figure 8-1 a photograph from the Corel Professional Photo CD-ROM Sampler is shown loaded into Corel PHOTO-PAINT without any image enhancement. Figure 8-2 is the same image with 10 percent Brightness, 30 percent Contrast, and 30 percent Intensity applied. You will hear many rules about ratios of Brightness to Contrast. Ignore them. Many of the rules are carryovers from disciplines other than digital imagery. Use the Results preview window to experiment and discover what works for you and your output device.

IP: *Make as many initial corrections as you can when you bring the image into the system. This includes the scanning process and applying color correction when loading Photo-CDs. Consider applying color correction even if the image is going to be converted to a grayscale image.*

An unenhanced image from the original Corel Professional Photo-CD Sampler

FIGURE 8-1

By adding a little brightness and equal amounts of contrast and intensity, we are able to make the photo a little more usable. At least we can see the subject is a duck

FIGURE 8-2

Now that we have explored brightness, contrast and intensity, let's look at some filters in the Effects menu that really make a difference. First is the Unsharp Mask filter.

The Unsharp Mask Filter

This filter, along with the other Sharpen filters, is discussed in detail in Chapter 21, but I want to give you a brief introduction here since the use of this filter is so important to overall image tonal enhancement. The Unsharp Mask effect accentuates edge detail, as well as sharpening a certain amount of the smooth areas in an image. Generally, any photograph will benefit from an application of Unsharp Masking. Despite its odd name, which comes from its photomechanical origins, this filter will sharpen a dull image without producing the highlights (small areas that are too bright) normally associated with Sharpen filters.

IP: *While it is best to apply sharpening when the image is scanned, applying it in Corel PHOTO-PAINT is the next best thing.*

The Equalize Filter

This filter may be one of the most misunderstood and underused of all the filters. Many Corel PHOTO-PAINT users are reluctant to use this filter because they don't understand what the filter is or what it does.

The Equalize filter is used to redistribute the brightness values of the pixels in an image so that they are spread out more uniformly throughout the image. The classic way to show how the brightness values of the pixels (shades) are distributed in an image from the lightest to the darkest is with a histogram.

The Histogram and How to Read It

Look at Figure 8-3, which shows the histogram of a dark photograph. The bottom of the histogram shows the range and distribution of shades in the image. Shades to the left of the Low-point arrow are black (darker). Shades to the right of the

The histogram for our low contrast and dark photograph is shown in the dialog box so you can see how the tones of the image are concentrated in the dark end of the range of tones

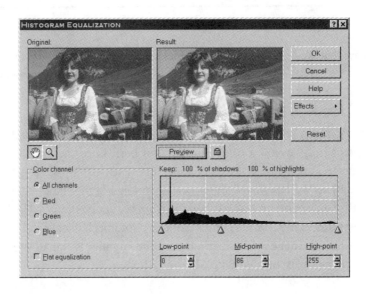

FIGURE 8-3

High-point arrow are white (brighter). The Mid-point is supposed to be neutral (gray). The vertical scale indicates the number of pixels of each shade in the image. Knowing this, let's look at what this histogram is telling us.

Because the photograph in Figure 8-3 is dark, the greatest concentration of shades is on the left (which is the dark side, Luke). Since the photograph is low contrast, there are very few shades outside of this main area of concentration on the left. The numbers in the three boxes below the histogram represent the numerical readout of the range of pixels in the photograph, with 0 representing the darkest possible shade in the image, 255 representing the brightest possible shade, and 128 representing the midpoint.

 OTE: *Grayscale images can display 256 possible shades (0-255). Color is composed of three channels (Red, Green, and Blue—RGB), each one capable of displaying 256 possible shades.*

Using the Equalize Filter

We can redistribute the shades in a photograph using Equalize. This filter can make the darkest colors black and the lightest colors white and stretch all of the shades between. In this particular photograph, the histogram tells us that the darkest shade in the image has a value of 10, the brightest shade a value of 217, and Corel PHOTO-PAINT has determined the midpoint to be 113. By sliding the Mid-point arrow to the left, we are telling the Equalize filter to redistribute the shades in this image so they spread out over a greater range. In Figure 8-4 we have used the Equalize filter to do just that to create a much brighter photograph. Please note that the histogram shown in the photograph does not appear during normal operation. I used Corel Capture to make a screen capture shot of the photograph's histogram and then used Corel PHOTO-PAINT to crop and paste it into the photograph.

The Equalize Filter Dialog Box

The controls of the Equalize Filter dialog box operate in the same manner as the Brightness-Contrast-Intensity dialog box described at the beginning of the chapter. Only the controls that are unique will be listed here. The dialog box contains the following elements:

Histogram	Displays distribution of pixels in an image according to brightness.
Low-point Arrow	Shades to the left of the Low-point arrow are darker.
Mid-point Arrow	Position determines the tonal quality of the midpoint tones.
High-point Arrow	Shades to the right of the High-point arrow are brighter.
Flat Equalization	Disables the Mid-point arrow and uniformly distributes the tones between the High-point and Low-point arrow settings.
Color Channel	Allows application of the Equalization to individual color channels.
Keep % of Shadows	*Shadows* are the shades between the Low-point and Mid-point values. Displays percentage loss (if any) of Shadows caused by current Low-point arrow setting.
Keep % of Highlights	*Highlights* are the shades between the High-point and Mid-point values. Displays percentage loss (if any) of Shadows caused by current High-point arrow setting.

Our photograph no longer looks like it was shot in a swamp at twilight. The histogram displays the new distribution of tones (shades)

FIGURE 8-4

One way to get a feel for how the Equalize filter works is to try different variations with the Equalize filter on a file that has a basic 11-step gradient fill from black to white (which results in 11 gray bars).

The effect of an adjustment using the Equalize filter is relatively evident with this image because the tones are spread out as equally as possible. Therefore, the redistribution of tones that a given Equalize setting applies is obvious. As long as you keep in mind that most photographic images do not have an equal distribution of tones the way a Linear gradient fill from black to white does, it can be useful to learn about the Equalize filter in this way.

Exploring the Equalize Filter Further

1. Create a new file with the following parameters: Grayscale, 2 inches by .66 inches at 100 dpi. After the file has been created, double-click the Fill tool (looks like a bucket) button in the Toolbox, which opens the Tool Settings roll-up. Select the Gradient fill button (second from the left). Click the Edit button, opening the Fountain Fill dialog box. Enter the following values: Type: **Linear**; Angle: **180**; Steps: **11**; From: **Black**; To: **White.** Click the OK button. Now with the Fill tool still selected, click anywhere in the new image area. The results should look like the illustration below.

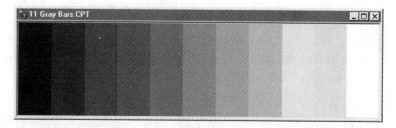

2. From the Effects menu, choose Color Adjust and then Equalize. The Equalize dialog box opens as shown. Notice that the histogram shows an even distribution of tones.

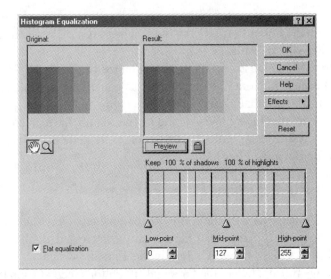

A histogram of a Linear Gradient Blend from black to white shows that the tones are evenly distributed.

3. Make sure the Auto Preview and the Flat Equalization check boxes are not enabled. To show the effect of redistribution, reduce the values of Mid-point and High-point by half. Next, we enter a value of 63 for the Mid-point setting and 127 for the High-point setting, then hit OK. The Equalize filter will redistribute the tones according to these settings by taking all of the values from 127 to 256, making them white, and then redistributing the gradient from black to white so that it goes from 0 to 127, with the midpoint being at 63.

4. Close the file we just modified and do not save changes when asked.

Recommendations for Using the Equalize Filter

While there is a science to using the Equalize filter, it takes a significant amount of experience to use it effectively. Equalize provides some of the most powerful controls to adjust the overall appearance of the image. The other filters deal with specific areas of the image, that is, special effects, adjustment of softness/sharpness, and so on. The Equalize filter enables you to take a dark murky image and make it bright and clear, or to make a washed-out color appear more vivid. All of these effects are best accomplished through experimentation with the filter.

A good starting point—after you have used the Preview button to see the effects that the default settings made—is moving the Mid-point arrow a small amount to the left or right and checking the preview window to see the results.

Generally, though, if you have an image with a lot of dark tones and you need to lighten it up, start by adjusting the Mid-point setting to the left to bring more light tones into the image. You can also try moving the High-point setting left.

 IP: *Be cautious when moving the High-point and Low-point settings toward the Mid-point, as this reduces the tonal range of the image. What is tonal range? See the following explanation.*

8

Tonal Range

To better understand the operation of the Equalization filter, it would be helpful to understand what tonal range is. Most photographs have wide tonal ranges. The tonal range is the difference between the lightest and the darkest pixels (tones) in an image. Different types of media have different tonal ranges. This range of difference is expressed in a logarithmic density scale. Such a wide tonal range is impossible to reproduce in printing. As a point of reference, the tonal range of a color slide (the best) is 2.7. The best range possible for printing (on very high quality paper) is about 1.9, and the worst is newsprint with a range of 0.9. So what happens when a color image with a tonal range of 2.7 is printed on newsprint? Similar tones merge into a single tone, resulting in uncontrolled and undesired color range reduction.

If the image is too light, you can try adjusting the Mid-point setting to the right to ease more dark tones into the image. If the midtones are the only problem, you would only adjust the Mid-point setting to redistribute midtones.

Don't be concerned with the numerical data presented on the bottom when you are making adjustments, although this data is useful for commercial applications where critical adjustments are required. Keep moving the arrows, making note of the effects. All of the settings interact with one another, so moving the High-point arrow to the right has an effect that is different, depending on where the Mid-point arrow is located. It bears repeating: Experiment with the settings on the histogram. The time invested will pay great dividends later on. Expertise comes from repeated use and familiarity with the results of different settings on the Equalize filter. The following are more hints on using the Equalize filter:

▶ It is often best to equalize a scanned image first to improve its appearance before using other filters.

▶ Use Equalize when you have applied a Canvas that has been washed out from applying it at a high transparency value.

▶ The Equalize filter can be used several times on the same image until the right effect is achieved. It can be done, but don't make a habit of it. Be sure to use Checkpoint before attempting this approach.

▶ If you get lost while moving the arrows around, click the Reset button to return to the original values.

▶ Experiment! Experiment! Experiment!

What about the Color Channels?

Color channels are not available if the image you are working with is not color. The application of Equalization to individual color channels is beyond the scope of this chapter.

The Gamma Filter

I wish there was a quick and slick way to explain gamma. Many people work with gamma and don't know what it is. Australians refer to sunbathing as "catching gammas." Gamma Hydra 4 is one of the more popular names for a planet in the old *Star Trek* series. Monitors have gamma settings and scanner hardware and software offer gamma correction. Corel PHOTO-PAINT offers a gamma filter. So the question remains: What is gamma and what does it do?

What Gamma Is (Boring Technical Stuff)

A *gamma curve* is the name for a mathematical function that describes the nonlinear tonal response of many printers and monitors. That is the best and most concise official technical description I have been able to find. What does it say? Gamma is a mathematical curve that describes how inaccurately scanners, monitors, or printers reproduce a tonal range. Still fuzzy? Read on.

What the Gamma Filter Really Does

The Gamma filter controls the Gamma curve of an image in a very simple manner. The Gamma curve is a graphical representation of the balance of shadows, midtones, and highlights. Use the Gamma filter to enhance detail by adjusting middle grayscale values (midtones). This will not affect shadow areas (darkest black areas), or highlight areas (lightest white areas). Visually, it will look and act like a combination of Brightness, Contrast, and Intensity. It will pick up some additional detail in low-contrast images without the graininess of the Contrast Filter. For those experienced users who are accustomed to working with Gamma values, a value of 180 in the Gamma filter dialog box represents a normal gamma of 1.8.

The Gamma Filter Dialog Box

The controls of the Gamma filter dialog box operate in the same manner as the Brightness-Contrast-Intensity dialog box described at the beginning of the chapter. Only the control that is unique will be listed. The dialog box is displayed here.

GAMMA VALUE   The Gamma slider displays gamma values as a percentage. The range is from 10-1000 percent. Values below 100 will darken the image. Values above 100 will increase the brightness of the image.

So, What Can I Do with the Gamma Filter?

You can use the Gamma filter to correct a poorly adjusted scan. The Gamma filter provides a method of making an image brighter without losing the midtones. The result of using Gamma is that the image isn't as washed out as it would be using Brightness. A small increase in Gamma can have a significant effect on an image without washing the image out. It has been my experience that Gamma works best when applied selectively to objects or masked areas rather than the entire image. My favorite use for the filter is to make text into a mask and then apply a high setting of Gamma to the mask as shown below.

Applying the Gamma filter to a masked area can really make it stand out.

Enhancing the Color
of an Image

B efore getting into the area of image color enhancement, let's make sure we are all using the same terms. Color is an area where even the brave become fainthearted. While it is easy to see color on your display, it is harder to control color and even harder to get color output from a printer that makes you and your client happy. Since we will only be discussing the most basic color enhancements, this will be a short chapter. We need to understand some of the terms we will be using. These are not necessarily industry standard terms (there is no such thing as a standard term in this business), but they are the terms used throughout this book.

Color Enhancement Versus Color Correction

So what is the difference between enhancement and correction? Is it possible to have an absolutely accurate scan and display of a color photograph and have it not be correct? Of course it is. Many color photographs do not match the original subjects. The negative may have been overexposed, or it may have been a dull, gray day when the photograph is taken and you want a bright and sunny photograph. I have a photograph of the sphinx from the first Corel Sampler. The first time I saw it I thought that it didn't look "right." How did I know? I have never been to Egypt to see it myself. Yet, I had a perception of what I thought it should look like. Looking at the photograph I felt the overall colors should be changed. This is what color enhancement is all about, changing the colors of an image to make it look like you think it should. Color correction, on the other hand, is about making the color in the image match the original photograph, though not necessarily the original subject. We will not be discussing color correction in this chapter; that topic is explored in Chapter 26.

The color accuracy of your monitor is critical when working with color enhancement, since you will be making judgments based on what you seen on the screen. When you consider the expense factors involved in four-color press work compared to single or even two-color printing, mistakes in color are very costly.

IP: *Before you do any serious color work that you expect to send out to a printer, you absolutely must calibrate your system using the Color Wizard (located in the Tools menu).*

In this chapter we are going to look at some of the simple things we can do to the entire image to improve its color and not force a printer to run screaming into the night the next time you bring in a job. Let us start with the most basic of the color controls: Hue/Saturation/Lightness in the Color Adjust portion of the Effects menu.

The Hue Filter

What can you do with hue? That's the first question I had when I began working seriously with color back with the Corel PHOTO-PAINT 5 book. While it's possible to use hue for color correction, this is not recommended. The demonstration of Hue I generally see in other books is someone taking a color photograph of a rose and turning the red roses on green stems into blue roses on purple stems. There are many effects that look great, or at least interesting, but have no practical application. The color-shifted rose falls into that category. I have yet to have someone ask me to produce a color-shifted rose.

What can you do with hue? The good news is that there are several useful things that you can do with both hue and saturation. The best effects with both hue and saturation are made by applying them selectively to parts of the image. Let's first look at hue.

Using the Hue/Saturation/Lightness Filter to Enhance Color

The Hue/Saturation portion of this filter is one you are more familiar with than you may realize. You have both of these "filters" on your color television. You know them by a different name. Hue acts like the tint control, and Saturation acts like the color control. Although all three filters are grouped together in the Effects menu, we will look at them and their effects separately.

Hue is a term used to describe the entire range of colors of the spectrum. In HSB (Hue-Saturation-Brightness) and HLS (Hue-Luminance-Saturation) color models, hue is the component that determines just what color you are using. The Hue filter changes the selected color from shade to shade until you have gone through the entire spectrum. Changing the Hue in an image shifts all of the colors in one direction or another. To understand this better, we need to use the color wheel.

The Color Wheel

Have you ever seen a color wheel? There isn't one displayed in this chapter because it is difficult to use a grayscale color wheel. The color wheel displays all of the colors in the visible spectrum in a circle. When you pick a point on the color wheel and travel halfway around the wheel, you are at the inverse, or complement, of the color. Color wheels are wonderful tools for picking complementary colors. Did you know that? Just pick a color that you want to use and the color that is opposite it on the wheel is the complementary color.

How the Hue Filter Works

The Hue filter expresses color value change in degrees of rotation around the color wheel. All of the other filters describe color change in values of shade (0-255). The extremes of the Hue filter are –180 and +180 degrees (a value of 180 degrees in either direction selects a point exactly halfway around the color wheel).

Every pixel that has the Hue filter applied to it will have its color value changed. Hue affects all pixels by changing their color value. This is important to remember since applying the Hue filter to make one part of the image look "better" may make another portion of the image look "weird."

IP: *Every pixel in an image that a Hue filter is applied to will have its color value changed.*

Using the Hue/Saturation/Lightness Filter

This filter is only available for color images. Select Hue/Saturation/Lightness..., located under Color Adjust in the Effects menu, from the drop-down list that appears. The Hue/Saturation/Lightness filter dialog box appears after a few moments, as shown below. The dialog boxes of all of the filters share many common elements. The common controls for this filter are described in detail in Chapter 8. Only the controls that are unique to this filter are discussed here.

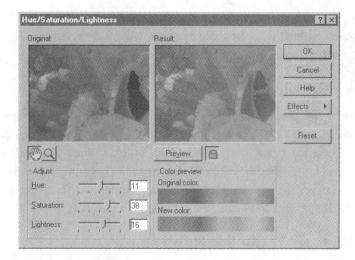

The Hue Slider

The Hue slider controls the amount of Hue filter action applied to the image. To operate, you may set the Hue slider in the dialog box to a value between –180 and +180 degrees to specify the degree to which you want to change the colors in the selected image. Higher values produce greater color shift. Use the Result window to see the effects of different slider settings on the image.

The Saturation Percentage Slider

The Saturation slider controls the amount of Saturation in the image. To operate, set the Saturation percentage slider in the dialog box to a value between –100% and +100% to specify the amount of saturation you want to apply to the image. Positive values (more than zero percent) produce more intense colors. Large positive values actually decrease the tonal range of the photograph, resulting in an effect known as *posterization.* Negative values (less than zero percent) decrease the amount of color in the image. At a setting of –100%, a color picture appears to be a grayscale image. Use the Result window to see the effects of different slider settings.

Lightness Slider

Until now, we haven't mentioned lightness. *Lightness* refers to the amount of white in the color. This control determines the lightness or darkness of the colors and affects all selected pixels. This effect does not change the brightness of an image.

Confusing, isn't it? Large values entered with this control can quickly turn a photograph into either the La Brea Tar Pits or a white screen. Any adjustments made using this control should be very small, that is, in the range of 1-3.

The Color Preview

The Color preview portion of the dialog box displays two vertical color spectrums (Original color and New color) to let you visually see the changes being made between the original colors and the resulting colors. When you shift the Hue of colors, you will notice that the entire spectrum on the bottom shifts either to the left or the right, depending on whether a positive or negative shift was applied. The effects of the Saturation and Lightness are displayed as well.

Three Ways to Apply the Hue Filter

There are three ways to apply the Hue filter. First, it can be applied to the entire image for overall enhancement or correction. Second, it can be applied selectively to a portion of the image. While selective application of the Hue filter is generally discouraged by professionals, there are times when it can be used very effectively. Third, it can be applied to individual color channels for effects of advanced correction techniques. In this chapter, we will only explore applying Hue to the entire image or selectively to portions of the image.

The Effects of the Hue Filter

To see the effects that the Hue filter produces, look at the samples I created in the color insert. As the amount of color shift in a color image approaches 180 degrees from either the positive or negative direction, several things become apparent. First, the changes in the image begin to look more alike the closer they get to the 180-degree point. Second, at 180 degrees, the image has been inverted and looks like a photographic negative.

Summary of the Hue Filter

The Hue filter is very powerful. There are many times when colors will need to be changed, and the Hue/Saturation filter is the best way to accomplish this quickly. I have one last note on Hue. Theoretically, you can get every color in the rainbow using the Hue filter. However, I find that in practice it is sometimes difficult to get an exact match, even using one-degree increments in the filter. Now we'll move on to Saturation and a special effect that is becoming very popular in advertising.

Saturation

When we discuss *saturation* of an image, we are referring to the strength or intensity of color applied to the image. Did you ever turn the color control knob on the TV set (back when they had control knobs) all the way up? If you did, the colors became saturated and began to look surrealistic (in the 1960s, we would have called them "psychedelic"). The Saturate filter expresses values as a percentage. The extremes are –100 percent (no color; the image becomes grayscale) and +100 percent (image takes on an unreal, comic-strip look). Saturation affects every pixel in an image, increasing the amount of color in each pixel to its maximum intensity. Adjusting Saturation on selected portions of a color photograph can be a very effective attention-getter by removing the color from everything in the photograph except that part you want to bring to the viewer's attention.

The Desaturate Filter

The Desaturate filter in Effects|Color Adjust accomplishes the same thing as the Hue/Saturation/Lightness filter when Saturation was set to –100%. So why did they put in two filters that do the same thing? Well, first of all they don't do the same thing. With the Hue/Saturation/Lightness filter, the user can control the amount of saturation. With the Desaturate filter, it is always –100% saturation.

The Desaturate filter provides a quick way to change a color image into one that looks like a grayscale while actually remaining a color image. This can be very useful if you wanted to add color to highlight or colorize a grayscale image. Remember, you cannot recover lost color information. For example, if you apply Desaturate to a color photograph and then in the next step use the Hue/Saturation to apply a saturation of +100 percent, the color will not return.

 IP: *When you Desaturate a color image, the colors are not suppressed, but lost permanently. The image loses all of its original color information.*

Color Hue Control

This filter and its counterpart, Color Tone Control, are new additions with Corel PHOTO-PAINT 6. It is used to correct the color cast in photographs. If you are not familiar with color cast, think of it as a light tint that affects the entire image. The Color Hue Control, found in the Adjust group of the Effects menu, lets you visually select and then apply correction as your image may require it. The dialog box displays six thumbnails of your image, each representing individual color-correction filters as shown below.

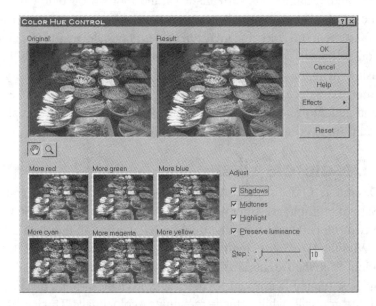

The thumbnails are arranged so that each color is above its complement (or opposite). To add an effect, simply click one of the thumbnails across the top row containing the three primary colors (Red-Green-Blue). The Steps slider controls the amount of an effect that is applied when a particular thumbnail is depressed. To subtract one of the primary colors, click one of the colors below it. For example, to reduce the amount of red in an image, you only need to click the More Cyan thumbnail. The Result window and every thumbnail change to reflect your choice. The effects are additive, meaning that you can click the More Red twice at a Step setting of 10 and the More Blue once at a Step setting of 5. Click the Reset button to restore the default settings.

Choose the portions of the image that you wish to affect from options in the Adjust settings area. Shadows applies the color changes only to the darkest areas of the image. Midtones changes midrange areas. Highlight applies changes to the lightest areas, and Preserve Luminance ensures that the brightness of the colors in the image does not change.

Using the Color Hue Control Filter

For a brief demonstration of what the Color Hue Control filter can do, I have included the following exercise:

1. Open the file \IMAGES\PHOTOS\FOOD\091015.JPG located on CorelDRAW Disk #3. This is a colorful photograph but it has cool cast. To give it more warmth, we will use the Color Hue Control filter.

2. From the Effects menu, choose Adjust and select Color Hue, opening the Color Hue Control dialog box. Each thumbnail shows what the image area would look like if that thumbnail were applied.

3. Click the More Red thumbnail and the More Green thumbnail once. Notice that after each thumbnail is clicked, the change occurs in both the thumbnail and the Preview window. Keep the Steps at 10. Click the OK button. The colors in the image now have a warmer cast.

4. To more readily see the effect of the filter, you need to use the Undo feature. Hold down the CTRL key and click the Z key (Undo), and the image returns to its original state. Still holding down the CTRL key, clicking the Z key again (now it becomes a Redo key) reapplies the last effect. This is a quick way to compare the effects of any filter. So is the color now correct? As I said at the beginning of the chapter, the correct color is less important in most cases than the desired color.

Color Tone Control

The Color Tone Control located under Adjust in the Effects menu lets you visually select the type of color tone (color contrast, color saturation, and color brightness) effect your image may require. It operates in the same manner as the Color Hue Control except in what effect it controls. The dialog box displays several thumbnails of your image with a number of applied color tone correction and image enhancement filters. As with the Color Hue Control, you can add an effect by simply clicking on the thumbnail or combination of thumbnails that best reflects the type of effect you want. The other noticeable difference between the two controls is that the Color Tone Control effects appear in the preview almost instantly. The Color Tone Controls take a few moments to generate.

Introducing Masks

10

Now that we have covered some of the basics of applying enhancements to the entire image, we need to understand how *masks*, *objects*, and *layers* operate. It is the creation, manipulation, and transformation of masks and objects that form the foundation of any advanced work done in Corel PHOTO-PAINT. With that said, let us begin this chapter by introducing masks.

What Is a Mask?

The official Corel definition of a mask is "a defined area that covers part of an image or the entire image." Another way to say the same thing is that by using a mask, we can control exactly where on the image an effect will be applied. For example, if I have a picture of a jet and I want to change the background but leave the image of the jet unaffected, I need to make a mask that protects the jet from changes.

Here's an analogy. If you have ever painted a room in a house, you know that one of the most tedious jobs is painting around the window sills and baseboards. The objective is to get the paint on the wall but not on the surrounding area, so either you paint very carefully (and slowly) or you get a roll of masking tape and put tape over the area where you don't want the paint to go. In using the tape, you have created a mask.

Another example of a mask is a stencil. When a stencil is placed over an object and then painted, only the portion of the stencil that is cut out allows paint to be applied to the surface. Both stencils and masking tape are examples of masks.

Corel PHOTO-PAINT masks are much more versatile than a stencil or masking tape (and not as difficult to remove when you are done). The masks used in Corel PHOTO-PAINT enable you to control both where and how much of an effect is applied to a portion of an image.

To the human eye, this is a picture of a jet. To the computer, it appears to be something else entirely.

Masks as Fences

Because the concept of masks is so important, I want to give another illustration to help you understand the need for masks in Corel PHOTO-PAINT applications. Look at the preceding photograph. To our eyes, it appears to be a jet flying in the sky. To the computer, there is no distinction between the jet and the sky. It is just a rectangle filled with blue, gray, and white pixels. (The original I am looking at is a color photo.) To the computer, a bitmap image is like a large field of land. When you look at a map of an area, you can see where one lot ends and another begins. When you look at the actual property, there are no property lines, only dirt. The only way to separate the property into lots is to put up boundary markers or fences.

Masks are the equivalent of fences to Corel PHOTO-PAINT. They tell the program where one area ends and another begins. Without masks, it would be difficult, if not impossible, to accomplish even the simplest of image-editing tasks.

How Masks Are Created

Corel PHOTO-PAINT provides a variety of mask-creation and selection tools. Figure 10-1 shows the flyout menu of mask-creation tools.

These tools, used in combination with the related buttons shown in the toolbars in Figure 10-2, provide the Corel PHOTO-PAINT user with an almost limitless selection of masks.

Don't be concerned about the names of tools for the moment. We will be examining each one of these so that you can understand their functions and the best times to use them.

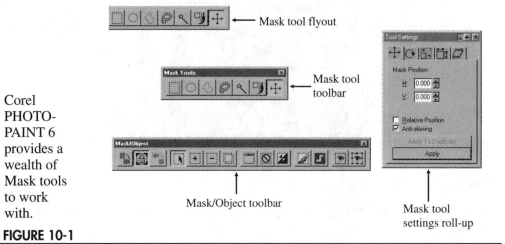

Corel PHOTO-PAINT 6 provides a wealth of Mask tools to work with.

← Mask tool flyout

← Mask tool toolbar

↑ Mask/Object toolbar

↑ Mask tool settings roll-up

FIGURE 10-1

Magic Wand Mask tool

Mask Brush tool

Mask Transform tool

Rectangle Mask tool

Freehand Mask tool

Circle Mask tool

Lasso Mask tool

Invert Mask

Overlay Mask

Show Object Marquee

Create Object

Create Mask

Add to Mask

XOR Mask

Remove Mask

Show Mask Marquee

Preserve Image

Normal

Subtract from Mask

Mask All

Paint on Mask

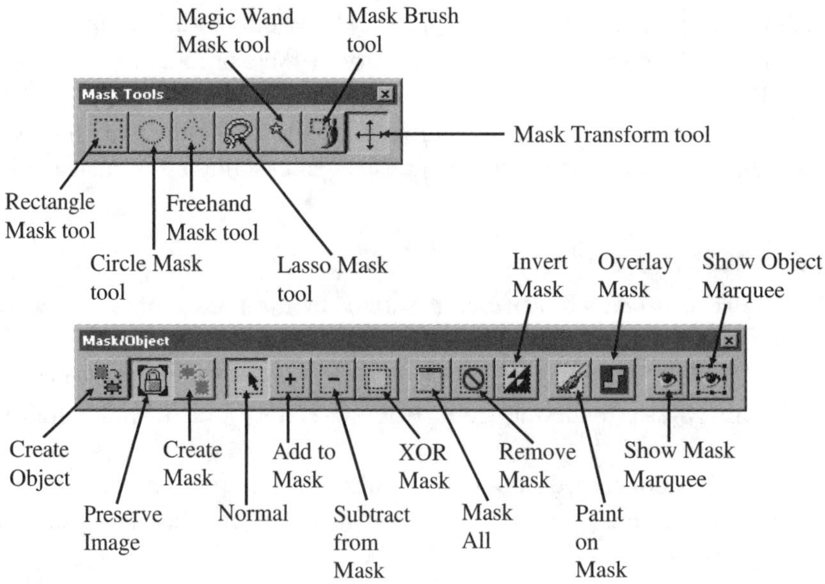

The Mask buttons/icons

FIGURE 10-2

Two Groups of Masks

The mask tools shown on the flyout in Figure 10-2 can be divided into two basic groups: *regular* mask tools and *color-sensitive* mask tools. Regular masks are created by the user, who defines their size and location within the image by using the mouse or other pointing device. The regular mask tools are the Rectangle, Circle, and Freehand mask tools. Unlike the Regular mask, the boundaries of the color-sensitive masks are created by Corel PHOTO-PAINT based on information entered by the user in conjunction with the color values of the image. Color-sensitive mask tools are the Lasso and Magic Wand. The last button on the Mask Tool flyout is the Path Node Edit tool, which is used to alter both the regular and color-sensitive masks.

Simple and Complex Masks

Regardless of which mask tool is used, you can create one of two types of masks: *simple* and *complex*. (Corel calls them "complex," but they should be called "compound.") Simple masks are those made with a single operation. For example, if you take a Circle Mask tool and drag it until you have a circle, you have created a simple mask. Complex masks are made up by combining two or more smaller masks. (Knowing the difference between simple and complex masking will save you some head scratching later when we discuss complex masks.)

Creating a Simple Mask

We will use the following steps to create a simple mask and learn a clever way to add text to a photograph at the same time.

1. Before we can create a mask, we need an image to work with. On CorelDRAW Disk #3 of the Corel CD-ROM, locate the file 065084B.JPG in the folder \IMAGES\PHOTOS\PEOPLE. Open the file. If you don't have a CD-ROM drive, run out immediately and buy one. If you bought Corel PHOTO-PAINT 6 and not CorelDRAW 6 you will not have this photograph. You can use almost any photograph in the Corel PHOTO-PAINT 6 series for this exercise. Find one you like and use it.

 IP: *A quick way to reopen a file that was recently opened or saved is to use the keyboard combination* ALT-F *and then enter the number for the file near the bottom of the menu.*

2. Click and hold the left mouse button on the Mask Tool button in the toolbox. After one second, a flyout menu appears. A faster way to do the same thing is to click on the tiny black control arrow in the lower-right corner of the tool and the flyout opens immediately. Release the mouse button (the flyout remains open) and click on the Rectangle Mask tool. The flyout disappears and the Rectangle Mask tool is now the visible button on the toolbox.

3. Move the cursor into the image area. The cursor becomes a crosshair. Click at a point in the image and, holding down the mouse button, drag a rectangle ending at a point near the bottom of the railing as shown below. You have just created a simple mask, as shown in the following illustration. Notice that the outline of the mask is composed of a black-and-white line that seems to move. This is known as "marching ants" to Adobe Photoshop users. The color of the mask is used to differentiate it from other marquees used in Corel PHOTO-PAINT.

4. That's it! That's all it takes to make a mask. Let's do something
constructive with the mask. Open the Effects menu and select Color
Adjust. A drop-down list appears. Choose Gamma and a dialog box will
open. Be aware that Gamma, like many other filters, requires the file be
24-bit color to be available to the user. Change the Gamma Value setting
to 500 and click the OK button. The results are shown in the following
illustration. If you want to save the file, you must use the Save As
command in the File menu. So what can you do with it?

5. The reason I had you apply Gamma was to lighten the area without
washing it out. Next the mask was removed, and the image was saved and
imported into CorelDRAW. The text was copied into the clipboard from
the Word 6.0 file for this chapter and pasted into paragraph text in
CorelDRAW. The finished product is shown here.

What is a Mask?
The official Corel
definition of a mask
is as follows:
"A Mask is a defined
area that covers part
of an image or the
entire image."
We have just created
a mask for this
demonstration.

The Importance of Looking for the Mask Icon

Whenever a mask is created, a tiny icon appears in the lower-right corner of the main screen. This tells the user there is a mask on the image. This tiny icon will save you a great deal of frustration once you train yourself to look for it. As a rule, users do not look for icons placed almost off of the screen. I am working on a 17-inch, high-resolution monitor, and the icon is small; finding it on a 14-inch screen must be even harder. *Make it a habit to look for the icon.*

This is important because when a mask has been placed on an image, it prevents any effect from being applied to the image *except to the area inside of the mask.* Thus, if you have created a small mask or have zoomed in on a corner of the image and can't see the masked area, Corel PHOTO-PAINT will not allow any effect to be applied to the image. Here's the best part: you will attempt to apply the effect and Corel PHOTO-PAINT will tell you that it completed the action, yet nothing will have been done. Talk about frustration!

Rule: If you are unable to apply an effect to an image, check first to see if the Mask icon is present. Even if you can't see the mask, the computer thinks the mask is there and will prevent you from applying any effect. Knowing this will save you time and money (for the cost of aspirin and tech-support calls).

The Properties of Masks

These four points summarize the general properties of masks:

- ▶ A mask "sits on top" of the image but is not part of the image.

- ▶ A mask can be moved, rotated, distorted, node-edited, and even combined with other masks to achieve a desired effect.

- ▶ A mask can remain as part of an image when the image is saved as a Corel PHOTO-PAINT (CPT) or a TARGA image.

- ▶ Masks can be saved separately and loaded later as masks.

The Basic Mask-Creation Tools

This section describes the basic mask-creation and mask-selection tools that are available in the toolbox.

The Rectangle Mask Tool

This is the tool you have already used in the previous demonstration. It is used for making square and rectangular masks. A mask is made by clicking and holding down the left mouse button and dragging until the desired shape is achieved. Holding down the SHIFT key produces a mask that increases or decreases proportionally from the starting point. Hold down the CTRL key to constrain the mask to a square.

The Circle Mask Tool

The Circle Mask tool enables you to define oval or circular masks. A mask is made by clicking and holding down the left mouse button and dragging until the desired shape is achieved. Holding down the SHIFT key produces a mask that increases or decreases proportionally from the starting point. Hold down the CTRL key to constrain the mask to a circle.

The Freehand Mask Tool

This mask tool has changed considerably since Corel PHOTO-PAINT 5. For those of you familiar with Corel PHOTO-PAINT 5, the Freehand mask tool is a combination of the Polygon Mask and the Freehand mask tool. Traditionally, a freehand-type tool is difficult to use with a mouse. By combining the two mask tools, it becomes possible with a mouse to effectively mask irregularly-shaped objects with some degree of accuracy. The concept behind the operation of this tool is as follows: As long as the left mouse button is clicked and held down, it acts as a traditional freehand tool. Wherever the cursor is moved the mask is applied. What makes this mask tool so good is that, unlike the Freehand tool in Corel PHOTO-PAINT 5, when the mouse button is released, the mask does not immediately join its end points. Instead, the mask can be continued until all of the subject is masked. Then, by double-clicking the left mouse button, the mask becomes complete. Here is a little exercise to familiarize you with the Freehand mask tool.

Using the Freehand Mask Tool

In this exercise we have a lovely photograph of an Australian dollar photographed on top of the flag. Many times in photo-editing, we need to emphasize a subject. One way to do that is by masking the background and slightly blurring it. We cannot use a rectangle mask because the bill is slightly skewed. This is a good choice for the Freehand mask tool.

1. On Disk #3 of the CorelDRAW CD-ROM, locate the file 125026.JPG in the folder \IMAGES\PHOTOS\COINS. Open the file. If you bought

Corel PHOTO-PAINT 6 and not CorelDRAW 6 you will not have this photograph. You can download it from the World Wide Web as described in the Introduction of this book.

2. Select the Freehand mask tool from either the Mask tool flyout or the Mask toolbar, if it is visible.

3. At the upper-left corner of the bill, click the left mouse button. Now move the mouse to the right and you will notice that a line is attached to the cursor. You could next click the upper-right corner of the bill, but I would recommend clicking at the point where the white stops. Next, click at the next junction where the bill becomes white again. As with so many things, this involves personal taste and technique. I choose to do the smaller jumps between the points so the mask more closely follows the edge of the bill. This is most important on the right edge of the bill, which is curved. Continue to do this until you return to the starting point.

4. Double-click the mouse to complete the mask. You have just completed a Freehand mask. Your mask should look like the illustration below. Don't worry if you are a little inside or outside of the bill. It isn't critical in this exercise.

10

5. Now that we have the bill masked, how do we work on the background? Easy! From the Mask menu, select Invert. Presto! Everything that was masked is now unmasked, and everything that wasn't masked is now masked. The Invert Mask command is one of the most powerful features in the Mask menu. OK, we have now masked the background.

6. Select Blur in the Effects menu. From the drop-down list that appears, choose Gaussian Blur…. When the Gaussian filter dialog box opens, ensure it is set to the default setting of 5 and click the OK button. (The Blur filters and their use are explained in Chapter 20.) Click the OK button. The Gaussian Blur makes the background appear slightly out of focus. The results are shown below.

Operational Points of the Freehand Mask Tool

The Freehand Mask tool is a very versatile tool for creating irregular masks. Unlike the Freehand tool in Corel PHOTO-PAINT 5, this tool does not complete its action when the mouse button is released but when the left mouse button is double-clicked.

▶ Begin by clicking the left mouse button to anchor the starting point.

▶ Move to the next point, and click there. When you click the mouse button, a line is drawn from the last point to the cursor. A closed polygon now exists between the two points (the anchor and the second point) and the cursor.

▶ Move the cursor to continually reshape the polygon based on the points placed and the current cursor position.

▶ End by double-clicking a point that finishes the last line and completes the mask.

▶ When the shape you are masking is not composed of straight lines, you can either make many small increments of lines or click and hold the left mouse button and drag the cursor around the image area to be masked.

▶ If you accidentally place a point that is not where you want it to be, just use the DEL key to remove the last point on the mask. Each successive DEL continues to remove mask points until the starting point is reached.

▶ Holding down the CTRL key when placing points constrains the angle of the next point to 45-degree increments.

IP: *Consider using the Freehand Mask tool when creating a large and complicated mask, even if it doesn't have a single straight line in it. The advantage of the Polygon tool is that you can stop at any point and rest, whereas with other mask tools, as soon as you let go of the mouse, the mask completes.*

The Mask Brush Tool

The Mask Brush tool enables you to brush or paint the area to be masked. Instead of applying a color, you are applying a mask. The size and shape of the Mask Brush tool is set from the Tool Settings roll-up. The roll-up is accessed through the View Roll-ups in the View menu or by using CTRL-F8, which reflects the settings of the currently selected tool. New to Corel PHOTO-PAINT 6 is another variation of this mask tool called Paint On Mask.

10

Operational Summary of the Mask Brush Tool

Here are the main points you need to know when working with the Mask Brush tool:

► To use the Mask Brush tool, position the cursor over the area to be masked, click the left mouse button, and drag the brush.

► Holding down the CTRL key while dragging the brush produces a straight horizontal line. While the brush can be moved outside of the original horizontal line, it only has an effect on that horizontal line until the CTRL key is released. For example, if the brush has a setting of a 10-pixels square, and you begin a line with the CTRL key depressed, Corel PHOTO-PAINT will protect every part of the image outside of a 10-pixel-wide straight line. So you could move the Brush tool all over the image and only produce a mask inside the 10-pixel horizontal line until the CTRL is released.

► Holding down the CTRL and the SHIFT keys produces the same effect, except in the vertical.

► Releasing the mouse button completes the mask.

► The Mask Brush tool is one of the handiest tools in Corel PHOTO-PAINT for doing touch-up on masks.

The Lasso Mask Tool

If you are an experienced Photoshop or PhotoStyler user, you might think you know what this tool does, but you're probably wrong. The Lasso Mask tool is a very handy tool that unfortunately bears the same name as a different tool in both of the aforementioned programs.

The lasso metaphor is perfect for this tool. On a ranch, a lasso surrounds an object, and when you pull on the rope, the lasso closes until it fits tightly around the object. The Lasso tool works very much in the same way, but without the rope.

How the Lasso Mask Tool Works

The Lasso Mask tool enables you to define a mask that is irregular in shape in much the same way as the Freehand tool. When the mouse button is released, the mask shrinks until it surrounds an area of colors that fall within the limits set by Tolerance slider in the Tool Settings roll-up. The mask will contain the area surrounded by the Lasso Mask tool. The Lasso tool acts as a localized version of the Magic Wand Mask tool (which is explored later in this chapter). It is used when it is necessary to restrict the region where the mask is to be placed.

Whereas the Magic Wand Mask begins at the pixel starting point and *expands* until it reaches its limits, the Lasso Mask *shrinks* until it reaches its limits. The range of color sensitivity is set using the Color Tolerance command on the Tool Settings roll-up.

Operational Summary of the Lasso Mask Tool

The Lasso Mask tool operates much like the Freehand Mask tool.

► Click and hold either mouse button to anchor the starting point for the mask.

► Still holding the mouse button, drag the cursor around the area to be masked. This causes a line to be drawn around the object. The pixel underneath the cursor when the line is started determines the starting color value.

► Continue to drag the cursor around the area until you are near the starting point.

► When the button is double-clicked, the computer will complete the line and compute the masked area.

Replacing a Background Using the Lasso Mask Tool

Here is a common application. The client wants a picture for a brochure. Unfortunately, you do not have it. Your choices are to hire a photographer (big bucks) or combine two existing photographs. Guess which one we are going to do in this exercise? You're right if you said "combine two photographs." We'll be using the Lasso Mask tool and a few other tools and commands to make these two photographs into one.

1. On Disk #3 of the CorelDRAW CD-ROM, locate the file 070054B.JPG in the folder \IMAGES\PHOTOS\ANIMALS. Open the file. If you bought Corel PHOTO-PAINT 6 and not CorelDRAW 6 you will find this photograph in IMAGES\PHOTOS\BIRD\070054B.JPG.

2. Select the Lasso Mask tool from the mask flyout or the Mask toolbar, if it is available.

10

3. Open the Tool-Settings roll-up by double-clicking on the Lasso Mask button, and make the settings match those shown below. The setting of 17 tells Corel PHOTO-PAINT to compare pixels as the mask is shrinking and to keep going until it reaches a pixel that is greater by 17 shades than the starting pixel value. It does this with all of the pixels in the enclosed area until it is finished. Anti-aliasing tells it to make the resulting mask smooth.

4. Start at the point outside of the hawk indicated by the arrow. Click the cursor to establish the starting (anchor) point. Now click around the hawk until you have surrounded it completely. Double-click the last point and the mask is created.

5. The mask we just created still includes some dark blue area that is next to the bird. To remove this, we are going to use the Feather command in the Mask menu. The Feather Mask command creates a gradual transition between the pixels along the mask's edge or directly inside the mask and the surrounding pixels. You can control the direction and hardness of the feathered edge by selecting different options in the Feather dialog box. When the dialog box appears, change the settings to match those shown in the following illustration. When they are the same, click the OK button.

6. To replace the background, we must invert the mask by either using the Invert command in the Mask menu or clicking the Invert button in the toolbar. From this point, there are several ways we could add the other photograph to form the background. We will use the Paste from File command only because it takes the fewest number of steps. From the Edit menu, select Paste from File. When the Paste Image from Disk dialog box opens (you recognize it as the File Open dialog box—only the name has been changed), select the file 044009.JPG from the Corel Disk #3 in the \IMAGE\PHOTO\MOUNTAIN folder. Click the OK button. If you bought Corel PHOTO-PAINT 6 and not CorelDRAW 6 you will need to load a different photograph. My choice would be \IMAGE\PHOTO\MOUNTAINS\36183.JPG.

7. After a few moments, the new photograph covers the entire photograph as shown in the following illustration. The mountain photograph is an object on top of the photograph. Notice that the mask is still visible because the mask is always on top of the everything in the image.

10

8. In the Object menu, choose Clip Object to Mask. We are telling Corel PHOTO-PAINT to use the mask as a cookie cutter. The result is that all of the masked area will be filled with the mountain photograph. All of the area outside of the mask (the hawk) will remain unchanged. The result is shown in Figure 10-3. In Chapter 13 we'll learn some different ways to do the same kind of background replacement.

The Magic Wand Mask Tool

The Magic Wand Mask tool is used to create masks both quickly and automatically. The ability of the tool to make an accurate mask is dependent upon the Tolerance settings in the Tool Settings roll-up and the actual color-value composition of the image. In other words, it takes a little time to get the hang of using this tool correctly. However, once you do, it is a very handy tool to have. The Color Mask tool masks all colors in the image that match the values entered. The Magic Wand Mask tool differs in that the Magic Wand mask expands from a starting point until all of the adjacent colors that meet the selection criteria are included.

How the Magic Wand Mask Tool Performs Its Magic

Two simple facts about the Magic Wand tool are: (1) there is nothing magic about it; and (2) it is very simple to use once you understand the concept behind its

The finished photograph is a composite of the two originals.

FIGURE 10-3

operation. In theory, you simply click on the area that needs to be masked or the area that surrounds the area to be masked, and Corel PHOTO-PAINT does the rest. There are actually times when this will work as intended.

Corel PHOTO-PAINT treats the pixel under the cursor when it is clicked as the starting point. The program reads the color value of the pixel, then, using the limits entered in the Tolerance setting of the Tool Settings roll-up, expands a mask pixel by pixel until it can no longer find pixels that are within the limits. For example, if the starting pixel has a hue value of 60 and the Tolerance value has been set to 50, the mask will continue to expand from its starting point until every adjacent pixel with a value between 10 (60 minus 50) and 110 (60 plus 50) has been included in the mask.

IP: *When using the Magic Wand mask tool, the most important decision to make is the choice of whether to mask the object or the area around the object. If the area to be masked is filled with a wide variety of colors or the colors in it have a wide tonal range, then look at the area surrounding it. Remember, it only takes one click of the button to invert the mask.*

Taking the Magic Wand Mask Tool for a Test Drive

How about some real-life situations? Fair enough. Let's use the Magic Wand tool to do a simple background replacement like we did with the Lasso mask tool and the background.

The sky in the preceding figure looks dull and flat. To make it more appealing, it needs some fireworks. No problem. The CorelDRAW CD has several photographs of fireworks. Using the Lasso tool would not be a good choice to isolate the existing skywork. We need to mask the sky with the Magic Wand mask tool, invert the mask, and paste the fireworks picture on it.

1. On Disk #3 of the CorelDRAW CD-ROM, locate the file 244000.JPG in the folder \IMAGES\PHOTOS\USACITIE. Open the file. If you bought Corel PHOTO-PAINT 6 and not CorelDRAW 6 you do not have this photograph. You can download the photograph from the World Wide Web as described in the Introduction of this book.

2. Select the Magic Wand mask tool from the Mask flyout.

3. Open the Tool Settings roll-up and adjust the slider to a value to 7. Make sure Normal and Anti-aliasing are selected. Did you wonder where the number 7 came from? It would be nice to give you some complicated mathematical formula, but experience and experimentation are my only explanation for where the number came from.

 IP: *In Corel PHOTO-PAINT 5, a setting of 40 is a good starting point for the Color Tolerance value. In Corel PHOTO-PAINT 6, the best overall starting number for the Tolerance setting seems to be between 15 and 20.*

4. Click on the blue sky in the lower-right corner. The mask fills only part of the blue sky. This is because the darker shade of blue in the upper portion of the sky was more than 7 shades (color tolerance number) different from the color at the starting point. We'll fix it in a moment. Notice that the sky inside of the crown between the points was also not included as part of the mask, and it needs to be included. To include it in the mask, we must venture into a new area of the Mask tools.

Introducing the Add to Mask Mode

Up until now, every time you created a mask, it wiped out any existing mask. In this case, we need to add the portion of sky that was missed to the mask made by the Magic Wand tool without losing that mask. To do that, we need to change the mode of the Mask tools from Normal to Add to Mask. When the Add to Mask mode is enabled, any mask that is applied to the image is added to the existing mask. We can do this in a variety of ways. We can:

► Click the Add to Mask button in the tool bar (if the Mask Tools toolbar is enabled).

► Choose the Add to Mask mode in the Mask menu.

► Use the keyboard shortcut CTRL-+ (plus key from keypad).

10

5. Select Add to Mask mode (whichever way you want to do it), and click the Magic Wand cursor in the upper-right corner of the picture. We nearly have a complete mask.

6. With the Magic Wand mask tool, click on each of the two areas of sky showing between its left arm and the crown. We are still in Add to Mask mode, so clicking the tool will add the areas that are currently unmasked to the big mask. The illustration below shows the completed mask. Now we want to place the fireworks photo on top of the existing photograph. Because we used the Magic Wand, the sky is masked and we do not need to invert the mask as we did in the previous exercise.

7. Select Paste from File in the Edit menu. When the dialog box opens, select \IMAGES\PHOTOS\HOLIDAYS\040091b.JPG.

8. After a few moments, the fireworks cover the entire photograph. The photograph of the fireworks is an object on top of the photograph. Notice that the mask is still visible because the mask is always on top of everything in the image.

9. In the Object menu, choose Clip to Mask. We are telling Corel PHOTO-PAINT to use the mask as a cookie cutter. The result is that all of the masked area will be filled with the photograph of the fireworks. All of the area outside of the mask will remain unchanged. The result is shown below.

10

Managing Masks

11

Allmasks created in Corel PHOTO-PAINT can be saved and reloaded. This ability to save masks is essential because:

▶ Only one regular mask can be on an image at a time. Other masks such as a color mask can coexist on the same image.

▶ Masks are valuable. If you spent several hours creating a mask, it is essential to have a copy.

▶ It is a great way to copy the same size image area out of several different images.

How Masks Are Saved with Images

An image containing a regular mask that is saved in Corel PHOTO-PAINT format (.CPT) will have its mask saved with the image automatically. In addition to Corel PHOTO-PAINT format, masks can be saved in Targa (.TGA) and TIFF (.TIF) formats. The ability to save a mask apart from the image allows a mask created in one image to be loaded and applied to other images for special effects or accurate placement of objects. How another application uses the saved mask information depends on the application. For example, the mask information in a .TIF or .TGA file is interpreted by Photoshop as an alpha channel.

Saving a Mask

Saving a mask is just like saving an image file. The mask does not have a unique file extension. In fact you can save a mask in almost any graphics format you desire. After a mask has been created, it can be saved two ways. It can be saved to disk or saved in temporary storage in a channel. Use of the Mask channel is explained later in this chapter. The following procedure is for saving a mask to disk:

1. Select the mask with the Mask Picker tool.

2. Choose Save from the Mask menu. At this point you have two choices: Save to Disk and Save to Channel. Select Save to Disk and the Save An Image to Disk dialog box opens.

3. Name the mask and click the Save button. The mask has been saved and can be recalled at a later time.

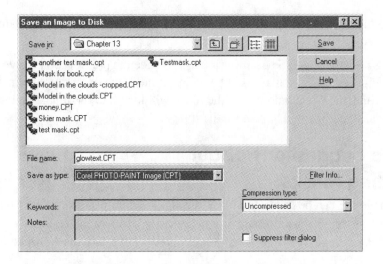

Notes about Saving Masks

When naming masks, try to include the fact that the file is a mask as part of the name (e.g., Mask for Project 22.CPT or Tree mask.TIF). One of the benefits of using WIN'95 is the ability to assign 256-character filenames. Do not use a unique extension such as .MSK for the mask. This three-character extension is used by Corel PHOTO-PAINT and most other Windows applications to determine the correct import filter to use. Although the mask can be saved in any bitmap format (i.e., PCX, TIF, BMP, etc.), it is recommended to save masks in Corel PHOTO-PAINT's native CPT format.

Loading a Mask

The Load Mask function allows a wide variety of image file formats to be loaded as masks. Loading a mask into an image involves the following procedure:

1. Select the image to which the mask being loaded will be applied.

IP: *If you have several images open on your screen, make sure that the one you want to load the mask into is active. If you load the mask into another image, the mask will replace any existing mask in that image.*

2. Choose Load in the Mask menu. The Load A Mask from Disk dialog box opens.

3. Select the file to be used for a mask. Notice the preview box shown in Figure 11-1. The mask will be a black-and-white or a grayscale image. Click the Open button, and the mask will load into the image and the mask outline will appear on the image.

Some Suggestions about Loading Masks

Any image file can be used for a mask. Using photographs or other non-mask files may give unpredictable, although not necessarily undesirable, results. A non-mask file is any image file that was not created using the mask tools in Corel PHOTO-PAINT.

In Corel PHOTO-PAINT 5, the mask must be a one-bit (black-and-white) image file, while the Transparency mask is a grayscale image. In Corel PHOTO-PAINT 6, the two have been combined. The regular mask now is a grayscale image.

When loading a mask, it is important to be aware that Corel PHOTO-PAINT *will resize the mask to fit the image!* At first reading this automatic resizing of masks may appear to be a slick feature; it's not. It can cause you headaches if you are not careful. Let's look at some examples to demonstrate the point.

In Figure 11-2 we have masked a skier in the photograph. Notice how the mask fits around his body. Now let's use the automatic resizing feature on this picture.

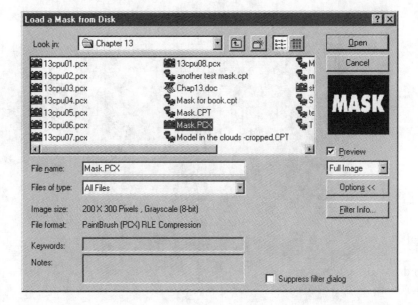

The dialog box that is used to load masks. Notice the mask in the preview box

FIGURE 11-1

1. The mask is saved and then removed from the image using the None command in the Mask menu.

2. The Crop tool from the Toolbox is used to crop the image to a smaller size.

3. After loading the mask just saved, Corel PHOTO-PAINT resizes the mask to fit the new image dimensions, as shown in Figure 11-3. The mask is no longer the correct size or in the correct position.

So how would you get the mask to maintain the proper size and position on the image when you crop or resample? Good question. Corel PHOTO-PAINT does it for you automatically. The only reason the mask did not work in this example is because by saving and removing it, we separated it from the image. Therefore, when we reloaded it, it was the original size and not the new size. If you leave any mask

Original
mask
surrounds
the skier

FIGURE 11-2

The
reloaded
mask no
longer fits
the resized
image

FIGURE 11-3

The resized photograph and mask are correctly placed and sized

FIGURE 11-4

in position when you crop or resample, Corel PHOTO-PAINT will automatically resize the mask and maintain it in the proper position. In Figure 11-4, the image was cropped with the mask in place, resulting in the correctly placed and sized mask.

 IP: *If you have a mask on an image, always do cropping or resampling with the mask in place. This way Corel PHOTO-PAINT can resize and reposition the mask correctly.*

In the following figures I have provided some examples of loading different mask files. Loading non-mask files to make masks can produce some neat effects, but it takes experimentation. I recommend it to those who are looking for special effects or those who have time on their hands.

Loading a Photograph as a Mask

In the following image, a photograph of a model has been loaded as a mask. Whenever you load a photograph to use as a mask, you need to invert the mask or the results will appear as a negative. To make sure the mask did not become distorted when it was loaded, I checked the size of the image to be used as the mask before making the base image. After noting the mask size, I created the image so that it was the same size as the mask.

 IP: *Always invert masks created from photographs, or the images they create will appear as a photographic negative.*

Next, pasting a photograph of clouds into the image using Paste From File, the clouds and the mask are in the same image as shown.

The last step is to use the mask to apply the cloud photograph to the image. This is done with the Clip to Mask command in the Object menu.

11

The operation of masks with objects has changed in Corel PHOTO-PAINT 6. With Corel PHOTO-PAINT 5 you can merge the object to the background with a mask in place and create the effect in the previous figure. This technique no longer works in Corel PHOTO-PAINT 6 and has been replaced by the Clip to Mask feature in the Object Menu.

Removing a Mask

There are several ways to remove a mask. One of the quickest is to click the None button on the Mask toolbar. One of the Mask tools must be selected for the Mask buttons in the toolbar to be available. The mask may also be removed by selecting None in the Mask menu. A mask may also be removed with the DEL key if the mask is selected. The mask is selected whenever the Mask Transform tool is selected. (The mask will have control handles on it.) If the mask is not selected, *the contents of the mask will be cleared when the DEL key is depressed*. Therefore, use the DEL key with caution.

Inverting a Mask

One of the more useful mask functions is the Invert Mask command. When a mask is created, the area inside the mask can be modified while the area outside the mask is protected. The Invert Mask command reverses the mask so that the area that was inside the mask now becomes protected and the area outside can be modified. The Invert Mask command can be accessed through the Mask menu or by clicking on the Invert Mask button.

Suggestions about Using the Invert Mask Command

Some masks are so complex it is difficult to determine what part of the image lies inside or outside of the mask. A quick way to check is to select a brush and paint across the area in question to see where the paint is applied. If it is being applied in the wrong area, invert the mask. Immediately after applying the paint, perform an undo (CTRL-Z) to remove the paint *before you invert the mask*. Remember: Corel PHOTO-PAINT can only undo the last action. To do more than that requires the use of the Undo List in Edit mode. Depending on how many keystrokes deep you are into the image, this can take a long time to use.

Mask All

To mask the entire image, select the Mask All command from the Mask menu. The mask will encompass the entire image inside of the image window. If the image is only partially visible because you have zoomed into an area, the entire image is still masked. In this situation, you will not be able to see the entire mask. There are several shortcuts for the Mask All command: clicking the All button in the Mask toolbar, or double-clicking any of the basic Mask selection tools in the toolbox—Rectangle, Circle, or Freehand.

Mask Channel Operations

The mask channel is new to Corel PHOTO-PAINT 6, and if you do any amount of work with masks, you have got to love this feature. You can temporarily store masks in mask channels by using the Channels roll-up. A mask channel is temporary storage area for masks. When you create a mask channel, Corel PHOTO-PAINT makes a copy of the current mask and stores it in a channel where you can access and reuse it in the image as many times as you wish. You can also save a mask channel to a file or open a previously saved channel into the current image.

Once saved in a channel, a mask can be selected and reused within an image. When you change a mask in an image, you can reflect the changes in the channel by clicking the Update Channel button in the roll-up. There are also commands for saving a mask channel to a separate file or opening a previously saved mask channel.

The Channels Roll-Up

The Channels roll-up provides several different command functions. In this chapter we are only concerned with the bottom portion of the Mask Channels roll-up. The Mask channels section displays the mask channels that are currently occupied. In Figure 11-5, we have opened the Channels roll-up in order to see the contents.

To Create a Mask Channel

1. Create a mask using one or more mask tools.

2. Open the Channels roll-up.

3. Click the Save Mask to New Channel button at the bottom of the roll-up. A thumbnail representing the mask appears in the Mask Channels box.

4. To change the name of a mask channel, double-click the default channel name, delete the default name (i.e., Mask 1), and then type a new name.

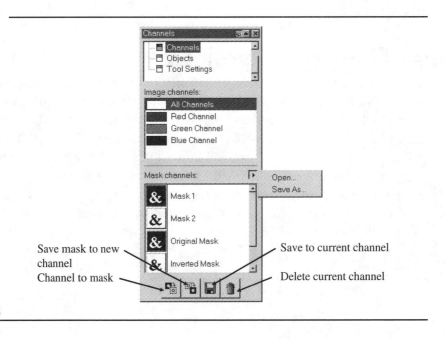

The Channels roll-up

FIGURE 11-5

To Delete a Mask Channel

1. Open the Channels roll-up.

2. Choose a mask channel by clicking its thumbnail in the Mask Channels box.

3. Click the Delete Current Channel button (looks like a trash can) at the bottom of the roll-up. The channel's thumbnail disappears from the list.

To Open a Previously Saved Mask Channel

1. Open the Channels roll-up.

2. Click the right-facing arrow to the right of the Mask channels title and click Open from the menu.

3. Locate and select the mask file in the Load a Mask Channel from Disk dialog box.

4. Click the Open button to open the file. A thumbnail representing the mask channel appears in the Mask Channel box.

To Save a Mask Channel to Disk

1. Open the Channels roll-up.

2. Click the right-facing arrow to the right of the Mask channel's title and click Save As… from the menu.

3. Locate and select the location for the file on the disk.

4. Give the mask a filename and click the OK button.

To Update a Mask Channel

1. With a mask on the image, open the Channels roll-up.

2. Choose the mask channel you wish to update by clicking its icon in the Mask Channels box.

3. Click the Save to Current Mask Channel button (looks like a floppy disk) at the bottom of the roll-up. Any changes to the current mask on the image are reflected in the selected mask channel's thumbnail.

Using the Grid System with Masks

12

A new feature of Corel PHOTO-PAINT 6 is the grid system. Before they added the grid system, all alignment of objects had to be accomplished using a calibrated eyeball. In other words, it took a lot of work and the results were not always excellent. When the grid is enabled, you can both see the spots for visual alignment and turn on the Snap To Grid function to align masks and objects with the grid.

Using the Grid

The grid system is enabled through the View menu by selecting Grid Setup..., which opens the Grid Setup dialog box shown below.

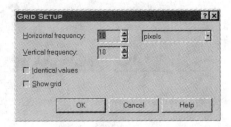

The Grid Setup Dialog Box

The Grid Setup dialog box lets you define grid attributes, including horizontal and vertical grid line spacing, and measurement units. Enabling the Identical values check box lets you keep the X and Y values the same. Any value entered in one box will automatically cause the other to reflect the change. Enable the Show grid check box to apply the grid to the image immediately.

 IP: *If you use inches as the units of measure for the grid settings, be aware that using the default value of 10 for spacing results produces a decimal grid system. For a traditional measuring system, enter a value of 12.*

If you did not enable the Show grid check box when you set up the grid, you can turn the grid on or off by selecting Show Grid in the View menu.

You can enable Snap To Grid by choosing the option in the View menu or by using the keyboard combination CTRL-Y. Snap To Grid affects all of the creation tools like Rectangle, ellipse, and so on, as well as the mask tools. In the creation of the figures for a book, I often need to create multiple samples to show what different fills look like, as in the following illustration. The sample of bitmap fills was created in only a few minutes using the Snap To Grid feature to size the mask, move it precisely to each of the four corners, and center.

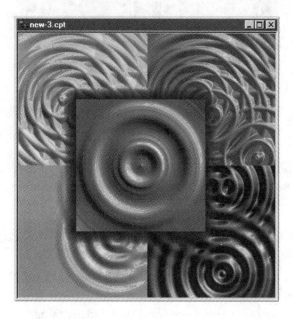

Tales from the Grid

When I was making the sample of bitmap fills, I had difficulty making the squares line up. There were two problems, both of my own making. First, while I wanted to divide the square into four equal parts, I made the image 3 x 3 inches. While it is possible to equally divide that size image, it is impossible to do so with Snap To Grid enabled. I also discovered that even though the image was set up in inches, the grid was set up in pixels. By making the measurements the same, I was able to make the image you see here in less than four minutes.

12

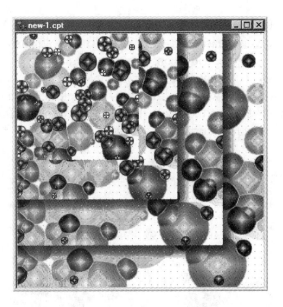

 IP: *To achieve accurate placement of masks and objects, use the same unit of measurement for the Grid setup as you use for the image.*

A Demonstration of Several Mask Features

In the previous chapters we learned how to make a simple mask. Now we need to learn more about how masks act and interact. The power of Corel PHOTO-PAINT is in its ability to create a mask that will meet the needs of the project you are working on. In this demonstration we will see some of the many things you can do with the Mask tools.

How many masks can you see in Figure 12-1? The answer is one mask. This is an important point to understand. There can only be one mask on an image at any given time. In the next example, the one mask is composed of four square areas. It was created with the Rectangle Mask tool with Add To Mask Mode enabled (which allowed the addition of three squares to the mask) and Snap To Grid enabled so that the squares would line up.

To show how the mask (not masks) works, another image is pasted on top of the mask using the Paste From File command in the Edit menu, as shown in Figure 12-2.

Pay close attention to what happens next because it is the operating principle of Corel PHOTO-PAINT 6 and it is different from Corel PHOTO-PAINT 5. The photograph of a sunset has been pasted on top of the image as an object as indicated

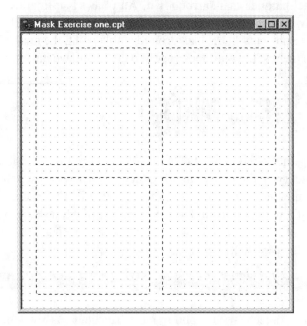

How many masks can you see in this picture?

FIGURE 12-1

The photograph of the sunset has been placed on the original image as an object

FIGURE 12-2

12

by the blue marquee that surrounds it. An object is a floating bitmap image. The mask is always on top of the image, which is why we can still see it. If we were to combine the object with the background at this point, the mask would not affect the image and the result would look just like the image we have right now.

In Corel PHOTO-PAINT 5, combining the object with the background is called merging (don't you love it when they change the names of commands?). In Corel PHOTO-PAINT 5, merging the object with the background is affected by the mask. Not so in Corel PHOTO-PAINT 6. A new command has been added, which leads us to the next step.

With the object (sunset photograph) selected (as evidenced by the control handles), open the Object menu and select Clip Object to Mask. Only the portion of the object that was inside the mask remains as shown in Figure 12-3.

At this point the object (sunset photograph) is still floating, so we need to nail it down. Selecting Combine All Objects with Background from the Object menu makes the object part of the image. If you didn't quite understand what an object is, don't worry. It isn't an object any more—it and the background have become one (sounds Zen, doesn't it?). Objects are explained in much greater detail in Chapter 15.

We now want to apply a fill to the remaining white area. To do this, we must invert the existing mask by selecting Invert from the Mask menu (you can also click the Invert Mask button in the Toolbar). With the mask inverted, all of the area that was protected is no longer protected and vice versa.

We are going to place another image on top of this one using the Paste From File command in the Edit menu again. This fill was created from a photograph in the Textures by James Dawson Corel Photo CD. It is cropped to a 4 x 4-inch image in order to fit perfectly in the existing image.

Using Clip Object to Mask, as with the sunset photograph, only the portion of the object that was inside the mask remains. The clipped object is combined with the background. The image in Figure 12-4 shows the photograph at this point. With

Using the Clip Object to Mask feature, I was able to use the mask like a cookie cutter

FIGURE 12-3

Inverting the mask allows us to fill in the remainder of the image with a wood texture

FIGURE 12-4

12

the original mask inverted, we were able to fill only the white area with a wood texture from a photograph, yet the wood does not convey a sense of depth.

Funny thing about the way the human mind operates. Both photographs are real, yet the frame we created doesn't look real. One of the reasons it doesn't appear real is that all of the wood grain is going in the same direction. That will be corrected first. A copy of the original mask is saved to a channel for later use, then the mask on the image is removed by selecting None in the Mask menu.

In Corel PHOTO-PAINT 6, select None to remove a mask. In Corel PHOTO-PAINT 5 this is done with the Remove command.

With the help of the grid, it is easy to mask the vertical elements of the wood. We need to mask the four vertical elements of the frame, as shown in Figure 12-5. Selecting the Rectangle Mask tool from the Toolbox, the left vertical portion of the mask is created. It is only necessary to get near the spot and the grid will snap the mask to the edge. Notice that the rectangle mask on the left doesn't begin at the top or go to the bottom of the image.

Snap To Grid and Its Effect on Masks

The Snap To Grid can do its work too well, sometimes placing the mask where you don't want it. If you begin to drag a mask and notice that it has jumped to a grid point that you did not want, move the cursor back as close to the point of origin as possible and let go of it. Corel PHOTO-PAINT will not make a mask if the mask area is less than a few pixels. If you do make a mask you don't want and it is too late to undo it by the previously described technique there are several other ways to remedy the situation. First, select Undo (CTRL-Z) and the last mask added will be deleted. Another way to remove an unwanted portion of a mask is to choose the Subtract From Mask mode and place a mask over the portion of the mask you did not want. Any portion of a mask you enclose with the new mask is removed from the mask. If you use this method, don't forget to return the Mask mode back to Add To Mask or Normal. If you don't, the next mask you produce may both mystify and surprise you.

Creating an Illusion

The object is to create the illusion of a window frame. To do this, we must imagine what a window frame looks like. There should be a horizontal piece that runs across the top and bottom and a piece in the center. Therefore, mask only the areas that are

All of the vertical components are included in the mask

FIGURE 12-5

12

vertical; do not include the expected horizontal pieces. Choosing Add to Mask (CTRL-F10), we added three additional rectangles to the mask until it looks like Figure 12-5.

From the Effect menu, choose Blur and then Motion Blur.... We will learn all about this filter in Chapter 20; for now we need to know that it will smear the masked portions of the photograph in a specific direction. The vertical portions of the frame are now blurred so that they look different from the horizontal parts. The grid and mask marquee are not clearly visible.

After removing the latest mask, our window frame still doesn't look real. In fact it looks very flat. To give it some depth, we need to add shadows. Normally, brushing in shadows can be tricky, but we going to take advantage of some of the new mask features in Corel PHOTO-PAINT 6. To do this, we need to load the original mask we had saved to a channel previously. The Load Mask from Channel command causes the mask to return.

To add depth to our window frame, we need to add shading on the inside of each window frame. Very simple. From the Mask menu, choose Shape and then pick Border... from the drop-down list. When the dialog box opens, a width of 3 pixels and a Hard edge are chosen. Corel PHOTO-PAINT turns all of the squares that comprised our mask into three-pixel-wide borders as shown in Figure 12-6.

Our window now has a border mask surrounding each of the "panes"

FIGURE 12-6

The Border Dialog Box

The Border mask command lets you add a border around the existing mask, which creates a mask frame. The Width option determines the number of pixels between the original mask frame and the position of the new mask border. Edges lets you choose a border with a hard or soft edge.

To add a darker color to the area inside the border mask we could pick a dark color from the onscreen palette. Let's look at how I added this professional touch.

Using the Eyedropper to Pick a Color

At the bottom of the wood frame is a dark area of wood to the right of the center. The color we want to use is in the dark area inside of the grain, and it is easy to get it. Holding down the E key changes the cursor into an eyedropper. With the eyedropper over that dark area and continuing to hold down the E key, press the SHIFT key. The dark color in the frame becomes the Fill color, as indicated in the color swatch in the status bar at the bottom of the screen.

Selecting the Rectangle tool (F6) and dragging a rectangle across the entire image (start and end outside of the file) fills all of the masked border area with the darker color picked from the photograph; this will give the appearance of shading to the window panes. That's it for the basic stuff.

Some Advanced Stuff

The Road Window is finished, but for the more adventurous, here are some more complex things you can do with the same image.

Reloading the original mask, we invert it so only the wood of the frame is selected. Visually the wood looks too smooth, too perfect. This perfection is what alerts the mind to the fact that the picture is a fake. So let's make our perfect world a little less perfect with the addition of some noise. In the Effect menu, select Noise, and from the drop-down list, select Add Noise…. If you have never worked with noise before, don't worry; it's covered in Chapter 18. Using the Uniform Noise button at a Density of 100 and a Level of 8 produces some "grit" that gives the wood an appearance of texture, as shown below. Note that the preview window of filter dialog boxes does not accurately represent areas that will be affected by the filter when the mask is complex, like the one we are working on. The completed frame is shown in Figure 12-7.

Now for a special effect, we will mask the area above the horizon. To do that, we must invert the mask again so that only the panes of the windows are selected. Next, we need to remove the lower portions of the two bottom frames from the mask

12

The Noise filter gives the window frame a more realistic appearance

FIGURE 12-7

(the portion of the mask below the horizon). The Subtract from Mask mode is selected by any of several methods: choosing Mode in the Mask menu and selecting Subtract from Mask; clicking the Subtract from Mask button in the Mask toolbar; or clicking CTRL-F11. When this mode is selected, anything we mask will be removed from the existing mask.

We must first ensure the Snap To Grid feature is not enabled. This is a case where Snap To Grid would make our task impossible. The Freehand mask tool is selected from the Toolbox. Clicking at the point on the left side where the horizon and the lower-left frame meet, we click to anchor the Freehand mask. Next, we continue to click at points along the horizon so that the mask follows the edge of the horizon. When we get to the right side of the lower-right side, we click a point in the middle of the wood outside of the existing mask. To complete the mask, we need two more points: one point in the lower-right corner of the image, and then we double-click the lower-left corner of the image. You get the idea. We are making sure the mask we are creating includes all of the mask below the horizon. Double-clicking the last point causes the Freehand tool to complete its action. Figure 12-8 shows what your mask should look like.

The completed mask ready to produce the next effect

FIGURE 12-8

Lens Flare Filter

Now for a filter that is new in Corel PHOTO-PAINT 6 and can be a lot of fun. We use it to produce a light at the end of the road. To do that, we will use the Len Flare filter. Located in the Effects menu under Render, the Lens Flare filter simulates the refraction caused by shining a bright light into a camera lens. After opening the Lens Flare dialog box and enabling the 35mm Prime lens button, we change the Brightness setting slider to 90. The Preview window only shows the masked area. The point where the Lens Flare effect is centered is determined by where on the Preview image you click the mouse button. Clicking on the right side of the center frame at the point where the horizontal and vertical pieces meet produces the image shown. Now we have a light at the end of the road as shown in Figure 12-9.

More New Mask Features

There are so many things that can be done in the creation and positioning of masks, I could continue writing until the release of Corel PHOTO-PAINT 22 and still not

There is now a light at the end of the road— the result of using the Lens Flare filter

FIGURE 12-9

be finished. That said, let's cover some more of the new features of Corel PHOTO-PAINT 6.

Mask Overlay

I like Mask Overlay. My wife and I used to go look at houses under construction. As we would walk through the framed home, I would have trouble imagining what the rooms looked like. It wasn't until they got the sheet rock up that I could visualize the rooms. That's what Mask Overlay is to me, electronic sheet rock. When the Mask Overlay is selected in the Mask menu, it covers all of the masked area with red (default color) to help people like me see exactly what the mask does and does not cover. This is especially important with feathered edges and grayscale portions of masks. The mask marquee helps considerably in situations like this. I have included some samples to show the Mask Overlay action. To demonstrate Mask Overlay, I have brought back an earlier version of the previous image. The mask shown here protects all the area inside the panes.

Figure 12-10 shows the Mask Overlay made active. Any area covered in red (I know you can't see red, since it is a grayscale book) is protected from all Corel PHOTO-PAINT actions.

Next, we feather the mask so that a portion of the area inside the panes is not protected. It is not until we use the Mask Overlay that we can actually see what is and is not protected.

Couldn't resist the opportunity to use the Clip Object to Mask feature. I call it the "Tire Meets the Road with Clip Object to Mask" feature. This time I pasted in a photograph of a tire and clipped it to the mask. The Mask Overlay is turned off in this illustration for clarity.

Pasting in a photograph of a tire and using the Clip Object to Mask feature we used in the previous exercise, I have replaced the wood frame with the tire as shown below. The edges of the original background look fuzzy (soft) because we feathered the mask. With that introduction, let's talk about the Feather mask feature.

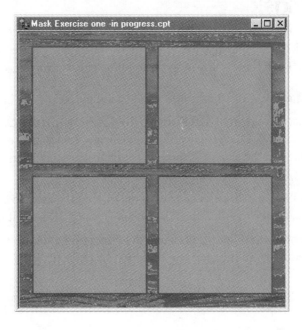

No, the windows aren't dirty, the Mask Overlay feature is enabled

FIGURE 12-10

Feather Mask

The ability to feather a mask gives the user a lot of control over how well an effect can be blended into an image. There are many things that can be done with feathered masks. Next, I will show you how to create some effects that are used to highlight text.

1. Create a new file that is 400 pixels wide by 200 pixels in height at 100 dpi.

2. Select the Text tool and from the Tool Setting roll-up (CTRL-F8), select the Futura Xblk BT. Actually, you can use any font you like. If you use Futura, set the size to 72 points. If you use another font, pick a size that will fill most but not all of the screen.

3. Left-click the 20 percent gray in the onscreen palette to set the Paint color, or double-click the left swatch to enter 20 percent in CMYK mode.

4. Enter the word you want to add the effect to. I am not very original after working on this chapter for 12 hours, so I picked "FEATHER" as shown.

5. Here is a great way to make a mask. Select the Object picker from the Toolbox, which selects the text since it is the only object in the image. From the Mask menu choose Create from Object(s). This will produce a mask that surrounds each of the characters as shown below.

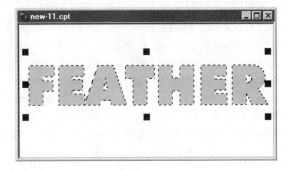

6. From the Mask menu, choose Feather… and the Feather dialog box opens.

The Feather Mask Dialog Box

The Feather dialog box, shown below, determines the direction of the feather: Inside, Outside, or Middle. The Width option determines the number of pixels between the original mask frame and the position of the new mask boundary. Edges lets you choose a border with a hard or soft edge. A hard feather produces a more abrupt change, while a soft creates a gradual transition over the width of the feather.

12

7. Enter the values Width: 10 (pixels), Direction: Outside, and Edge: Soft; and then click OK. The result will be that the mask is not only enlarged but it has a gradual transition at the mask boundaries. You will not be able to see the transitions in the mask marquee.

8. Select a black uniform fill by right-clicking on black in the onscreen palette. Open the Objects roll-up by double-clicking the Object Pointer tool in the Toolbox. When the Objects roll-up opens, click on the lock icon of the text object to prevent any action from affecting it. Make sure the Background lock icon is unlocked.

9. Double-click the Rectangle tool to open the Fill roll-up. By default, the Rectangle Tool is set to produce a rectangle with a border that is 20 pixels wide. Locate the Width setting on the first tab of the roll-up and change it to zero. Now drag a rectangle across all of the text and the mask area in a single action. The result will look like the illustration below. Actually, it won't look exactly like the figure unless you follow up by applying a Gaussian blur (under Blur in the Effect menu) at a setting of 10. Sorry about that, I always blur shadows out of habit.

10. Now for the finishing touches. Remove the mask by selecting None in the Mask menu. Unlock the object in the Objects roll-up, and select the text by clicking on it with the Object pointer from the Toolbox.

11. From the Mask menu, choose Create from Object(s). This will produce a mask like the one created in Step 5.

12. From the Mask menu, choose Feather... This time, when the dialog box opens, enter a width of 4 pixels and change the Direction setting to Inside. Leave the Edge setting as Soft. Click OK. This time the mask appears inside of the text. Invert the mask using the Invert command in the Mask menu. Open the Object roll-up (CTRL-F7) and click on the lock icon in the background layer.

13. From the Effects menu, choose Noise. From the drop-down list, select Add Noise.... When the dialog box opens, choose Gaussian Noise and put both settings at 100%. Click the OK button. The results are shown here.

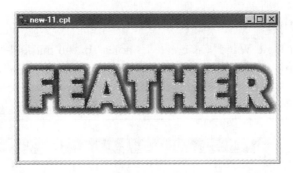

Slick Trick to Align a Mask

The Align command works only with objects, so it cannot be used to align masks. With a few extra steps, it can be used to align a mask. Watch!

1. Create the mask you wish to align to the image area. Figure 12-11 shows a simple mask in a large image area.

2. From the Object menu, choose Create From Mask. The mask then becomes an object. Converting the mask to an object removes the mask, leaving only the object indicated by the control handles.

3. Now that the mask has become an object, we can align it to the center of the page using the Align command. From the Object Menu, select Align. When the Align dialog box opens, as shown in the next illustration, enable the Align to Center of Page button, and click the OK button.

12

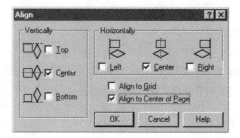

4. From the Mask menu, choose Create From Object(s). A mask is created from the object as shown in Figure 12-12. If Preserve Image was enabled, the object remained. To remove the object, select Delete from the Object menu.

Remove Holes

Ever since the Magic Wand was created, "holes" in the masks left by the Magic Wand have been a problem. Holes are the tiny excluded areas of a mask that are produced when the program creates the masks. Because these areas have a color

A simple
mask

FIGURE 12-11

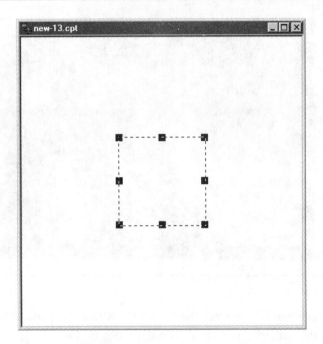

A mask
created
from an
object

FIGURE 12-12

threshold that is higher than the color tolerance setting, the holes could not be included in the mask. In cases like this, raising the tolerance levels will reduce the number of holes but may cause the mask to go beyond the desired boundary area. To solve this, Corel provided the Remove Holes command.

Look at the photograph shown in Figure 12-13. After the Magic Wand was applied to the wall there were tiny holes left. They can be seen at the edges and in the middle of the wall itself.

To apply the Remove Holes command, select Shape in the Mask menu; from the drop-down list that appears, choose Remove Holes. That is all there is to it; the result is shown in Figure 12-14. The mask edge is smoother and the tiny mask holes in the middle are gone.

About Floating Masks

An important concept in Corel PHOTO-PAINT 6 is the difference between a floating and a non-floating mask. If you are like me, you ran into floating masks without

Tiny holes
left behind
by the
Magic Wand

FIGURE 12-13

realizing it. When I discovered them, all I knew was that sometimes when I moved
the mask, the background moved with it. I wondered why.

The
Remove
Holes
command
causes the
holes to
disappear

FIGURE 12-14

In Corel PHOTO-PAINT 5 you cannot remove the portion of an image enclosed by a mask unless the mask was created using the right mouse button. In Corel PHOTO-PAINT 6 you can.

After you mask part of an image, you can drag the mask to a new location on the image with the mask tool still selected using either the left mouse button or the arrow keys and the pixels in the mask will float with the mask. The pixels in the original location of the mask are replaced with the paint (background) color. If the mask is moved with the Mask Transform tool, only the mask moves, leaving the original background unchanged.

If you drag the mask (with a mask tool still selected) with the right mouse button, you will be presented with a choice of Copy or Cut. If you choose Copy, the background will remain unchanged. If you choose Cut, the original location of the mask is replaced with the paint (background) color. Regardless of which option is chosen, the mask will float containing the original background pixels.

The mask is considered "floating" because it sits on a plane above the background. In effect, a floating mask is a temporary layer. Floating masks are most useful for copying, cutting, pasting, and moving. When you remove a floating mask, the contents of the mask become part of the background.

For more complex editing, it's best to convert a floating mask into an object. Once the mask is an object, you can try out different blending effects and positions without merging the data into the underlying layer.

Floating or Defloating a Mask

Here is the basic procedure to float and defloat a mask.

1. Create a mask with any mask tool.

2. To Float a mask: With any mask tool (other than the Brush Mask tool or the Mask Transform tool) selected, click and drag the mask. This action moves the mask and its contents, leaving the paint color. This is like a cut and paste operation.

12

3. To Defloat a mask, remove the mask. The contents of the mask will be merged with the background.

Figure 12-15 shows an example of what you can do with the float/defloat capabilities.

Using the Grow and Similar Commands

The Grow and Similar commands in the Mask menu allow you to expand a mask to include areas similar in color to the current mask. These commands use the tolerance value specified in the Tool Setting roll-up to define the color range of pixels to be included in the expanded mask.

The Grow command expands a mask to include all adjacent areas of the image with similar pixel colors. The mask continues to expand until all of the adjacent colors that meet the selection criteria are included. The criteria for including pixels are set by using the Magic Wand Tool Settings Roll-Up Tolerance slider.

Here is a quick image I put together using the float/defloat capabilities of the masks

FIGURE 12-15

 **OTE:** *You cannot use the Grow or Similar command on line art (1-bit) images.*

The Similar command creates a new color mask based on the currently selected mask. When this command is chosen, the current mask expands to include all of the areas in the image that have the same or similarly colored pixels as those that fall along the edges of the mask marquee. For example, if a rectangular mask is created and the mask marquee contacts a red, white, and blue pixel, the mask will expand to include all red, white, and blue areas of the image even if they are not adjacent to the mask. Use the Magic Wand Tool Settings Roll-Up Tolerance slider to determine the tolerance level for color inclusion of both the Grow and Similar commands. A tolerance of 0 will include only those pixels with the exact pixel color value as those that come into contact with the mask marquee. A tolerance of 100 will include pixels of similar color to those that come into contact with the mask marquee.

Extending a Mask with the Grow or Similar Command

1. Create a mask.

2. Choose Grow from the Mask menu to include adjacent pixels that fall within the specified tolerance range.

3. Choose Similar from the Mask menu to include pixels throughout the image, not just the ones next to the mask, that fall within the specified tolerance range.

4. Choose either command repeatedly to increase the mask in increments.

Image Editing

13

This and the following chapter examine the tools that are used to edit and retouch images. Several of the tools perform filter functions already discussed in previous chapters. These tools enable you to apply the filter functions selectively to small areas to achieve effects such as increasing contrast in a small part of an image or removing a shadow. By using these tools, you will also be able to quickly access some commands and functions without going through multiple menus and drop-down lists.

The Eyedropper Tool

The first tool we are going to talk about has been mentioned before, but now we will explore it in depth. It is the Eyedropper tool and it is located in the Toolbox.

The Eyedropper tool is used to pick a specific color from an image by clicking on it. This tool has more uses than might first be apparent. For instance, while the Eyedropper tool is active, the color value of the pixel under the cursor is displayed in the status bar. I'll explain the usefulness of this in a moment. First, let's go through the basics of how to use the Eyedropper.

There are three color areas that can be selected using the Eyedropper tool—the paint, paper, and fill color, displayed from left to right, respectively, in three color icons at the bottom of the screen.

- ▶ **PAINT** color—To select the paint (foreground) color, click on the desired color in the image with the left mouse button.

- ▶ **PAPER** color—To select the paper (background) color, click on the desired color with the mouse button while holding down the CTRL key.

- ▶ **FILL** color—To select the fill color, click the right mouse button.

 OTE: *The right mouse button only works as a Fill selector if the "Use right mouse button for fill color" box is enabled in the Tool Setting roll-up.*

Eyedropper Shortcut

To temporarily select the Eyedropper tool without leaving your currently selected tool, place the cursor in the image area and hold down the E key. This turns the cursor into an Eyedropper as long as the E key is held down. (All of the key combinations just described work with the E key, although you may feel like you are playing the keyboard version of Twister when selecting the background color.)

Eyedropper Sample Size

The Tool Settings roll-up is used to set the sample size of the Eyedropper tool. By default, the Eyedropper tool samples an area one-pixel wide to determine a color value. Sometimes when retouching photographs, you want an average color from an area. This is why Corel PHOTO-PAINT gives you the ability to select different sample sizes.

To change the sample size, open the Tool Settings roll-up (CTRL-F8) and click an alternate sample size in the list box. The roll-up in the next illustration has a drop-down list containing the following choices:

► Point (1 pixel)—default setting

► 3x3 Area (9 pixels)

► 5x5 Area (25 pixels)

► Custom Area—enables you to use the Eyedropper tool to define any size sample area

With every sample size (except Point), the color selected when the mouse button is clicked represents the average of all the colors in the sample area. Obviously with the Point setting, it represents the color value of the single pixel underneath the cursor. Be aware when using samples larger than the default setting of 1 pixel on areas of high contrast that the averaged color may be different than any individual color in the sampled area. The settings made in the Tool Settings roll-up only affect the Eyedropper tool, and they have no effect on other tools that may use an Eyedropper to define colors, such as Color Mask.

Notes on Using the Eyedropper Tool

If there are multiple objects on the image, the Eyedropper tool can only read the colors on the top object. Good rule of thumb: If you can't see it, the Eyedropper can't see it either.

When a large area is sampled and averaged, the result may be a color that, while representing the average color in the image, may not exist per se in the image. An example of this would be an area that had the same number of white and red pixels. The resulting color would be pink, even though there was no pink in the image.

Use the Eyedropper quick key (E) when you want to see what the color value(s) is for a part of the image to help set the Tolerance Values. An example of using this is when determining where a Magic Wand mask in an image is to be created. I use the E quick key to see what the color value is of the starting area (where I click to start the mask).

IP: *Use the quick key E when retouching images. It provides a fast and easy way to pick up adjoining colors, which is critical when touching up an imperfection on a picture of someone's face. The E key shortcut is also a quick way to get a numerical color value for a spot or area. This information is very helpful when setting Color Tolerance values for the Color Mask roll-up or the Magic Wand mask tool.*

Eyedropper Demonstration

Here is a demonstration that shows some practical uses for the Eyedropper tool. In this session I am going to take a photograph that is tall and narrow and change it so it can be used to run across several columns in Corel VENTURA.

Our original photograph from the PhotoDisc collection, shown here, is tall and narrow. A simple Image rotation will only produce a wide and short photograph. To make it wide and tall, we must use the Paper Size command and a few other tools.

Our first step is to rotate the image 90 degrees Clockwise. Choose Rotate from the Image menu and select 90 degrees Clockwise. The image may appear cut off on the ends. If so, just grab one of the sides of the photo and stretch it until the entire image fits. Now, let's make it taller.

Selecting the Paper Size command in the Image menu opens the Paper Size dialog box, as shown here. Since we will be changing the height and not the width of the photograph, we turn off the Maintain aspect ratio check box first. Then we enter the new values shown into the dialog box, click the Bottom Center option for Placement and then click the OK button.

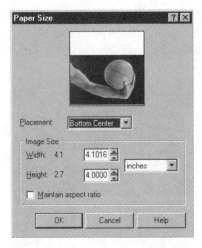

We now have a photograph with the top portion set to the same color as the Paper color. The one shown below is white because that is what the Paper color was set to. We want to fill in the white area at the top with a color that is identical (or very close) to the original.

To get the exact match we will use the Eyedropper tool. Open the Tool Settings roll-up (CTRL-F8) and choose the 3x3 Area for the Sample size. Because we need to extend the background, we need to make the Fill color match the existing background. So, we click the check box beside Use right button for fill color.

Placing the cursor on the white area of the background transforms the cursor into an eyedropper. The status line at the bottom left of the screen continually displays the color value of the pixels (in RGB numbers) under the eyedropper. This is very handy when looking for darker or lighter areas that may appear identical on the screen. The rules for color values are: the darker the shade, the lower the RGB numbers; the lighter the shade, the higher the number. In Figure 13-1 the cursor was over the white area when the screen capture shot was made. Hence the values displayed are 255,255,255.

End of color lesson and back to work. By moving the eyedropper over the black background and clicking the right mouse button—not the left—the display at the bottom of the screen now indicates the fill is the same color as the background.

Now that we have a Fill color that matches, we only need to select the Fill tool (looks like a bucket) from the Toolbox and click on the white area on top of the photograph. The white area floods with the same color as the original background. Well, not completely. Look on the left side of the photograph for a faint red gradient. We will learn how to fix that later when we work with the clone tools.

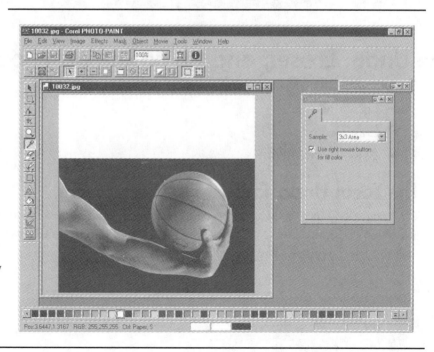

With the Eyedropper tool selected the status bar continuously displays the color under the cursor

FIGURE 13-1

In the next illustration I have imported some text from CorelDRAW 6 and placed it into the photograph. If this had been a real job, I would have imported the Corel PHOTO-PAINT image into CorelDRAW and applied the text there.

The Undo, Eraser, and Color Replacer Tools

The following three tools are located together on the same flyout:

▶ Local Undo tool

▶ Eraser tool

▶ Color Replacer tool

The Local Undo Tool

The Local Undo tool enables you to paint over areas where you wish to undo the last action performed by the previously used paint tool. There are two uses for this tool: to correct a mistake and to create an effect.

Controlling the Undo Tool

▶ Holding down the CTRL key while using the Local Undo tool constrains the movements of the tool to the horizontal or vertical. Depressing the SHIFT key changes the direction of constraint.

▶ The shape, size, rotation, and flatten characteristics of the Local Undo tool are determined by the Tool Settings roll-up (CTRL-F8).

▶ The Transparency of the Local Undo function is fixed at 0 percent.

▶ Double-clicking the Local Undo tool button acts the same as the CTRL-Z keyboard command—that is, it toggles the Undo/Redo function for the entire image or selected area.

 IP: *The Local Undo tool only works on fill and paintbrush applications. It does not partially undo filter effects or object merges.*

Things to Do with the Local Undo Tool

The Local Undo tool is very useful for removing part of whatever effect was last applied. Many times a filter will affect more of the image than was desired. By using the Local Undo tool, it is simple to remove "extra" effects.

The Local Undo tool can also be used for effects. The image shown in Figure 13-2 was created by placing the brick bitmap flood fill over the Photo-CD image of the building. Then, using the Local Undo tool (Square brush), we removed some bricks of the flood fill to give the appearance of looking through a hole in a brick wall. The whole image took less than five minutes to complete.

 IP: *Local Undo only operates on the last effect or last paint that was applied, so be careful to ensure that additional steps are not unintentionally performed either before or while the Local Undo tool is being used.*

The Eraser Tool

Big secret: The Eraser tool doesn't erase anything. Instead, the Eraser tool paints over the image with the current paper color. Remember how Corel PHOTO-PAINT and all other bitmap editing programs operate: they don't cover each pixel with a color but rather replace an existing color with a new color. This has the desired effect of "erasing" the image underneath it.

Controlling the Eraser Tool

▶ Hold down the CTRL key to constrain the Eraser tool to horizontal and vertical movements, and hold down the SHIFT key to change the direction of constraint.

▶ The size and shape of the Eraser tool are set from the Tool Settings roll-up in the View menu.

▶ Transparency of the Eraser Tool is not fixed, making a fade effect available.

▶ When the Eraser tool is applied to an object, only the object is affected; the image under the object remains unchanged. The rule remains: If you can't see it, Corel PHOTO-PAINT cannot affect it.

In the previous "Hole in the Wall" image, I used the Eraser Tool constrained horizontally to erase the bricks. It made the job much easier.

An example of the effects created with the Local Undo tool

FIGURE 13-2

IP: *If you need to erase a large area of an image, don't use the Eraser tool. Mask the area to be erased and select Clear from the Edit menu.*

The Color Replacer Tool

The Color Replacer tool replaces a range of colors using the current paint (foreground) color as the reference point with the paper (background) color. The advantage of the Color Replacer tool is that it can be applied selectively to an area of an image.

Controlling the Color Replacer Tool

▶ The size and shape of the Color Replacer tool is set from the Tool Settings roll-up in the View menu (CTRL-F8).

▶ Transparency of the Color Replacer tool is fixed at 0 percent, and there is no fade available.

▶ Holding down the CTRL key constrains the tool to horizontal and vertical movements. Holding down the SHIFT key changes the direction of constraint.

▶ Double-clicking the Color Replacer tool will cause a color replacement for the entire image.

Notes on Using the Color Replacer Tool

While this is a useful tool to selectively go into an image area and replace one color with another, be careful in using it. Remember that this tool replaces a range of colors (the range of colors selected is determined by the setting in Color Tolerance) with a single color. Unless the image you are working on is composed of solid colors or a limited number of shades, it is difficult to get all of the shades correctly matched and replaced. If it is your desire to change the color of an object that is composed of many shades of color, you may want to use the Hue tool instead.

Although the color of paint (foreground) to be replaced can be selected from the Color roll-up, a more accurate (and practical) way is to use the Eyedropper to pick out the exact color that needs to be replaced. To date, I can't recall someone ever giving me a project and saying, "Please replace all of the Trumatch 10-b2 with 11-a." It just doesn't happen in real life.

As said before, the range of colors that will be replaced is determined by the Tolerance setting in the Tool Settings roll-up. A greater number of shades increases

13

the colors that are replaced by the Color Replacer tool. You could think of it as a quick color-mask/paintbrush combination.

So what can you do with this tool? Good question. I really had to scratch my head on this one. It makes great silhouettes, and it does a nice but limited job of posterization. Other than that, I couldn't really figure out any eye-popping applications for this one.

Maximizing the Work Area

With all of the Toolbars, Palettes, and other things that clutter up the screen, it is sometimes necessary to clear the screen temporarily of the Title and Menu bars to make the image area larger. When you click Maximize Work Area in the View menu, the Title and Menu bars disappear from the screen. The problem with this command is trying to figure out how to restore things to normal when the menu bar has disappeared. That is why I stuck the following tip in the book.

 IP: *To un-Maximize the work area and restore the title and menu bars, right-click in the Toolbar area and select the Maximize Work Area command (which de-selects it) or use the keyboard shortcut ALT-V-W.*

Getting A Closer Look with the Zoom Tool

Before we can do any worthwhile image editing, we need to review some tools and techniques that will make your photo-editing and photo touch-up work more productive.

Most work in photo-manipulation requires the ability to zoom in very close to catch some fine detail in the work. Corel has provided some excellent tools for zooming in and out quickly; they have also provided a way for us to zoom in and remain zoomed in until we are finished. Let's review these magnification tools as they would be used with the freehand editing tools. The three tools are the Zoom tool, the Hand tool, and the Navigator roll-up.

The Zoom Tool

There are many way to access the Zoom tool:

▶ Zoom controls from the View menu

▶ Zoom tool in the Toolbox

► Zoom settings in the toolbar
► Shortcut z key

Zoom Controls from the View Menu

Zoom tools are essential for quality photo-editing. Corel PHOTO-PAINT provides a large number of Zoom options as described below.

Zoom Percentage Factors

The Zoom tool lets you magnify or diminish the active image by either choosing the zoom percentage you want from the drop-down list or entering the exact percentage you want.

The maximum zoom magnification is 1600%. Any percentage value less than 100% will reduce the size of the image as it appears onscreen.

Zoom 100%   This returns an image to one-to-one view (100%) after the Zoom tool has been used to magnify or diminish the size of an image.

 IP: *The two ways to quickly return an image to 100% zoom are to double-click the Zoom tool in the toolbox and to use the keyboard combination CTRL-1 (the number one).*

Zoom 1:1   This displays the image at its actual size (the size at which it was originally created).

Zoom To Fit   This shrinks or magnifies your image to fit within the Corel PHOTO-PAINT main window.

 IP: *The shortcut for Zoom to Fit is the F4 key.*

Zoom Tool

The Zoom tool can be selected either from the toolbox or by holding down the z key. After selecting the Zoom tool, the selected tool cursor changes into a Magnifying glass cursor when it is over the image. While holding down the left mouse button, drag a rectangular shape over the area to be edited. Release the mouse button, and after a few moments the image magnification will be reflected in the zoom factor in the toolbar.

13

IP: *You can zoom in or out with the* Z *key depressed. Each left mouse click zooms in while the* Z *key is held down. Each right mouse click zooms out in preset increments (10, 25, 33, 50, 100, 200, 300, 400, 600, 1600 percent) while the* Z *key is held down.*

The Navigator Roll-up

The benefit of being close is that you can see precisely what you are doing. The problem with being close is that you can't see what you are doing to the image as a whole. To see what you are doing both close up and far away, select the Navigator roll-up from the View menu (CTRL-F6).

The Navigator roll-up, shown here, makes it faster and easier to zoom in and out and reposition your image in the window. The Zoom tools of the Toolbox and display commands of the View menu are combined into this one, convenient roll-up. The Navigator roll-up lets you view specific areas of an active image. Like a map, this roll-up displays a thumbnail of the entire image. As you pan across the preview image, using the hand cursor to move the marquee, the main image mirrors the image information in the marquee. This lets you maintain image orientation when you are working with highly magnified areas of an image.

Using the Navigator Roll-up

The buttons at the bottom of the roll-up reflect the Zoom controls previously discussed. The buttons are (from left to right) Zoom 100%, Zoom to Fit, and Zoom 1:1. The two buttons on the right zoom in or out of the image each time they are clicked. The zoom percentages are determined by the preset percentages. For example, if the image is currently at 100% and I click the Zoom In (magnifying glass with the plus sign) twice, the image will be at 300% magnification. If the image is at 100% and the Zoom Out button is clicked, the image will be at 50%, since that is the first preset percentage below 100%.

USING THE ZOOM TOOL ON THE IMAGE   With the Zoom tool selected, you can place the cursor over the image and drag a zoom rectangle and it will zoom in on that area. The preview window in the Navigator roll-up will reflect the zoomed area with a rectangle.

PANNING AND ZOOMING WITH THE NAVIGATOR ROLL-UP   The cursor can be used inside the Preview window of the Navigator roll-up to redefine the zoom area or move the zoom rectangle.

Place the cursor in the preview window, outside of the zoom rectangle, and it becomes a magnifying glass. Use it in the Preview window to define an area to zoom. Place the cursor inside the zoom rectangle and it becomes a hand. Hold down the left mouse button and drag the rectangle to a different position. The image will reflect the new position.

New Window

As good as the Navigator roll-up is, there still is a need to view the area you are working on at high magnification at a lower zoom percentage. In Figure 13-3 I have opened a duplicate of the image using the New Window command from the Window menu. Since it is the first duplicate of the image, its title bar reflects the image filename followed by the number "2". Each image can be at a different magnification level. In this example the original is at a magnification of 800 percent and the duplicate image is shown at a zoom of 200 percent. If we were doing touch-up on the woman's face, we would use a setup similar to the previous illustration. This allows us to see how the effects we are applying appear in relation to the entire face or image.

The Duplicate command has been replaced with the New Window command.

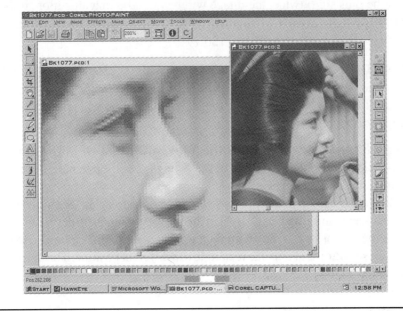

The New
Window
command
allows you
to view an
image at a
different
magnification
level

FIGURE 13-3

The Hand Tool

The best way to move short distances is not the scroll bars. Instead, either select the Hand tool in the Zoom flyout of the Toolbox, or hold down the H key and the cursor becomes a hand. Isn't that handy? (Sorry about the pun.) While still holding down the H key, click and drag the cursor. It is as if the hand were attached to the image, and it will move in the direction you drag it. It is much faster than the scroll bars.

To recap: Use the Z key to zoom in or out of an area without needing to change tools. You can watch the effect of your close-up work on a 100 percent image by selecting Duplicate in the Window menu. Use the H key (the Hand tool) to move short distances rapidly.

Exploring Corel PHOTO-PAINT's Editing Tools

14

In this chapter we are going to discuss the tools (now called Brushes) located in the Tool Settings roll-up when you select the Effect tool from the Toolbox. These tools offer a rich assortment of different effects. Many of these effects can be found in the Filter section. The advantage of the Effect tools is that the effects can be applied selectively in small areas without the necessity of creating a mask. In the following pages we are going to discuss the technical information about the tools and some of the uses for them. In Corel PHOTO-PAINT 5, these tools are called the Freehand Editing tools, and they are all located on a flyout. No longer. In Corel PHOTO-PAINT 6, they can only be accessed from the Tool Settings roll-up. There are ten categories of tools that constitute the Freehand Editing tools. I call them categories since, like their Corel PHOTO-PAINT 5 equivalent, the Brush Tool Settings roll-up, they offer multiple presets in each category. The ten general editing tool categories and their icons are shown here.

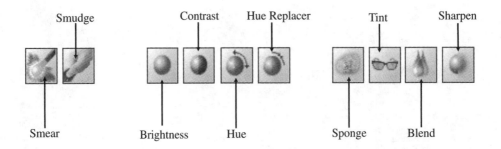

Each category contains at least nine different preset settings. For example, there are several presets for the Smear tool. Additionally, you can add a large number of custom presets of your own creation.

The effects provided by many of the tools can also be applied through various menu commands, while others are unique to the Toolbox and not available elsewhere in Corel PHOTO-PAINT. We will explore these tools in the order they appear in the Tool Settings roll-up, beginning with the Smear tool.

The Freehand Editing tools are no longer located on a flyout. They are now accessed through the Tool Settings roll-up.

Because all of the Edit tools (brushes) use a common dialog box, we will compare the dialog box as it relates to the Smear tool with other tools and point out differences. Each Edit tool has 26 categories of settings, and each setting interacts with other settings. This means that there are literally several billion combinations of settings. Since it is impossible to document all of the combinations, I have described what the settings do and leave it to you to experiment with them. I have included with most tools some tips on which settings have the greatest (useful) effects on particular tools.

The Smear Tool

The Smear tool smears colors. The same tool in Adobe Photoshop is called the Smudge tool (which can get confusing, because there is a Smudge tool in Corel PHOTO-PAINT). The Smear tool spreads colors in a picture, producing an effect similar to dragging your finger through wet oil paint. The size and shape of the Smear tool is set from the Tool Settings roll-up in the View menu.

Constraining the Smear Tool

Use the CTRL key to constrain the tool to a vertical or horizontal direction. Pressing the SHIFT key changes the direction of constraint.

14

Smear Tool Settings Roll-Up Options

All of the tools are controlled through the Tool Settings roll-up, shown here. The tool is referred to as a brush because it uses the same dialog box as the Brush settings. It is divided into three tabs. The first tab of the roll-up is the Brush control. It provides control over the brush shape, size, and transparency of the fill. Here is how the settings in the Brush tab work.

Type

This setting contains all of the saved styles for the selected brush. Many of these preset styles have names that indicate how they operate. Examples include Pointy Smear and Thick Smear.

Flyout Menu

The arrow (pointing outward) to the right of the Type box opens a menu that allows you to reset the brushes to their default values. You can reset a single brush, all of the brush styles, or all of the brush tools. This is really handy when you have been making all kinds of changes to the tools and need to return them to their original values.

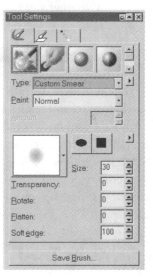

Paint

This setting determines the way the paint pixels are applied to the image. There are 20 different modes. The way each of these modes works is discussed later in this chapter.

Shape Buttons

These set the shape of the brush. The three available shapes are Oval, Square, and Preview Window. The custom preview area shows the size and shape of the selected brush. If the Custom preview area is chosen by clicking on it, a different screen appears showing a large selection of brush presets. Any custom brushes that are created by the user and saved will appear at the bottom of the type list. The red text in the corner indicates the size of the brush in pixels.

Size

This setting allows adjustment of Round or Square paintbrush sizes from 0 to 100 pixels. The size of brush selected is shown in the preview box. The size of the Custom brush is not adjustable.

Transparency

This setting sets the level of transparency of the brush stroke. It is similar to adjusting the amount of water mixed with watercolors. The higher the setting, the more transparent the brush stroke. At a very high setting, the color acts more like a tint. A setting of 0 has no transparency, whereas a setting of 100 makes the brush stroke invisible regardless of any other settings.

Rotate

This setting rotates the Round or Square brush by the amount entered. You can see the effect of the rotating in the preview window as the change is being applied. The Rotate control does not affect the custom brush. Value is in degrees, up to a maximum of 180 degrees. Obviously, rotating a Round brush serves no purpose, but rotating a flattened Round brush does.

Flatten

The Flatten slider controls the height of the Round and Square brushes. Values are in percentage of height. You can see the effect of the flattening in the preview window as the change is being applied.

Soft Edge

This sets the edges of the brush to either soft, hard, or in between. Soft edges make the brush stroke the least dense at the edges; Hard edges are dense up to the edge, with little to no softening, depending on the brush size and other brush settings. The preview box displays the edge selected. The higher the value, the greater the softness of the edges.

Save Brush

This saves a brush setting using a style name in the Type box.

Controlling Texture, Water Colors, and Brush Strokes Settings

The second tab, shown here, controls the Texture, Water Color, and Brush Stroke settings.

Brush Texture

This texture setting is new in Corel PHOTO-PAINT 6. It is similar to the paper setting in Fractal Design's PAINTER. The setting has a range of 0-100. A setting of zero produces no effect. A setting of 100 produces a rough texture when the Smear tool is applied.

To load a different texture, click the left-pointing arrow and select Load A Texture from the menu. Select a drive and folder in the Look-In list box, and double-click the texture file name to load it.

 IP: *The best images to use for brush textures possess high contrast. The dark area paints and the light area doesn't.*

Edge Texture

This works like Brush Texture, except it controls the amount of "texture" (0-100) that is applied to the edge of the stroke.

Bleed

In the Watercolors section, this setting determines how much the pixels in the image are smeared when the brush is dragged across the image. With a range from 0-100 the greatest effect is seen when set to 100 and no effect is seen when it is set to zero.

Sustain Color

This controls the amount of color variation in the image.

Smoothing

In combination with the anti-aliasing check box, this option determines how smooth the brush strokes of the tools are.

Dab Variation and Color Variation

The third tab is divided into two parts, Dab variation and Color variation, as shown below. This tab controls the number of dabs as well as the spacing, spread, and fade-out effects applied when any of the brush tools are applied.

Fade Out

This setting determines the length of the brush stroke before it fades entirely by adjusting the rate at which the brush stroke disappears. This is similar to adjusting the pressure of the brush against the canvas as the paint is applied. The greater the Fade Out value, the more fade-out is applied and the quicker the fade-out of the brush stroke occurs. As the Fade Out value decreases, the amount of fade-out applied to the brush stroke diminishes; a value of 0 turns off the Fade Out function completely.

Fade Out works by counting the number of brush applications to determine when to begin applying the gradual fade-out function. This is important for the following reason. Spacing, the next parameter, controls the distance between brush applications. Increasing spacing between brush applications increases the distance that the brush stroke will go before Fade Out begins.

Spacing

This sets the distance, in pixels, between applications of the brush. To create a brush stroke, the pointing device draws a line across the image. At a frequency determined by the Spacing setting, the brush is applied to the line. For example, if a brush stroke is made with a setting of 5 (pixels), Corel PHOTO-PAINT will produce the selected brush on the image area at a spacing of every 5 pixels. While it may seem that a setting of 1 would be desired, a lower setting slows down the generation of the brush stroke considerably. It can be really slow on some systems. When a large brush is being used, the setting can be larger (and this is recommended) because of the overlap caused by the larger brush.

Spread

This sets the distance between individual strokes. Higher values make the distance between stroke lines greater.

Number of Dabs

This sets the number of times the brush strokes are applied. This has the effect of having more paint on the brush. This value, like the Spacing value, can have a significant effect on the speed at which your computer renders an image. It is recommended that you keep the number of lines very low and the spacing as high as practical.

Using the Smear Tool

The purpose of this tool is to smear colors. I know I said that before, but it's worth repeating, because many first-time users of Corel PHOTO-PAINT misuse the Smear tool. That is, they use it to soften color transitions. That is the purpose of the Blur tool. Think of it this way: The results of using the Smear tool are not that much different from finger painting (except you don't have to wash your hands after you're done). Blending an area causes the distinction between colors to become less pronounced. Choosing a blending amount of 0% in the Tool Settings roll-up causes no blending to occur, while an amount of 100% will give you the maximum amount of blending possible. Adjacent pixels must be different colors for the effect to work.

 IP: *Make a practice of using the Checkpoint command (which makes a temporary copy of the image that can be quickly restored) before you begin application of the Smear tool or any other freehand editing tool.*

Have the Smear Tool Settings roll-up open when you work with this tool. For retouching, Soft Edge and Transparency should be adjusted to produce the greatest effect without being obvious. Remember that a higher Soft Edge setting causes the edges of the Smear tool to appear more feathered, which is desirable for most Smear tool applications. Fade Out and Spacing are not the critical settings. That said, you might want to play with the Fade Out settings for applications where you do not want the effect to end abruptly. The effect of the Smear tool is additive. Every time you apply it to the image, it will smear the pixels, no matter how many times you apply it.

For retouching, you may end up "scrubbing" the area with the tool to get the effect desired. When retouching a photo, you do not want a solid color after you are done—you need to have texture for the subject to look real.

 IP: *If you start the Smear tool well off of the image, it pulls the pixels (Paper color) onto the image. This can be used to give the brush-stroke effect on the edge.*

The last application of the tool can be removed with the Undo command (CTRL-Z), provided it was applied with one continuous stroke without letting go of the mouse button.

Using the Smear Tool to Do Touch-Up

Here is a quick example of using the Smear tool to remove the glare from a young woman's nose, as shown in Figure 14-1. Again, the purpose of this tool is to smear colors. I am going to smear the colors from around the patch of glare on her nose into the glare spot. Using the default setting for "Pointy Smear," I drag the color from around the patch of glare (Figure 14-1) until the glare is gone, as shown in Figure 14-2.

 IP: *You could use this effect to blend the edges of a pasted object with the background to make it appear more natural.*

Creating Effects with the Smear Tool

The Smear tool is not limited to retouching photographs. In the following examples, I have made only a few samples of what can be done with the Smear tool.

In the next illustration, I applied the Smear tool across the text using the "Pointy Smear" setting. By using the constrain key while I applied the smear, I was able to keep the smear lines straight.

Here is the
original
photograph.
Even
though it
is a
professional
photo, the
lady forgot
to powder
her nose

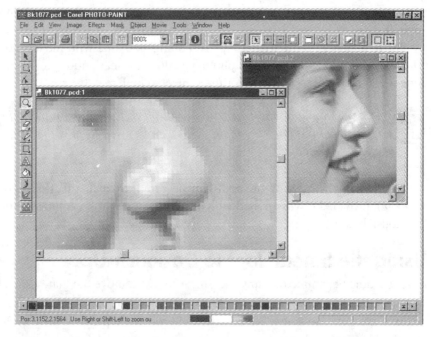

FIGURE 14-1

We have toned down, but not completely removed the glare on her nose. The Smear tool is more effective for this type of work since, if we used a Clone tool, we would lose highlights, which would make the final photo look flat

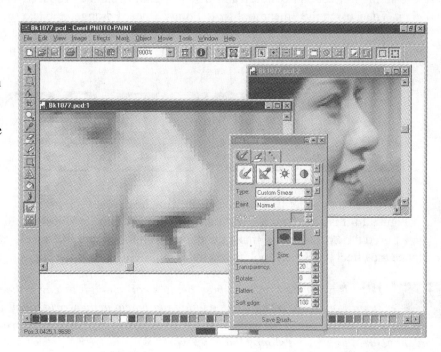

◼ FIGURE 14-2

By changing the brush size, shape, and rotation, and dragging the smear tool from right to left, I was able to give the cascaded appearance to the text shown here.

14

To create the next image, I applied a flip vertical to the original text, I skewed the resulting "reflection" to the left and, using the control handles, reduced its vertical height. Then, using the Smear tool set to Pointy Smear I dragged the text (using the Constrain key). For a final touch I placed a rectangle mask just below the original word and applied an airbrush stroke to create the light horizon below the text.

There are many other things you can do with the Smear tool.

Figure 14-3 is a photograph from the KPT Power Photos collection. In Figure 14-4 I used the Smear tool to make the photograph look more like an oil painting. Notice the effect the Smear tool has on the background and on the edges.

IP: *Never count on an image being small enough to cover the sins of sloppy touch-up. With all of the fancy equipment in the world today, it is too easy for people to get a photo blown up to poster size, and that is when they might get real ugly about sloppy touch-up work.*

The Smudge Tool

Maybe it is just me, but the first time I began exploring the freehand editing tools, I thought Smear and Smudge sounded like they did the same thing. The Smudge tool in Corel PHOTO-PAINT is different from the tool with the same name in Adobe Photoshop. As it turns out, the Smudge tool adds texture by randomly mixing pixels in a selected area. It is like a can of spray paint that sucks up color from the area that it is currently over and then sprays it back onto the subject. Technically, it acts like a local color noise filter. I am not aware of any equivalent of this tool in Photoshop.

The Smudge Tool Settings Roll-Up

All of the controls are identical to those shown for the Smear tool with one exception. The Rate of Flow setting determines how fast the noise (texture) is placed on the image. A rate of flow of 1 causes the noise texture to flow very slowly; therefore, to create a noticeable change, the tool has to be held at the same location for a longer period.

The original
photograph
from KPT
Power
Photos

FIGURE 14-3

The same
photo after
it was
modified
with the
Smear tool

FIGURE 14-4

14

Using the Smudge Tool

The Smudge tool adds texture. It is really color noise. The effect of the Smudge tool is additive. As long as you hold the button down, the effect is being applied, *even if the brush is not moving*. Look at the next image, a photograph that contains lots of highlights on the faces of two young people.

By applying the Smudge tool set to the Smudge A Little preset, we are able to tone down the highlights as shown below. However, the image now appears to be less sharp. If we had used the Smear tool to do areas this large, we might have ended up with what appeared to be scar tissue.

Thoughts about Retouching Photographs

While the Smudge tool removes highlights very well, it must be used with caution. Look at the original photograph that we just smudged again. Notice that when the bright highlights are removed, the image appears to be "flatter" than before. This is a drawback as we seek perfection in a photograph. Too many highlights may distract, but they also add contrast to the photograph, which deceives the human eye into thinking the image looks sharper. Another consideration when you are touching up photographs is whether what you are removing or modifying is necessary for the overall effect the photograph is trying to convey. Ultimately, you must make the call, but consider what you are changing before you change it. The only photographs that are digitally manipulated to perfection without regard to the original subject generally are the type that fold out of magazines.

IP: *Always remember when working with the Smudge tool that it acts like the Airbrush or Spraycan brush. That means that you do not need to drag it across the image unless you have a high Rate of Flow setting. Just put it over the area you want and hold down the mouse button until you get the desired effect.*

The Brightness Tool

Brightness is the degree of light reflected from an image or transmitted through it. The Brightness tool can be used to both lighten and darken areas of the image. This tool is similar to the Dodge-and-Burn tool in Photoshop. These tools are simulations of traditional darkroom techniques. Photographers can improve their work by using the dodge and burn technique to block out or add light from a negative in order to enhance an image. In photography, dodging is used to lighten shadow areas (the darkest portions of an image), and burning is used to darken the highlights (the brightest portions of an image). Both dodging and burning can increase the detail in a photograph. The Brightness/Darkness tools produce the same effect in a digital image.

Using the Brightness Tool

The Brightness brush brightens or darkens areas in an image. Choosing a brightness of 100% in the Tool Settings roll-up causes all the black to be removed from the affected area, resulting in a much lighter color. Conversely, choosing -100% turns the affected area black.

Special Effects with the Brightness Tool

This tool is great for giving a feeling of depth to images. In the following series of figures, I have shown the use of the Brightness tool to add shadows to an object to make it appear more real. Although this is not set up as a skill session for you to do, I have included all of the steps necessary to accomplish the task if you so choose.

The first step is to create the original shape. Filling a rectangular mask with one of the color bitmap fills provided in the Corel PHOTO-PAINT 6 package produced the following image.

Next, I removed the mask and applied the Ripple filter (Vertically with the settings Period: 90, Amplitude: 6). The results are shown here. The reason the rectangle mask had to be removed was that it would have clipped portions of the 2D Ripple effect that went outside of the mask. The rectangle is now rippled, but without shadows and highlights it appears flat.

Making Shadows and Highlights

Before we can apply the Brightness tool, we must create a new mask. With the Magic Wand mask tool, I click anywhere in the white area. After the mask is formed, I choose Invert from the Mask menu. Now, only the rippled area is masked. The reason for the new mask is to prevent the Darken setting of the Brighten tool from getting on the white background. The first application of the Brightness tool uses the Darken setting to make the shadows. Starting outside the rippled area, I drag the Brighten (darken) tool in a vertical line using the Constrain key to keep the line vertical. You must think three-dimensionally to decide where to put the shadows. I think of this image as a rug. I decided the light source should come from the upper right. Next, I decide where the shadows would appear. After that I use the Brighten setting to produce the highlights on the portions that would be near the top if it were a real rug or just near the light source. The rug begins to appear to have some depth, as shown below.

Shadow for the Rug

Because the human eye doesn't register something it sees as real unless it sees a shadow, we should create one. To make the shadow, I used the Create Object from Mask command in the Object menu. Next, I created a duplicate of the object. After locking the top object in the Objects roll-up, I used the rectangle tool to paint the duplicate black. I combined the black object with the background using the Combine command in the Object menu. To make it look like a shadow and not an oil spill, I applied a Gaussian blur at a setting of 10. The result is displayed below.

Using the Brighten Tool

When using this tool, remember that you want the changes to be subtle, so make them in small increments using a Brighten tool with a round shape unless you are working near straight lines, as in a geometric figure. The effect of the tool is not additive. It will apply the effect at the level set in the Tool Setting dialog box the first time it is applied. Progressive applications cannot make any changes unless the Tool Settings options are changed.

Any single application of the tool can be removed with the Undo command (CTRL-Z) as long as it was applied with one continuous stroke without letting go of the mouse button. If you must be zoomed in at great magnification to do your work, keep a duplicate window open at a lower zoom value so you can see the effect in perspective.

To achieve any subtle effects in areas that have no naturally occurring visual boundaries, you must be prepared to apply the brush in several stages to reduce the sharp transition of the contrast effect.

The Contrast Tool

Contrast is the difference between the lightest and the darkest parts of an image. The Contrast tool intensifies the distinction between light and dark. It operates in the same manner as the Contrast filter, except that it can be applied to small areas without the need to create masks. The size, shape, and level of the Contrast tool is set from the Tool Settings roll-up in the View menu. The Contrast Tool Presets are Custom Contrast, Increase Contrast, and Decrease Contrast, plus small, medium, and large Soft and small, medium, and large Flat.

Using the Contrast Tool

Use the Contrast tool to bring out color in scanned photographs that appear dull or flat. Don't increase the contrast too much or the picture might appear overexposed. Some scanners have a tendency to darken the photographs when they are scanned, which causes them to lose contrast. Video images that are obtained through a frame grabber also tend to be dark. Both of these applications can benefit from the selective application of contrast.

Be careful not to overuse the Contrast tool, which can result in exaggerated white and dark areas. In the next illustration, I have loaded a Corel Photo-CD and created a mask composed of three separate rectangles. To the left rectangle I applied the Contrast tool at the Decrease Contrast setting. At this setting, the areas affected have reduced contrast, resulting in a gray image. The rectangle in the middle was painted with the Contrast tool at the Increase setting. It slightly darkened the image and increased the overall contrast. At the maximum Amount setting for Increase Contrast (rectangle on the right), the highlights and shadows are blown out. That is, the areas that are lighter become white and almost all shades are lost. It is as if the image were converted to *bi-level,* which means the image is composed of only black and white pixels.

 IP: *This is one of the advantages of the contrast tool over the contrast filter. It allows you to apply the filter to only a portion of the mask.*

The effect of the Contrast tool is additive. It will apply the effect at the level set by the Tool Setting dialog box the first time it is applied. After the mouse button is released, progressive applications add to the effect already applied.

The Hue Tool

There are two hue tools, the Hue tool and the Hue Replacer tool, that at first seem to do the same thing. I found their names to be especially confusing. The Hue tool shifts the pixels of the image the number of degrees specified in the roll-up. The Hue Replacer is used to replace the hue of pixels in the image with the hue of the selected Paint (foreground) color.

How the Hue Tool Works

The Hue tool actually changes the color of the pixels it touches by the amount of the setting. The number of degrees entered in the Amount setting relates to the color wheel. The maximum setting is halfway around the color wheel (180 degrees), which represents the complementary color of the changed pixel.

 IP: *The best way to get the most realistic color change is to experiment with the transparency settings for the Hue tool. I have found that the default setting has insufficient transparency.*

Using the Hue Tool

► Adjust the amount of color change by typing a new value in the Amount number box.

► Adjust the size and shape of the brush by choosing options in the roll-up.

► Click and drag over the area to change the colors.

Limiting the Effect of the Hue Tool

Using the Hue tool is like using the tint control on your color TV. The difficulty with using this tool is that it will shift every pixel you paint with the tool. To prevent unwanted hue shifts, it is best to mask the area first. By using the Color Mask roll-up, you can create a mask that is limited to the colors that you want to change. The best part about this combination of Color Mask and Hue tools is that you need not concern yourself if the Color Mask exists in an unwanted portion of the image, since you will limit the application of the Hue shift by where you place the Hue tool.

In the color insert is an example of the application of the Hue tool. By applying the Hue tool to the pink portions of the water skier's board and life vest, I was able to change the color to fluorescent green.

 IP: *Use the Hue brush to create interesting shifts in color within your image.*

The effect of the Hue brush tool is additive. It will apply the effect at the level set by the Tool Setting dialog box the first time it is applied. Progressive applications after the mouse button is released will shift the hue of the pixels that much again.

The Hue Replacer Tool

The Hue Replacer tool replaces the hue of pixels in the image with the hue of the selected Paint (foreground) color. By changing the Hue, the color changes but the other two components (saturation and brightness) remain unchanged. The same considerations exist with the tool's masking and other settings, as mentioned with the Hue tool. The Hue Replacer brush changes the colors of pixels by the value set in the Amount number box. For instance, if you select an amount of 180 and brush over a red area with a color value of 1, the color changes to cyan (181). The color values relate to the degrees on the HSB Color Wheel.

Using the Hue Replacer Tool

► Select the Hue Replacer tool.

► Adjust the size and shape of the brush by choosing options in the roll-up.

► Choose a paint color from the onscreen color palette or from the Color roll-up.

► Click and drag over the area. The affected pixels change to the hue of the paint color.

Mixing Colors and Other Confusion

The amount of the original hue that remains is determined by the Amount setting in the Tool Settings roll-up. For example, in the color insert we used the Hue tool to shift the hue of the pixels to change the color of the skier's equipment from pink to green. If I select green for the Paint color and have the Amount setting at 100 (percent), anywhere I paint on the pink becomes green. If I set the Amount setting to 50 (percent), then it will mix the pink (50%) with green (50%). The result in this example is not what you might expect. All of the traditional rules of color you learned, like yellow + blue = green, do not apply with digital color. To complicate matters further with regard to predicting the color outcome the default color model of Corel PHOTO-PAINT is RGB. To accomplish the Hue mix, Corel PHOTO-PAINT must temporarily convert the model to HSB. This text is not here to discourage you, only to help you understand that predicting the color outcome is very difficult, and the best method I am aware of is experimentation.

IP: *Use this Hue Replacer effect tool to replace the color of an object without removing its shading and highlights. For instance, you can change the color of a red dress to yellow, while still retaining the shading that distinguishes the folds in the skirt.*

The Sponge (Saturation) Tool

The Sponge tool acts in the same manner as the Saturation filter, discussed in Chapter 11. The Sponge tool is used to increase the saturation or intensity of a color. When saturation is added to a color, the gray level of a color diminishes; thus it becomes less neutral. The Sponge tool can also be used to desaturate or diminish the intensity of a color. When Saturation is reduced to –100 percent, the result is a grayscale image. The size, shape, and level of the Saturation tool are set from the Tool Settings roll-up in the View menu.

IP: *Also use the Sponge brush to make colors more vibrant. For the amount, select a low positive value (5, for example) and brush over the desired area.*

Using the Sponge Tool

The Sponge tool actually removes the color of the pixels it touches by the amount of the setting. The effect of the tool is not additive. It will apply the effect at the level set by the Tool Setting dialog box the first time it is applied. Progressive applications will not make any changes to the previously affected area unless the tool settings are changed.

The Tint Tool

The Tint tool tints an area in the current paint color. This may seem the same as painting with a high-transparency paintbrush, but it is not. The paintbrush is additive. That is, when the same area continues to have the brush applied to it, the paint builds up until it reaches 100 percent. The Tint tool will apply the paint color as specified by the Tint setting, regardless of how many times it is applied. The amount of tint set in the Tool Settings roll-up is the maximum level of the paint color that can be applied to the pixels in the image.

14

Using the Tint Tool

The first thing to remember with the Tint tool is that 100 percent tint is a solid color without any transparency. The Tint tool provides a way to highlight a selected area with a color. The same effect can also be achieved over larger areas by using the Rectangle, Ellipse, or Polygon Draw tool and controlling the Transparency setting through the Tool Settings roll-up.

Another use of the Tint tool is for touching up an image. The technique is simple. When you have a discoloration to cover, pick an area of the image that is the desired color. Using the Eyedropper tool, select a large enough sample to get the average color that is needed to match the adjoining areas. Now apply the tint to the area with progressively larger percentage settings until the discolored areas disappear into the surrounding area. If the resulting tint application looks too smooth, use the Smudge Brush to add texture. You can also use the Blend tool to reduce spots where there are large differences in the shades.

The Blend Tool

This is a better tool to use for some types of retouching than the Smear tool. The Blend tool enables you to blend colors in your picture. Blending is the mixing of different colors to cause less distinction among them. For example, if you have two areas of different colors and they overlap, it is possible to blend the two different colors so that the separation of the two areas is indistinct. You can use the Blend tool to soften hard edges in an image and to correct any pixelation caused by oversharpening.

 IP: *You could use this effect to blend the edges of a pasted object with the background to make it appear more natural.*

Blending an area causes the distinction between colors to become less pronounced. Choosing a blending amount of 0% in the Tool Settings roll-up causes no blending to occur, while an amount of 100% will give you the maximum amount of blending possible. Adjacent pixels must be different colors for the effect to work.

Using the Blend Tool

The Blend tool acts like applying water to a watercolor. The effect of the tool is additive. It will apply the effect at the level set by the Tool Settings dialogs box each time it is applied.

The Sharpen Tool

The Sharpen tool sharpens selected areas of the image by increasing the contrast between neighboring pixels. It operates in the same manner as the Sharpen filter except that it can be applied without the need to create masks. The size and shape of the Sharpen tool are set from the Tool Settings roll-up in the View menu.

Using the Sharpen Tool

Avoid overusing the Sharpen tool, which results in exaggerated white spots (pixelation) wherever the white component of the image approaches its maximum value. The effect of this tool is additive. It will apply the Sharpen effect to the Sharpen level set in the Tool Settings dialog box every time it is applied. Progressive applications intensify the changes. Any application of the tool can be removed with the Undo command (CTRL-Z) as long as it was applied with one continuous stroke without letting go of the mouse button. If you must be zoomed in at great magnification to do your work, keep a duplicate window open to a lower zoom value so you can see the effect in perspective.

The Clone Tools

This is the last set of tools in the Toolbox. The ability to clone images in Corel PHOTO-PAINT is one of the more valuable features in the program. Contrary to public opinion, Clone tools are not what was used to make the dinosaurs in *Jurassic Park*. (Did you know that the Tyrannosaurus Rex that attacked the cars in the movie wasn't a model but a whopping 23-ton robot? There is a little fact to chew on.) Here is the official Corel definition of the Clone tool:

> *"A clone is an identical duplicate of an area on the image. The Clone tool creates an identical replica, whereas the Pointillism Clone tool and the Impressionism Clone tool create a duplicate in the style of Pointillism (dots) and Impressionism (lines)."*

In the world of Corel PHOTO-PAINT, Clone tools are used to take part of an image and apply it to another part of the image. This is important when part of an image needs to be removed and something is needed to replace the removed section. Another use is to duplicate an area of one image into another.

14

The Clone Tool Settings Roll-up

There are several ways to open the Clone Tool Settings roll-up shown in the next illustration. Through the View menu, use the keyboard combination of CTRL-F8 or double-click the Clone tool on the toolbox. The Clone Tool Settings roll-up is identical to the Brush Tool Settings roll-up except for the Clone selections. The category headings are:

► Normal Clone

► Impressionism Clone

► Pointillism Clone

► Custom From Saved

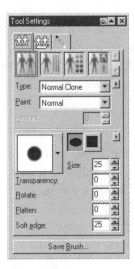

Normal Clone

In this mode the Clone tool does not modify the pixels. The pixels from the source are painted precisely as they appear in the source. The following is a demonstration of the Normal Clone tool. In this demonstration we are taking a good stock photograph and cloning the grapes so there are more of them. The process of cloning one object to another to create something that is missing is commonly used both in still photography and motion pictures. In the movie *Forrest Gump,* the actor who played Lt. Dan had special blue socks on when they shot the scenes that showed his legs. By using a blue screen process, anywhere his blue socks appeared would not record on film. They used clone tools as in Corel PHOTO-PAINT 6 to clone other parts of the background to replace the areas covered by his legs. Our object is for the grapes to look real and not cloned.

The picture shown here is from the Corel Grapes and Wine collection. It is an excellent photo but we need some more grapes.

Select the Normal Clone brush from the large selection of brushes available. Applying the Clone tool can be tricky if you do not create a mask to limit where the clone is applied. Before cloning, I made a mask to ensure the cloned grapes did not end up on the leaves.

To create a mask, select the Magic Wand mask tool. Now click the cursor at a point in the lower middle. It is the area that has the stronger green hues. The resulting mask, shown here, has outlined the leaves. Don't worry about the part of the mask that covers the grapes. Our object is to protect the leaves.

One last thing to change before beginning the process of cloning is to select Options in the Tools menu and enable the Use Shape Cursor function. The Use Shape Cursor feature allows the cursor shape to indicate the size of the selected brush or tool. By default, the cursor is an icon that reflects the type of tool selected. The reason the cursor size is not used as the default is because it slows the brush action slightly. In most cases I do not advise enabling this feature unless you have a fast system.

Now that we can see the cursor size, the size of the Clone tool is changed to 50 pixels so that it is approximately the same size as the grapes. Finally, we can begin cloning.

Place the cursor, which looks like a circle with a plus in it, over one of the grapes. Clicking the left mouse button anchors the source point. The indication that the source point is anchored is that the plus symbol remains when we move the circle cursor. When we click the left mouse button, we establish an aligned relationship between the source and the Clone tool.

Aligned and Non-Aligned Clone Modes

The clone has two modes in which it can operate: aligned and non-aligned. When it is in aligned mode, the source point moves in relation to the Clone tool. This mode is used to clone whole images, like the grapes. When it is in non-aligned mode (which we will show later in this session), the Clone tool can move about but the source is restricted by the user. This is generally used to clone nondetailed areas like clouds or abstract backgrounds.

Holding down the left mouse button, we begin dragging the Clone tool while watching the crosshair cursor. Remembering that the crosshair is the center of the circle, we drag the crosshair down the right side and up the left side. We are not concerned about the lighter or darker background that may get cloned along with the grapes. We will correct the background later. Continue to drag the Clone tool inside the grapes until all of the grapes have been cloned and it looks like the image shown here.

Changing the settings of the Clone tool settings roll-up, our object is to make a smaller clone tool that will allow us to get into smaller places. We also want to give our clone tool a softer edge with greater transparency so that the cloning will not be evident. Now we are going to use the non-aligned mode.

Non-Align Mode and Resetting the Clone Tool

Before we use non-aligned mode, we must first reset the Clone tool by placing it over a point in the background that contains the colors we want to clone. Holding down the SHIFT key and pressing the left mouse button at the same time resets the Clone tool. The source point is now anchored at the new location. First, I place the

Clone tool cursor over a point that contains the pattern/color pixels I want to clone. Second, while holding down the S key, I drag the Clone tool a very short distance and release the mouse button without releasing the S key. When the mouse button is released, the source crosshair jumps back to the original anchor point. This is what non-align mode is all about. It operates, like the mouse, in relative mode. As long as you hold down the S key, each time you release the mouse button, the source point will return to its previous (not the anchor) point. This allows us to "paint" an area using clones of the pixels under the source. I continue to select areas of the background that look like they would help hide the portions of the background that were unintentionally cloned with the grapes. We are close to being finished, but there are still a few touch-ups to complete.

Finishing Touches

In this age of mass production, a common goal is to have every manufactured unit be identical to every other. When we see identical things in nature, our mind is alerted to the fact that someone has been fooling with Mother Nature. So the way to make the new grapes not look phony is to make them different. We can do that by changing the position of some grapes. To do this I will change the size of the Clone tool to 50 (pixels) and leave the other settings unchanged.

Selecting one of the round grapes in the center of a cluster, I place the Clone tool cursor over it, and holding down the SHIFT key, I press down the left mouse button. Releasing the SHIFT key and the mouse button anchors the grape as the source. Holding down the S key, I place the Clone tool cursor over one of the brightly-lit grapes near the top of the cloned cluster. Next, I hold down the left mouse button and move it around the grape slightly so that the darker grape color covers all of the grape. Keeping the S key held down, I repeat the procedure on several of the brightly-lit grapes.

Next we use the Hue tool to change the colors of the cloned grapes slightly. Selecting the Hue Replacer function and setting the Amount (of Hue shift in degrees) at –13 (degrees), I paint over all of the grapes. The shift of –13 degrees will give the cloned grapes a slightly more reddish hue. If you think that it is too much, cut back the percentage. As a former resident of the Napa Valley in California, I think they look perfect.

The final task is to use the Blend tool and apply the default setting of "Blend A Lot." I apply the blend to the entire bunch of cloned grapes. Since they are further from the viewer, the eye expects them to be slightly out of focus. Blending them produces that slightly out-of-focus look. That's it! All you need now is some new age music and a mellow-toned narrator and you have a good wine commercial. The finished image is shown in Figure 14-5. The color version is in the color insert of the book.

Recap: How to Use the Clone Tools to Clone an Area

► Double-click the Clone tool on the toolbox to open the Tool Settings roll-up.

► Select the type of clone tool desired.

► Set a clone point on the area you want reproduced and then move the Clone tool to the new location. The cloned area can be on the same image or in a different image window.

► To re-anchor the clone point place the cursor over the area you want to clone, hold down the SHIFT key, and click.

► To operate in non-align mode, hold down the S key.

► Holding down the CTRL key constrains the Clone tool to horizontal/vertical movements.

► Holding down the CTRL and the SHIFT keys changes the direction of constraint.

► To draw a straight line in any direction with the Clone tool, click to establish a starting point, hold down the ALT key, move to where you wish the line to end, and click again to create the line.

 IP: *You can use the Normal Clone tool to retouch photographs that contain scratches or other defects. Clone an area containing similar color and copy over the damaged section of the photograph.*

Removing Clutter from a Photograph with the Clone Tool

Probably the most common use for the Clone tool is removing things from a photograph. In 1993, they restored the film *My Fair Lady;* even though the film is only 20 years old, it was in very poor condition. In the opening credits, several frames of film had scratches, leaving black spots on the screen. Technicians used clone tools

The
completed
project. All
that is
missing is
some New
Age music
and a
mellow-toned
narrator

FIGURE 14-5

to clone part of another background to cover the spots. The result was that the blacks spots were gone without a trace.

Because removing background from a photograph can take some serious time, I am demonstrating the procedure I used on a cover from a PhotoDisc catalog.

IP: *A serious warning. In the next session, we will demonstrate the use of the Clone tool to restore a scan of a PhotoDisc catalog. I want all of you to be aware that scanners can be a pathway to legal entanglements. By that I mean that I obtained permission from PhotoDisc to use a scan of their cover. Make sure you have the rights to use any image that you intend to publish. While all of the images that shipped with the Corel 6 Suite are royalty-free, this is not true with all vendors. Ignorance of the copyright law doesn't protect you.*

We have scanned the cover as shown here. The object is to (1) remove all of the clutter at the bottom of the photograph, (2) remove the punched holes in the page, and (3) replace the part of the sign that was deleted with the hole punch.

Setting the Zoom at 100 percent shows all of the clutter at the bottom of the photograph that must be cloned out, as shown here.

The first step, after zooming in, is to use the non-align Clone mode to clone the sky from another portion of the photograph to the lower-right corner. After some work, I have removed all but the portion underneath the wheel to the right of the pole and the portion of the traffic signal that is in front of the signpost at the bottom. I also got a little sloppy on the white border. Hey! I was in a rush. Deep thought: Have you ever noticed that it seems we never have time to do it right but can find time to do it over again?

Using the non-align Clone mode, almost everything on the bottom-right of the photo, shown next, has been removed except the area in front of the post and the small portion on the bottom-right of the wheel sign.

By zooming in to a very high zoom ratio I was able to remove the portion that was close to the wheel using the same clone technique. Next, I did a combination of non-aligned and aligned cloning to remove the traffic signal from the pole as shown here.

Using the same techniques used on the right side, the bottom of the image is finished. The damage done to the borders on the left is repaired with a paint tool and the borders on the right were wisely protected beforehand with a mask.

On to the top, where there are several specks on the border—I really need to clean the glass on my scanner—which you may not be able to see. Also to be repaired are the holes and the missing portion of the sign.

The holes and defects on the border were quite simple. The missing portion of the sign required a little more effort. In the following figure you can see that by zooming in to 600% and creating a 200% zoom window using the New Window command, we can see what we are doing. Using the non-align Clone mode, we have begun to remove the white circle.

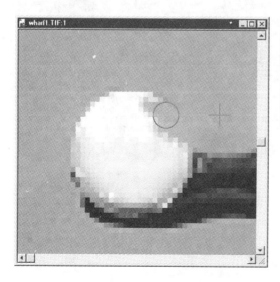

The Clone tool effectively removes the white hole and replaces it with the sky. Resetting the anchor point for the source on the shaft near the edge gives us the material needed to fill in the white area. Watch the 200 percent zoom area when doing this. Next, the Blend tool was applied to bring the different clone pieces together as shown here.

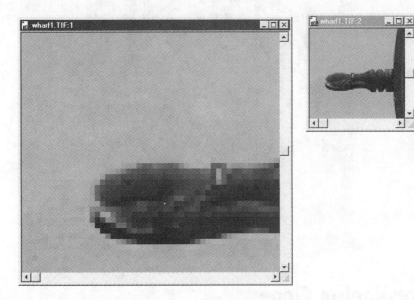

Because the edges looked fuzzy after applying the Blend tool, I went back over the edges with the Sharpen tool set to Sharpen A Little. We could do some more fine tuning, but we have now restored it enough. Always remember that if the area you are repairing is not the focus of the photograph, don't waste time on it.

The finished area is shown here. The only improvement that might be justified at this point is to go back with the Smear tool and drag out a slight point on the restored section.

Impressionism Clone

In this mode the pixels from the source are modified using the Impressionist effect. The Impressionist effect applies brush strokes to the image, causing it to look like an Impressionist painting. Impressionist paintings are marked by the use of unmixed primary colors and small brush strokes to simulate reflected light. Notable Impressionist painters include Monet, Cezanne, and Degas.

This tool wins the big prize: I have been unable to find any practical use for this tool whatsoever. Think about it for a moment. A clone is an exact copy of the original, right? The Impressionist Clone tool makes randomly distorted copies of the original. Am I missing something here?

In using the tool, remember that by keeping your brush size and number of line settings small, your result will more closely approximate the original. At least the outcome will be recognizable. The results with this tool are unpredictable, so be sure to use the Checkpoint command before beginning your work.

Pointillism Clone

In this mode the pixels from the source are modified using the Pointillist effect. Pointillism adds a dotlike appearance to the image. The brush stroke made with the Clone tool incorporates a selected number of dots in colors that are similar (e.g., eight shades of red). The size, shape, and qualities of the Pointillist Clone tool are set from the Variation Tab in the Tool Settings roll-up. The effect can be subtle, retaining the overall appearance of the original image, or you can vary the dots and the colors to create very unusual special effects. The Pointillism Clone tool selects colors in an image and paints with those colors in a pointillist style. It does not reproduce areas in an image as does the Normal Clone tool.

Experiment with this tool when you have lots of time on your hands and no deadlines. Use it to create special effects. Keeping the brush size very small (a setting between 2 and 5) enables the creation of a clone that looks vaguely similar to the original. As with the Impressionism filter, use objects that have definite shapes, making them easily recognizable as the Clone tool distorts their appearance. The results with this tool can be unpredictable, so use the Checkpoint command before beginning your work.

Custom From Saved

This is new with Corel PHOTO-PAINT 6. It has several presets to it, each producing a different effect. The Presets are:

- ► Light Eraser
- ► Eraser
- ► Scrambler

The Eraser and Light Eraser Presets

This is a wonderful feature for when you are cloning images. After you have cloned a portion of an image, you may end up with cloned material that you do not want. The Eraser and the Light Eraser allow you to restore the original pixels from the last saved version of the image. This restores areas to their saved states. The Light eraser allows you to control how much of the changes you want to remove, requiring multiple passes to achieve the full restoration. The Eraser removes all of the cloned pixels.

IP: *To restore background with the Clone From Saved feature, I recommend you use the Eraser setting with a soft edge setting of 60-80. This way the transition is gradual and you won't need to go over the area later with a Smear or Blend tool.*

Working with Objects

15

U p to now we have been manipulating images with the help of various types of masks. In this chapter we will begin to work with one of the more powerful features of Corel PHOTO-PAINT, which is the ability to create and control objects. The use of objects falls into a category I call fun stuff. There is a tabloid sold in the United States called *The Sun*, which may be one of the leading forums for unique photo-editing. If you live in the United States, you have probably seen *The Sun* while standing in grocery lines. Last night, the headline was "Baby Born with Three Heads." The photograph showed a woman holding an infant who fit the headline's description. Someone on *The Sun* staff had masked the face of a small child, made several copies, and placed them on the body of the baby. Like I said, this is fun stuff. If you are an avid reader of *The Sun*, do not take what I say as criticism of the tabloid. I love *The Sun*! I stand in a lot of grocery lines, and it provides entertainment during an otherwise boring wait.

In this chapter we will explore the Objects and Transform roll-ups and all that can be done with them. The Objects roll-up has been substantially improved in Corel PHOTO-PAINT 6 from previous versions.

Pixels and Crazy Glue

When an image is placed in a bitmap program like Corel PHOTO-PAINT, it becomes part of the background of the image. Traditionally with bitmap programs (like Microsoft PAINT), there is only one layer. With these one-layer programs, if we were to take a brush from the Toolbox and draw a wide brush stroke across an image, every pixel the brush touches would change to the color assigned to the brush. If we then removed the brush color, the original image would have vanished, because the brush color did not go on *top* of the original color, it replaced it. It is as if every pixel that is applied has super glue on it. When an action is applied to an image, it "sticks" to the image and cannot be moved. This is one of the reasons the Undo command can only "remember" what color(s) it replaced in the last action. Each Undo operation requires the entire image area to be replaced, a process which consumes large amounts of system resources. Anyone who has spent hours and hours trying to achieve an effect with these older one-layer bitmap programs will testify that the process by which bitmaps merge into and become part of the base image is the major drawback to photo-editing programs.

Objects Defined

So what is an object? Here is the official Corel definition:

An object is an independent bitmap selection created with object tools and layered above the base image.

Let's expand that definition. In Corel PHOTO-PAINT, an object is a bitmap that "floats" above the background, which is also called the *base image.* Because it is not a part of the base image, but instead floats above the image, an object can be moved as many times as needed without limit. Objects can also be scaled, resized, rotated, and distorted.

Corel PHOTO-PAINT 5 has *simple* and *complex* objects. Corel PHOTO-PAINT 6 has only one kind of object. Here is the best part: objects are much easier to create in Corel PHOTO-PAINT 6 than they are with Corel PHOTO-PAINT 5. You are about to learn how to do some amazing things with objects. Most of the rules you learned in previous chapters regarding masks also apply to objects.

The Objects Roll-Up

The Objects roll-up is the control center for all object manipulations. With the Objects roll-up, you can do the following:

▶ Select objects.

▶ Lock or unlock objects.

▶ Make objects visible or invisible.

▶ Create objects from masks.

▶ Create masks from objects.

▶ Move objects to change their order.

▶ Control the transparency/opacity of objects.

▶ Select merge modes for individual objects.

▶ Label different objects.

▶ Combine objects with the background.

▶ Combine individual objects together.

▶ Delete objects.

The Objects roll-up has been changed substantially from the Layers/Objects roll-up of Corel PHOTO-PAINT 5. The feathering control has been placed in the Object menu.

Exploring the Objects Roll-Up

The Objects roll-up, shown here, is a multifaceted roll-up. It can be opened by double-clicking on the Object Pointer in the Toolbox, with the keyboard combination CTRL-F7, or by selecting it from the Roll-up list in the View menu.

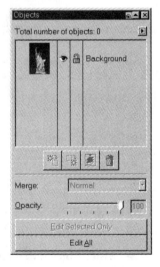

The display is divided into four columns. The column on the far right shows the name of the object/layer. For purposes of clarification, the terms *object* and *layer* are used interchangeably. This is because each layer can contain only one object, and without an object there cannot be a layer. The bottom layer is named background. It cannot be moved. Each time an object is created, Corel PHOTO-PAINT assigns it a default name unless the user changes it.

The column next to it contains an icon that shows if an object is locked or unlocked. When an object is locked, it cannot be selected, and it is protected from any effects being applied to it. Locking an object in Corel PHOTO-PAINT 6 is equivalent to "hiding" the object in Corel PHOTO-PAINT 5. The advantage of being able to lock an object is that it remains visible, whereas in Corel PHOTO-PAINT 5 the hiding object disappears.

The "Eye" icon in the center column is either open or closed, indicating the object is either visible or invisible. When an object is invisible, it is automatically locked. The column on the left displays a thumbnail of the object in the layer.

The status line shows the Total Number of Objects in the image. When an image is first opened, it contains zero objects. To the right of the status line is a small right-arrow button. Pushing it opens a drop-down list that determines the size of the thumbnails displayed. The choices are Small, Medium, and Large. The buttons at the bottom are not available when there are no objects or masks in the image.

There are several buttons on the bottom of the roll-up that we will explain as we go along. So, are you still awake? Let's take a guided tour though the wild world of objects that will demonstrate most of their features and capabilities.

A Guided Tour of Objects

In this exercise we will be creating a single image from two different photographs. If you bought Corel PHOTO-PAINT 6 and not CorelDRAW 6, you will not have the first photograph. You can download this file from the World Wide Web as described in the Introduction of this book.

1. Open the image IMAGES\PHOTOS\USACITIE\244001.JPG located on CD-ROM Disk #3.

2. Our first step is to mask the Statue of Liberty. Select the Magic Wand mask tool from the Toolbox. Change the mask mode to Add to Mask through the Mode section of the Mask menu.

3. Place the cursor on the blue sky and click the left mouse button. This will create a partial mask. Click on another spot in the unmasked area of the sky. Continue to do this until all of the sky is masked. To ensure that the mask fits as closely to the statue as possible, make sure that at least one point you click with the Magic Wand mask tool is on the blue that is close to the statue.

4. We have now masked the sky. Since we want to mask the Statue of Liberty, we must next invert the mask by selecting Invert from the Mask menu. Now only the statue should be masked.

5. Open the Objects roll-up by double-clicking the Object pointer at the top of the Toolbox. Because there is a mask on the image, one of the four buttons at the bottom of the roll-up is enabled. The button that is enabled is the Create from Mask button. This feature and its counterpart, From Mask (Create Mask from Object), are new with Corel PHOTO-PAINT 6. How they work is influenced by the Preserve Image command. Before proceeding, we need to discuss this command and its features.

Preserve Image—A New and Powerful Feature

The Preserve Image command protects the pixels within an image from being altered when creating masks and objects.

To create an object, you define an area with a mask tool, click Create From Mask, and the pixels inside the mask marquee become the new object. The Preserve Image command determines whether the pixels inside the marquee are cut or copied from the image to create the new object. Enabling the command copies the pixels, thus preserving the image, whereas disabling the command cuts the pixels inside the marquee, leaving a paper-colored hole in the image that is obvious when the object is moved.

Preserve Image also influences the way masks are created from objects. If you create a mask from an object with the Preserve Image command enabled, the newly created mask is superimposed over the original object. Without the command enabled, the mask simply replaces the object and the object is lost.

6. Disable the Preserve Image by ensuring it is unchecked in the Image menu. Click the Create Object From Mask button at the bottom of the roll-up. Note that several things changed in the roll-up, as shown in Figure 15-1. First, an object appeared in the roll-up. Second, the thumbnail for the background changed, indicating that the masked area had been cut and replaced with the current Paper (background) color. Third, many of the grayed-out features of the roll-up became active. On the image, the mask was replaced by a blue marquee that indicates it is an object.

7. To change the name of the object in the roll-up, click once on the default name and it becomes highlighted. Type in the name **Statue** and hit ENTER. The name of the object now reflects the subject contained in the layer. This ability to name layers is a very useful feature when working with multiple objects whose thumbnails look nearly identical.

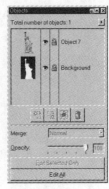

The new
Object
roll-up
offers
greater
control of
objects in
an image

FIGURE 15-1

8. Now we are going to add another photograph that will serve as the background. From the Edit menu, select Paste From File. When the dialog box opens, select the file IMAGES\PHOTOS\COINS\125000.JPG and click the OK button. The image loads as an object on top of the statue layer. If you bought Corel PHOTO-PAINT 6 and not CorelDRAW 6, you will need to load the file PHOTOS\BUSINESS\125000.JPG from the CD-ROM.

9. The orientation of the flag and coin shown in Figure 15-2 is different than the original photograph. To correct this, we need only rotate the object 90 degrees. Select Rotate from the Object menu and choose 90 degrees Clockwise from the drop-down list. The flag object is rotated and now covers the original photograph entirely.

10. For our next step, we want to put the flag into the background. To accomplish this, we only need click on the object's text in the roll-up and, while holding the mouse button down, drag the title so that it is between the background and the Statue object. After a moment or two, the roll-up and the image will reflect the changes made.

The roll-up
now shows
two objects
on top
of the
background

FIGURE 15-2

11. Rotating the flag made it fit, but the text of the coin was also rotated. In our next few steps we will correct that. The first step is to make the top object invisible so it is easier to see what we are doing. Click on the Eye icon for the Statue object. The Eye icon closes and the object disappears from the image.

12. To rotate the coin back to its original position, we must select the Circle Mask tool and drag a circle mask that covers the coin. It may take several attempts to produce a mask that fits the coin. Here is a technique to make the job easier. First, change the mask mode back to Normal. By doing this, any time you make another mask, it eliminates the previous one. Place the cursor in the center of the coin and hold down both the SHIFT (expand from center) key and the Constrain (CTRL) key as you make the mask. The mask will expand from the center. When you get the right size, you may find out you did not start in the exact center. No problem. Select the Mask Transform tool from the Mask flyout in the Toolbox. It is the one that has arrows pointing in four different directions. Now use the arrow keys on your keyboard to nudge the mask so it fits snugly over the coin (not the shadow). Don't waste a lot of time making an exact fit; this isn't brain surgery.

13. Now that we have masked the coin, we will make it into an object. Before we do that, enable the Preserve Image command by selecting it in the Image menu so that the original coin will not be removed.

14. With the Object Picker tool, click on the coin. Select Create From Mask in the Object menu. The mask around the coin disappears and the coin becomes an object and appears in the top of the layer. Click and drag the name of the coin object in the roll-up so it is between the statue and the flag photograph.

15. To rotate the coin select Rotate in the Object menu and select 90 degrees Counter-clockwise. Now that the coin is in the right position, we are going to use one of the Merge Modes to change the color of the coin. Verify that only the coin is selected by looking at the roll-up. The selected object has a frame around it. Change the Merge mode to Invert. The coin will have a bronze appearance.

16. Next, we will combine the flag object into the background. Deselect the coin by clicking on its thumbnail in the roll-up and then select the flag object by clicking on its thumbnail. Click the Combine button (it's next to the Trash Can button) near the bottom of the roll-up. The object is merged and the flag photograph becomes the background.

17. We are going to apply an effect to the background. To prevent the other two object from being affected, we must lock them. The Statue of Liberty is hidden, so it is already locked. To lock the Coin object, click on the Padlock icon in the Objects roll-up. To make the flag background a little more abstract, open the Effects menu and select Artistic. Choose Alchemy from the drop-down list, and the Paint Alchemy dialog box opens. In the Saved Styles box under the preview window, click the down arrow button to see a portion of the alphabetical list containing 75 styles included with Corel PHOTO-PAINT. Find the style called Brush Strokes Random. Click the OK button. Notice that even though the coin was visible, it wasn't affected.

18. Unlock the coin object, click on the thumbnail, and combine it with the background by clicking the Combine button on the roll-up.

19. Click on the Eye icon to make the statue visible, and then click on the thumbnail. The edge of the statue object still has a fringe of the original blue sky around it edges. To remove this fringe select Matting in the Object menu and choose Defringe, which is used to decrease the harsh edges that are sometimes found on an object. Defringe Object replaces the color of the edges of an object with the colors of the adjacent background pixels, creating a smooth blending effect. Choose a width of two pixels and click OK. For the last step, combine the statue with the background. The finished project is shown in Figure 15-3 and in the color insert.

This was a whirlwind tour, but it gave you an idea of some of the things that can be down with Objects. The next roll-up that we will be looking at also is used to control Objects. It is the Transform roll-up.

Object Tool Settings Roll-Up

The functionality of the Transform roll-up from CorelDRAW first became apparent with the release of Corel PHOTO-PAINT 5. It is structured so that when you have the Object Picker selected and bring up the Tool Settings roll-up (CTRL-F8), the Transform roll-up is displayed as shown in the illustration on the next page.

Take two photographs, add Corel PHOTO-PAINT 6, and presto! A new image

FIGURE 15-3

The Tool Settings roll-up for objects provides a very powerful and easy way to make precise manipulations to objects. There are five tabs that control the following:

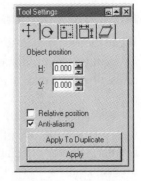

► Object Position

► Object Rotation

► Object Scaling/Mirror

► Object Resizing

► Object Skewing

Each of the Tabs within the Tool Settings dialog box for objects has three common functions. They are:

► **Apply To Duplicate button**   This button, when selected, creates a copy of the selected object with the effects applied, while leaving the original object unchanged. For example, the Object Rotation tab was selected and a value of 15 degrees was entered. Clicking the Apply to Duplicate would create a copy of the object that was rotated 15 degrees while leaving the original unchanged.

► **Apply button**   This button, when selected, applies the effect to the original.

► **Anti-Aliasing check box**   This check box, when enabled, causes Corel PHOTO-PAINT to process the image though a more sophisticated process to produce smoother lines and prevent "jaggies." Use of this feature may increase processing time.

Object Position

Going from left to right, clicking on the first tab accesses the Object Position. These controls are used to reposition or move objects. The default units are pixels, but you can change this in the Preferences dialog box.

If you attempt to move an object with a setting that will place the object outside of the image area, the object will be placed outside of the image area. The object is still there, just not in the viewing area. When these controls are used in conjunction with the rulers, you can position objects very precisely and quickly anywhere within the image.

Absolute Positioning

When the Relative Position option is unchecked, the Horizontal listing displays the leftmost position of the object and the Vertical listing displays the topmost position of the object in relation to the 0,0 point of the image (upper-left corner). Moving the object is accomplished by changing these values.

While precise positioning, such as centering an object on the page, can be done with this roll-up, use of the Align command in Corel PHOTO-PAINT 6 is much simpler. Objects of equal size can be positioned on top of one another by entering the same values for each object in these settings.

Relative Position

When the Relative Position option is checked, the Horizontal and Vertical Settings start out at zero pixels in both the horizontal and vertical axes in reference to the object. Movement is applied relative to the apex of the topmost and leftmost lines of an object. Entering a positive value for the Horizontal setting moves the image to the right, and a negative value moves the image to the left. Entering a positive value for the Vertical setting moves the object down, while a negative value moves the object up. After a setting is applied, the settings both return to 0. Values that place the object outside of the image area will move the object off of the page.

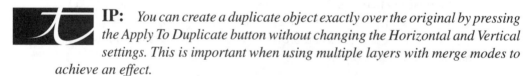

IP: *You can create a duplicate object exactly over the original by pressing the Apply To Duplicate button without changing the Horizontal and Vertical settings. This is important when using multiple layers with merge modes to* achieve an effect.

Object Rotation

The second tab provides access to the Object Rotation controls as shown below. While rotation of objects can be accomplished from the Objects menu or by dragging the Rotation handles, the Transform roll-up allows for precision rotation, which is very handy when you are applying it to multiple objects. Control of rotation is divided into two parts.

Angle of Rotation

The first set controls the amount of the Angle of Rotation. There is nothing mystical here, the value is in degrees. The range of rotation is +360 degrees through – 360

degrees. It is important to note that you can enter a number for the Angle of Rotation as low as one one-thousandth of a degree. For example, if you rotate an object 15 degrees, close the Object Tool Settings roll-up, and then reopen it three hours later after having worked on several other files, the setting will still be 15 degrees for the Angle of Rotation. If you close and reopen Corel PHOTO-PAINT, the setting will default back to 0 degrees. Regardless of what rotation values are entered into this setting, the Center of Rotation setting remains centered on the object.

Center of Rotation

The next set of controls is a little more interesting. With the Center of Rotation controls, you can precisely position the center of rotation. With the Relative Center option turned off, the controls for Center of Rotation report where the center of rotation is located on the currently selected object. Whenever you need to reposition the center of rotation, simply use the rulers to locate the new position and enter those values into the Center of Rotation controls. For example, if your currently selected object has a center of rotation at the Horizontal and Vertical position of 1 inch each, you could easily change that to, say, 2 inches Horizontal and 3 inches Vertical by simply entering those values in the Center of Rotation Controls.

Relative to Center

When the Relative to Center option is turned on, the controls for Center of Rotation start off at 0. Units are controlled by the Preferences dialog box. Values entered in the Center of Rotation controls will move the center of rotation according to the values relative to its current position. For example, if you are working in inches and you enter a Center of Rotation value of 1 inch for both the Horizontal and Vertical settings, the center of rotation would be repositioned one inch down and to the right of the current center of rotation.

IP: *A quick way to rotate an object is to select it with the Object Picker and then click on the object a second time. The control handles will change to indicate it is in rotation mode. By holding down the CTRL key on the keyboard while dragging the handles, you get rotation in 15-degree increments.*

Object Scale/Mirror

Object Scale enables you to do exactly what its name suggests: scale objects. An object can be scaled by percentages of the object's size. You cannot enter negative numbers for the Object Scaling settings. Rather, numbers larger than 100 percent scale the object larger than its current size; numbers smaller than 100 percent scale the object smaller than its current size.

When Maintain Aspect is selected, the Horizontal and Vertical settings within Object Scaling remain the same. The Object Mirror buttons flip the objects horizontally and vertically. The Object Scale settings and the Mirror buttons can work in conjunction with one another. For example, if you have 50 percent Horizontal and Vertical settings for Object Scale with the Vertical Mirror button on, the selected object will be flipped vertically at 50 percent of its original size when the Apply button is pressed.

 IP: *You can create a duplicate object exactly over another by hitting the Apply To Duplicate button with 100 percent Horizontal and Vertical Object Scale settings and the Mirror buttons not selected.*

Object Size

The Object Size settings are a more accurate way to resize an object than Object Scale. The Object Size settings list the dimensions of the currently selected object. To change the dimensions of the currently selected object, simply enter in the new values and select Apply or Apply To Duplicate. Units are determined by the default setting in the Options dialog box. Negative numbers should not be entered for the Object Size settings.

Maintain Aspect

When the Maintain Aspect option is checked, the aspect of the object will be maintained when you enter a new value in one of the Horizontal or Vertical settings. For example, if you have an object that is 1 inch horizontal and 2 inches vertical, and you enter 2 inches in the Horizontal setting with the Maintain Aspect option checked, the Vertical option will automatically maintain the aspect ratio of the object by changing to 4 inches.

Object Skew

Object Skew allows you to numerically skew objects. Like all of the other settings in the Object Tool Settings roll-up, Object Skew simply provides a way to accurately enter in values for alterations that could otherwise be performed manually. Negative degree values can be used. Once new values are entered into this setting, the Object Skew settings will remain the same until they are changed, even if the file you are working on is closed and another is opened.

Additional Tips for Working with Objects

► Transform Options will be unavailable when anything other than the Object Picker is selected from the Toolbox.

► Objects do not have to be the same size as the page. You can paste or drag-and-drop an object that is larger than the page size.

► While Corel PHOTO-PAINT does not have a paste-inside feature, you can emulate this effect by creating a compound object with a hole(s) in it. For instance, if you have an image with a TV screen on it and you want to change what's on the TV, simply create an object with a hole where the TV screen is, and then position the new image behind it. With this functionality, a paste-inside feature is unnecessary.

► It is the ability to create, modify, and position objects that makes Corel PHOTO-PAINT 6 such a powerful photo-editing program. We have only covered the basics to this point.

New Text Features of
Corel PHOTO-PAINT 6

16

There have been some new features added to the text capabilities with the release of Corel PHOTO-PAINT 6. The major improvement has been the addition of editable text. This means that once text is entered and becomes a Corel PHOTO-PAINT object, it remains editable as text. In Corel PHOTO-PAINT 5, the text becomes a bitmap image after it is entered and becomes an object. In Corel PHOTO-PAINT 6, we can return to text and change the fonts, size, or other attributes at any time. Only when the text is combined with the background does it cease to be editable. The Text tool, used in combination with the fill capabilities and layers/objects, can produce stunning effects quickly.

Before Adding Text in Corel PHOTO-PAINT

The best way to add general copy text in a Corel PHOTO-PAINT image is to use another program like CorelDRAW. It is a simple procedure. Just finish whatever enhancements to the image are needed and save it as a CPT file. Next, import the file into CorelDRAW or a similar graphics program and add the text at that time. While I have mentioned this before, it bears repeating. Text in a program like CorelDRAW is resolution-independent. When text is created in Corel PHOTO-PAINT, it is a bitmap image that is resolution-dependent. This means that text placed in Corel PHOTO-PAINT will be the resolution of the image. If it is 300 dpi (dots per inch), then the text will be a bitmap image that is 300 dpi regardless if it is printed to a 300 dpi laser printer or a 2450 dpi imagesetter. If the same text is placed in CorelDRAW, it remains as text. If it is output to a 2450 dpi imagesetter, then the resolution of the text will be 2450 dpi. The result is sharper text.

Basics of the Text Tool

The Text tool (the icon with the letter "A" on it) is located in the toolbox. The best way to quickly get through the basics of using this tool is to participate in a quick skill session. In this session you will learn how all of the associated buttons work, along with some general principles about working with the Text tool.

1. Open a new image file either by selecting New in the File menu or by clicking on the New File icon in the Ribbon Bar. Either accept system defaults for the new image or select 3.0 inch width by a 1.5 inch height, 24-bit colors with a white paper color. Resolution is not important; mine is set for 96 dpi.

 IP: *The Text tool will not work unless you have an image selected.*

2. Click on the Text tool in the toolbox. At this point you can control the text in two different ways. You can open the Text toolbar (right-click) or use the Tool Settings roll-up (double-click). The Text toolbar appears as shown here.

3. If you have worked with recent versions of word processors in Windows, everything on the Text toolbar should be familiar to you. The first box shows all of the available fonts that are installed in WIN'95 . The second box displays the selected font sizes in points (72 points = 1 inch). While the font size drop-down list shows a long list of available sizes, you can select any size you need by typing the desired font size (in points) in the Font Size box.

OTE: *There are no system default settings for the Text tool's font selection. The typeface is always the first element of the list of installed fonts. Since lists in WIN'95 are maintained alphabetically, the typeface whose name is first alphabetically (i.e., AARDVARK) will always appear as the default. The last settings of the Text toolbar remain until changed again or until Corel PHOTO-PAINT is shut down.*

4. The next three buttons are controls for the **bold**, *italics*, and <u>underline</u> attributes. The last three buttons are for left, center, and right alignment.

5. Select Times New Roman from the Font drop-down list, a font size of 48, and click on the Center text button. As you move the cursor inside the image area, it changes into a Text toolbar. With the Paint color set to

Black, click near the middle of the image and type in the word **TEXAS**. You now have the word "TEXAS" surrounded by an inverted rectangle as shown here. This inverted area tells you that you are in text edit mode. Do not select any other tools at this point, as that will turn the text into an object.

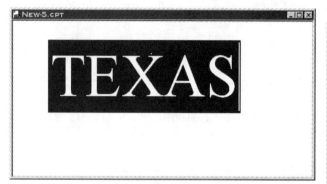 

6. Before we go further, here are the facts about the Corel PHOTO-PAINT Text Tool:

   ▶ Character, word, and line spacing (leading) are controlled by Corel PHOTO-PAINT. If you need to control any of these attributes, you need to import the Corel PHOTO-PAINT image into a program like CorelDRAW or Corel VENTURA. The exception to that is leading (space between lines). If you only have a few lines of text, you can type each line separately and use the alignment and group functions to control the leading.

   ▶ The color of the text is determined by the setting of the paint (foreground) color. It is very easy to change the color of the text in Corel PHOTO-PAINT 6. If you have the onscreen palette open, click on any color in the palette with the left mouse button. If you currently have text selected, it will change the color of the text to match the color you just clicked.

   ▶ To correct a text entry, use the BACKSPACE or DELETE key.

   ▶ To check the spelling of text, use a dictionary.

► The selected alignment of text (left, center, or right) does not occur until the ENTER key is pressed.

► There is no automatic line wrap (soft carriage returns) of text. This is because Corel PHOTO-PAINT has no idea where to wrap the line.

7. From the Tool Settings roll-up or Text toolbar, change the name of the Font to PLAYBILL (it is one of the fonts provided by Corel; if you do not wish to install it, keep the Times New Roman font, but be aware the font sizes will be different).

8. Change the Font Size to 72 and click the Bold button. The word "TEXAS" is still too small for this typeface, but 72 points is as large as the preset list goes. This is easy to fix. In the font size window, highlight the 72 point value and type in **99**. Notice that the font size did not change. Now hit the ENTER key and the font will reflect the requested size. If the word "TEXAS" went off of the screen when you changed sizes, do not be concerned—it is still there, just out of the image area.

IP: *The font, font size, and characteristics can all be altered at this stage. Any change you make in the Text toolbar is instantly reflected in the text displayed in the image area. You can also move the rectangle containing the text by clicking on it and dragging it with the left mouse button.*

In Corel PHOTO-PAINT 5, the text is a bitmap after it becomes an object. In Corel PHOTO-PAINT 6, the text remains editable as text after it becomes an object until it is combined with the background or another object.

9. Click on the Object Picker (top button of the Toolbox). The action of selecting another tool causes the text to become an object, as indicated by the ugly blue marquee that surrounds it. If you want to turn off the blue marquee, click on Marquee Visible in the Object menu. Because the text is now an object, we can see it with the Objects roll-up. Depress the

CTRL-F7 key to open the Objects roll-up box as shown in Figure 16-1. Since it is an object, we can resize (by dragging the control handles), rotate, or distort it.

10. Next, we will add some color to this text, but not to the background. To do that, we must lock (protect) the background. Click the background Lock icon in the Object roll-up to protect the background. Any effects applied to the image will only affect the word "TEXAS".

11. Select the Rectangle tool (F6) in the Toolbox. Now select the Tool Settings roll-up (by using the keyboard combination CTRL-F8, double-clicking the icon, or right-clicking in the image and choosing the Tool Settings roll-up). Because the Rectangle tool is selected, the Tool Settings is the Fill roll-up. Set width, transparency, and roundness values in the Tool Settings roll-up to zero. When it opens, select Uniform Color Fill (first button on the left) and click the Edit button. Pick any shade of blue for the Fill color.

The Fill roll-up is no longer a stand-alone roll-up. The Tool Settings roll-up becomes the Fill roll-up when either the Fill or Draw tools are selected. It may seem confusing at first, but by the time Corel PHOTO-PAINT 7 is released, you will be used to it. Of course, then it may change again.

12. With the Rectangle tool (F6) in the Toolbox still selected, and starting above and to the left of the word "TEXAS," click the left mouse button and drag a rectangle that covers the entire word. When you release the mouse button, the text fills with blue. Let us examine what you have just done. This is an important principle of applying fills to text.

How to Apply Color to Text Using the Rectangle Tool

When the Rectangle tool was used, it did not make a rectangle, as happens in CorelDRAW. Instead, we filled an area with the selected color that was defined by

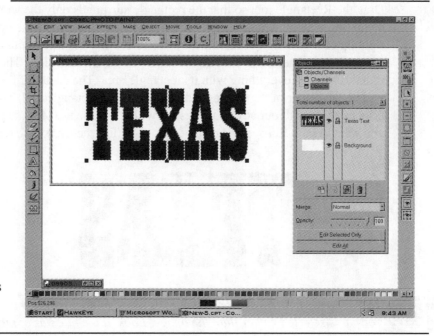

The text
is now an
object and
it appears as
a layer

FIGURE 16-1

the rectangle drawn. After the area was filled with the fill color, the rectangle boundary ceased to exist. Anything under the rectangle is filled with color. The exceptions are objects that are locked or areas protected by masks.

Because we locked the background, nothing was applied to it. The text object was unlocked, so when we applied the Rectangle tool, the text was filled with color. This is how we apply color to text. If you are thinking that we could have applied a solid (or uniform) color when we originally made the text, you're right. This technique has more advantages with different types of fills.

Next, we will change the type of fill being applied to the text to demonstrate the way the Rectangle tool places fills.

1. Select the Fountain fill mode in the Tool Settings roll-up. (It is the button to the right of the Uniform Color Fill.) Click the Edit button. Select Radial fill in the upper-left corner of the dialog box. Select blue for the From color and red for the To color. Set Steps to 10 steps. The fill pattern we created will not look pretty; it is meant to help us see just how the Rectangle tool applies a fill. When you have completed all of that, click the OK button.

2. Drag the Rectangle tool so that the rectangle surrounds only the word, beginning with the uppermost corner of the "T" and ending at the bottom right tip of the "S" in "TEXAS." Now the entire word is filled with one fill, with the center being around the letter "X" as shown below. The radial fill floods everything with its rectangle area. The center of the fill will be the center of the rectangle drawn with the Rectangle tool. This principle works to our advantage, as we will see in the next few steps. If you want to see a full-screen preview, press F9. Click the ESC key to return.

IP: *If your full-screen preview doesn't work, many times it is because a roll-up is selected rather than the image. Look at the title bar of the image to see if it is selected.*

3. Drag the Rectangle tool over the word "TEXAS," beginning at the extreme upper-left corner of the image window—not the word. End at the lower-right corner of the letter "S." The result is shown here. Now the fill has changed its center as a result of being applied with the Rectangle tool in the larger offset area shown by the dotted lines. Because the rectangle was offset in relation to the word "TEXAS," the center of the fill is somewhere below the letter "X" in "TEXAS."

4. Did you also notice that the second application of the Rectangle tool was applied over the previous fill? As long as transparency for the Rectangle tool is set to zero, fill colors are not additive.

IP: *When using the Rectangle tool at zero percent Transparency setting, any existing color is wiped out by the application of a new color; the previous fill (color) and the new fill are not combined.*

Using the Fill Tool to Apply Fills to Text

There are other ways we can control the fill in text. Before we do the next step, we must return the text-color fill to a uniform color. In the Tool Settings roll-up, select the Uniform Fill button (any color will work) and drag a rectangle over the entire word "TEXAS." We apply the Uniform Fill before the next step because the Fill tool will only be applied until it reaches a color boundary as determined by the Tolerance setting. Did that make sense? It will make sense later on. Using the Fill tool on a multicolor (shade) area can produce some funky-looking fills, which is why we are returning the text to a uniform color.

1. Select the Fill tool from the Toolbox. The cursor changes to a Fill icon, which looks like a little bucket.

2. In the Tool Settings roll-up, select the Fountain Fill icon and click the Fill tool in each letter. Now each letter in the text exhibits an individual linear fill, as shown below. It doesn't matter where in the letter that you click the tool. The program calculates where the edges of the character are and applies the fill accordingly.

The possible combinations of fills and tools are almost infinite. In the next few steps we will learn how to use the Text tool in combination with the other tools of Corel PHOTO-PAINT.

Creating Text Effects Skill Session

Many times when creating brochures we are required to put title size text on a photograph. While this could be done in CorelDRAW as discussed at the beginning of the chapter, we can use Corel PHOTO-PAINT to make the characters stand out. In this skill session we will use several techniques to create a brochure cover for the Southwest Studies Program. Some of the techniques involve the use of masks, which was covered in previous chapters.

1. Open the file IMAGES\PHOTOS\ANCIENT\089037B.JPG located on Corel Disk #3.

2. Select the Text tool and type **SOUTHWEST STUDIES PROGRAM**. The text used in Figure 16-2 is FUTURA Md BT at 72 points and with the Bold and Center buttons selected in the Text Tool Setting roll-up.

Changing Text Color

After entering the type and with the Text tool still selected, click on any one of the colors in the onscreen palette. Notice that the color of the text changes automatically each time a different color is chosen. Even after the text becomes an object, you can go back, select the text tool, and change the colors.

With Corel PHOTO-PAINT 6, you can change the color of the text without the need to open the Tool Settings (Fill) roll-up by selecting the Text tool and clicking on any color in the onscreen palette.

Creating Blurred Shadows Behind Text

Next, we want to create a blurred shadow behind the text. To do this, we need to create a mask. In Corel PHOTO-PAINT 5, this step takes some serious effort. With Corel PHOTO-PAINT 6 it is easy. Do not confuse the shadow we are making in this portion of the session with a drop shadow, which only appears on one side of the text or object.

1. We are about to create a mask from an object. In this exercise we want to make the mask and also keep the object we are making the mask from. To do that, we must select Preserve Image by either depressing the Preserve

FIGURE 1

FIGURE 2

FIGURES 1 & 2

WHILE MAKING IMAGINATIVE AND PATENTLY RIDICULOUS BACKGROUNDS IS FUN, ONE OF THE MORE USEFUL APPLICATIONS OF THE CLONE TOOL IS TO DUPLICATE PORTIONS OF EXISTING BACKGROUNDS TO ENHANCE OR CHANGE THE CONTENT OF THE ORIGINAL PHOTOGRAPH. CHAPTER 14 SHOWS THE STEP-BY-STEP PROCEDURE THAT WAS USED TO CHANGE THE ORIGINAL PHOTOGRAPH (FIGURE 1) INTO THE ONE SHOWN BELOW IT (FIGURE 2). PLEASE NOTE THAT JUST BECAUSE THE CLUSTER OF GRAPES IS CLONED DOESN'T MEAN IT MUST LOOK LIKE IT WAS CLONED. USING TECHNIQUES DESCRIBED IN CHAPTER 14, WE ARE ABLE TO MAKE THE DUPLICATE LOOK LIKE IT'S ANYTHING BUT A DUPLICATE.

Figure 3

In Chapter 9 we explore the Hue-Saturation filter. To illustrate the effect of Hue shift, the green apples in the photograph had six different settings of the Hue filter applied. From left to right: $-180°$, $-90°$, $-45°$, $0°$, $+45°$, $+90°$, and $+180°$. Please note that the effect on the image on the extreme ends appears identical.

Figures 4 & 5

Many times we are faced with photographs that have colors in them that need to be changed. In Chapter 14 we learn the technique of using several Corel PHOTO-PAINT tools together to obtain an effect. In the original photograph (Figure 4), the board and all of the trim on the skier's equipment is pink. By masking all of the shades of pink with the Color Mask tool and applying a Hue shift with the Hue Replacer tool, we are able to change all of the pink colors to a fluorescent green (Figure 5).

Figure 3

Figure 4

Figure 5

Figure 6

With Corel PHOTO-PAINT we can use objects to create composite photographs. This composite image was created from two separate photographs in the step-by-step tutorial found in Chapter 15.

Figure 7

This is an example of a photo montage that was created for a book cover. The background is a photograph of ice from Corel's Ice and Frost Photo-CD collection. The images on top are from four other photographs. The title text looks like it is cut into the stone to create the shadowing.

Figures 8 & 9

The new mask features of Corel PHOTO-PAINT provide users with greater levels of imaginative power tools. The original photograph (Figure 8) is from a Corel Photo-CD. First, I masked the blue sky. Next, I feathered the mask to make a subtle transition. Finally, I applied one of the Corel PHOTO-PAINT texture fills to the masked area to create a completely different photograph (Figure 9).

FIGURE 6

FIGURE 7

FIGURE 8

FIGURE 9

Figures 10 & 11

Sometimes you need to convey an attitude, yet animals are not famous for their acting skills (sorry, Flipper). By using the Mesh Warp filter described in Chapter 23, you can turn a curious owl (Figure 10) into one that looks like he had a real bad hair (feather) day (Figure 11).

Figures 12 & 13

What happens when you can't find the attention-getting photograph you need? Clone it! The original photograph is a typical winter sports action shot (Figure 12). To make it more interesting, I protected the two individuals in the photo by creating a mask using several of the Corel PHOTO-PAINT Mask tools. Taking another photograph of some surf, I used the Clone tool to replace the background. The operation of the Clone tool is explored in Chapter 14.

FIGURE 10

FIGURE 11

FIGURE 12

FIGURE 13

FIGURE 14

FIGURE 15

FIGURES 14 & 15

OF ALL THE DAZZLING EFFECTS AND ARTISTIC WONDERS THAT CAN BE CREATED WITH COREL PHOTO-PAINT, THE MOST IMPORTANT TASK IS THAT OF IMPROVING THE QUALITY OF PHOTOGRAPHS FOR PRODUCTION. THE FIRST FIGURE IS THE ORIGINAL COLOR PHOTOGRAPH FROM A PHOTO-CD THAT WAS CONVERTED TO GRAYSCALE USING COREL PHOTO-PAINT. IT WAS A DARK PHOTOGRAPH LACKING ANY DETAIL. SOME OF THE SEALS DOWN BY THE WATERLINE ARE DARK ENOUGH THAT THEY BLEND TOGETHER.

THE FIRST STEP WAS TO APPLY THE EQUALIZE FILTER (CHAPTER 8) WHICH LIGHTENED UP THE PICTURE. NEXT, I USED SEVERAL PASSES OF THE UNSHARP MASK FILTER (CHAPTER 21) TO ADD SOME EDGE DETAIL. THE INDIVIDUAL SEALS HAVE ADDITIONAL SHARPENING APPLIED USING THE SHARPEN EDITING TOOL (CHAPTER 14). DID YOU NOTICE THE SEAGULL IN THE VERY CENTER OF THE PHOTOGRAPH HAS NO FEATURES ON ITS HEAD IN THE ORIGINAL PHOTOGRAPH? ENHANCING THE PHOTO DID NOT BRING OUT THE DETAIL, SINCE IT WASN'T THERE TO BEGIN WITH. I USED THE CLONE TOOL (CHAPTER 14) AND BORROWED THE FEATURES FROM THE GULL IN THE UPPER-LEFT. (HE DIDN'T SEEM TO MIND.) THE FINAL RESULT (FIGURE 15) SHOWS THE DIFFERENCE COREL PHOTO-PAINT CAN MAKE.

This
shows the
photograph
with the
text added.
If this was
all we were
going to do,
then we
would have
done it in
CorelDRAW.

FIGURE 16-2

Image button on the Mask toolbar or ensuring that Preserve Image is
checked in the Image menu.

2. Select the Object picker in the Toolbox. Next, open the Mask menu and
    select Create From Object(s). After a few moments the mask will surround
    the text. The mask we created fits the existing text precisely, so if we are
    going to see a shadow, we will need to make the mask a little larger.

3. Select the Feather Mask feature located in the Mask menu. When the
    Feather Mask dialog box opens, enter the values as shown in the figure
    below and click the OK button. After a few moments the mask will be
    modified. If you cannot see the mask, the Marquee Visible feature in the
    Mask menu may not be enabled.

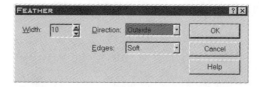

4. To create the shadow, we must protect the text while making sure we can apply effects to the background. First, open the Object roll-up (CTRL-F7). From the roll-up, ensure that the background is unlocked and then lock the text by clicking on its respective Lock icon.

5. Select the Rectangle tool (F6). Place the cursor over the color black (far left side) on the onscreen palette, and click the right mouse button. This changes the fill color of the Rectangle tool to black. It also changes the type of fill to Uniform fill.

6. Holding down the left mouse button, drag the cursor to cover all of the text with a rectangle. When released, the masked area will be filled with black. Because we feathered the mask, it will gradually fade from solid black to a very faint black as it approaches the edge of the mask. The result is a blurred shadow as shown below.

7. We could quit at this point, but I think its contrast is too stark. So, let's modify it a little. Open the Tool Settings roll-up. Change the fill to

Fountain fill (second tab from the left). Click the edit button, and when the dialog box opens, change the settings to match those shown below. Change the From color by clicking the color sample in the dialog box. When the color palette opens, move down the palette until you find a peach color. Repeat this process, this time making the To color a pale yellow. Color choice is *not* critical, only a suggestion. Delete the mask by selecting None in the Mask menu.

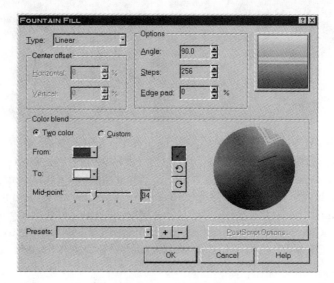

8. We are going to use the Rectangle tool again to apply the fill to the text, but this time we are going to apply it to each word individually. By applying it to each word, the darker color appears as shading at the bottom of the characters of each word. In the Tool Settings roll-up, unlock the text and lock the background. Next, drag a rectangle so that it covers the first word: "SOUTHWEST". After the fill is applied, repeat the same procedure on the second and third word, resulting in the following image.

9. For a final touch, we are going to give the letters some texture using the Noise filter. Select Noise in the Effects menu. From the drop-down list that appears, choose Add Noise… When the dialog box opens, click on the button next to Gaussian Noise. Don't be concerned about the Noise dialog box at this time. The Noise filter is explored thoroughly in Chapter 24. Change the Level setting to 11 and the Density setting to 100. Click the OK button and the noise will be applied to the text as demonstrated below.

10. Close the file and save it if you wish.

Going Back to Change the Text Attributes

If, after the text has become an object, you wish to return and make changes, it can be done very easily.

1. Select the Text tool.

2. Click on the text you wish to change. When it is selected, it changes into text edit mode. If you cannot select the text, make sure it is not locked in the Object roll-up or part of a group (explained later in this chapter).

3. Make the changes with the Text Tool Settings roll-up, and then select a different tool which will take the text out of edit mode and return it to an object.

 IP: *When you go into Text Edit mode, the text will look pretty ugly (lots of jaggies). Don't worry! It will look fine once you exit text edit mode by selecting a different tool.*

The Shadow Knows

A drop shadow is the shadow created when the object is between the light source and the reflecting surface. This results in a shadow being cast on the background. The viewer's mind can be tricked, but not easily. When making drop shadows, look at any other object in the image to see if there is a visual indication of the light source. If the background appears to have a light source in the upper-left corner, you do not want to create a shadow that makes it appear the light source is in the lower right. The resulting figure will seem to be "wrong" to viewers, although they probably cannot tell you why. So, when creating shadows, you must consider the entire image before deciding where to place your shadows.

Hard and Soft Shadows

The intensity of the light source and the distance of the object from the background determine how sharp or soft the shadows should be. If the light source is very bright and the text (object) is close to the background, the shadows will have a sharply defined edge.

If there are multiple light sources or if the object is farther away from the background, the shadows will be softer.

Comparing Shadows

In the next illustration we have the text against a bitmap fill. Traditionally, light sources come from the upper-right direction; in the second image, we added a simple drop shadow to illustrate this. It is a hard shadow (meaning it has a sharply defined edge), and it is very close to the original text. The transparency of the shadow was reduced, making it a softer, less distracting shadow.

The drop shadow gives the appearance of the text floating just slightly above the background. The next illustration is another drop shadow, but it has been moved a greater distance from the original text. The text appears to be suspended above the background at a greater distance.

Next, the shadow is returned to its original position. The only change has been feathering the edges of the shadow, which makes the shadows softer.

A different variation of a shadow is shown in the next image. Here, we have flipped and distorted the shadow to make the text appear to be backlit. Other visual clues were added, including the bright light (Lens Flare filter) and the dark surface (Smoked Glass filter).

The most important tip I can give you about making shadows is not to get lost in them. Shadows are never the focus of an image, so you want to avoid a shadow that attracts attention. Shadows need to be subtle. So much for the basics of shadows; let's learn how to make basic drop shadows for text.

Making Basic Drop Shadows for Text

In the previous session we produced blur shadows behind text to make it stand out from the background. In this section we will create simple cast shadows to make text appear more realistic. The first type is the easiest:

1. Open a New file (3.0 x 1.5 inches) at 100 dpi resolution. If you want to create the same background I have in the illustration, use the Fill tool and apply a linear fill. After applying the fill, apply Gaussian Noise at a Level of 7 and a Density of 100.

2. Select the Text tool from the Toolbox. Click the cursor anywhere on the image and type the word **COOL**.

3. From the Text Tool Settings roll-up, pick a typeface you like. I have chosen Dutch801 Xbd BT at 72 points. Click on the Object picker tool and the text will become an object. If you like, you can turn off the blue marquee surrounding the text from the Object menu.

A Slight Detour to Learn about the Align Command

This step has nothing to do with making a drop shadow, but it seems like the best time to introduce the Align command that was added to Corel PHOTO-PAINT. The align command is great. To center an object in an image, click on the text with the Object picker tool. Depress CTRL-A (you can also open the Object menu and select Align...), and the Align dialog box opens. If you are a user of CorelDRAW, the Align dialog box should look familiar. Click the button that says Align to Center of Page. The text is now centered on the page as shown here. Now, back to the shadows.

4. Our next step is to make a duplicate of the word so we have a shadow to work with. With the text still selected, depress CTRL-D (you can also open the Object menu and choose Duplicate). There are now two copies of the text, as shown in the next illustration.

5. To help visually distinguish the shadow from the text, we are going to change the color of the text—the easy way.

6. Select the text tool from the Toolbox and click on the duplicate you just created (it is the one down and to the right of the original). Now, pick a color for the text by clicking on the color in the onscreen palette with the left mouse button. I used a brown but you pick a color that you like.

7. Use the Object picker to select and move the text up and to the right, as shown in the following illustration. Now we have a hard drop shadow. Pretty ugly, isn't it?

Improving the Drop Shadow

1. To make the shadow look less like black letters and more like a shadow, we need to open the Object roll-up (CTRL-F7). When the Object roll-up opens, select the shadow object by clicking on the thumbnail image in the left column. It should be the object just above the background. If the text (top object) is also selected, click on it in the Object roll-up to deselect it. Now, with the shadow text selected, click on the Opacity slider and move it over to 20 (meaning 20% opacity, which is the same as 80% transparency). Now the shadow is much softer, as shown in the next illustration.

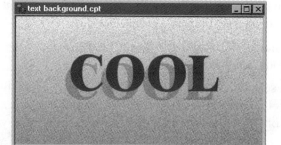

2. The final touch is to soften the edges of the shadow. This is accomplished by feathering. Feathering an object works the same as feathering a mask. From the Object menu, select Feather and a Feather dialog box appears. Feathering is defined by how many pixels in from the edge the feathering will occur. In this example, I selected four pixels based on some experimentation. On a huge image you may need to use a much larger number. Use the preview window to determine the correct amount of feathering to apply. For now, set the Width value to 4 (pixels) and the Edges setting to Soft. Click OK and the shadow object is made much softer.

Groups, Text, and Shadows—Keeping It All Together

We can't leave this section without discussing a new feature in Corel PHOTO-PAINT 6 that is a real timesaver when it comes to shadows. I am referring to the ability to group objects. Before Corel PHOTO-PAINT had grouping, you made a shadow like we did in the previous session and positioned it in the "perfect" spot. If you then needed to move the text to another position on the image, you had to move and reposition the shadow as well. Now it is possible to group them both together as a group of objects, just as you can do in CorelDRAW.

How to Group Objects

To group objects, you must have two or more objects selected. There are several ways to select objects for grouping in an image.

▶ Using the Object picker, you can drag a rectangle over the objects you want grouped together.

▶ From the Objects roll-up you can select (by clicking on the thumbnail image) the objects you want selected.

▶ If you want to select all of the objects in the image, you can choose Select All... from the Object menu.

▶ You can select the first object, and then, holding down the SHIFT key, select more objects. Each time you select an object, it is added to the number of Objects selected. The action is a toggle, so if you select an object you do not want, click it again to deselect it. (Did you know "deselect" is not a real word? Isn't it amazing what we learn from our spelling checkers?)

After you have selected the objects, depress the keyboard combination CTRL-G. All of the selected objects will become grouped together. How will you know the objects are grouped together? Looking at the Object roll-up gives a visual clue of what objects are grouped. When objects are grouped, they are joined together with a black bar in the far left column of the Objects roll-up. Now, anytime the text is moved, its shadow moves with it. To ungroup the objects, select the group and depress CTRL-U or choose Ungroup from the Object menu.

The Artistic Filters

T he Artistic filters contain some of the most powerful and unique filters in Corel PHOTO-PAINT. Two of the filters, Paint Alchemy and Terrazzo, stand out more than any other in the set. Since there is almost no documentation for these filters and they are, without a doubt, the most complex ones, I have discussed these in greater detail than the others.

Paint Alchemy

Paint Alchemy and its counterpart Terrazzo were only available for the Macintosh until their release in Corel PHOTO-PAINT 5 Plus. They are both incredible filters. To provide the most accurate documentation, I have been assisted greatly by Xaos Tool's documentation for the Macintosh and their tech-support people, who have been a world of help. Acknowledgments and kudos given, let's play with Paint Alchemy.

Paint Alchemy applies brush strokes to selected areas of your image in a precisely controlled manner. As with all filters, you can apply Paint Alchemy on part of an image or the entire image. You can use preexisting brushes or create your own brushes. It is not hard to create effects and control Paint Alchemy. The key to using and enjoying this filter is experimentation.

 IP: *As you learn how to make changes to the Paint Alchemy filter styles, I recommend limiting your changes to one at a time so that you can keep track of the effects.*

Starting Paint Alchemy

The Paint Alchemy filter is located under Artistic in the Effects menu. Clicking Alchemy in the drop-down list opens the Paint Alchemy dialog box as shown in the next illustration.

 OTE: *Paint Alchemy is only available when 24-bit color images are selected. If a grayscale, black-and-white, 16-color, 256-color, or 32-bit color image is open, the Alchemy filter is unavailable (grayed out).*

The Paint Alchemy Dialog Box

The dialog box is divided into three sections: control cards, style controls, and preview controls.

THE CONTROL CARDS   These are the controls that let you customize Paint Alchemy. They are arranged on five control cards. Only one card can be visible at a time, but the controls on all five cards are always active. To switch between cards, click on the labeled tabs at the top of the cards.

THE STYLE CONTROLS   The style controls let you select one of the 75 preset styles included with Paint Alchemy, modify an existing style so that it may be saved as a new style, or remove an old style. Before you begin modifying the preset styles, I encourage you to work with and learn the preset styles to get a feel for what they do. If you do change a style and like the results, you can save these settings as a style.

THE PREVIEW CONTROLS   The preview controls allow you to zoom in or out of the preview image. They also allow you to move the image inside of the preview window. Clicking the left mouse button in the preview area zooms the preview image in; right-clicking zooms it out. Clicking the left mouse button and dragging produces a hand for moving the image around in the preview window. Two seconds after any change is made in the preview window, the filter preview is automatically invoked.

If you have used Paint Alchemy on the Macintosh, the preview area is the only place where you will notice a difference between the two platforms. The Macintosh version shows a before-and-after thumbnail, whereas Corel opted for the larger single display area.

IP: *After you click the OK button to apply the Paint Alchemy filter, you will see a message in the Status Bar: "Press ESC to cancel." Clicking the ESC key at any time before the filter has completed its action will not cancel the filter action. I think this is because the Alchemy filter doesn't ever check to see if the ESC key was pressed.*

A Quick Tour of Paint Alchemy

Paint Alchemy is fun. That said, here is a quick tour of the filter to help you get familiar with how it works.

1. For this quick tour, open \IMAGES\PHOTOS\FOOD\091002B.JPG from Corel Disk #3. If you bought Corel PHOTO-PAINT 6 and not CorelDRAW 6, you will need to load \IMAGES\PHOTOS\FOOD\ 332032.JPG. This is a different photograph but shows the effect as well as, if not better than, the original.

2. Selecting Artistic in the Effects menu, choose Alchemy. The Paint Alchemy dialog box opens. Let's say you need to use the produce in this photograph as a background insert for a cookbook chapter head. While one of the photographs has a slight color cast, it doesn't prevent us from giving it the appearance of an abstract painting, which is what we want for the chapter head.

3. Click on the down arrow in the Saved Styles section. Scroll down the list and select the Pastel style.

4. Click the Preview button to see the results of the selected style. If the image in the preview window is zoomed in too closely, right-click the mouse button in the preview window to zoom out.

5. Click the OK button, and the photograph of the vegetables is transformed into what appears to be a painting, as shown in the following illustration.

6. Close the file without saving and open a new file, IMAGES\PHOTOS\ANCIENT\067079B.JPG, located on Corel Disk #3. If you bought Corel PHOTO-PAINT 6 and not CorelDRAW 6, you will load IMAGES\PHOTOS\LANDMARK\67079.JPG.

7. Open the Paint Alchemy dialog box again. This time, select the style called Mosaic Medium. This style makes the photograph look like it was composed of mosaic tiles. Click the OK button and the photograph now looks like a mosaic tile, as shown here. Close the file without saving.

8. Open the file IMAGES\PHOTOS\PLANTS\251057.JPG, which contains the photograph of a sunflower on Corel Disk #3. If you bought Corel PHOTO-PAINT 6 and not CorelDRAW 6, you will open IMAGES\PHOTOS\NATURE\479075.JPG (different photo, same subject matter). Next, open the Paint Alchemy dialog box. Choose the Ripple Detail style and click OK. Close the file without saving.

9. In all of the previous examples, I have selected combinations of photographs and styles that allowed the viewer to recognize the subject of the photograph after the effect has been applied. In this step we will create a colorful abstract background. Load the file \IMAGES\PHOTOS\DESIGN\057041.JPG. If you bought Corel PHOTO-PAINT 6 and not CorelDRAW 6, open IMAGES\PHOTOS\ASIA\057042B.JPG. Open the Paint Alchemy dialog box again and select Ice Cubes. Click OK. The result is a very colorful abstract. Close the file without saving.

10. For the last stop on the tour, we are going to use Corel PHOTO-PAINT to manipulate the output of one of the Alchemy filters to produce an unusual effect. Open the file \IMAGES\PHOTOS\DESIGN\265082.JPG. It is the same file and location in Corel PHOTO-PAINT 6 (stand-alone).

11. Open Alchemy, select the Molecules Sparse style, and click the OK button. As with many of the Alchemy filters, we have created an effect that makes the original image barely recognizable.

17

12. From the Edit menu, choose Paste From File. When the dialog box opens, select the same file (265082.JPG) again. Click the Open button and the image is placed on top of the original as an object. Our goal is to use part of the original to "beef up" what was removed by the Alchemy filter. To do that, we need the use of the Objects roll-up. So, double-click the Object Picker tool in the Toolbox to open the Objects roll-up.

13. From the Objects roll-up, move the Opacity slider to 50. Next, change the Merge mode to Add. This adds the Object (original) and the one changed by the Alchemy filter, producing a unique effect on the objects in the photograph as shown here. If this were a real job, you would click the Combine Object(s) with Background button on the lower-part of the roll-up (the button next to the Trash Can button) and then save the image in a standard image format file. For now, close the file without saving it.

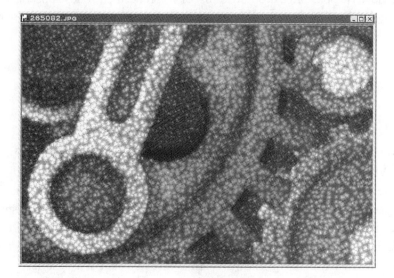

IP: *A quick way to return to the default setting for any style is to click on the style name. Then use either the UP ARROW or DOWN ARROW key to move to an adjacent style, and then, using the opposite arrow key, return to the original setting.*

This concludes our quick look at some of the many things that Paint Alchemy can do. The remaining information about Paint Alchemy is highly detailed and, let's face it, a little dry. I have included the following reference material because the Paint Alchemy filter is not documented anywhere else. Let's begin by looking into Styles.

Using Styles

You can use Paint Alchemy to create an enormous variety of effects. With 30 parameters to change and the ability to use custom brushes in addition to the brushes provided, the number of possibilities is virtually infinite. To allow the user to keep track of favorite settings, the Paint Alchemy filter offers the ability to record all of the filter settings as styles.

Each style is a complete record of the settings of all the controls. By loading a style, you can reproduce exactly that incredible filter effect that so wowed your client.

Loading a style is very simple. You only need to click on the down arrow to the right of the Style box, and a drop-down list of 75 predefined styles appears. You can use the styles that Corel provides with Paint Alchemy, or you can create your own. The styles can be customized using any of the Paint Alchemy controls.

 IP: *Altering existing styles and saving the new settings under a new name are often the best ways to begin creating your own styles.*

Creating a Custom Style

Paint Alchemy, like many paint-oriented filters, can take a long time to apply to an image. When you begin experimentation in search of the custom look that is going to win the Corel Design contest for you, either select a small area of the total image by using a mask, or pick one of the smaller image configurations, such as snapshot or wallet, if you are working from a photo-CD. Smaller image areas can be processed much faster. When you find the style you want, you can then apply it to a larger image to make sure all of the settings work before you save it as a style.

The people at Xaos Tools have a wealth of experience making custom styles. I have extracted the following procedural approach from their Mac manuals and from suggestions I received from Mac Paint Alchemy users via online services.

► Find an existing style that is closest to the style you want to create. Use the settings from that style as your starting point.

► Reduce the number of brush strokes (the Density) on the Brush card until you can see what the individual brushes are doing. Using the Zoom feature of the preview window, zoom in on individual brush strokes and make necessary adjustments to appropriate parameters (i.e., size, transparency, etc.).

▶ Change the attributes on the Color control card until you can see how the controls change each brush stroke. Once you are comfortable with the color controls, adjust your colors.

▶ Increase the density (number of brush strokes) until the angle of application becomes clear. Now you can adjust the brush stroke angle.

▶ To save a new custom style, click the Save As button. You are asked to enter a name for the new file (it can seemingly be a name of endless length, but you can only see the first 40 characters in the Style box). The current settings are saved with the name you provide, and the new style is added to the Style Controls drop-down list in alphabetical order. When you create a custom style, all of the style information is stored in the Alchemy.ini file located either in the COREL50\CONFIG directory (Corel PHOTO-PAINT 5) or the COREL\PHOTOPNT folder (Corel PHOTO-PAINT 6).

If the style name's length exceeds 80 characters (which would be dumb), it causes the name to wrap in the INI file. This means that the filter won't work and can't be removed using the Remove button. The only way to remove it is to go into the ALCHEMY.INI file and manually delete it and the description of the setting near the bottom of the file.

Changing a Custom Style

To change a custom style, do the following:

1. Select the style to be changed.

2. Make the changes desired.

3. Click the Save button. (You cannot change and save a preset style. With preset styles, only the Save As button is available.)

Saving a custom style will substitute the current style settings for those of the Paint Alchemy style with the same name.

Removing a Custom Style

To delete a custom style, you need only select the style you want to delete and click the Remove button. A warning box (I like to call them "second chance" boxes) asks you if you are sure that you want to remove the style. If you click OK, it's all over.

The Brush Card

The Brush card is the card you see when Paint Alchemy is first opened. This card is the heart of Paint Alchemy. The description that is in the Xaos Tool's Paint Alchemy manual can't be beat: "The simplest description of what Paint Alchemy does it this: It applies a whole bunch of brush strokes to your image. As a result, the shape of the brush has a profound effect on the look that is produced."

The Brush card displays six of the standard brushes. When I first began working with this program, I thought that they displayed the best brush for the application and then showed brushes that were also likely candidates for the effects. Wow, was I ever wrong! The six standard brushes that are displayed never change, regardless of the current brush that is loaded. The currently selected brush has a highlighted border around it. (On my system, it is red.)

Loading a Custom Brush

There are 30 custom brushes included with Paint Alchemy. They are located in the COREL50\PLGBRUSH directory (Corel PHOTO-PAINT 5) or the COREL\PHOTOPNT\PLGBRUSH folder (Corel PHOTO-PAINT 6). Click on the Load button and the Load Brush dialog box opens.

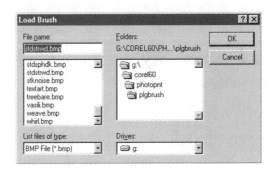

It allows you to select any BMP file as a custom brush. Here are the general rules regarding brushes.

You can load any size of BMP file as a brush as long as it meets the following parameters: 128 x 128 pixels and 300 dpi. If any of these parameters are different, the custom brush won't work. The exception is that the resolution can be 100 dpi. The brush icon will appear but the resulting brush may be distorted.

Using the default settings, brushes are completely opaque where white and transparent where black. Gray areas are semi-transparent; the darker they are, the more transparent they are. Black portions of your brush will not change your image, while the white portions define the area in which your selected effect is applied.

IP: *When making brushes in Corel PHOTO-PAINT, it is not necessary to paint white-on-black. Do all of your work in black-on-white, and then use the Invert filter.*

Styles that are built around custom brushes depend on the brushes remaining in the PLGBRUSH folder. If the brush that a selected style needs is not available when the style is selected, a default brush is loaded in its place.

Density

The Density slider controls the number of brush strokes that will be applied to the selected area. The density is a factor that is used to calculate how many brush strokes should be used for a given image size. The absolute number of strokes that will be used with the current image size is displayed above the slider. All of the calculations are based on the image size, not the mask size. Unlike the Texture Bitmap fills, the size of the brush effects does not increase or decrease as a result of the image size or the mask size.

IP: *The time required to apply the effect depends directly on the number of brush strokes: the more strokes, the longer the effect will take. The other factor that determines the amount of time that it takes to apply an effect is the size of the image or the size of the mask. If the image is large and the mask is small, the processing will still occur more quickly because the effect is only calculated for and applied to the masked area.*

Positioning

These sliders are far less than self-explanatory. They add randomness to the position of the brush strokes. When the sliders are both set at 0, the strokes are placed on a regular grid. The Horizontal Variation slider controls side-to-side brush stroke deviation. The Vertical Variation slider controls the up-and-down motion of the brush stroke deviation. With most of the styles applying brush strokes one on top of another multiple times, there are many styles that seemed to be changed very little by the positioning controls.

Layering Methods

There are three choices for layering methods in the Brush card: Random, Ordered, and Paint Layering.

RANDOM LAYERING   The brush strokes are applied so that they randomly overlap each other.

ORDERED LAYERING   The brush strokes are applied so that strokes that are above and to the left always overlap those that are below and to the right. With a square brush, this can look like roofing shingles. With a round brush, it can look like fish scales.

PAINT LAYERING   With Paint layering, the brightest portions of each brush stroke take priority in the layering. The effect it produces is highly dependent on the shape and coloring of the brush. You will need to experiment with Paint layering to find out what it can do. Paint layering can also cause brush shape to be lost when brushes overlap too much. The overlapping brush problem is resolved by lowering the brush-density setting or reducing the brush size to reveal more of the brush.

 OTE: *The Paint method of layering can cause aliasing (the dreaded "jaggies") when a brush that has hard black-and-white (or bright) edges is used.*

Randomize

Before you read this, click the Randomize button and see if you can figure out what it does. For those of you who understand techno-babble, it is a *random-seed generator.* For those who do not speak the language, it is the Randomize setting, which lets you set the initial value used in the random-number generation, a value that is called the *seed number.*

Clicking the Randomize button will randomly change the seed. You can also type a number directly into the box that is adjacent to the button. As a rule, forget the button. The fine folks at Xaos Tools, however, give two examples where you might actually want to use this function, as follows.

CHANGING THE SEED TO SUBTLY CHANGE THE EFFECT   You may want to change the seed if you like the general effect that Paint Alchemy is producing but there are some brushes that don't quite work the way you would like them to. Changing the seed puts the brush strokes in slightly different random positions, and this may produce that final correction you were looking for.

MAINTAINING THE SEED TO ENSURE REPEATABILITY   Using the same seed number guarantees that the exact same series of random numbers will be used for Paint Alchemy's internal calculations and thus all of the effects will be identical. This application, however, sounds a little fishy to me. How can it be a true random-number generator if identical results occur every time you use it?

BONUS: PICKING THE NUMBERS FOR YOUR STATE LOTTERY   This is my idea. The numbers that you get each time you click the Random button are indeed random, so you can use this function to pick lottery numbers in much the same way that they are picked by the state, untainted by the sentimental and unscientific "favorite numbers" technique. The only hitch is that most big-money lotteries are based on two-digit numbers. No problem—just use the last two digits of the random number for the lottery. By the way, if you win using this method, it is only fair for you to split the winnings with me and the editors who let this piece of nonsense get into print.

Creating Your Own Brushes

Creating brushes is one of the slicker things you can do with Paint Alchemy. It is easy to make a brush, but it is a little more difficult to make one that looks great when it is used in Paint Alchemy. Here is a summary of brush-making tips from Xaos Tools and from my own experience working with Corel PHOTO-PAINT and Paint Alchemy.

You can open the existing brush files in Corel PHOTO-PAINT. (The brushes are BMP files located in the PLGBRUSH folder.) You can then use Corel

PHOTO-PAINT to alter the appearance of the brushes. If you change one of the original brushes that came with Corel PHOTO-PAINT Plus, make sure you only save it under a new name. All of the styles in Paint Alchemy were designed to use one of these brushes. If you change the brush, you will need to reinstall PAINT Plus to restore the original brushes. If you want to save changes you made, use the Save As feature of Corel PHOTO-PAINT.

When you create a new brush from scratch, use an image size of 128 x 128 pixels with a resolution of 300 dpi. Also, remember to make the image a grayscale. If the brush you create is too large, it will not load into Paint Alchemy.

For more texture in the effect, create brush designs with a lot of gradation between black and white. Xaos Tools offers a collection called Floppy Full Of Brushes. This collection is only available at this time for the Macintosh. However, the brushes on the Mac side are PICT files (.PCT in DOS lingo). To use them, I took the Mac disk to a copy center, where we copied the Xaos Tools original diskette to a high-density disk (it comes from Xaos on a low-density disk which cannot be read on a PC) and had the PICT files saved in a format that my IBM could read. Finally, I loaded each one into Corel PHOTO-PAINT as Mac PCT files (did you remember that we could read Mac files?) and saved them as BMP files. I know that may seem like a lot of work, but it's worth it. The best part is they all have long descriptive filenames, which meant changing the names under Corel PHOTO-PAINT 5. I was able to keep the names under WIN'95's file-naming convention.

IP: *To change the brush that is used by a style, select the style before you select the brush. This is because every style has a brush associated with it. If you load the brush and then the style, the style will load its own brush, forcing you to reload your brush.*

The Color Card

You can use the Color card, shown below, to create effects such as pastel-like colors or even create improved black-and-white styles.

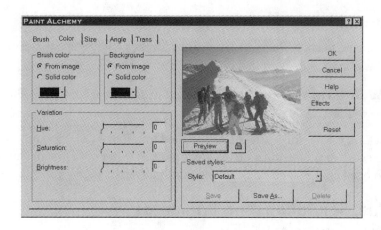

If you use a single solid color for your brush (instead of using the From Image setting), you can vary hue, saturation, and brightness controls to get a range of colors.

 IP: *To create pastel-like colors using the Color card, set the Brush color to From Image and the Background color to Solid Color (white). Then set your brush strokes to be partially transparent.*

Brush Color

Each brush stroke is a single, solid color. To determine the color of your brush strokes, use the Color card. You can set the colors of your brush strokes by using the colors of the image you are working on or by selecting a specific color using the Brush Color controls.

FROM IMAGE The color of each brush stroke is based on the color of the image at the center of each brush stroke.

SOLID COLOR The color of all the brush strokes is based on the color that you select. To select the color, click on the color preview window below the Solid Color button to open up the standard color-selection palette.

Background

You can choose to apply Paint Alchemy brush strokes with a Paper (background) of solid color using the Background controls.

FROM IMAGE   The brush strokes are applied to your image based on the color of each brush stroke.

SOLID COLOR   The brush strokes are applied to a Paper (background) of a solid color. To select the color, click on the color preview window below the Solid Color button to open up the standard color-selection palette.

The Hue, Saturation, and Brightness Variation Controls

These controls operate in a similar manner to the Impressionism or Pointillism brush tools. They allow you to vary from the initial Brush Color settings. The amount of variation can be controlled independently for the hue, saturation, and brightness of the brush color. These controls affect the brush stroke of both the From Image and the Solid Color settings.

HUE VARIATION   Hue Variation controls how much the color varies from the starting color. A small setting causes the colors in the brush to vary just a few shades to either side of the original color. A large setting produces a rainbow of colors, producing a confetti-like effect.

SATURATION VARIATION   Saturation Variation has the least noticeable effect of the three. It controls the amount of gray level in the image. It isn't a simple relationship; for example, 100 percent gives lots of gray. It has a greater effect in images where the color scheme of things contains large quantities of gray. Play with this control, but expect subtle rather than great changes in the image.

BRIGHTNESS VARIATION   Brightness Variation has the effect of controlling contrast. Officially, it controls the amount of variance there is in brightness between the starting color and the additional colors that are created by Paint Alchemy.

Image Enhancement

As with many of the other filters, you can increase the effectiveness of the Color card by using the other controls and filters in Corel PHOTO-PAINT to modify the image before working on it with the Paint Alchemy filter. If you have a low-contrast image, you should consider applying the Equalization filter to stretch the dynamic range of the image or increase the contrast of the image to produce more dramatic results.

The Size Card

The Size card, shown below, does just what it says: It enables you to vary the size of the brush strokes that are applied. There are several controls on this card that are evident when you open it. They are Vary Brush Size, Adjust Size, and Variation. The setting for Vary Brush Size then determines what controls are available in the rest of the Size card. When I first opened the Vary Brush Size drop-down list, I was greeted by a lengthy list of, shall we say, interesting names. However, once you understand the thinking behind the designers at Xaos, these might make a little more sense.

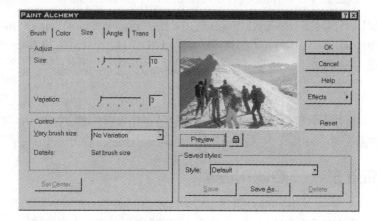

The Vary Brush Size Control

Clicking on the arrow button to the right of the name box produces a list of eight sets of brush variations. The names of the presets are the same for all three brush cards: Size, Angle, and Transparency. No variation is available through the By Brightness setting. What follows is a description of the action of each of these variation sets.

NO VARIATION   Here's the only set that is self-explanatory. Well, sort of. When this option is selected, all of the brush strokes will be the same size. The size of the brush is set using the Size slider. The size is scaled from the actual size of the brush image selected. In practice, it is a percentage of the size of the original. For example, if the BMP file that makes up the brush is 128 x 128 pixels, a size value of 128 would produce brush strokes of the same size. If the value was set for 50 (50 percent), the brush strokes would be 64 x 64 pixels in size. All of the brushes included in Paint Alchemy are 128 x 128 pixels. Now for the weirdness.

What does a Variation slider do in a No Variation setting? It overrides the No Variations In Size option, of course. Thus, larger numbers cause larger variations in brush size in the No Variation setting. Is that clear? I think I'm getting a headache. By the way, the preceding explanation applies to all of the Variation sliders.

RANDOMLY When this option is selected, the brush strokes vary in size randomly. I love the two settings for this one: This and That. You use This and That to set the minimum and maximum size allowed. It doesn't matter which is which. The larger setting will be the Maximum and the smaller setting will be the Minimum. Look at the bottom of the card. Another Variation slider! This one does the same thing as the Variation slider in No Variation: It overrides the This and That slider settings.

BY RADIAL DISTANCE With this option, the brush strokes will change smoothly in size, in a circular manner. The brush strokes start out one size in the center and gradually change to another size at the edge of the circle. Because the size of the brush varies as a function of its distance, two sliders control how the brush stroke will appear:

► **Center slider:** Determines the size of the brush at the center of the circle.

► **Edge slider:** Sets the size of the brush at the edge of the circle.

Variation Slider: Overrides

To set the location of the center point, click the Set Center button. This brings up a dialog box that contains a thumbnail of the image or of the area selected by the mask. If more than one area is masked, an area of the image that is determined by the boundaries of the various masks makes up the preview image. By clicking on the place that you want to be the center of the circle, a small crosshair is placed on the image at the point where you clicked.

Below the thumbnail is exact X/Y-position information (in pixels) for the point where the circle is centered. Actually, I haven't got a clue why this information is provided. It wasn't in the Mac version, and when I asked some members of the Paint development team, they didn't know either, except that it had been requested from higher up in the command chain.

𝓃 **OTE:**   *The Set Center point determines the center of the circle used by the Size, Angle, and Transparency cards. The Set Center point is available on the Size, Angle, and Transparency cards when By Radial Distance is selected on each.*

BY VERTICAL POSITION   With this option, the brush strokes change smoothly in size from the top to the bottom of the image. You set the sizes using the Top and Bottom sliders.

BY HORIZONTAL POSITION   With this option, the brush strokes change smoothly in size from the left to the right of the image. The sizes of the brushes are set using the Left and Right sliders.

BY HUE   With this option, each brush stroke is scaled according to the hue of the image at the location of each brush stroke. You set the minimum and maximum sizes using the Warm and Cool sliders. For example, the default setting for the Spatula style is Warm 5, Cool 30. The warmer colors will be limited to variations of up to 5 percent of the brush size, while the cool colors will be allowed to become up to 30 percent of brush size. So what do we mean by cool and warm? On a color wheel, the dividing line between cool and warm runs through red. Therefore, by using the By Hue option for determining brush size, brush strokes that are applied to areas of the image that contain colors on the yellow side of red are given the Warm size values. Those colors that fall on the magenta side of red are given the Cool size values. (This detailed explanation is so that you know how it works. I have yet to sit down with a color wheel that can calculate this stuff. Experiment on small images or the preview window.)

BY SATURATION   With this selection, each brush stroke is scaled according to the saturation of the image color at the location of the brush stroke. You set the minimum and maximum sizes using the Unsaturated and Saturated sliders. If you are very health conscious, you can use these setting to make images that are high in unsaturates (just kidding). Setting the values for Saturated to be larger than the values for Unsaturated results in brush strokes over richly colored areas that will be larger than the brush strokes over black, white, or gray areas.

 IP: *While working with this larger/smaller brush stroke thing, remember that smaller brush strokes retain more detail of the original image and may be more desirable than larger brush strokes.*

BY BRIGHTNESS   With this option, each brush stroke is scaled according to the brightness of the image color at the location of the brush stroke. You set the minimum and maximum sizes using the Bright and Dark sliders. Setting the value for Bright to be larger than the value for Dark results in brush strokes over bright areas of the image that will be larger than brush strokes over dark areas.

Variation Size Slider

See description in the Size card section.

The Angle Card

You use the Angle card, shown below, to set the angle of your brush stroke and to change brush angle based on its position in your image. Based on the Control option chosen, the Adjust options vary. You can also control brush angle based on the color content of your image, or you can change brush angle randomly. This card is similar in operation to the Size card.

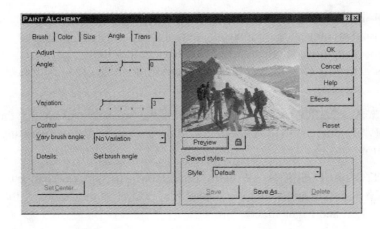

Vary Brush Angle

The Vary Brush Angle drop-down list lets you specify what should control the orientation (the amount of rotation) of your brush strokes. You can apply all of the brush strokes at the same angle, or you can have them vary randomly, according to information in the image, or by their position. The following is what each option does.

NO VARIATION   When this option is selected, all of the brush strokes will be rotated by the same angular amount. The amount of rotation (−180 to +180) is set using the Angle slider. If the Angle is set to 0, the brush strokes will not be rotated at all; they will have the same orientation as the picture of the brush that is displayed on the Brush card. If the angle is set to 180 degrees, the brushes will be upside-down.

RANDOMLY   With this option, the brush stroke angle varies randomly. You use This and That to set the minimum and maximum angles. It doesn't matter which is which. The larger setting will be the Maximum and the smaller setting will be the Minimum.

BY RADIAL DISTANCE   With this option, the brush strokes will change their orientation smoothly in a circular manner, starting at one angle in the center and gradually changing to another angle at the edge of the circle. The operation of these controls is described in the earlier discussion of the Size card controls called "By Radial Distance."

BY VERTICAL POSITION   Using this selection, the brush strokes change their angle smoothly from the top to the bottom of the image. You set the angles using the Top and Bottom sliders.

BY HORIZONTAL POSITION   With this option, the brush strokes change their angle smoothly from the left to the right of the image. You set the angles of the brushes using the Left and Right sliders.

BY HUE   With By Hue selected, each brush stroke is rotated according to the hue of the image at the location of each brush stroke. You set the minimum and maximum angles using the Warm and Cool sliders. Therefore, when using By Hue for determining brush stroke angles, areas of the image that contain colors on the yellow side of red are given the Warm size values. Those colors that fall on the magenta side of the red are given the Cool size values. If you set the angle for Cool to be larger than the angle for Warm, brush strokes over the blue areas of the image will be rotated more than brush strokes over yellow areas. (You should feel free to experiment on small images or the preview window.)

BY SATURATION   With this option, each brush stroke is rotated according to the saturation of the image color at the location of the brush stroke. You set the minimum and maximum angles using the Saturated and Unsaturated sliders. Setting the values for Saturated to be larger than the values for Unsaturated results in brush strokes over richly colored areas that will be rotated more than brush strokes over black, white, or gray areas.

BY BRIGHTNESS   With this option, each brush stroke is rotated according to the brightness of the image color at the location of the brush stroke. You set the minimum and maximum angles using the Bright and Dark sliders. Setting the values for Bright to be larger than the values for Dark results in brush strokes over bright areas of the image that will be larger than brush strokes over dark areas.

Angle Variation

The Variation slider lets you add randomness to the stroke angles. The higher this value, the more your strokes will vary from their set angles.

The variation is calculated as degrees of offset from the brush angle. Thus, if you set Vary Brush Angle to No Variation, the Angle to 90, and the Variation to 10, you will get brush strokes that range in angle from 80 to 100 degrees.

The Transparency Card

The Transparency card, shown below, is used to control brush stroke transparency and to change the transparency based on brush position in your image. Based on the Control option chosen, the adjust options vary. You can also control transparency based on the color content of your image, or you can control it randomly. This card is similar in operation to the Size card.

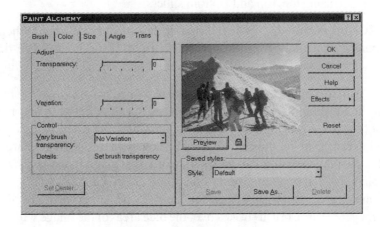

The Vary Brush Transparency Controls

The Vary Brush Transparency drop-down list lets you specify what controls the transparency of your brush strokes. The following are brief explanations of what each option does.

NO VARIATION   With this option, all of the brush strokes are equally transparent. You set the degree of transparency using the Transparency slider. If the Transparency is set to 0, the brush strokes will be completely opaque. If it is set to 100, the brush strokes will be completely transparent (in other words, invisible).

OTE: *The gray areas of the brushes are partially transparent when the Transparency is set to 0. The transparency that you set with the slider is added to the normal transparency of each pixel in the brush.*

RANDOMLY   The transparency of your brush strokes can vary randomly. The maximum and minimum transparency is set using the This and That sliders. It doesn't matter which is larger or smaller.

BY RADIAL DISTANCE   With this option, the brush strokes smoothly change their transparency in a circular manner, starting at one angle of transparency in the center and gradually changing to another at the edge of the circle. The operation of these controls is described in the earlier discussion of the Size card controls called "By Radial Distance."

BY VERTICAL POSITION   With this option, the brush strokes change their degree of transparency smoothly from the top to the bottom of the image. You set the degree of transparency using the Top and Bottom sliders.

BY HORIZONTAL POSITION   With this option, the brush strokes change their degree of transparency smoothly from the left to the right of the image. The degree of transparency of the brushes are set using the Left and Right sliders.

BY HUE   With this option, each brush stroke is rotated according to the hue of the image at the location of each brush stroke. You set the minimum and maximum degree of transparency using the Warm and Cool sliders. Thus, by using By Hue for determining brush stroke, the degree of transparency that is applied to areas of the image that contain colors on the yellow side of red is given the Warm size values. Those colors that fall on the magenta side of red are given the Cool size values. If you set the degree of transparency for Cool to be larger than the degree of transparency for Warm, brush strokes over the blue areas of the image will be rotated more than brush strokes over yellow areas. Experiment on small images or the preview window.

BY SATURATION   With this option, each brush stroke is rotated according to the saturation of the image color at the location of the brush stroke. You set the minimum and maximum degrees of transparency using the Saturated and Unsaturated sliders. Setting the values for Saturated to be larger than the values for Unsaturated results in brush strokes over richly colored areas that will be rotated more than brush strokes over black, white, or gray areas.

BY BRIGHTNESS   With this option, each brush stroke is rotated according to the brightness of the image color at the location of the brush stroke. You set the minimum and maximum degrees of transparency using the Bright and Dark sliders. Setting the value for Bright to be larger than the value for Dark results in brush strokes over bright areas of the image that will be larger than brush strokes over dark areas.

Transparency Variation Slider

The Variation slider lets you add randomness to the degree of brush stroke transparency. The higher this value, the more your strokes will vary from their set degree of transparency.

The variation is calculated as degrees of offset from the brush's selected degree of transparency. Thus, if you set Vary Brush Transparency to No Variation, set the Transparency to 90, and set the Variation to 10, you will get brush strokes that range in transparency from 80 to 100 degrees.

The Power of Paint Alchemy

I have given you many pages of reference material about the Paint Alchemy filter. While perhaps not the most exciting reading, this material will be very useful when you begin experimenting with creating your own brushes and styles.

The Canvas Filter

In Corel PHOTO-PAINT 5, the Canvas filter is a roll-up. Changing it to a filter was a good move on Corel's part. The Canvas does not need to be kept available as other roll-ups do. Actually, Canvas was always a filter that thought it was a roll-up. The Canvas filter lets you apply any tile pattern or bitmap for use as an image background. If you set the transparency level to a higher percentage, the canvas can also be used to overlay an existing image.

Using the Canvas Filter

The Canvas filter is a simple filter that will allow you to achieve professional-looking effects with little experience or effort. A Corel PHOTO-PAINT Canvas can be made from any color (mono or grayscale images have to be converted to color first) bitmap image. Although these images can be used for a canvas, the Canvas filter is only available with 24-bit and 32-bit images. The Canvas filter applies the selected bitmap pattern to the background of an image to give the appearance of a canvas. The canvas can also be used with a high transparency to overlay an existing picture. The canvas shows through the image and any future application of paint. You can set the transparency and the level of embossing. A low transparency value allows you to view more of the canvas. Embossing creates a relief effect. The Canvas effect is used to load a bitmap pattern over an existing image (creating a screening effect) or to serve as a background image (or canvas). The transparency and embossing levels let you create unique special effects, as do the X, Y, Row, and Column options, which let you control the position of tiled bitmaps onscreen. If you select a bitmap that is smaller than the image to which it is to be applied, the bitmap is tiled to fit the image.

The Canvas Filter Dialog Box

The Canvas filter is accessed by selecting Artistic in the Effects menu and choosing Canvas. The dialog box shown here consists of two viewing windows arranged in an Original and Result format. The window on the left shows a thumbnail of the existing image (before). The window on the right is a preview window that displays the results of the filter action based on the current settings (after). The description of the settings in the dialog box that are unique follows.

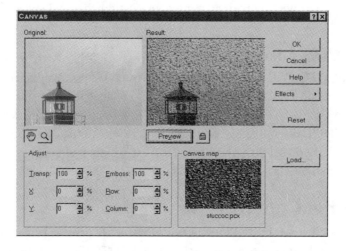

CANVAS PREVIEW   Located below the Preview window, the Canvas Preview displays the selected canvas. If no canvas has been loaded, the Canvas Preview will be blank except for a large "X" in the center.

TRANSP (TRANSPARENCY)   This sets the level of transparency, expressed in percentage. High levels make the canvas more transparent and the underlying image more visible. Lower levels make the canvas opaque and less of the image is visible.

X/Y VALUES   The X/Y values allow you to control the size/placement of the bitmap tiles through scaling. You cannot always see the results of changing the values in the Result window.

EMBOSS   Emboss gives the canvas a raised relief effect. Use the slider to change the percentage of embossing or enter the number directly into the value box.

ROW/COLUMN   The Row and Column settings provide control over the placement of the bitmap tiles in relation to one another. Changing the Row value to 50% means that each successive row of bitmap tiles will overlap by 50 percent. Row and Column settings are mutually exclusive, meaning that if a value is entered in one, the other is zeroed out.

LOAD BUTTON   Clicking the Load button displays the Load a Canvas from Disk dialog box. Select a canvas from the PHOTOPNT\CANVAS directory, or choose another image.

Corel PHOTO-PAINT 6 installs ten PCX files for Canvases. Each PCX file is 128 x 128 pixels at 300 dpi in 256-color mode. They are located in the COREL\PHOTOPNT\CANVAS folder.

In Corel PHOTO-PAINT 5 there are a total of 120 canvases located on the CD-ROM Disk under COREL50\PHOTOPNT\CANVAS. Now the 120 additional canvases are actually 40 canvases that each come in three different sizes. The different size files are identified by the last letter of the filename, not by extension. The files are designated as follows:

Coarse: *filename*C.*pcx* (128 x 128 pixels). Example: Paper01C.pcx
Medium: *filename*M.*pcx* (96 x 96 pixels). Example: Paper01M.pcx
Fine: *filename*F.*pcx* (64 x 64 pixels). Example: Paper01F.pcx

Finding Custom Bitmaps to Use for Canvas

You can use any color bitmap file that can be imported by Corel PHOTO-PAINT to create a new canvas by loading it into the Canvas roll-up through the Load a Canvas from Disk dialog box. The files that can be used for canvases include Photo-CDs and the files that you create with Corel PHOTO-PAINT 6. If you have a vector-based file that you want to use, simply load it into Corel PHOTO-PAINT and save it as a color bitmap file.

If the Canvas Bitmap Is the Wrong Size

If the bitmap image that is selected for use as a canvas is too small to fit the image area where it is being applied, the image will be tiled by Corel PHOTO-PAINT to fit the image area. If the Image used for a canvas is too large to fit into the image area, it will be cropped (not resized) to fit the image area.

IP: *If the image is going to be tiled, you may want to consider cropping the bitmap with the Cropping tool, feathering the edge of the object with a small value, and dragging the image into the Corel PHOTO-PAINT workspace to create a new cropped image. The feathering will reduce the lines and therefore the "kitchen tile" look.*

Considerations About Using the Canvas Filter

If you are going to apply the canvas to an image, be aware that it will make the image more opaque to some extent. The best canvases are those with little color, lots of white area, and contrast. Cement is a good example of a canvas to place on top. It is a high-contrast canvas and therefore the effect of the embossing really stands out.

There is good news and bad news about using the Canvas filter. The bad news is? One of the effects of applying the canvas filter is that the resulting image looks washed out. The good news? There is a cure. After you have applied the canvas, apply the Equalize filter in the Effects|Color Adjust menu using the default setting. Applying this filter generally restores most of the color depth that is lost when the canvas is applied.

Canvases can be placed on top of and behind images. Canvases can be applied to objects. In fact, the canvas provides a way to add texture only to an object.

Although it has been mentioned before, remember that the preview for this filter does not always faithfully reflect what the final output will look like.

Adding texture to text or other objects is another use for the Canvas filter. Figure 17-1 shows the application of a canvas first to the background and then to the text with the background locked. Only the objects that are unlocked have the canvas applied to them.

The Glass Block Filter

This filter, which is only available with 24-bit, 32-bit color, and grayscale images, creates the effect of viewing the image through thick transparent blocks of glass. The dialog box is very simple, as shown in the following illustration. With the exception of the Width and Height settings, the operation of this dialog box is identical to the Canvas filter dialog box described earlier in this chapter. The two settings, width and height of the glass blocks in pixels, can be set independently of each other. The setting range is 1 through 100. The lowest setting (1 Width, 1 Height) produces glass blocks that are 1 x 1 pixels in the image area.

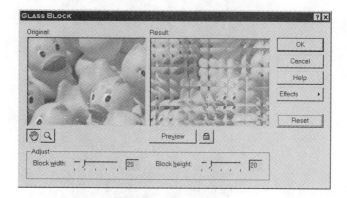

Here is something unique to do with the Glass Block filter. In Figure 17-2 I took a photograph of flowers, rotated the image 45 degrees, and applied the Glass Block filter to it. Next, I rotated the image back to its original position. The shadow was made by creating an object of the photograph, duplicating it, merging it with the background, and applying a Gaussian blur.

The application of the Canvas filter to the text and then the background gives the image a photo-realistic texture

FIGURE 17-1

Here is
something
exciting that
can be done
with the
Glass Block
filter

FIGURE 17-2

The Impressionist Filter

Like the Glass Block filter, the Impressionist filter is only available with 24-bit, 32-bit, and grayscale images. This filter gives an image the appearance of an impressionist brush. Not really, but that's the official description. The amount of Impressionist effect can be applied independently as Horizontal or Vertical values. The range is 1-100 and is measured in the amount of scatter (displacement) in pixels. For example, a setting of 10 in the Vertical will diffuse the image over a ten-pixel region in the vertical. Using a setting larger than the default (or 20) will scatter the pixels in the original image to the point it becomes unrecognizable.

The Smoked Glass Filter

The Smoked Glass filter applies a transparent mask over the image to give the appearance of smoked glass. You can determine the color of the tint (before opening the filter), the percentage of transparency, and the degree of blurring.

The color of the tint is determined by the Paint (foreground) color, which is controlled in the Tool Settings roll-up before opening the Filter dialog box. The Tint slider controls the Opacity of the tint being applied. Larger values mean greater amounts of color tint applied to the image. A value of 100 fills the area with a solid color. The Percentage slider controls the amount of blurring applied to the image to give the appearance of the distortion caused by glass. A value of 100 percent produces the greatest amount of blurring, while 0 percent produces no blurring of the image.

The Terrazzo Filter

The next plug-in filter we will discuss from Corel PHOTO-PAINT 6's Artistic filters group is called Terrazzo. (The name comes from the Italian word for "terrace" and originally referred to a kind of mosaic floor covering.) I again acknowledge my gratitude to the fine folks at Xaos, who have let me borrow heavily from their manual so that the material in this chapter would be accurate.

Terrazzo enables you to create beautiful, regular patterns taken from elements in existing source images. With Terrazzo, the patterns are very easy to create and infinitely repeatable. The best part is that Terrazzo is simple to use. Xaos Tools ships a wonderful manual with their product that covers Terrazzo in incredible detail. Since the User Manual is not available, I have done my best to give you a condensed version of the major features and functions of Terrazzo.

An Overview of Terrazzo

The regular patterns you can create with Terrazzo are based on 17 symmetry groups, which are known in the math and design worlds by several names, including "planar," "ornamental," or "wallpaper" symmetry groups. You choose the symmetry you want to use from a Symmetry selection box from the Terrazzo dialog box.

The 17 symmetries in the Terrazzo filter are named after common American patchwork quilt patterns. Each of these symmetries also has a mathematical name. Because these mathematical names (such as p-4m) aren't very exciting or as easy to remember as the quilt names (such as Sunflower), Xaos has only used the quilt names in the interface.

Tiles, Motifs, and Patterns

Each Terrazzo-generated pattern is made from a *motif,* which is the shape that builds a *tile* when a *symmetry* is applied to it. The tile, in turn, repeats to build a regular pattern. These three terms will be used throughout this discussion.

The motif in Terrazzo is very similar to the masks in Corel PHOTO-PAINT. The area that is enclosed by the motif is the foundation of the tile. There are eight different motif shapes. Different symmetries use different motifs.

Although each of the 17 symmetries produces different results, all of the symmetries perform one or more of the following operations:

► *Translations*, which move the motif up, down, right, left, or diagonally without changing the orientation

► *Rotations*, which turn the motif one or more times around a center at a specific angle

► *Mirror Reflections*, which create one or more mirror images of the motif

► *Glide Reflections*, which create one or more mirror images of a motif and move the motif up, down, right, left, or diagonally

The Terrazzo Filter Dialog Box

Terrazzo is located in the Effects menu under Artistic. Clicking on the name produces an hourglass for a moment. (Of all of the filters that were available at the time this book was written, Terrazzo takes the longest to initialize. Still, on my system we are only talking about ten seconds. And after it is initialized, Terrazzo operates very fast.)

Terrazzo works on grayscale, 24-bit, and 32-bit color images, but not on black-and-white (1-bit) images. Like Paint Alchemy and all of the other filters, you must have a image open before you can access the filter.

When you first open Terrazzo, you will see the opening screen as shown below. Let's take a closer look at it.

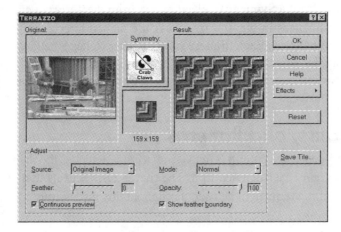

The large image on the left side of the Terrazzo dialog box displays the masked area of the image, or the entire source image if you haven't selected any areas with a mask. (Color masks don't count.)

The large image on the right of the dialog box displays the source image with the current symmetry applied to it. We'll refer to the image on the right as the *destination* image.

OTE: *The destination image is the one to which you are applying a pattern. Although you can open a new source image from within Terrazzo, you cannot open a new destination image without closing Terrazzo and returning to Corel PHOTO-PAINT 6's main screen.*

The Continuous Preview Option

When the Continuous Preview check box is checked, the destination image is continuously updated as you change any of the settings in the Terrazzo dialog box. This allows you to see the effects of your adjustments in real time as you are making them.

IP: *Leaving the Continuous Preview options selected may slow down some older systems. This is especially true if you are using a large motif, one of the triangular motifs such as Sunflower, or the kite-shaped motif such as Whirlpool. If you experience system slow-down, you may want to consider switching off the Continuous Preview option. That said, I find that having it on really helps in finding some nice patterns quickly.*

By default, Continuous Preview is turned off in the Terrazzo dialog box. When the Continuous Preview check box is not selected, the destination image is updated only when you release the mouse button after making an adjustment to one of the controls in the Terrazzo dialog box.

The Terrazzo Motifs

When you first open the Terrazzo dialog box, the motif is positioned in the center of the source image; if you have already opened the Terrazzo dialog box, the motif is in the position where you last placed it.

Adjusting a Motif

You can change the tile you are creating by moving the motif to a new position on the source image, thus selecting a different part of the image to make into a tile.

In addition to moving the motif, you can also adjust the size and, in the case of the Gold Brick symmetry, the shape of the motif. Each motif has a handle on it that enables you to resize it.

To Adjust the Motif's Position

Place the cursor anywhere inside the motif and hold down the left mouse button. The cursor becomes a hand, and while you hold down the mouse button you can drag the motif anywhere inside the source image.

If the Continuous Preview option is on, the destination image on the right side is constantly updated to show the results of repositioning the motif on the source image.

To Adjust the Motif's Size

Place the cursor over the motif control handle and drag it to increase or decrease the size. The only exception to this is the Gold Brick, which has two handles. The handle in the upper-right corner of the motif resizes the width, and the handle in the lower left lets you resize the height of the motif and skew its shape.

IP: *To constrain the Gold Brick motif to a rectangular shape, or to return to a rectangular motif after you have skewed the motif, hold down the SHIFT key as you drag the lower-left handle. The motif automatically becomes rectangular as long as you hold down the SHIFT key.*

Selecting a Symmetry

The first time you open Terrazzo, the active symmetry is Pinwheel. This symmetry is displayed between the source and the destination images in the Terrazzo dialog box. Each symmetry swatch displays a simple representation of the selected symmetry.

To select a different symmetry, click on the currently displayed symmetry swatch and the Symmetry selection box opens as shown in the following illustration. Clicking the desired symmetry causes it to be highlighted with a blue border. Click the OK button when you are satisfied with your selection, and the selected symmetry appears between the source and destination image.

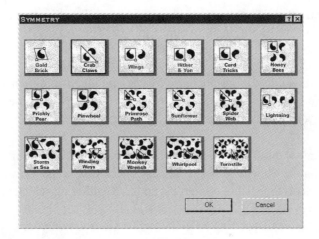

Creating Seamless Patterns

With most of the Terrazzo symmetries, you may notice a visible edge or seam between the tiles. The feather option in the Terrazzo dialog box allows you to feather the edge of a motif so that the seams between tiles fade away.

When you turn on feathering in Terrazzo, an area outside the motif (called the *feather boundary*) is selected, and the pixels inside the feather boundary are dispersed, thus creating a gradual transition between motifs.

 IP: *Sometimes there is such a thing as too much of a good thing. With certain patterns, using too large a feathering value causes faint black seams to develop on certain patterns.*

Using the Feather Option

You use the Feather option in the Terrazzo dialog box to set the width of the feather edge around the motif. The feather option is dimmed (not available) if you have selected the Sunflower, Prickly Pear, Turnstile, or Winding Way symmetry. The option is not available because these four symmetries are kaleidoscopic and therefore always seamless.

To adjust a motif's feather edge, drag the slider to increase or decrease the feather edge around the motif, or enter a value directly into the data box to the right of the slider. The value is a percentage based upon the size of the image. For example, setting the Feather value to 25 creates a feather with a width of 25 percent of the distance from the edge of the motif to its center.

When you set the feather value above 0, you will notice that a second border appears around the motif in the source image. This border represents the area included in the feather edge of the motif.

IP: *You cannot move the motif by clicking and dragging inside the feather border. You must be inside the motif itself to move a feathered motif. (This little jewel drove me crazy till I figured it out.)*

If you don't want to see the feather boundary around the motif, you can turn it off by clearing the Show Feather Boundary check box in the Terrazzo dialog box. This only turns off the visible border; if you have feathering selected, the feathering is still applied.

You may notice that setting a Feather value slows down your system a wee bit. The folks at Corel have done a wonderful job of speeding up these filters in comparison to the Mac versions. However, if you noticed that the feathering is slowing your system down, keep it off until you are ready to fine-tune your image.

IP: *Some symmetries create mirror lines as they reflect a motif to create a pattern. Feathering does not occur on mirror lines, because these are "seamless" lines; feathering only appears on edges with visible seams.*

Feather Boundary Constraints

If the Show Feather Boundary is off and you have some value of feathering entered, you will discover that you cannot position the motif any closer to the edge of the source image than the feather boundary.

If the motif is already positioned near the edge of the source image and you attempt to enter a value for Feather, that would create a boundary that goes beyond the image edge. You would then receive a warning and the maximum allowable value would automatically be entered in the Feather value box. The slider or values will not exceed that value unless the motif is moved.

One last feathering note: If you have a very small motif, you may not be able to see the feather boundary, even if you have the Show Feather Boundary option turned on. Although you can't see it, the feather will still appear when you apply the pattern.

The Mode Settings

The Mode drop-down list in the Terrazzo dialog box lets you control the way a pattern is applied to a selection. The following sections contain explanations for each of Terrazzo's mode choices. In each of the accompanying figures, the same tile was applied to the same image. The only setting that was changed was the mode.

Normal

This mode applies the pattern uniformly to all the pixels of the destination image.

Darken

This mode applies only to those pixels in the pattern that are darker than those in the destination image. The pixels in the destination image that are darker than those in the pattern remain unchanged.

Lighten

This mode applies only to those pixels in the pattern that are lighter than those in the destination image. The pixels in the destination image that are lighter than those in the pattern remain unchanged.

Hue

This mode applies the pattern by changing only the hues (colors) of the destination image, without affecting the saturation (intensity of colors) or the luminosity (lightness and darkness) values of pixels in the destination image. This mode is not available if the destination image is in grayscale.

Saturation

This mode applies the pattern by changing only the saturation values of the destination image, without affecting the hue or the luminosity values of the pixels in the destination image. This mode is not available if the destination image is in grayscale.

Color

This mode applies the pattern by changing both the hue and saturation values of the destination image without changing the luminosity values of pixels in the destination image. This mode is not available if the destination image is in grayscale.

Luminosity

This mode applies the pattern by changing only the luminosity values of the destination range, without affecting the hue or saturation values of the pixels in the destination image. This mode is the inverse of Color mode. (It can also produce some surprising results.)

Multiply

This mode causes the color pattern to combine with the color in the destination image, creating colors that are darker than those in either the pattern or the destination image.

Screen

This mode causes the colors in the pattern to combine with the colors in the destination image, creating colors that are lighter than those in either the pattern or the destination image. This mode is the inverse of Multiply mode.

The Opacity Slider

The Opacity slider in the Terrazzo dialog box lets you adjust the opacity of the pattern when you apply it to a selection. You may want the effect of an almost invisible pattern (low opacity), or you may want a bold application of a pattern, covering the destination image entirely (high opacity). An opacity value of 100 (100 percent) means that the pattern is completely opaque; an opacity value of 1 means that the pattern is almost invisible (which is not very useful).

Previewing Tiles

A preview of the current tile appears below the symmetry swatch. The pixel dimensions of the current tile are also displayed below the tile. You are provided with a constant preview of the tile you are creating.

Saving a Tile

One of the benefits of having the Terrazzo filter integrated into Corel PHOTO-PAINT 6 is that saving a tile button becomes a real time saver. The Save Tile feature saves the tile created by Terrazzo as a BMP file in the default location for the Bitmap Fill tiles. This way you can quickly use Terrazzo to make a tile, and by saving it as a tile, you can use it immediately as a bitmap fill.

To save a Terrazzo tile:

1. Choose the symmetry, and position the motif where you want it in the source image.

2. Click the Save Tile button in the Terrazzo dialog box. The Save Tile dialog box opens.

3. Name the file and confirm where you want the file saved. Click the OK button. When you return to the Terrazzo, click Cancel if you do not want the pattern applied to the image.

The Vignette Filter

The Vignette filter applies a mask over the image that has a transparent oval in the center. The remainder of the mask is opaque. It is designed to appear as an old-style photograph when the image is placed in an oval.

A Vignette can be applied to the entire image or just a masked area. By clicking and dragging the Offset slider, you can control how large the oval is about the center of the image. The larger the percentage, the smaller the transparent oval. The Fade slider controls the fade (feathering) at the edge of the oval. Using the Vignette dialog box, you can determine the color of the mask by selecting black, white, or Paint color. The Paint color must be selected before applying the Vignette filter.

The Noise Filters

18

T he Noise filters are very important to photo-editing. Noise, which is composed of random pixels, can be used to add an apparent sharpness to a soft image. It can be used to add "grit" to an otherwise smooth surface. Naturally occurring noise in an image can result from poorly scanned images or from the film grain of certain film types. Whether noise needs to be removed or even added, Corel PHOTO-PAINT 6 provides the necessary filters to accomplish it. The Noise subgroup in the Effects menu has the following seven filters: Add Noise, Diffuse, Dust & Scratch, Maximum, Median, Minimum, and Remove Noise.

The Add Noise Filter

Why would you want to add noise? Actually, adding noise has more uses than you would first imagine. Noise (random pixels) can give the effect of grit and texture to a picture. It can add a dusting of pixels to an image in a way that emulates film grain. When the grain color is not quite compatible with the image, adding noise can be helpful in softening the look of stark image areas. When you are retouching photographs that have existing film-grain texture, it can be helpful to add noise so the blending is less apparent. If you are an old hand with Photoshop, you probably know much of this already.

The Add Noise filter creates a granular effect that adds texture to a flat or overly blended image. There are several neat tricks that can be done with this filter. Let's begin with a description of how the filter operates.

The Add Noise Filter Dialog Box

The dialog box, as shown here, consists of two viewing windows arranged in a Before and After format. The window on the left shows a thumbnail of the original image. The window on the right is the Result window that displays the results of the filter action based on the current settings.

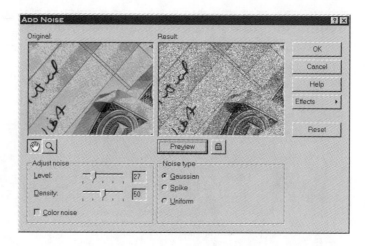

LEVEL   The Level slider controls the Intensity of the noise pixels. The slider operates on a percentage scale of 0-100%. A lower setting makes the noise barely visible. A higher setting produces higher-visibility noise pixels.

DENSITY   The Density slider controls the amount of noise pixels added to the image. The slider operates on a percentage scale of 0-100%. A lower setting adds very few noise pixels. A higher setting produces a higher density of noise pixels.

COLOR NOISE   When Color Noise is checked, the Noise filter uses the color values of the image pixels to create noise that contains color values. When left unchecked, the noise that is introduced is grayscale.

TYPE   Three types of noise are available. They are Gaussian, Spike, and Uniform. The differences are displayed in Figures 18-1 through 18-3.

► **Gaussian**: Using this option prioritizes colors along a Gaussian distribution curve. The effect is that most colors added by the filter either closely resemble the original colors or they slightly push the boundaries of the specified range. The results are more light and dark pixels than with the Uniform Noise option, thus producing a more dramatic effect.

► **Spike**: This filter uses colors that are distributed around a narrow curve (spike). It produces a thinner, lighter-colored grain.

Gaussian noise applied to an image at an 8% Level and 100% Density

FIGURE 18-1

▶ **Uniform**: This filter provides an overall grainy appearance. Use this option to apply colors in an absolutely random fashion, with the range specified by the Noise Level percentage slider.

Spike noise applied at a 75% level and 100% density. Due to its nature, Spike noise requires a high-level setting to produce a visible result in the image

FIGURE 18-2

Uniform noise applied at a 25% Level setting and a 100% Density setting

FIGURE 18-3

Noise Filter Effects

The Noise filters are used to create a wide variety of background effects. In this chapter we can only show a few of them.

Removing Banding from a Radial Fill

Many times if a radial fill (or any gradient fill, for that matter) is applied to a large area, some banding occurs. *Banding* is the phenomenon wherein the changes of color or shades appear as bands in the image. This effect is more pronounced in low-resolution than in higher-resolution output. It is also more apparent in grayscale or 256-color fills than in 24-bit color. Figure 18-4 shows a 50-step fountain fill. The fill in Figure 18-5 had a Gaussian Noise with a Level setting of 8 and a Density setting of 100 applied to it.

Making Metallic Effects

Not only can the Noise filter add texture to fills, it can also be used to create some very unusual backgrounds.

A fountain fill background that will exhibit banding when printed on a low-resolution printer. It is also boring

FIGURE 18-4

To create the metallic effect shown here:

1. Apply Gaussian Noise to a linear fountain fill.

2. Next, apply Motion Blur (setting of 5). The blur direction can be any one of your choosing.

3. Apply the Sharpen filter to the resulting blur. Don't make the Edge level setting too high (30 or less should do it).

The same fill that has had a Gaussian Noise applied with a Level setting of 8 and a Density setting of 100. Now the fill has texture

FIGURE 18-5

Noise and Embossing

Noise serves as the foundation for many textures and effects. Using a combination of noise and embossing to make a stucco-like texture is a favorite technique of mine. Try this effect:

1. Using the Text tool, type the word **NOISE** (Futura XBLK BT was used in the example).

2. In the Object roll-up, lock the background by clicking on the Lock icon.

3. Apply a Gaussian noise at a Level of 50% and a Density of 100%.

4. Next apply the Emboss filter under 3D Effects in the Effects menu. Select an emboss color (I chose gray for this sample). The resulting text texture is shown here. I placed a bitmap fill background behind the text so the image wouldn't appear to be sterile.

5. Apply a Motion Blur (Lower-Right with a setting of 5). This filter action smears the noise we applied to the text to give it a different texture. The pixels that are dragged off of the background onto the text provide subtle shading for the characters. The finished product is shown below (I added a simple drop shadow behind the text for a finishing touch).

Noise and Focus

Noise also has the ability to make the focus of an image appear sharper than it actually is. This is because the human eye believes images are in sharper focus when it see areas of higher contrast. So the viewer can be tricked into seeing an image as being in sharper focus by introducing a very small amount of Uniform noise onto a soft image. Applying small amounts of Uniform Noise to an image is often referred to as "dusting" the image. When you see the results you may think, at first, that nothing was accomplished. In fact, to the operator the image appears noisier. That's because (1) it does have more noise, and (2) you know what the original looked like before you added the noise. To a first time viewer of the photograph, it will appear sharper.

The Diffuse Filter

Before the Gaussian blur filter was added to Corel PHOTO-PAINT 5, the Diffuse filter was all that was available to blur an image. Corel's PHOTO-PAINT team received so many requests for Gaussian blur that it was added to Corel PHOTO-PAINT 5 in the first Maintenance release. So where does that leave the Diffuse filter? It still has uses. First, the Diffuse filter scatters colors in an image or a selected area, creating a smooth appearance. Unlike the Gaussian blur, the Diffuse filter scatters the pixels producing a harsher or grittier blur. So why is it in the Noise section of Effects? Because its operation is based on noise.

The Diffuse Filter Dialog Box

The Diffuse Filter dialog box is shown below. The operation of a majority of the controls on the dialog box is described in Chapter 8. Only the controls unique to this dialog box are described here.

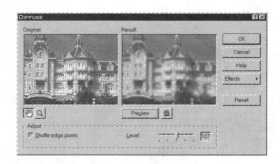

LEVEL The Level slider controls the amount of diffusion in the image. Set the level slider in the dialog box to a value between 1 and 255. The number specifies the number of shades that adjoining pixels are shifted, which controls the amount of diffusion of the selected image. Higher values produce more pronounced effects. Use the preview window to see the effects of different slider settings.

SHUFFLE EDGE PIXELS This check box, when enabled, causes the pixels that make up edges (areas of high contrast) to be affected. When it is not selected, the edges are maintained. In Figure 18-6, Shuffle edge pixels was not selected. As a result, the edges of the sailboat masts and numbers on the sails have been preserved. In Figure 18-7, Shuffle edge pixels was selected and the entire image has been diffused.

Notes on Using the Diffuse Filter

When selecting a level setting, watch the preview window for the appearance of an edge. When some objects are diffused at too high a setting, they develop an outline, which may be undesirable. To overcome this, do multiple applications of the diffuse filter at lower settings.

The Diffuse filter applied without Shuffle edge pixels selected preserves the edges in the photo

FIGURE 18-6

The Diffuse
filter applied
with Shuffle
edge pixels
selected
causes
the entire
photograph
to be
diffused

FIGURE 18-7

The Dust & Scratch Filter

The Dust & Scratch filter reduces image noise. Use this effect to eliminate dust and
scratch faults in an image. Located in the Effects menu under Noise, the Dust &
Scratch filter is not a magic cure-all. The best use of this filter is to first apply a mask
around the damaged areas of the image before selecting the effect. This will let you
eliminate the problem areas without affecting the rest of the image. The filter will
cause the area to which it is applied to have a softer appearance. To avoid the areas
affected being visible, when you create a mask, you should feather it before applying
the filter.

Dust & Scratch Filter Dialog Box

The dialog box, shown in the next illustration, operates like the others described in
this chapter. The controls unique to this filter are described below.

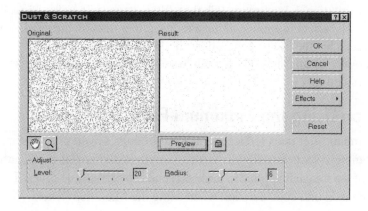

LEVEL   Adjust the Level slider to reduce image noise. The lower the setting, the greater the amount of noise removed. This is setting a threshold level; in other words, by setting it low, you are telling the filter that above the Level setting is considered noise.

RADIUS   Adjust the Radius slider to set the range of the effect. The Radius setting determines the number of pixels surrounding the noise that will be included in the removal process. Be advised that increasing the Radius setting increases the processing time for the filter's operation.

The Maximum Filter

The Maximum filter is not a traditional noise filter. Actually, it is a bit of a mystery why it's under Noise in the Effect menu. The Maximum filter lightens an image by adjusting the pixel values of the image, decreasing the number of colors. By using the slider, you can control the percentage of filtering that is applied. This filter provides a method of lightening an image without washing it out (as would happen with brightness or intensity adjustments). If you are an experienced Photoshop user, the Maximum filter that you are already used to does something different.

Fundamentally, Maximum as used in Photoshop creates a spread trap. In layman's terms, the Maximum filter spreads the white areas and chokes the black areas. Spreading and choking are used to compensate for minute misalignments in the printing process. While the Maximum filter in Corel PHOTO-PAINT can be used as a traditional Maximum (Choke) filter, it doesn't work as well as other programs. The effect is applied along a radius rather than on the pixel edge. (If you didn't understand the last sentence, don't bother rereading it. It will not become any clearer the second time around. If you live and breathe digital imaging and prepress, you understood it.)

Notes on Using the Maximum Filter

The Maximum filter does reduce the number of colors in an image area to achieve the lightening effect. In addition to color-depth reduction, it also causes a mild blurring of the image if applied in large percentages or multiple times. This blurring should be taken into consideration when using the Maximum filter.

The Median Filter

This filter reads the brightness of the pixels within a selection and averages them. Median simplifies an image by reducing noise (produced when pixels of different brightness levels adjoin one another) and by averaging the differences out of the selection.

The Median filter is used to smooth the rough areas in scanned images that have a grainy appearance. This filter uses a slider to set the percentage of Noise removal that is applied. The filter looks for pixels that are isolated and, based on the percentage setting in the dialog box, removes them.

Notes on Using the Median Filter

There is nothing magic about the Median filter. Its ability to remove noise is dependent on the type of noise (sharp and high-contrast or blurred and low-contrast) that is in the image. The Median filter tends to blur the image if it is set too high. Use the Result window to experiment with various settings. If a particular area of the image has noise, mask it off and apply the filter to the noisy areas rather than to the entire image.

The Minimum Filter

The Minimum filter, like the Maximum filter, is not a traditional noise filter. This filter darkens an image by adjusting the pixel values of the image, decreasing the number of colors. By using the slider, the percentage of filtering applied can be controlled. This filter provides a method of lightening an image without washing it out (as would occur using brightness or intensity). Converse to the Maximum filter, this filter spreads out black or dark areas into the white or light areas of an image.

Notes on Using the Minimum Filter

The Minimum filter reduces the number of colors in an image area to achieve the darkening effect. In addition to color-depth reduction, it also causes a mild blurring of the image if applied in large percentages or multiple times. This should be taken into consideration when using the Minimum filter.

What's Really Going On with the Maximum, Median, and Minimum Filters

These filters are each taking a look at an image's brightness values, pixel by pixel, and replacing adjacent pixels with the maximum or minimum brightness value of the neighboring pixel. Thus the name Maximum and Minimum. (The Median filter is, obviously, named after that thing in the middle of the highway.)

The Remove Noise Filter

This filter acts like a combination Jaggy Despeckle and Median filter. The Remove Noise filter softens edges and reduces the speckled effect created by the scanning process or from line noise in faxes. Each pixel is compared to surrounding pixels and an average value is computed. The pixels that then exceed the threshold set with the slider control in the dialog box are removed. This operates in the same manner as the Jaggy Despeckle does on objects (it reduces jaggies by softening edges), but, unlike Jaggy Despeckle, it also removes random pixels (noise) in the image.

The Remove Noise Dialog Box

The Remove Noise dialog box is shown in the next illustration. The operation of a majority of the controls on the dialog box is identical to the Add Noise filter described at the beginning of the chapter. The most important setting on this dialog box is the Auto check box. Use it!

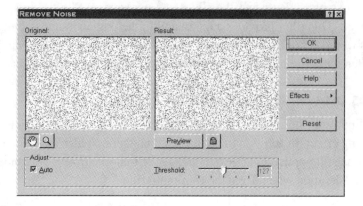

AUTO   The Auto check box, when enabled, automatically analyzes the image and determines the best Threshold setting for the image. The Threshold setting is not available when Auto is set.

THRESHOLD LEVEL   The Threshold slider controls the amount of threshold the program uses to differentiate between noise and non-noise. Set the level slider in the dialog box to a value between 1 and 255. Use the Preview Window to see the effects of different slider settings. While this slider can be set manually, I don't recommend it.

This filter is good for cleaning up faxes and poor scans. Like the other Noise filters, it cannot take a real garbage scan and make it look pristine. It can, however, take a poor scan and make it better.

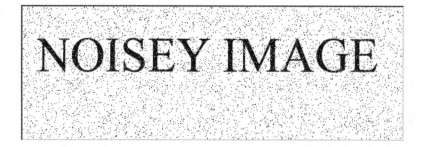

In the image above I applied Spike noise to a black-and-white image. This most closely resembles the noise one can expect in real life. Using the Auto setting, the Remove Noise filter lived up to its name and did an excellent job cleaning up the noise as shown below.

NOISEY IMAGE

IP: *The way to improve the performance of this filter on really trashy scans is to mask the worst areas and apply the Remove Noise filter to them first. This speeds up the operation (because the area is smaller) and also keeps the filter from modifying areas that do not need to have any noise removed.*

The Color Transform
Filters

19

This is a collection of six filters that cover the gamut of usefulness from the essential to the strange. Filters marked with an asterisk (*) are available with color only.

► Bit Planes filter
► Halftone filter*
► Invert filter
► Posterize filter
► Psychedelic filter*
► Solarize filter

The Bit Planes Filter

This filter, available with grayscale, 24-bit, and 32-bit color images, applies a posterization-style effect to each channel individually. The Bit Planes effect can be a powerful tool for analyzing gradients in images. The effect reduces the image to basic RGB color components and emphasizes tone changes. For example, different areas would appear as solid blocks since there is little change in tone. Since gradient fills have a high degree of color tone change, the Bit Planes effect is very useful for analyzing the number of steps in gradients.

The Color plane sliders control the sensitivity of the effect. Higher settings display fewer tone changes and gradient steps. At the highest setting, the image contains a large amount of black and white areas since the effect is displaying only extreme tone changes. Lower Color plane settings display more tone changes and gradations. At the lowest setting, a photographic image will appear like color noise, as subtle changes are virtually random. A graphic or computer-generated image will show salient contours of change in tone.

The Color sliders can be used separately to see the tone changes in a specific component color, or together to see all tone changes. The Bit Planes filter is used to provide unusual color effects to an image.

The Bit Planes Dialog Box

The Bit Planes dialog box is shown here. The operation of the common controls of the Bit Plane is described in Chapter 8. The controls that are unique to this filter are described as follows.

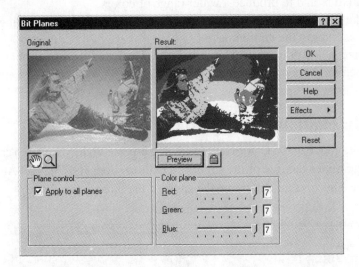

APPLY TO ALL PLANES When enabled, all of the color plane values change so that all of the plane values are identical.

COLOR PLANE Adjust the Color Plane sliders (Red-Green-Blue) to set the sensitivity of the color effect. Higher values display more course changes in tone. At the highest settings, the image will show large, flat areas with or without color, where the image is brightest and darkest. At the lowest settings, the image will show the finest level of tone variation. The result depends on the type of image to which you are applying the effect.

The Halftone Filter

The Color Halftone filter, only available with 24- and 32-bit color images, simulates the effect of using an enlarged halftone screen on each channel of the image. For each channel, the filter divides the image into rectangles and replaces each rectangle with a circle. The circle size is proportional to the brightness of the rectangle.

The Halftone filter converts color images into color halftone images. Use the Max Radius slider to control the maximum radius of a halftone dot, and the Cyan, Magenta, and Yellow slider bars to control the channel angle in order to determine the color mixture and to produce a wider range of colors.

Click the Preview button to display the effects of the current filter settings before applying this filter to the entire image.

So what can you do with the Halftone filter? The best I have been able to figure is to take perfectly good art and make it look like the DC Comics that were around when I was growing up.

The Color Halftone Dialog Box

The controls unique to the Color Halftone dialog box are divided into two areas. Dot Control determines the size of the simulated halftone dot. The Channel Angle area contains the controls that determine the angle of the three color channels.

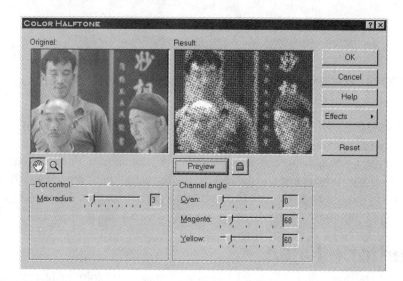

Using the Color Halftone Filter

▶ Select Color Transform from the Effects menu, and choose Color Halftone from the drop-down list. The Color Halftone dialog box will appear.

▶ Enter a value in the Dot Control section from 2 to 10, for the maximum radius of a halftone dot.

▶ Enter a screen-angle value for each channel. Click Reset to return all the screen angles to their default values. The values indicate the angle of the dot from true horizontal.

The Invert Filter

This filter, available with all images, is both the simplest and most essential filter. The Invert filter changes the colors in an image so that they appear as a photographic negative. While the ability to make a photographic negative is rarely needed, the Invert filter can be used to reverse a portion of the image to create interesting effects.

The dialog box doesn't have any settings. Click the Preview button to display the effects of the current filter settings before applying it to the entire image.

The uses for this filter are demonstrated throughout this book.

The Posterize Filter

This is the second most useful filter in this group. The Posterize filter, which only works on grayscale, 24-bit, and 32-bit color images, removes gradations, creating areas of solid colors or gray shades. This is useful when there is a need to simplify a complex color image without converting it to 256- or 16-color mode.

Another way to use this filter is to apply the Posterize effect selectively to individual channels through the Channels roll-up. Please note that individual color channels are grayscale images. Posterizing an image with a setting of three and four shades is a standard use of this filter. In Figures 19-1 through 19-4, I have created two examples with the Posterize filter.

Original
photograph
from
Corel's
World's
Best Digital
Photographs
collection

FIGURE 19-1

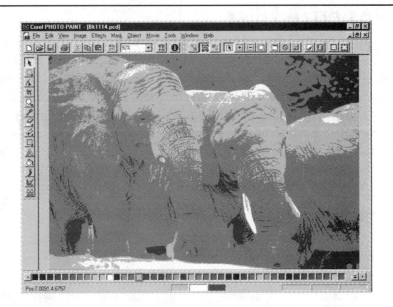

After the
application
of the
Posterize
filter at a
setting of 3

FIGURE 19-2

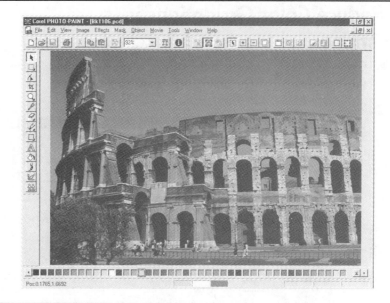

Original
photograph
from
Corel's
World's
Best Digital
Photographs
collection

FIGURE 19-3

Another
example of
posterization

FIGURE 19-4

To Reduce Color Gradations in an Image

▶ Choose Color Transform in the Effects menu and choose Posterize from the drop-down list. The dialog box opens as shown here.

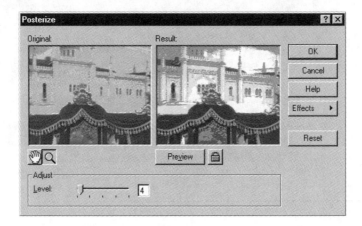

▶ Adjust the Level slider to specify the number of gray or color channels. The lower the value, the more pronounced the poster effect will be.

The Psychedelic Filter

If it isn't bad enough that the '60s are showing up in the fashion world, we now have this filter in the Corel PHOTO-PAINT program. (It has been said that if you clearly remember the '60s, you weren't really there. Perhaps this filter will bring them back to you.) The Psychedelic filter, only available with 24- and 32-bit color images, changes the colors in selected areas or images to bright, electric colors such as orange, hot pink, electric-banana yellow, cyan, lime green, and so on.

The Adjust level spans a range of 256 shades (0-255). Use in large doses and it can induce flashbacks. Use in small amounts to achieve the best effects..

 IP: *Use the Psychedelic filter to achieve bizarre or unusual effects with color backgrounds.*

The Solarize Filter

The Solarize filter, which is only available with grayscale, 24- and 32-bit color images, enables you to make an image look like a photographic negative. The effect will be more pronounced in color images. Solarize is an effect that, when applied to its maximum (255 shades), results in a negative or inverted image. It simulates an old photographic technique that required the photographic plate to be briefly exposed to sunlight outside of the camera. This resulted in the darkest areas being washed out. How washed out they were was determined by how long the plate was exposed. (The emulsions they had in the old days were very low speed and very, very slow.)

The Corel PHOTO-PAINT Solarize filter operates in a similar fashion, except that instead of entering in the time the image is in the sun, you can control the shades of color that will be affected by the filter (0 through 255). A setting of zero has no effect on the image. A maximum setting of 255 shades makes the image a complete negative.

The Solarize filter, like the Invert filter, transforms colors to appear like those of a negative photographic image. Unlike with the Invert filter (which produces an absolute effect where the image colors are completely inverted), you control the intensity of the effect to achieve different results. This effect will be more pronounced when applied to color images.

Its best use is to apply a partial inverted effect to an image. This limits its application to special effects and to backgrounds on color images. Although it can be applied to grayscale images, I only recommend its use with color images unless you are trying to create an artistic effect.

The Blur Filters

20

This is a fun chapter for me. There are so many things that you can do with the Blur filters, it's almost scary. Let's look at what filters are available under the name of Blur in the Effects menu. These filters are not listed in order of their appearance in the menu, but in order of their day-to-day usefulness. The first is the Gaussian Blur filter.

Gaussian Blur

This filter, although deceptively simple, is used every day to make shadows, produce glows, diffuse backgrounds, and in many of the special effects that are created with Corel PHOTO-PAINT. The Gaussian Blur filter produces a hazy effect that gives the image a slightly out-of-focus look. The filter can also be used to improve the quality of images with jaggies, although with some loss of detail. In digital photo-editing, you often hear the term *Gaussian*. I have been asked why Gaussian is capitalized and who is this person with a Blur filter named after him. Here is the scoop on Dr. Gauss.

How It Works

The term *Gaussian* comes from Dr. Carl Friedrich Gauss, a German mathematician who was born in 1777. Dr. Gauss did not invent the Gaussian Blur but he did discover the mathematical principles that the programmers use to create it. I thought it might be nice to show a picture of him, so I searched the archives of CompuServe and found the one shown here.

Dr. Gauss demonstrated the mathematical principle of normal distribution, which is the distribution of values described by what is called a *normal curve*. The few of you who actually stayed awake in Statistics 101 recognize normal distribution as one of the first things you were shown just before you dozed off. Because the shape resembles that of a bell, the curve is also known as a *bell-shaped* or *bell curve*.

When I was going to school (way back when) and everyone in the class was doing poorly, the teacher often graded "on the curve," meaning that all of the grades would have been distributed uniformly above and below the average of all the test scores. The result would have been a few "A"s, more "B"s, mostly "C"s, some "D"s, and a few "F"s. That is because the score necessary to get a grade of "C" would be the center of the curve (the average of all the scores), rather than an absolute, like 70 percent. This principle of Gaussian distribution is the principle on which the Gaussian Blur filter and many other tools in Corel PHOTO-PAINT work.

In photo-editing, the Gaussian Blur filter distributes the blur effect based on a bell-shaped curve. This curve is generated by mapping the color values of the pixels in the selected area and then distributing the blurring around the center value. So what's so hot about Gaussian blurring? Good question. It provides a true blurring, not a smearing, of the pixels, resulting in the blurred area appearing to be out of focus. End of history and math lessons. Next, you will learn how to use the filter and some of the effects you can create with it.

The Gaussian Blur Filter Dialog Box

The Gaussian Blur dialog box is opened by selecting Blur|Guassian Blur in the Effects menu. Here is the dialog box.

The dialog boxes of all of the filters in this chapter share many common elements. The description of the common controls can be found in Chapter 8. The controls that are unique to the filter dialog box are described in each filter description.

The Radius Slider

The Radius slider controls the amount of filter action. Adobe Photoshop users are accustomed to seeing three separate controls for Gaussian Blur. Corel PHOTO-PAINT has combined the functionality of three controls so that a single percentage setting will allow you to determine the filter's effect. While it can be argued that three separate control settings give the user a greater degree of control, I have found the single slider to be more than sufficient to produce the necessary blur.

To operate, set the Radius slider in the dialog box to a value between 1 and 50 percent to specify the degree to which you want to blur the selected image or masked area. For the more technically minded, the percentage would be more accurately described as *pixel radius*. With a setting of 5, the blur will be averaged over a radius of 5 pixels around each pixel in the image. The greater the Percentage slider setting, the greater the amount of blurring of the image. High percentage values (more than 30) can turn almost any image into fog. Use the preview window to see the effects of different slider settings before applying the filter. Click the OK button to apply the filter.

Subtle Emphasis by Creating a Depth of Field with Blurring

Look at Figure 20-1. This still life of some pears is pretty nifty (I think it was created in Painter 3.0). By applying a mild amount of blur to everything in the painting except the two pears in the foreground, we are able to make the pears appear to be closer to the viewer, as shown in Figure 20-2. This creation of a pseudo depth of field is a good way to subtly emphasize a subject without making a big show of it.

A second example is shown in Figures 20-3 through 20-5. With this photograph, if I had isolated the flowers and applied a Gaussian blur to the entire image, as was done with the pears, it would have looked strange. This is one of those situations in photo-manipulation where you have to remember how the human eye sees things. Objects near the viewer are usually slightly out of focus, while those further away are more out of focus. If you create effects that go against what our mind expects to see, it looks fake or artificial—even though the viewer in most cases cannot tell you why it looks fake.

To achieve the effect shown in Figure 20-5, I first masked the background and applied a Gaussian blur at a setting of 6 percent.

Next, the foreground (bottom of the photograph) was masked with a gradient fill mask that allowed the greatest amount of the blur to be applied to the bottom of

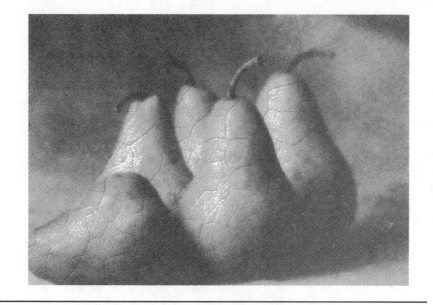

This is a great still life, but you want to emphasize the pear in the foreground

FIGURE 20-1

20

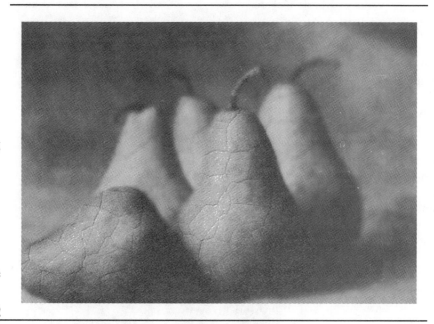

By applying a mild blur to everything but the two pears, you can make them stand out from the rest

FIGURE 20-2

Another example of selective blurring begins with this photograph, which is visually very busy

FIGURE 20-3

The gradient mask (shown by enabling the Mask Overlay feature) used to apply the blur effect to the bottom (foreground) prevents an abrupt transition that would be distracting

FIGURE 20-4

flower-blur-original.cpt

the other
flowers are
made less
distracting
by
application
of a
Gaussian
Blur

FIGURE 20-5

the photograph (the viewer's foreground). This is necessary for the blur to gradually blend into the flowers that are in focus. I have shown the mask (using the Mask Overlay feature) used for the application of blur in Figure 20-4. The amount of Gaussian Blur in the front is less because it needs to appear less out of focus than the background (top of photo). Finally, I applied the Gaussian Blur at a setting of 2 percent to the masked area. The finished product is shown in Figure 20-5.

The Shadow Knows...

One of the more useful features of the Gaussian blur is its ability to make very realistic-looking shadows. First, we will learn how to make a basic drop shadow against a solid background.

Drop Shadows

Drop shadows make objects appear real to the viewer. The first time I made a drop shadow in CorelDRAW, I thought it looked really slick. It looked a little like the next illustration, which I created in Corel PHOTO-PAINT.

Like I said, it looked slick but not very real. Next, in Corel PHOTO-PAINT I learned to use the Opacity control to give the shadows some transparency and then used the Feather in the Objects menu to take away some of the hard edges of the shadows. I have shown an example of this in the following illustration.

The best results are obtained when the text that makes the shadow has a Gaussian blur applied to it as shown below.

Making Shadows Using Gaussian Blur

This is a brief tutorial on how to make a simple but realistic drop shadow.

1. Create a new image file that is 600 x 200 pixels at a resolution of 100 dpi. Set the Color to grayscale, 24-bit, or 32-bit, and the Paper color to White.

2. Select the Text tool and click inside the image window.

3. Right-click inside the image window and a drop-down menu will appear. Choose Tool Settings roll-up.

 IP: *The right mouse button allows you to quickly get to related roll-ups of selected tools.*

4. From the Tool Settings roll-up, select PosterBodoni BT at a size of 72 points and check the anti-aliasing box. Click back in the image window and type **BIG SALE TODAY** (all caps). While this exercise can be done with any typeface, using the one specified will make your results look like the following illustration.

5. Select the Object Picker tool in the Toolbox. The text in the image window is automatically selected.

 IP: *If you don't want the blue marquee surrounding the text, select Marquee Visible in the Object menu.*

6. Choose Duplicate in the Object menu. A second copy of the text is created. Now there are two objects containing the same text. Right-click inside the image area. Choose the Objects roll-up from the drop-down list, which opens the Objects roll-up. You could name the objects in the

Objects roll-up "text" and "shadow," but with only two objects, it isn't really worth the effort.

7. At this point you are going to change the color of the top layer so that you can visually see what you are doing when you place the shadow in position. In the Objects roll-up, lock both the background and the bottom object by clicking on the lock icons. This prevents colors from being applied to either the shadow or the background.

8. Select the Draw Rectangle tool (F6) and, after checking the Tool Settings roll-up to make sure the fill color is set to a Uniform color (I used red), make sure the Width size is set to zero. With the left mouse button, click and drag a rectangle that covers all of the text. Because the top layer is unlocked, it (and nothing else) will change colors.

9. Select the text in the Objects roll-up and, using the Object Picker, click on the text in the image window and position the text above and to the left of the shadow as shown. Now we have two objects on the background. The top object is our red text and the bottom is the shadow.

10. Deselect the (Red) Text object by clicking on its icon. Select the shadow in the Objects roll-up and click the Combine Object with Background button. You now have only one object and the background.

IP: *Applying a Gaussian Blur to an object sometimes produces undesirable white halos on the object edge. Therefore, for shadows, it is recommended that the object be Combined with the background before applying the blur.*

11. In the Objects roll-up, unlock the background and lock the text. Select Blur from the Effects menu and choose Gaussian Blur from the drop-down list. From the filter dialog box, change the Percentage slider to

a setting of 6 and click the OK button. Your image should look like the following figure.

BIG SALE TODAY

Making Better Shadows

While the previous method makes great shadows, it doesn't work if you have a background that is not a uniform color. If the background has any pattern or detail to it, the application of the Blur filter will blur it as well. A second disadvantage to the previous method is that the shadow becomes combined with the background and cannot be moved. Here is a second method to produce a shadow that does not blur the background or produce a fixed position shadow.

1. Create a new image file that is 600 x 200 pixels at a resolution of 100 dpi.

2. Select the Text tool and click inside the image window.

3. Right-click inside the image window and a drop-down menu will appear. Choose Tool Settings roll-up.

4. From the Tool Settings roll-up, select any typeface (Lydian BT at a size of 72 points) and check the anti-aliasing box. Click back in the image window and type **BETTER SHADOWS** (all caps). Fill with Black.

5. Select the Object Picker and select the text. From the Object menu, choose Duplicate (or use CTRL-D). You now have two copies of the text.

6. Open the Objects roll-up (CTRL-F7) and hide the top object. This action also locks the object, preventing any actions from affecting it.

7. Select the other text object (which will become our shadow) and combine with the background by clicking the Combine button on the roll-up. It's the button to the left of the Trash Can (object delete) button. Don't worry about its placement in the image. At this point you have the text object (hidden for the moment) and a shadow that are combined with the background. With the text hidden (not necessary but visually easier to

20

work with), you are going to create a floating shadow with the blurred visible text.

8. Select the Rectangular Mask tool from the Toolbox and create a rectangular mask around the text as shown in the next illustration. Apply the Gaussian Blur effect from the Blur category in the Effects menu. Now the text is masked and ready to be created into an object using the Create Object button as indicated. Click the Create Object button in the Toolbar.

9. When an object was created from the mask, the new object was placed on the top layer. Since shadows need to be behind the subject, you need to change the order of the objects. Place your cursor on the description of the top object in the Objects roll-up. Click and drag the object so it is under the invisible text. Finally, hide (which automatically locks) the shadow object.

10. Either fill the background with a light detailed fill of your choice or use a fill provided on the Corel CD-ROM Disk #1 called …\FILLS\TILES \METAL\METAL04M. To use the Bitmap fill, select the Fill tool in the Toolbox. Open the Tool Settings roll-up and select Bitmap fill (checkerboard button). Click the Load button and in the next dialog box, click the Import button. In this dialog box locate the file …\FILLS\TILES \METAL\METAL04M. After the fill has been loaded, place the cursor in the image area and click the left mouse button. You can use the Fill tool or the Draw Rectangle tool to fill the image. The only difference is that to use the Fill tool, you must first erase the shadow in the background or the fill will go around it. To quickly remove it, select All from the Mask menu and then choose Clear in the Edit menu. The background must be unlocked in the Objects roll-up for that to work. Remove the mask when you are done by selecting None in the Mask menu.

11. Click on the Eye icon in the Objects roll-up to reveal the shadow text. Your image will look like the following figure. It doesn't look like a very realistic shadow at this point. It isn't necessary to name the layers in the Objects roll-up. I have only done it for clarity in the figures.

12. Here is the magic trick. With the shadow layer selected, choose Texturize in the Merge section of the Objects layer (Multiply will also work). The Merge mode allows you to make the white background disappear, producing a lovely shadow. Everything in the object that is white becomes transparent, creating a shadow on the background that is semi-transparent as shown in the next illustration.

IP: *If your shadow is too dark, don't attempt to change it using the Opacity settings. Because of the way the Merge mode works, decreasing the Opacity will cause the white rectangle object to begin to appear as a dark object. To change a shadow that is too dark, you must either go back and make another one using a lighter shade of gray, or lock all the other objects, return the Merge to normal, and apply the Gamma filter to the shadow.*

13. Reveal the text layer by clicking on its Eye icon. To make the text in this example stand out from the background, you need to make it a lighter color. Lock the shadow and background in the Objects roll-up. Select the

Draw Rectangle tool and, from the Tool Settings roll-up, choose the Uniform Color button and select a color you like. I picked white for the sample file because it gave the greatest contrast for the grayscale printing in this book. Drag a rectangle across the text and you are finished.

While there are many more things you can do with the Blur filter, they are discussed under different topics in the book. Now let's move on to my second favorite, the Motion Blur filter.

The Motion Blur Filter

The Motion Blur filter was designed to create the impression of movement in an image. It is supposed to achieve this effect by determining the edges of the image for the direction selected and smearing them into the adjacent pixels. I must point out that I rarely use the Motion Blur filter to give a sense of motion to a photo.

So what special effect can you achieve with the Motion Blur filter? The answer is shading of objects. When it is combined with other effects, this filter makes objects look 3D. Now for some basics.

The Motion Blur Filter Dialog Box

The dialog box is shown in the next illustration. There is a Percentage slider that provides speed value selection. The higher the speed percentage, the more blurring is applied. It also has a unique set of eight direction arrow buttons that allow the user to determine the direction of Motion.

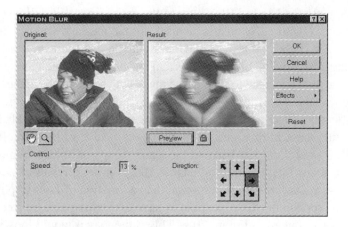

Using the Motion Blur Filter

The Motion Blur filter has many uses other than what its name describes. Throughout the book you will learn several techniques that can be done with the Motion Blur filter using tricks its original programmers never thought of. Remember not to let the name of a filter limit your imagination. The only way to find out what the large variety of filters included in Corel PHOTO-PAINT can do is to experiment with them. After all of this talk about non-motion special effects for the filter, it is only fair to actually show an example of using Motion Blur to give a sense of motion.

Using the Motion Filter to Give the Effect of Motion

The effectiveness of a motion blur filter depends a lot on selection of source material. Excluding surrealistic effects, the mind associates motion with certain subjects and not with others. An example of this association with motion is race cars. OK, I know it is trite, but it was all I could think of at the moment. Where was I? Oh yes, race cars. Let's look at how to apply the Motion Blur filter to a race car scene. Figure 20-6 shows a classic race car scene. Unfortunately, because high-speed film works so well, the image loses the feeling of speed. The cars all look like they are parked.

If you apply the Motion Blur filter to the entire image, it will just appear to be an out-of-focus picture. By creating a mask around the cars, you can limit the effect to just the cars. If you create a normal mask with hard borders, you will end up with hard borders, causing the blur to begins and end abruptly, which looks very strange. To eliminate this, you need to feather the mask with a wide soft feather. This is what was done with the race track photograph. The result is shown in Figure 20-7. Notice the front (leading edge) of the car that is in the center of the photograph. I deliberately left very little mask in that area so that it would receive little to no effect from the Motion Blur filter. I did this because the leading edge of objects in motion tends to be more in focus than the trailing edges. This is more a result of perceptions we humans have regarding things in motion than a function of laws of physics.

Another version of this concept is to have everything else blurred, leaving the cars in focus as shown in Figure 20-8. This is the way it would look if the camera was traveling at the same speed as the car it was photographing.

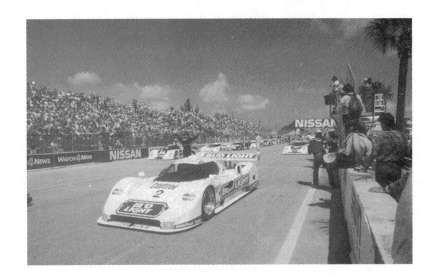

Without blurring, the race cars look like they are parked

FIGURE 20-6

Blurring makes the car look like it's moving

FIGURE 20-7

20

Blurring the background also gives the impression of speed

FIGURE 20-8

More Motion for Effect

I couldn't leave well enough alone. So here is another example of an ad made using the Motion filter. The original photograph of a race car driver is shown in Figure 20-9. Recognize the driver? If not, you are not spending enough time standing in grocery lines reading the cover of *The Sun.* The answer is . . . the UFO alien that visits all of the heads of governments. If you said it was Elvis, you get half credit for your answer. The ad wants to show the helmet made by the Fast Lane Helmet company of Toadsuck, Arkansas. The photograph of the helmet is very detailed. To give the ad some pizzazz, I masked off the front portion of the helmet and the man wearing it. Next, I feathered the mask with a big fat (40 pixels) soft feather. Then I applied a very small amount (setting of 2) of Motion Blur to this masked area so it won't look out of place when it is finished. This is important because if I did not do this, the masked area would look visibly different from the blurred area, thereby drawing attention to itself. Also, the Camel on the front of the helmet would be in crystal-clear focus and that too would be distracting. By adding a little bit of Motion Blur, I made it blend well with the rest of the helmet and helped impressionable children everywhere not see the name Camel and be overcome by an irresistible desire to begin smoking.

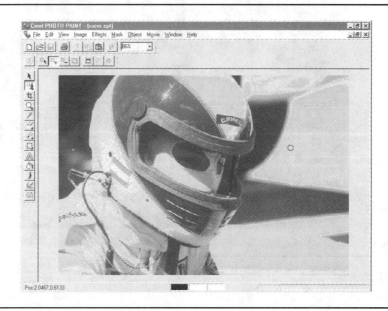

Excellent, highly detailed photograph of race car driver

FIGURE 20-9

The next step is to Invert the mask, apply a large setting (35) of the Motion Blur filter three times, and then apply a very small amount of the Sharpen filter to accentuate the blur lines. The result is shown in Figure 20-10.

 IP: *If you need to apply a large amount of the filter to create a special effect, you should make several applications of smaller values rather than one large application.*

The Jaggy Despeckle Filter

The Jaggy Despeckle filter scatters colors in an image to create a soft, blurred effect with very little distortion. It also smoothes out jagged edges (jaggies) on images. It is most effective in removing "jaggies" on high-contrast images. If the image has "jaggies," the Jaggy Despeckle filter will probably work well for you.

The Jaggy Despeckle Dialog Box

The Jaggy Despeckle dialog box, shown in the next illustration, offers options to control Height and Width values of diffusion separately or to keep the values identical if the Symmetrical check box is selected. Setting the values independently

After multiple applications of the Motion Blur filter and a little text, we have an ad for Fast Lane Helmets

FIGURE 20-10

offers a mild diffusing of the image while keeping image detail loss to a minimum.

Using the Jaggy Despeckle Filter

This filter will not work with line art, images composed of only black-and-white pixels. The image must be either grayscale or color. When applied to a photograph, it has a tendency to blur the image slightly, depending on your setting. Jaggy Despeckle operates by performing edge detection on the image. After the filter thinks it knows where all the hard edges are, it applies anti-aliasing to the edges to give them a smoother appearance. Figure 20-11 shows a portion of a script letter magnified at 500 percent. This is a worst case for a bitmap graphic. Diagonal lines, zoomed in at 500 percent, and little to no gray areas. A perfect candidate for Jaggy Despeckle.

The Jaggy Despeckle was applied at the default settings, resulting in the improvement you see in Figure 20-12. After the application of the Jaggy Despeckle filter, the "jaggies" have been visibly reduced. Don't forget you are looking at 500 percent zoom level. In day-to-day operations, I have found very little use for this filter. Maybe you will be more fortunate.

The Directional Smooth Filter

The Directional Smooth filter analyzes values of pixels of similar color shades to determine in which direction to apply the greatest amount of smoothing. Sounds great, right? As great as the description sounds, it is a Blur filter. It and the following

This is a
close-up of
some text at
500% zoom

FIGURE 20-11

The Jaggy
Despeckle
filter helps
smooth the
edges

FIGURE 20-12

two filters (Smooth and Soften filters) are nearly identical in their operation, although the results obtained are mildly different.

The Directional Smooth Filter Dialog Box

All of the controls in the Directional Smooth dialog box are the same as those previously described in the Gaussian Blur dialog box.

Using the Directional Smooth Filter

Set the Percentage slider in the dialog box to enter a value between 1 and 100 percent to specify the degree to which you want to apply directional smoothing to the selected image. Higher values produce more pronounced effects. Use the preview window to see the effects of different slider settings.

The Smooth Filter

The Smooth filter tones down differences in adjacent pixels, resulting in only a slight loss of detail while smoothing the image or the selected area. The differences between the effect of the Smooth and Soften filters is subtle and may only be apparent on a high-resolution display and sometimes not even then.

The Soften Filter

The Soften filter smoothes and tones down harshness without losing detail. The differences between the effect of the Smooth and Soften filters is subtle and may only be apparent on a high-resolution display or in the mind of the person who programmed this filter.

Where's the Beef?

So what is the difference between the way that Smooth and Soften work? Very little. Don't spend a lot of time trying to determine if you need to use Soften or Smooth. The results obtained with each filter will appear to be identical in most cases. When trying to decide which one to use, choose the Gaussian Blur.

Getting It All Together—the Blur Control

New to Corel PHOTO-PAINT 6 is the Blur option, found in the Effect menu, under Adjust. Enabling this opens a very large dialog box called Blur Control, shown in the following illustration, that displays thumbnails side by side, showing the results of applying each of the five Blur filters—Gaussian Blur, Motion Blur, Smooth, Directional Smooth, and Soften—to the current image. Blur control should not be confused with government information agencies.

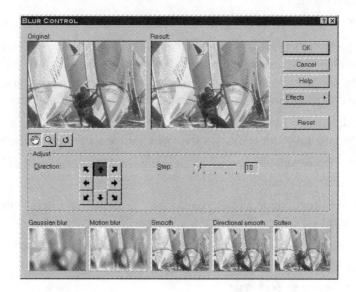

The Blur Control Dialog Box

This provides a quick way to compare the results of different filters side by side. The operation is centered on the Before/After format, which appears in windows called Original and Result at the top of the dialog box. Clicking the thumbnail of the desired filter applies the filter to the image in the Result window. To Undo the last filter application, you can click the Undo button that is to the right of the Zoom button. Repeatedly clicking this button lets you step back through a group of effects applied. Different filters can be applied multiple times using the Blur Control dialog box.

- ▶ The **Original** (before) window never changes and always reflects the current image or the portion of the image that is masked.

- ▶ The **Result** (after) window shows the effects of the applied filter.

- ▶ The **Steps** slider controls the number of steps for all of the filters simultaneously. For example, a setting at 10 means this setting would be applied each time the Motion Blur thumbnail, or any of the other filters, is clicked. This is important since a setting of 10 would be very small and therefore impossible to see with either the Smooth, Soften, or Directional Smooth filter.

- ▶ **Direction Arrows** are used to select the direction of the Motion Blur.

- ▶ The **Help** button opens our ever-sensitive context-sensitive Help screen. You can also display information about a specific button by right-clicking the button or control. When the What's This? message appears, click on it with the left mouse button. A description of the tool/function is displayed.

- ▶ Click on the **Undo** button to undo the last action taken. Repeatedly clicking this button lets you step back through a group of effects applied.

- ▶ The **Reset** button resets all of the images and settings in Blur Control to their default values.

- ▶ The **Filters** button allows you to open up additional filters without closing this dialog box.

- ▶ If you are wondering what **Cancel** does, I am seriously worried about you.

The Low Pass Filter

Also found in the Blur drop-down list, the Low Pass filter is not a traditional Blur filter, which is why it has been mentioned only at the end of the chapter. The effect of this filter is to remove highlights and color from an image, leaving shadows and low-frequency detail. The dialog box contains two Slider bars, one for Percentage and the other for Radius. The Percentage value controls the intensity of the effect and Radius controls the range of pixels that are affected. At higher settings, the Low Pass filter creates a blurring effect, which is why it is in the Blur filter section. This action erases much of the image's detail. If you need only to deemphasize (smooth) highlights, use a lower percentage setting.

Congratulations, you have made it through yet another chapter of filters. The next chapter is how to use the Sharpen filters. I figured after you had blurred the image, you might want to know how to sharpen it up.

The Sharpen Filters

21

The Sharpen subgroup of the Effects menu contains six filters that provide a wide range of sharpening effects that can be used to both improve image quality and create special effects. By increasing the contrast between neighboring pixels, sharpening filters enable you to compensate for images or image elements that were photographed or scanned slightly out of focus. Without some degree of sharpening, a scanned or Photo-CD image will look "soft" when printed. The human eye looks for edges, and so edges are accentuated through contrast. If too much sharpening is applied, the images gain too much contrast.

The best time to apply sharpening is when an image is scanned. I have seen several comparisons between images that were sharpened during scanning and those done with Sharpen filters after the scan. The scanned images were visibly sharper. Of course, if you are using a Photo-CD or other source, your image is already scanned, so if you want to sharpen it, you will need to use one of the filters included with Corel PHOTO-PAINT 6. Before we discuss the various Sharpen filters, it would be beneficial to understand a little about how these very important filters operate—most importantly, how they affect different parts and types of images.

How Sharpening Affects Noise

All computer images include noise. Noise is unwanted pixels that may appear as a grainy pattern or as the odd dark or light spot. Images from photographs will always have noise. The noise associated with camera film is called *grain*. Actually, any image, including those captured with digital cameras, will have noise of some sort. The most pristine photo in your stock photo collection that was scanned on a ten-zillion dollar drum scanner will exhibit some noise. The only exception to this concept of universal noise is a Uniform color fill which has no noise—or detail. Are you beginning to wonder if this chapter was supposed to be in another part of the book, on noise? Not to worry. This really is the Sharpen chapter, and there is a reason for this noisy introduction.

So why do we care about noise in the Sharpen chapter? Because when we sharpen an image, we "sharpen" the noise as well. In fact, the noise generally sharpens up much better and faster than the rest of the image, which is undesirable.

Why does noise sharpen up so well? Because noise (like the tiny white specks in a black background) appears in sharp contrast to its background. These unwanted high-contrast visitors are usually so small as to not be noticed. But, since they are high contrast, they contain the one component that sharpening filters look for, which is differences between adjoining pixels. The act of sharpening seeks out the differences (edges) and increases the contrast at those edges. That's what makes noise so noticeable after a Sharpen filter is applied. The existing edges of the noise are enhanced and enlarged more than the rest of the pixels in the image. That is why they show up against the adjacent pixels so well.

A Noisy Demonstration

To illustrate how noise rears its ugly head, I have scanned in a photograph of Sandy, a good friend of mine who has always wanted to have her picture in a nationally published book (not the kind with fold-out pages). Figure 21-1a shows a normal scan with no sharpening applied. It is one of those "glamour shots"—always (intentionally) a little out of focus—so popular these days at the shopping malls.

Next, I masked only the dark areas of the photograph (background and gloves) and applied a large amount of the Sharpen filter to the masked area. The result, shown in Figure 21-1b, looks like she had dandruff and it got on the black curtain. The white specks in the background are the enhanced noise. The noise in the background was always there; the application of the Sharpen filter made it visible. As point of clarification, there are a group of filters called the Sharpen filters and in that group there is a filter called the Sharpen filter. When I talk about the Sharpen filter, I am referring to the specific filter and not to a general type of filter.

So, does this mean you can't use the Sharpen filter or the other Sharpen filters? Not at all. We are discussing this because it's important to be aware of potential pitfalls lurking in your photographs, especially those that are scanned on a machine that hasn't had its glass cleaned in a while. Now we will see how the filters that are categorized as Unsharp filters get around this noise problem.

Unsharping the Noise

If we can't sharpen the image without enhancing the noise, we can minimize the effect of the noise by distorting the image. Don't panic—when I say distortion, I mean distortion in the technical sense, not the kind that produces a distorted image. The distortion I am referring to has the effect of toning down the sharp borders of noise while providing general sharpening of the other pixels in the image. The result is an overall sharpening of the image without enhancing the noise. This is how the

a) Here is Sandy before Sharpening is applied. b) After Sharpening, the photo looks like a dandruff commercial

FIGURE 21-1

Unsharp filters in Corel PHOTO-PAINT work. These filters have a strange name. In the trade they are generically referred to as Unsharp Masking filters (USM). The name *unsharping* is confusing to first-time users of photo-editing programs. Unsharping is named after a traditional film compositing technique that highlights the edges in an image by combining a blurred film negative with the original film positive, which results in a sharper image without enhancing the noise.

The Sharpen Filters

Now, let's actually look at the filters and what they do and don't do. The Sharpen subgroup of the Effects menu has the following filters:

- ► Adaptive Unsharp
- ► Directional Sharpen
- ► Find Edges
- ► High Pass
- ► Sharpen
- ► Unsharp Mask

Three of these filters, Adaptive Unsharp, Unsharp Mask, and Directional Sharpen, act in roughly the same way and can be grouped together. Like the Unsharp filters mentioned previously, they enhance the image while introducing small amounts of distortion to reduce noise enhancement. The Sharpen filter is a true Sharpen filter that sharpens both the image and its noise equally. The last filter is the Find Edges, which is not a traditional sharpening filter. It is in the Sharpen group because internally it uses the same sharpening techniques to determine the edges in an image. Let's look at the filters a little more closely.

Adaptive Unsharp, Unsharp Mask, and Directional Sharpen Filters

I have grouped these filters together because the difference between their operation and the results they produce is very slight. I have spent quite a bit of time making sample images and trying to see the differences between them at various settings. I have come to the following conclusions.

- ► **The Unsharp Mask and Adaptive Unsharp filters** both sharpen the image while controlling the enhancement of noise.

► **The Adaptive Unsharp filter** produces good sharpening with a slightly higher contrast than the Unsharp Mask.

► **The Directional Sharpen** also produces good sharpening, but with higher contrast than the other two. Please note that the differences in contrast between all three of these filters is very slight.

The Filter Dialog Box

The dialog boxes of all of the filters share many common elements. The common controls for this filter are discussed in Chapter 8. Only the controls unique to the filter are described in this chapter.

THE PERCENTAGE SLIDER   This slider controls the amount of filter action. Traditionally, Unsharp-style filters have two or three separate controls. Corel PHOTO-PAINT has combined the functionality of three controls so that a single percentage setting will allow you to control the filter's effect. The exception is the Unsharp Mask filter.

To operate, you may set the percentage slider in the dialog box to a value between 1 and 100 percent to specify the degree to which you want to sharpen the selected image. Higher values produce more pronounced effects. Use the preview window to see the effects of different slider settings.

THE RADIUS SLIDER   This slider has a range of 1 to 20 pixels. It controls the size of the sampling area (in pixels).

Notes Common to Adaptive Unsharp, Unsharp Mask, and Directional Sharpen

These filters produce a subtle effect. It is not uncommon to make several applications of 100 percent. Beware of applying too much sharpening, however. At some point the image will begin to take on a distorted look when too much Unsharp masking is applied.

The best approach for applying these filters is to use the Checkpoint Command to save a copy of the image before you begin to apply the filters. Next, apply the filter in 50 percent increments and evaluate how it looks after each application by using the Full Screen Preview (F9). Use the ESC or ENTER key to return.

Notes about Adaptive Unsharp

The effect of the Adaptive Unsharp filter is very similar to the other two Unsharp filters. Testing done while writing the book has shown some subtle differences. The

Adaptive Unsharp seems to produce slightly less contrast than either the Unsharp Mask or Directional Sharpen filters.

Directional Sharpen

The Directional Sharpen filter analyzes values of pixels of similar color shades to determine the direction in which to apply the greatest amount of sharpening. That's what the help file says it is supposed to do. I have found that the Directional Sharpen filter usually increases the contrast of the image more than the Unsharp Mask filter does.

Sharpen

The most important thing to remember about sharpening an image is that the Sharpen filter is rarely the best filter to use. Use one of the three filters discussed in the previous paragraphs. Why? Because the Sharpen filter doesn't care about noise, it just sharpens everything in the photograph. It is a powerful filter that will blow the socks off of your image if you are not careful. The Sharpen filter, shown in the next illustration, sharpens the appearance of the image or a masked area by intensifying the contrast of neighboring pixels. There are times when this filter may be preferred over any of the previously described filters, but they are rare.

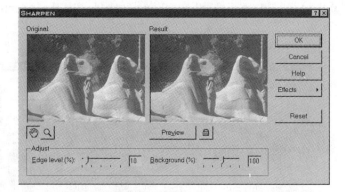

Using the Sharpen Filter

Most of the controls on the Sharpen filter dialog box operate in the same manner as the filters previously discussed in this chapter. The new controls are Edge Level (0-100%) and Background (0-200%).

THE EDGE LEVEL SLIDER   This slider controls the amount of sharpening applied to the photograph. Use this filter at higher settings with some degree of caution. I have included several images to show you the effects of different Edge Level settings. The Background setting in all of this is kept at its default setting of 100 percent (which we will see later is functionally a zero setting). Set the Edge Level slider in the dialog box to a value between 1 and 100 percent to specify the degree to which you want to sharpen the selected image. Higher values produce more pronounced effects. Use the preview window to see the effects of different slider settings.

 IP: *Unlike the previously discussed filters, the Sharpen filter has a much greater effect at 5 percent than the USM filters do at the 100 percent level.*

THE BACKGROUND SLIDER   The Background slider is a percentage slider that goes from zero to 200 percent.

Find Edges

This filter is unlike any other filter in this chapter. Even though it is not a general image enhancement tool like the Sharpen filters, it allows you to obtain some effects that would not be otherwise possible.

Find Edges dialog box

Operation of the Find Edges dialog box, shown here, is like the Adaptive Unmask filter dialog box.

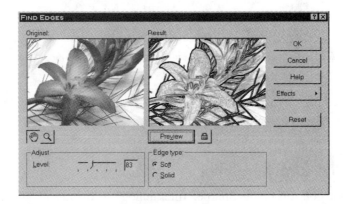

THE LEVEL SLIDER   The Level Slider controls the threshold that triggers the Find Edges filter. As the value increases, the threshold decreases, allowing the filter to include more of the edge. As the slider value decreases, less of the edge component is included, making the edges thinner and therefore lighter. Adjust the Level slider to define a sensitivity value. The higher the number, the more edges are enhanced.

THE EDGE TYPE SETTING   The Edge Type Setting determines the type of outline produced. For dark bold lines, choose Solid. For lighter, more diffused outlines, choose Soft.

So What Can You Do with Find Edges?

I have given you two sets of images to demonstrate both the range of the filter and some different applications with which it can be used. At a setting of 50, the flower shown in Figure 21-2a appears to be a charcoal outline. Changing the Level slider to 80 causes the edges to expand, making it darker as shown in Figure 21-2b.

The Find Edges filter can also create an outline effect. The first step is to place some text over the photographs of leaves, as shown in Figure 21-3a. The Find Edges filter determines the edges on everything in the image and removes everything that is not an edge. The Level Setting for the image shown in Figure 21-3b was 80, which produced darker lines.

Making Pencil Sketches with Find Edges

One of the unique things you can do with Find Edges is make fake pencil sketches. The next illustration is a beautiful flower shot against a black background. Because Find Edges looks only for edges, the black background will go away immediately when the filter is applied.

Now, if I wanted to use it for a brochure or a flyer, I could mask out the background and have a photograph of a flower. Or, I could apply the Find Edges to it and have what appears to be a pencil sketch of the same flower, as shown on page 11.

The effect
of different
level
settings
with the
Find Edges
filter is
shown:
a) at 50 and
b) at 80

FIGURE 21-2

a) Original
photograph.
b) After
applying the
Find Edges
filter

FIGURE 21-3

I saved the flower as a CPT file and then imported it into CorelDRAW. Next, I duplicated it several times and added text as shown in Figure 21-4. It took a total of four minutes. When trying to make what looks like a pencil sketch, dark images work better than light images. Your subject should be easily recognizable, for example, a person, a barn, or a flower. If the photograph is complex, try masking the part that you want before applying the filter. Finally, if you are not getting satisfactory results, you may want to apply a large amount (20-40) of Contrast (located in Effects|Color Adjust|Brightness-Contrast-Intensity) and then apply the Find Edges filter.

Using a single photograph of a flower and the Find Edges filter, we were able to make an attractive banner for a menu

FIGURE 21-4

High Pass Filter

I placed this filter last because it is unique. Officially, the High Pass filter removes low-frequency detail and shading, and emphasizes highlights and luminous areas of an image. This filter enables you to isolate high-contrast image areas from their low-contrast counterparts. The action of the filter makes a high-contrast image into a murky gray one. Now you may rightly ask why you would ever want a filter to do something like that. The answer is that this filter is best used as preparation for other filter actions. The dialog box is shown in the next illustration, followed by a description of the slider actions.

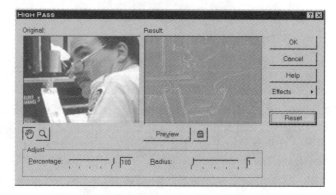

THE PERCENTAGE VALUE SLIDER   The Percentage value controls the intensity of the effect. The default setting is 100 percent, which is far too high for many applications. Low Percentage values distinguish areas of high and low contrast only slightly. Large values change all high-contrast areas to dark gray and low-contrast areas to a slightly lighter shade of gray. At higher settings, the High Pass effect removes most of the image detail, leaving only the edge details clearly visible. If you only want to emphasize highlights, use lower percentage settings.

THE RADIUS SLIDER   The Radius setting determines how many pixels near the edge (areas of high contrast) are included in the effect. The result is, the higher the setting, the more contrast is preserved.

So What Can You Do with the High Pass Filter?

The High Pass filter is especially useful as a precursor to the application of the Level Threshold filter. By first applying different levels of High Pass to an image, you can produce a wide variety of effects with the Level Threshold filter.

You can also use it to help differentiate objects in an image when creating a mask. This is because the High Pass filter sees an image in terms of contrast levels, which is one of the ways your eyes perceive images in real life. Using the High Pass filter as the first step helps in the creation of a mask of an image element that is visually unique but proves difficult to isolate with a mask. By applying the High Pass filter set to a Percentage level of 50 percent and a Radius of 20, you can often create an outline around the object you want to isolate. After the mask is created, save it and use the Revert command to restore the image to its last saved state. Then reload the mask.

Sharpen Control

Now that you know what all of the Sharpen filters do, you can see them all (except High Pass) at once with the Sharpen Control dialog box, shown in the following illustration, which is accessed by choosing Sharpness in the Adjust portion of the Effects menu.

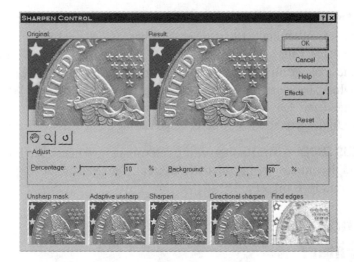

This provides a quick way to compare the results of different filters side by side. The operation is centered on the Before/After format. The windows, called Original/Result Pick, are at the top of the dialog box. Clicking the thumbnail of the desired filter applies the filter to the image in the Result window. To Undo the last filter application, you can click the Undo button that is to the right of the Zoom button. Repeatedly clicking this button lets you step back through a group of effects applied. Different filters can be applied multiple times using the Sharpen Control dialog box.

The 2D Effect Filters

22

This group of filters comprises some of the most unusual and complex in Corel PHOTO-PAINT 6. Many of the 2D filters are not needed for day-to-day photo editing but can be genuine life-savers in some situations. Many of the filters are new with the release of Corel PHOTO-PAINT 6; others are in Corel PHOTO-PAINT 5 under different names or categories. Enough introduction; let's begin working with the filters.

The Band Pass Filter

Leading off the lineup in the 2D Effect category is the Band Pass filter. This is one of those "what does it do again?" filters. According to the excellent Corel online Help, this filter "lets you adjust the balance of sharp and smooth areas in an image." The description is accurate. The Band Pass allows you to define a specific portion of the image and either enhance or reduce that component. Still fuzzy? It may help to think of this as a visual graphic equalizer. Look at the dialog box, shown in the next illustration.

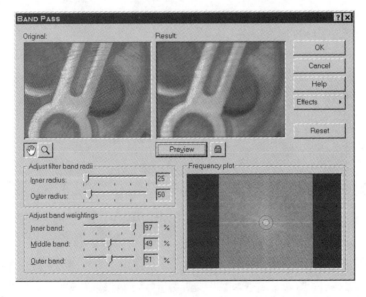

In the lower right is a frequency plot graph that shows the occurrence of sharp and smooth areas in the image. Smooth areas are displayed closer to the center, and sharp areas are shown around the edges of the graph. By adjusting the inner and outer radius sliders, you define what portion of the image's smooth/sharp areas are included or filtered out, which allows you to screen out unwanted features in your image. For example, a low weighting for the center of the plot will emphasize the image detail, while a low weighting for the outside of the plot will reduce image detail.

Reading the Frequency plot can be a little tricky at first. The area outside of the larger red circle is the Outer band; the area outside of the smaller red circle but inside the larger one is the Middle band. Everything inside of the smaller red circle is the Inner band. Use the Inner/Outer radius slider to determine which areas of the image (by frequency content) are in the Inner, Outer, and Middle bands. Then adjust the Inner, Outer, and Middle band sliders to set the intensity of each band. To eliminate either the sharp or smooth areas within a band, set the weighting to 0. To emphasize them, set the slider to the maximum of 100%.

Experiment with different weightings to see which provide the best results. For example, you can use the bands to eliminate unwanted noise by isolating the frequency of the noise within the middle band and reducing its weighting to 0. The only challenge you may experience with this filter is that it is very complex and therefore quite slow in its operation. I thought it was slow and I am using a Pentium at 90MHz.

The Displace Filter

This filter may be my favorite addition to the Corel PHOTO-PAINT 6 release. The Displace filter enables you to distort or add texture to an image by moving individual pixels. The direction and distance that the pixels move are determined by a second image called a *displacement map*. The brightness values of the pixels in the displacement map tell Corel PHOTO-PAINT 6 which pixels to move and how far to move them. It is important to remember that we are talking about Brightness values, so the following three values apply to grayscale and color images. The three determining brightness values are:

▶ **Black** Areas in the displacement map that contain black will move the corresponding pixels in an image being affected to the right and/or down by the maximum amount defined by the Scale settings in the Displace dialog box. Lighter values between black and 50 percent gray move pixels a shorter distance.

► **White**   Areas in the displacement map that contain white will move the corresponding pixels in an image being affected to the left and/or up by the maximum amount defined by the Scale settings in the Displace dialog box. Darker values between white and 50 percent gray move pixels a shorter distance.

► **Middle gray**   Areas in the displacement map that are composed of gray with a brightness of 50 percent cause the pixels to remain unmoved.

Are you confused? Let's look at some pictures. Figure 22-1a shows the original image from the Corel PHOTO-PAINT CD-ROM. In Figure 22-1b I have loaded one of the displacement maps provided with Corel PHOTO-PAINT 6. It is shown at a magnification of 1600 percent on the right. One the left is a duplicate of the displacement map at 100 percent so you can see how small it is in relation to the original. The results of applying the displacement filter using the pyramid displacement map are shown in Figure 22-1c.

A Quick Tour of the Displace Filter

Now let's take a quick tour of the Displace filter. In this simple exercise we are going to take an existing image and change its overall appearance to make it look like mosaic tile.

1. Using the File Open command in the File menu, open the image 265054.JPG located in THE IMAGES\PHOTOS\DESIGN folder of either CorelDRAW 6 CD-ROM Disk # 3 or the Corel PHOTO-PAINT 6 CD-ROM.

2. Under 2D Effects in the Effects menu, select Displace…. This opens the filter's dialog box. Locate and click the Load button on the right side of the dialog box. This opens the Import dialog box and COREL\PHOTOPNT\DISPLACE, which is the default location for the displacement maps provided with Corel PHOTO-PAINT 6.

3. Locate the file PIXELATE.PCX and either double-click on it or select it and click the Open button. On the left side of the dialog box under Undefined areas, select Warp around. By selecting this feature, we are instructing Corel PHOTO-PAINT to take pixels from the opposite side of the image to fill in any space left by the shifting of pixels near the edge. If we had left the Repeat Edges option set, Corel PHOTO-PAINT would have duplicated the edges to fill in the area. If the displacement is larger than a few pixels, the result would be a smearing of the pixels. Keep the

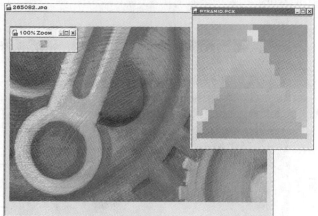

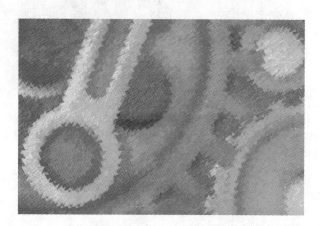

a) The original image. b) The displacement map used to modify the image. c) The result of applying the displacement map

FIGURE 22-1

Tile option selected and the Scale Values set to the default value of 10. Click the OK button and the image becomes "pixelated." Looks sort of like mosaic, but we are not done yet.

4. Many effects you see in covers for annual reports and book jackets have been created using more than one filter. To make the mosaic tile, we will next use the Emboss filter located under 3D Effects. Set the Direction setting to 45, Depth setting to 1, and ensure that the Emboss color is set to Original color. Click the OK button. The result is something that looks very much like mosaic tile.

The Displace Filter Dialog Box

Let's look at the Displace filter dialog box, shown here, and discuss how the rest of the controls work.

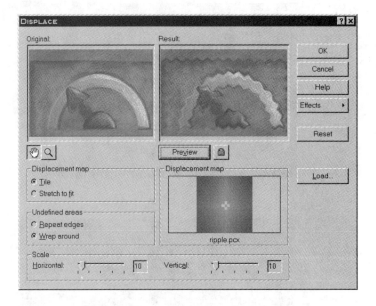

The Displace filter controls are divided into four general areas: Load Displacement Map, Displacement map controls, Undefined areas controls, and Scale sliders.

LOAD DISPLACEMENT MAP   This button opens the Import dialog box and is used to select and load the desired Displacement map.

DISPLACEMENT MAP PREVIEW   This area displays a thumbnail or the selected displacement map and the map's filename.

DISPLACEMENT MAP   The two buttons in this area allow the selected displacement map to be tiled or be stretched to fit. If the displacement map contains fewer pixels than the image, then the Tile option is selected and the displacement map is tiled beginning in the lower-left corner. The Stretch To Fit option makes the displacement map the same size and aspect ratio as the image. If the displacement map is very small in relation to the image, distortion of the map will result.

UNDEFINED AREAS   The two buttons control how shifted pixels on the edge will be replaced. The Repeat edges setting copies the edges of the image to fill in any undistorted areas. If the pixels are shifted a large distance in relation to the image, smearing results. The Warp around setting wraps the images so that the undistorted area is filled with the opposite side of the image. If the affected pixels are not near the edge of the image, then this setting has no effect.

SCALE   The Horizontal and Vertical sliders let you specify the distance the Displace filter moves the pixels as a percentage. At 100 percent, the black and white areas can move pixels a maximum distance of 128 pixels. That is because there are 256 shades of brightness, so each extreme (black or white) can displace the pixels in the image half of that distance ($256/2 = 128$). For example, if I have a black square in the displacement map, and the Horizontal set to 50 percent, the pixels in the image that are displaced by the black squares will move to the right 64 pixels (50 percent of 128).

Suggestions for Creating Displacement Maps

I know this filter sounds very complicated and I speak from experience when I tell you that it is possible to waste hours playing with it. Here are some practical suggestions for working with the Displace filter.

Remember that 50 percent gray is the neutral color that keeps the pixels from moving; therefore, it is a good background color when creating a displacement map.

Next, when making displacement maps, keep the image area small. Some of the most effective displacement maps that Corel provided are only 14 x 14 pixels. Keep the Horizontal and Vertical displacement settings small for the best effects. Also, you will find that the best displacement maps are those that contain smooth transitions between the bright and dark components. Resolution and file formats are not critical factors

The Edge Detect Filter

This filter is similar to the Find Edges filter in the Sharpen group of the Effects menu. This little jewel lets you make outlines of high-resolution photographs. In the original photograph, shown in Figure 22-2a, I have blurred the grass (removed edges) that surrounded the train so that it would be invisible to the filter.

The operation of the Edge Detect filter is extremely simple. The Edge Detect filter dialog box, shown in Figure 22-2b, has only two areas in which to make a choice. The first involves choosing the Background Color. The other is setting the Sensitivity slider (1-10), which determines the intensity of edge detection. Move the slider to the right to increase the effect, which means that more of the original area surrounding the edges is included.

The Edge Detect filter is then applied, making a fairly good pencil sketch of the train and the station, as seen in Figure 22-2c.

The Offset Filter

The Offset filter moves an image according to a specified number of pixels or a percentage of image size. We are not talking about moving an object. This filter actually moves pixels in an image. It is a favorite of those Photoshop users who were heavily involved in channel operations (CHOPS). This filter was critical to many operations before the advent of objects and layers. It allowed you to create an image and then save it to a channel, offset the duplicate, and create highlights and shadows. Today it is easier to do that by creating objects and positioning the objects. Having said that, there are still uses for the Offset filter. First, let's explore what it does and how it does it.

The Offset Filter Dialog box

The Offset filter dialog box, shown on page 436, provides many options for the Offset effect.

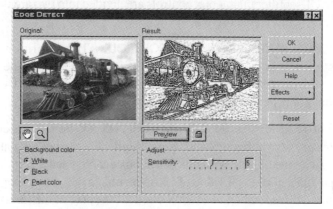

a) The original photograph.
b) The Edge Detect filter dialog box.
c) The result is a pencil sketch of the train

FIGURE 22-2

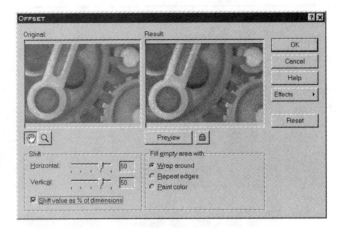

The Offset filter dialog box controls are divided into two areas: the Shift controls and the Fill empty area options.

HORIZONTAL AND VERTICAL SHIFT CONTROLS   These sliders determine the amount of shift in the Horizontal and Vertical. The values in the boxes to the right of the sliders represent either the number of pixels shifted or the percentage, depending on whether the Shift value box is checked.

SHIFT VALUE AS PERCENTAGE OF DIMENSIONS   When enabled, it causes the coordinates of the horizontal and vertical shift values to be calculated as a percentage of the size of the object. With this check box enabled and a vertical shift value of 50 selected and a horizontal value of zero, the image will shift along the vertical plane a distance corresponding to exactly one-half the size of the image.

FILL EMPTY AREA OPTIONS

► **Warp around**   When enabled, it wraps another part of the image around the edges of the window when shifted.

► **Repeat edges**   Enable this button to fill the space vacated by the shifted image with the color(s) currently appearing along the edge of the image.

► **Paint color**   This button is enabled to fill the space vacated by the shifted image with the current paint color.

Using the Offset Filter

There are a few things to consider when using this filter. First, the filter will shift either the entire image or an area enclosed by a mask. None of the pixels in the image being shifted will shift outside of the mask. Therefore, depending on the Fill Empty Area option chosen, all of the effects will happen inside the mask. If the object being masked is a solid color and Warp around is chosen as the option, it will appear as though nothing had happened. So what can you do with it? Not a lot. There are some special effects that can be achieved by applying Offsets to various masks and merging them.

The Pixelate Filter

The Pixelate filter gives a blocklike appearance to the selected area of an image. You have seen the effect many times before on newscasts where they pixelated their features to prevent viewers from seeing the face of the person talking. Because the pixelation was done on a frame-by-frame basis, the boundaries of the pixelation varied from frame to frame, which produced an apparent movement around the edges.

You can control the Pixelate effect by selecting either rectangular or circular mode and changing the size and opacity of the blocks. This filter can be used to create backgrounds that have the appearance of mosaic tiles.

Width and Height values (1-100 pixels) for the size of the pixel blocks can be entered independently. The effects of pixel block size are dependent on the image size. A value of 10 in a small image will create large pixel blocks. A value of 10 in a very large image will produce small pixel blocks. Use the opacity slider (range is 1-100%) to control the transparency of the pixel blocks. Lower values are more transparent. The shape of the blocks of pixels is controlled with the Mode Buttons. Rectangular mode arranges the pixel blocks on horizontal lines. The Circular mode bends the blocks of pixels and arranges them on concentric circles beginning at the center of the image or the masked area.

Using the Pixelate Filter

Since Corel PHOTO-PAINT 6 can import and work on video files (if you have a video capture board), the most obvious use for the Pixelate filter is to pixelate the faces of key witnesses to gangland murders for the local news station. If that opportunity is not readily available, Pixelate is very handy for creating unusual backdrops or converting background into something akin to mosaic tile. When working with backgrounds, remember that the best effects occur when there are contrasts in the image that is being pixelated. For example, if you pixelate a solid blue sky, you will hardly see any effect on the image. In Figure 22-3 I used the Color

Mask to isolate the flower and then pixelated the background with a Circular pattern to create a completely different background.

The Puzzle Filter

The Puzzle filter lets you break down the image into "puzzle-like pieces, or blocks, resembling a jigsaw puzzle." The preceding quotation is from the definition in the help file. Now, maybe the puzzles look different in Canada, but I have worked with puzzles most of my life, and the results of this filter look like several things, but a puzzle is not one of them. It does change images or the selected potions of them into nice blocks that can give the effect of mosaic tile.

The Puzzle Filter Dialog Box

In the Puzzle Filter dialog box, shown on the next page, there are a number of options available that let you control the puzzle (block?) effect, including Block Width and Height, Block Offset (space between pieces creating a segmented effect), and Fill Area.

The Pixelate filter can be used to create dazzling backgrounds

FIGURE 22-3

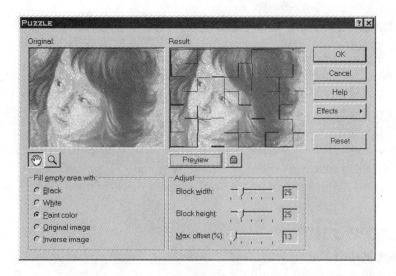

ADJUST BLOCK WIDTH AND HEIGHT SLIDERS   These two sliders control the width and height of the blocks. Their range is 0-100 pixels.

MAX OFFSET (PERCENTAGE)   This slider controls the offsetting, or shifting, of puzzle blocks. It is important to note that the offset is a percentage of the Block size. For example, if the Block size is set to a width of 50 pixels and the Max offset slider is set to 10 (percent), the Offset will have a maximum shift of 5 pixels (10% of 50 = 5). Therefore, increasing or decreasing block size changes the effect the Maximum amount of Offset has, even though the numbers don't change. To make the blocks look more realistic, the actual amount of offset for each block is random. This setting only determines the maximum amount of offset that can be applied.

FILL EMPTY SPACE WITH   When the blocks are offset, something must take their place. Choose from one of the following five options from the Fill empty areas with settings to fill the empty spaces.

▶ **Black**   Applies a black background.

▶ **White**   Applies a white background.

▶ **Paint color**   Applies the current Paint color.

▶ **Original image**   Uses the colors from the original image as a background.

▶ **Inverse image**   Inverts the image adjacent to the shifted blocks and applies it as the background.

An Example of Combining the Puzzle and Emboss Filters

In Figure 22-4, I took the original image and applied the setting shown previously in the Puzzle Filter dialog box. The Paint color I selected was picked off of the image using the Eyedropper tool. I next applied the Emboss located in the Effects menu under 3D Effects, using the Original color setting, a direction of 45 degrees, with a Depth setting of 3. This produced two effects: First, it gave the blocks a highlight that made them appear 3D. Second, it produced a raised graininess on the remainder of the painting which enhances the illusion that it was actually a tiled image.

The Ripple Filter

The Ripple filter is one of the "fun" filters. There is just so much you can do with it, although it is of little use in the day-to-day work of photo-editing. The Ripple filter creates vertical and/or horizontal rippled wave lengths through the image. This filter first appeared in Corel PHOTO-PAINT 5 and has been updated for Corel PHOTO-PAINT 6.

By combining filters you can achieve some unusual effects

FIGURE 22-4

The Ripple Filter Dialog Box

In the Ripple dialog box, shown in the following illustration, there have been several new controls added to provide even more control of the Ripple filter that was available in Corel PHOTO-PAINT 5. The two areas providing control are Ripple direction and Adjust.

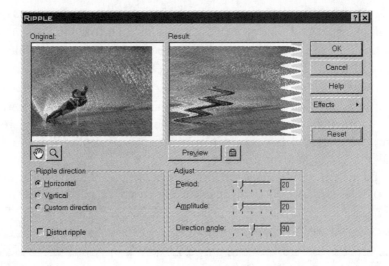

22

THE PERIOD SLIDER Located in the Adjust section, the Period slider sets the distance in pixels between each cycle of wave. A value of 100 pixels creates the greatest distance between each wave, resulting in the fewest number of waves. Be aware that since the Period setting doesn't work on a percentage basis, the larger the image, the larger the number of waves created.

THE AMPLITUDE SLIDER The Amplitude slider sets the amount of displacement the wave creates. The greater the value, the greater the displacement.

THE DIRECTION ANGLE SLIDER The Direction angle slider controls the angle of the ripple effect. It has a range (measured in degrees) between 1 and 180. Changing the Direction angle slider automatically enables the Custom direction button in the Ripple direction area of the dialog box.

RIPPLE DIRECTION Enabling one of the buttons sets the ripple direction to horizontal (from left to right at a default angle of 50 degrees), to vertical (from top to bottom with a default angle of zero), or to Custom. To use Custom direction, just move the Direction angle slider in the Adjust section to the right or left. The Custom direction button is automatically enabled when the slider is moved.

DISTORT RIPPLE Enabling the Distort Ripple option causes the ripple produced by the filter to be distorted. It works by placing a ripple on the ripple.

Doing Something with the Ripple

I don't know, maybe it's because I was raised in California, maybe it was the '60s, but just thinking about Ripple gives me a headache. Back to work. So what can you do with this filter? Like I told you before, have fun. The thing to remember about the Ripple filter is it only does part of the job. Look at the photograph of a water-skier shown in Figure 22-5a.

After the application of a Vertical ripple at maximum period (fewest waves) and a very low amplitude (6), we end up with the next picture, shown in Figure 22-5b. Now the ripple is correct, but it doesn't look like it has any depth. Why? No shadows or highlights. Like I said, the job isn't finished.

By adding a few strokes of the airbrush (white for highlights and black for shadows), it becomes a picture of a man surfing on a piece of corrugated fiberglass (something we see every day), as shown in Figure 22-5c. Playing with this filter can consume lots of time. You have been warned.

You probably noticed that one of the options for the Ripple filter, the one that applied both Horizontal and Vertical ripple effect simultaneously, did not make it into the Corel PHOTO-PAINT 6 release. I am sure the three people who used it are really disappointed.

The Shear Filter

Here is another distortion filter that is lots of fun—a real time waster. The Shear filter distorts an image, or the masked portion of it, along a path. When you open the Shear Filter under 2D Effects in the Effects menu, the dialog box shown on page 444 appears.

a) The original photograph. b) The Ripple has been applied but it appears flat. c) By adding shading and highlights we end up with a real ripple

FIGURE 22-5

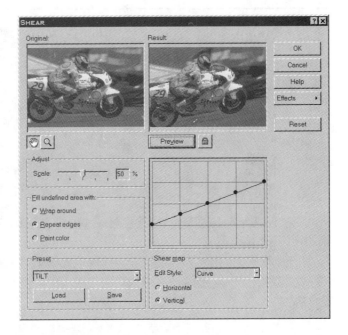

The Shear Filter Dialog Box

At first, the Shear filter dialog box appears to be a very complicated filter to operate. In fact, it is quite simple once you understand what the different parts are doing. As stated earlier, the Shear filter distorts an image along a path. The path that the distortion follows is the one shown under the Preview button. With that understood, let's look at the controls.

SHEAR MAP DISPLAY This displays the currently active Shear map and Shear map grid. This is the working area of the Shear dialog box where you manipulate nodes to create image altering curves. The Edit Style selected in the Shear map section determines how the response curve can be modified.

EDIT STYLE Choose from one of three styles in Edit Style.

► **Curve** In the Curve Edit Style you move nodes vertically along the grid lines to create a smooth, flowing Shear map curve. The movement depends on the setting of the Horizontal or Vertical button.

► **Freehand** In the Freehand mode the Shear map curve is modified using the mouse and the standard click-and-drag technique. There are no nodes that allow you to drag larger portions of the curve, which makes it difficult to create a Shear map. In this mode the movement is not controlled by either the Horizontal or the Vertical button.

► **Linear** Displays a flat line (no curve). Use the nodes located at each end of the line to adjust the angle of the line. Nodes can only be moved vertically when the Vertical button is selected, and Horizontally when the Horizontal button is selected.

HORIZONTAL/VERTICAL Enabling these buttons selects either a horizontal or vertical curve that extends across the Shear map grid.

THE SCALE SLIDER This slider controls the degree to which the image conforms to the curve. Choose 100% for absolute conformity (the image is distorted exactly as is the curve). In most cases you will not want to distort tightly to the curve as it often results in distortion that is not pleasing.

FILL UNDEFINED AREAS WITH Three options in this area determine what replaces pixels that are shifted. The choices and their actions are the same as described in the Displace or Puzzle filter.

PRESET SECTION This section contains two preset shear maps: Wave and Tilt (nothing to do with pinball machines). Choose a preset to apply a uniquely defined effect to the image. You can click the Load button to open the Load Shear Map Files dialog box, where you load saved shear maps located in the Shearmap folder or elsewhere on your system. Clicking the Save button opens the Save Shear File Map As dialog box, where you save the current shear map and assign a filename and description to it. You cannot save a SHR file to any directory other than the default directory Corel PHOTO-PAINT has assigned for this file type.

Using the Shear Filter

Figure 22-6a shows a good action photograph. By using the Shear filter with the Slant preset, we add more energy to the photograph as well as create space to add a short banner under the motorcycle if desired. The results are shown in Figure 22-6b.

a) The original photo of a racer. b) The Shear filter adds a little lift to the photograph

FIGURE 22-6

As I said, this is a fun filter. Using the Wave preset I was able to quickly create a flag for the land of Duck (where Howard sought asylum after his movie bombed). The flagpole is an object I created from a photograph of a flag and placed in the image, shown in Figure 22-7.

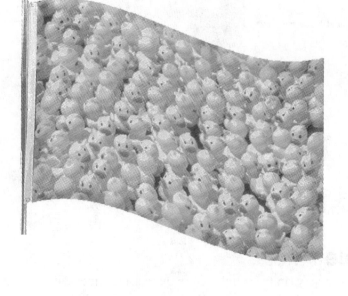

The official flag of "Rubber Ducky Land," courtesy of the Shear filter

FIGURE 22-7

The Swirl Filter

The Swirl filter rotates the center of the image or masked area while leaving the sides fixed. The direction of the movement is determined by the angle set with the Angle slider in the dialog box. It has a range of –360 to +360 degrees. Negative values rotate the image counterclockwise, positive values clockwise. Multiple applications produce a more pronounced effect.

Using the Swirl Filter

In the next illustration I have made a simple conical fill and applied it to a 200 x 200 pixels square. Next I applied the Swirl filter set to 360°. Using the CTRL-F keyboard shortcut, I applied the Swirl filter twice more. The last image shows the application a total of six times. By using the Swirl filter, you can make excellent ornaments and effects for your desktop publishing projects.

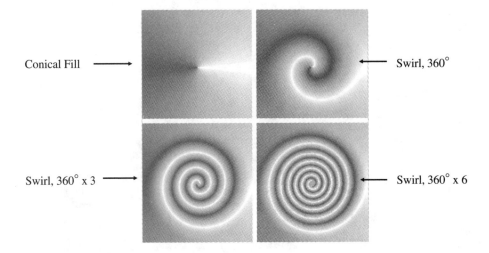

Conical Fill ⟶   ⟵ Swirl, 360°

Swirl, 360° x 3 ⟶   ⟵ Swirl, 360° x 6

The Tile Filter

This is a very simple and therefore quite useful filter. The Tile filter creates blocks of a selected image in a grid. You can adjust the width and height of the tiles using the Horizontal and Vertical sliders in the dialog box. The values entered represent the number of images duplicated on each axis. The Horizontal slider determines how many columns of the tile will be present in the image. The Vertical slider determines the number of Rows of tiles that will be produced.

The Tile effect can be used in combination with flood fills to create backgrounds as well as making wallpaper for Windows. The best effects are achieved when the number of tiles in relation to the original image is small. If you have a large number, then the original subject becomes so small as to be unrecognizable.

The Trace Contour Filter

The Trace Contour filter effect lets you outline the edges of an image. Use the Level slider in the dialog box to set the edge threshold level. The threshold slider in the dialog box ranges from 0 to 255. A lower setting leaves more of the image; a higher setting reduces the amount of the original image remaining after the effect is applied. Use this effect to provide unique and useful effects. The best effects are achieved when the subject matter is easily recognizable.

Choose an edge type from the Edge Type settings. The Lower setting will trace the inside edges of an image, and Upper will trace the outside edges.

The User Defined Filter

The User Defined effect lets you "roll your own." Yes, you can make your own filters. The User Defined filter enables you to design your own *convolution kernel,* which is a type of filter in which adjacent pixels get mixed together. The filter that you make can be a variation on sharpening, embossing, blurring, or almost any other effect you can name.

The dialog box, shown in the next illustration, displays a matrix that represents a single pixel of the image (shown at the center) and its adjacent pixels. The values you enter into the matrix determine the type of effect you create. You can enter positive or negative values. The range of the effect is determined by the number of the values you enter into the matrix. The more values you enter, the more pixels are affected.

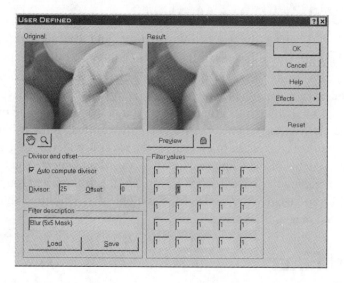

This filter is not for the faint of heart. To understand the operation of this filter would take a chapter in itself. So that you can see what the filter does, Corel has provided three sample user-defined effects. Use the Load button for this. These effects have been provided to help you determine what values to enter into the matrix.

The Wet Paint Filter

After applying the Wet Paint filter, the image has the appearance of wet paint. This filter can quickly create some neat effects, which have been improved in Corel PHOTO-PAINT 6. You can set the percentage and the degree of wetness. Percentage refers to the depth to which the wet paint look is applied. For example, if you set low percentages, the amount of wetness appears to affect only the surface of the image.

Technically, Percent controls the amount (how far down) the drip travels. The wetness values determine which colors drip. Negative (–) wetness values cause the dark colors to drip. Positive (+) wetness values cause light colors to drip. The magnitude of the wetness values determines how large a range of colors drip. Maximum values are +/–50 percent.

Wet paint can be used to provide many different effects. Several combinations of positive and negative wetness can be applied to the same object to produce drop shadows, giving a 3D appearance to rounded text.

The Wet Paint Filter Mystery

In Figure 22-8, I created the text with the text tool and then applied the Wet Paint filter to it. Pop quiz: How did I prevent the Wet Paint filter from affecting the brick wall?

"I don't care" is not the right answer. The trick is to place the text over a white background, merge it, and then apply the Wet Paint filter. Now you have what looks like Wet Paint on a white background. Next, you create a Rectangle mask around the text and cut it to the Clipboard. Are you still with me? Now using one of the many bitmap fills, I created the brick wall for the background. Click the Paste button to paste the contents of the Clipboard to the image as an Object. You have the text with a white rectangular background. To remove the white background, open the Object roll-up and change the mode of the text object to Multiply. All of the white disappears like magic. Slick trick!

The Wind Filter

The Wind filter creates the effect of wind blowing on the objects in the image. You can set the opacity and the strength of the wind. Click and drag the Opacity slider (1-100) to determine the visibility of the wind effect. Higher values make the effect more visible and lower values make the effect more subtle. The amount of the wind effect (distortion) applied is controlled by the Strength slider.

Here is an example made using the Wet Paint filter

FIGURE 22-8

Figure 22-9 is more what they had in mind when they made the filter. While this works fine if your object appears to be traveling from right to left, it does not let you change the direction of the wind. This is appropriate since, to quote Mark Twain,

The Wind filter gives the feeling of speed to this racing photograph from Figure 6a

FIGURE 22-9

22

"Everyone talks about the weather but no one never does anything about it." The solution, since the subject was traveling from left to right, was to flip the image using the Flip command in the Image menu and then, after the effect was applied, flip the image back again.

The 3D Effect Filters

23

Corel PHOTO-PAINT has is a rich collection of filters that can be loosely grouped under the 3D category. This can be confusing since there is a 3D program in the Corel 6 Suite. Some of the filters in this group give effects that appear to be 3D, but none are true 3D filters. The filters in this chapter are grouped by common function rather than by the order in which they appear. Please note that all of them are available with grayscale, Duotone®, 24-bit, and 32-bit color images with the exception of the Glass, The Boss, and Whirlpool filters, which are not available with 32-bit images.

3D Rotate Filter

The 3D Rotate filter rotates the image according to the horizontal and vertical limits set in the 3D Rotate dialog box. The rotation is applied as if the image were one side of a 3D box.

The 3D Rotate Filter Dialog Box

The dialog box is shown in the illustration on the right. The preview window shows the perspective of the image with the current slider settings. The plane of the box in the preview window that is shaded represents the image. By moving the vertical and horizontal sliders, the preview box can be oriented into the correct position. The preview window shows the result of the application of the 3D Rotate filter.

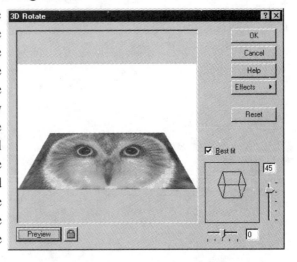

If the Best Fit check box is checked, the affected image or masked portion is scaled down to fit into the existing image window. If it is not checked, the image size will be increased to fit the corners of the newly rotated image.

Using the 3D Rotate Filter

In Corel PHOTO-PAINT 5, there isn't a zoom or automatic preview function in the preview window of the dialog box. In Corel PHOTO-PAINT 6, automatic preview has been added, making it a little easier to work with the filter. There still is no zoom in the preview window.

Applying the 3D Rotate filter to objects is not recommended, as the results may be unpredictable. The basic problem is that while the rotation of the image occurs within the object, the object retains the same shape. Using Corel PHOTO-PAINT, I have created a three-panel display of what happens when you apply the 3D Rotate filter to an object. In the next illustration the left panel displays an object with a gradient fill. The middle panel shows the application of the 3D Rotate filter. Note that the fill has been affected but the object shape remains unchanged, as shown by the bounding box. In the right panel the object is moved to show that part of the original object's fill has been painted on the background.

I recommend that you merge any objects before applying the filter to them. Lock or hide objects that the filter is not being applied to. The part of the image you want rotated should be masked, or the filter will ignore it.

There are some real limitations to this filter. Although you can apply rotation to both the horizontal and vertical axes simultaneously, it is not recommended. The resulting image loses varying degrees of perspective. Also note that the preview doesn't always display the 3D perspective correctly.

The image shown in Figure 23-1 was taken from the Sampler Photo-CD. The two sides were created using the 3D Rotate filter. After the image was created, each side was made into a separate object, and later the two were combined to produce the 3D look. The final touch of shading was done by applying the Smoked Glass filter to the left side at 40 percent. The cloud background is a bitmap texture fill.

The Perspective Filter

The Perspective filter creates the impression of 3D perspective to an image. There are two modes in the Perspective filter: *Perspective* and *Shear*. Perspective applies the look of 3D perspective to the image according to the movement of the four nodes in the preview box. The nodes are moved by clicking on them with the mouse and dragging them to the desired location. Shear also applies perspective, but it holds the original size and shape.

Using the Perspective Filter

Select the type of perspective to be applied: Perspective or Shear. Select Best Fit if the original image size must be maintained. Figure 23-2 shows the effects of Perspective (top) and Shear (bottom) settings of the Perspective filter next to the original photograph (middle).

Making a car in a block is simple work with the 3D Rotate filter

FIGURE 23-1

The
Perspective
filter shown
at three
different
settings

FIGURE 23-2

Notes on Using the Perspective Filter

This is another filter that I first considered rather pointless. However, after much experimentation with this filter, I have been able to obtain some good 3D perspectives. There are still some rough edges, however. One of the greatest challenges to using this filter is that its dialog box does not give any reading as to the changes being made. You must go strictly by the visual frame in the preview box. So, if you had grand ideas about using this filter to create 3D objects, you would be better to use CorelDREAM 3D.

You can only move the nodes along the horizontal and vertical planes in Shear mode. There are no zoom functions in the preview window of the dialog box. As with the 3D Rotate filter, applying the Perspective filter to objects is not recommended, because the results may be unpredictable; therefore, merge objects before applying the filter. Hide or lock objects that the filter is not being applied to.

Using the Perspective Filter to Make the "Tiger Wall"

The image "Tiger Wall," shown in Figure 23-3, was created almost by accident when I first began working with the Perspective filter. As with many such projects, as I explored the filter I found more and more things I could do with it. The photograph of a tiger has had the Perspective filter applied to it to create the illusion of a 3D folding wall. The shading on the opposite walls was created by applying the Smoked Glass filter. The floor is a gradient fill with noise applied to it. The sky is one of the sky settings in the Texture bitmap fill. The Tiger in the ball was done by using the Glass Lens, Normal filter from Kai's Power Tools. This effect can also be done with the Map To Object filter (which is called Map To Sphere in Corel PHOTO-PAINT 5).

The Emboss Filter

Corel PHOTO-PAINT 6 has two emboss filters. The first one is called Emboss; the other one, originally created by Alien Skin Software, is called The Boss and made its first appearance in Corel PHOTO-PAINT 5 Plus. The Emboss filter is an improvement over the Emboss filter of Corel PHOTO-PAINT 5. The most important change was the ability to use the original colors as part of the embossing instead of always using a solid color.

The folding wall of tigers was created with the Perspective filter

FIGURE 23-3

Embossing creates a 3D relief effect. Directional arrows point to the location of the light source and determine the angle of the highlights and shadows. The Emboss filter has its most dramatic effect on medium- to high-contrast images. Several filters can be used in combination with the Emboss filter to produce photo-realistic effects.

The Emboss Filter Dialog Box

The Emboss Filter dialog box, shown here, provides all of the controls necessary to produce a wide variety of embossing effects.

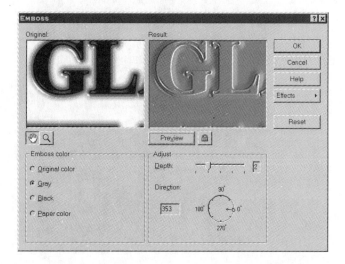

EMBOSS COLOR   Choose an option from the Emboss Color settings to set the color of the embossed image. When Original color is selected, the Emboss filter uses the colors of the image to simulate the relief effect. When Black or Gray is selected, the entire image becomes filled with that color. To select another solid color, other than black or gray, you must change the Paper Color (background color) to the desired color and select the Paper color button.

THE DEPTH SLIDER   Adjust the Depth slider to set the intensity of the embossing effect. Care should be taken not to use an excessive value since it can cause minor image displacement.

THE DIRECTION BUTTON   Drag the Direction button to specify the location of the light source, or enter a value directly in the value box. Light direction is very important. It can make the image look like it has either a raised or sunken surface.

23

The Effects of Applying Different Directions

In the next illustration I applied the Emboss filter to the text four times, each at a Depth setting of 2, but in the N,E,S,W directions. Be aware that when the Emboss direction is parallel with thin lines, thin lines can disappear. This is true if you use one of the solid colors but not if you use Original color.

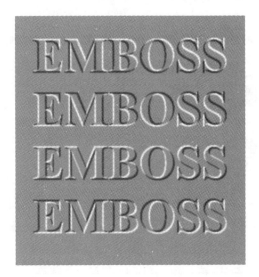

 IP: *To reduce the "jaggies" when applying the Emboss filter to high contrast images (like text), apply a Gaussian Blur filter at a setting of 1 before applying the Emboss filter.*

The Glass Filter

Unlike the Boss filter, the Glass filter (which was also originally created by Alien Skin Software) does not make the underlying image look 3D. Instead, the Glass filter seems to put a layer of glass on top of the image. Keep in mind that the sheet of glass is the 3D part, while the image remains flat. By adjusting the combination of light filtering, refraction, and highlights, you can achieve some striking effects with this filter.

The Glass filter requires a mask to do its job. The shape of the glass sheet is controlled by the shape of the mask. The top edge of the glass bevel occurs along the mask. Feathering the mask has no effect on this filter's operation.

The Glass Filter Dialog Box

The Glass filter dialog box, shown in the next illustration, is opened by selecting Glass in the 3D category of the Effects menu.

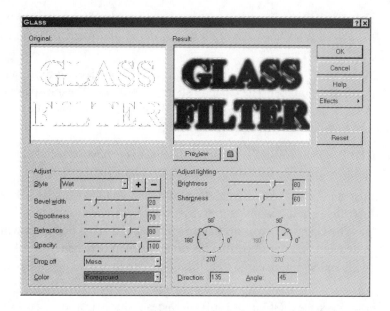

STYLE   This contains a drop-down list of presets that are provided with the Glass filter. Choosing any of the presets changes the controls in the dialog box for the selected presets. Custom settings are also saved in the Style area by changing the controls to the desired settings and clicking the plus button to the right of the Style name. Another dialog box opens that allows you to name the new style. The minus button is used to remove a saved style.

THE BEVEL WIDTH SLIDER   The Bevel Width slider is used to set the width of the bevel. The bevel is the area around a masked object that is slanted to produce the 3D look.

THE SMOOTHNESS SLIDER   The Smoothness slider is used to set the sharpness of the edges of the bevel. A low-level smoothness produces sharper edges but may also display the steps used to create the embossed look. A higher smoothness level removes the jagged edges and makes for rounded edges.

THE REFRACTION SLIDER   The most striking 3D effect of the Glass filter is *refraction,* which occurs when the direction of light rays is changed (bent) as a result of passing through a material such as glass or water. Since we are looking directly at the glass sheet, refraction only occurs at the beveled edges. The Refraction slider sets the angle at which the light is to be bent at the bevel. This distorts the image at the bevel location, which is the most striking effect of the Glass filter.

 IP: *To make the refraction effect more noticeable, try using a wider bevel. This will increase the area of glass that does not directly face the viewer.*

THE OPACITY SLIDER   Colored glass affects light, and it affects it more where the material (the glass) is thicker. The Opacity slider is used to set the transparency level of the glass sheet. The more opaque you make the glass, the stronger the underlying image will be tinted to look like the glass color.

DROP-OFF TYPE   The drop-off is the area adjacent to the bevel effect and is selected from a drop-down list. The following choices are available.

▶ **Gaussian**   Use the Gaussian drop-off when you want a very subtle affect. On a complex image it gives a wet appearance to the masked area edge. The Gaussian drop-off has an "S" shape; it starts and ends with a rounded and gradual slope that becomes steep in between. It results in a smooth and less noticeable transition between the bevel and the rest of the image.

▶ **Flat**   Because the Flat drop-off produces a sharp drop-off bevel, the areas around the edges are very sharp. The effect on text with dark colors may not even be noticeable. This effect works best with objects that have smooth, rounded edges. The Flat drop-off is a straight diagonal line starting at the bevel area and ending on the image. The transition is not as smooth as a rounded bevel, but the slope of the bevel is less steep.

▶ **Mesa**   This drop-off style probably gives the best overall glass effect of the three. The Mesa drop-off is a curve that begins abruptly (almost a 90-degree angle) and ends with a rounded gradual slope.

COLOR   The glass can be the Paint (foreground) color, the Paper (background) color, or leaded. *Leaded* is really the same as dark gray, but it makes it somehow seem a little more "real" to call it leaded. Dark glass colors the underlying image more strongly than light glass does, so if you are experiencing difficulty in getting a noticeable glass effect, try darkening the glass color. This is a drop-down list from which you choose a color for the glass, but background and foreground colors need to be chosen before you open the filters.

THE BRIGHTNESS SLIDER   The Brightness slider controls the intensity of the highlights in the glass. A higher setting produces more highlights on the glass.

THE SHARPNESS SLIDER   The Sharpness slider controls the sharpness of the light striking the edges of the bevel. So what is "Sharpness of light"? This setting actually controls the amount of sharpness that occurs as a function of light striking the affected area.

DIRECT AND ANGLE CONTROLS   You can control the direction that the sun comes by using the Light Direction and Light Angle controls. High light angle values illuminate the selection from directly above the surface, which tends to cause lighting that is bright and even. Low light angle values tend to make shadows stronger, thus accentuating the 3D effect. The angles are referenced to the horizon. High angle (90°) is similar to the sun being directly overhead, whereas low angle (0°) is like the sun sitting on the horizon.

▶ **Direction Dial and Value Box**   The Direction dial controls the direction of the light striking the bevel. The bevel is the area around a masked object which is slanted to produce the 3D look. You can drag the dial to point toward the light source, or you can enter an angle value directly in the value box.

▶ **Angle Dial and Value Box**   The Angle dial controls the angle at which the light is to be bent at the bevel. This distorts the image at the bevel location, which is the most striking effect of the Glass filter. The bevel is the area around a masked object that is slanted to produce the 3D look.

   IP: *You get better effects with Glass if you have a textured or high-contrast background to accentuate the glass effect.*

Using the Glass Filter

In Figure 23-4 I created two lines of text and then, with Preserve Image enabled, created a mask out of it. After the mask was created, I combined the text object with the background. With the mask still in place, I used the Glass filter to apply the Wet style to the image.

The Map To Object Filter

The Map To Object filter creates the impression that the image has been wrapped around a sphere, vertical cylinder, or horizontal cylinder. The sphere is easy to work

23

The Glass filter produces wet and shiny text effects

FIGURE 23-4

with. The vertical and horizontal require highlights and shadows to make them look like cylinders.

The Map To Object Dialog Box

The Map To Object dialog box, shown below, has controls that are common to many other dialog boxes. In addition, there are two unique areas: Mapping mode and Adjust.

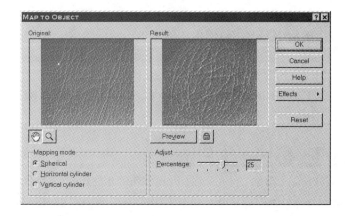

MAPPING MODE   Clicking Sphere, Vertical Cylinder, or Horizontal Cylinder allows selection of the model used for wrapping.

ADJUST SECTION   The Percentage slider is used to choose the amount of wrapping. Negative values wrap the image toward the back, and positive values wrap the image toward the front. The default setting for the dialog box is a good setting for Sphere. The amount needed to achieve a noticeable effect with the Vertical Cylinder or Horizontal Cylinder is generally the maximum.

Making the Glass Bubble with the Map To Object Filter

To make the glass bubble in Figure 23-5, I created a circle mask over the Sydney Opera House in the photograph and applied the Map To Object (sphere setting) to it. The glare on the glass was provided by applying the Lens Flare filter to it. The shadow is a feathered mask to which some dark airbrush was applied.

Map To Object is called Map To Sphere in Corel PHOTO-PAINT 5.

23

While the filter can be applied to the entire image, some of the most dramatic effects are achieved by applying the effect to a smaller area of the image that has been defined by a mask. The effect is more pronounced and effective if the object has horizontal and vertical lines. Almost all uses of the Map To Object filter will require the application of highlights and shadows with an airbrush to enhance their appearance. In Figure 23-6 the Horizontal Cylinder mapping mode was used to create the appearance of a glass rod lying on top of the money. The image did not look realistic until the shadows and highlights were added with the airbrush.

The Mesh Warp Filter

The Mesh Warp filter distorts the image according to the movement of the nodes on a grid in the Mesh Warp dialog box. The user, through the dialog box, determines the number of nodes positioned over the grid using the No. gridlines slider bar.

This glass sphere is a popular effect that is easy to create with the Map To Object filter

FIGURE 23-5

Making a glass bar with Map To Object and a little patience

FIGURE 23-6

(Generally, the greater the number of nodes selected, the smoother the Mesh Warp distortion.) Each node can be moved by clicking on it with a mouse and dragging it to a new position. Each node moves independently and can be positioned anywhere in the Preview window.

The Mesh Warp effect can be a little tricky to use at first. Use the Preview button to view the effects of a Mesh Warp transformation to ensure that it is acceptable before applying it to your entire image.

The Mesh Warp Filter Dialog Box

When the Mesh Warp dialog box opens, shown here, click and drag the No. gridlines slider to determine the number of nodes that will appear on the image. Lower values have fewer nodes, while higher values have more nodes. Use the Preview button to see the results of the node placement.

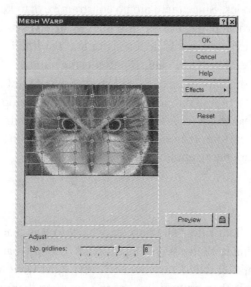

NO. GRIDLINES This controls the number of gridlines on the grid. At each point where a horizontal and a vertical gridline intersect, a node is positioned. It is the manipulation of the nodes along the grid that creates the effect. Each node moves independently of each another. Generally, the more nodes you use in the Mesh Warp operation, the smoother the effect will be. The first horizontal gridline lies along the top and the first vertical gridline is on the left. Be aware that they can be hard to see, depending on your display.

So... What Do You Do with It?

You can use the selective distortion capability to distort people and places. It does allow you to distort or "morph" images or photos with some interesting results. Figure 23-7a shows the original photograph of an owl, looking curious. After the application of the Warp Mesh filter, he looks mad enough to start a fight, as shown in Figure 23-7b.

Notes About Using the Mesh Warp Filter

As I said before, the greater the number of nodes, the smoother the transitions on the image. Because each node is independent, each must be individually moved. There is a trade-off between the smoothness of the transition and the time required to move all of the nodes. Since there are no constrain keys to keep the grid lines on the horizontal or vertical plane, use the grid lines themselves as your guide. As long as the line in the preview window appears straight, the line is still in line with its respective plane. The Mesh Grid value represents the number of nodes on each line of the grid. (The two end nodes on each grid line are out of view and not adjustable.) There is no zoom function in the preview window of the dialog box.

Applying the Mesh Warp filter to objects is not recommended, as the results may be unpredictable; therefore, merge objects before applying the filter. Hide or lock objects the filter is not being applied to.

Page Curl

This is a really excellent filter. The only drawback to it is that everybody and his uncle seem to be using it. I have seen a lot of flyers recently that have used the Page Curl filter. I wouldn't let that deter you, however; I just want to warn you in case your client seems less than enthusiastic when you show them something with the Page Curl filter. Page Curl simulates the effect of a page being peeled back, with a highlight running along the center of the curl and a shadow being thrown from beneath the image (if your image is light enough to contrast with a shadow). The area behind the image, revealed by the page curl, is filled with the current paper color.

a) A curious looking owl. b) With a little help from Mesh Warp—Owl with attitude

FIGURE 23-7

The Page Curl Dialog Box

The Page Curl dialog box, shown here, has been improved quite a bit with the release of Corel PHOTO-PAINT 6. The curl effect begins in one corner of your selection and follows a perfect diagonal line to the opposite corner. You also may notice a slight transparency to the curl if there is any pattern or texture in the selected portion of your image.

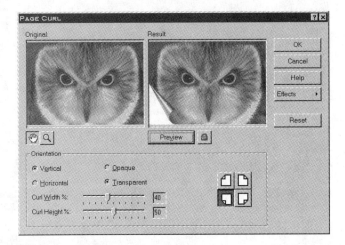

PAGE CURL CORNER BUTTONS   The origination point of the curl is controlled by using one of the four keys in the Page Curl dialog box.

VERTICAL ORIENTATION BUTTON   Click this button to create a vertically-oriented page curl, which curls the page across the image (from left to right or right to left). Experiment with this setting to achieve the page curl you want. The buttons are mutually exclusive; that is, selecting one deselects the other.

HORIZONTAL ORIENTATION BUTTON   Click to create a horizontally oriented page curl, which curls the page upward or downward through the image (from top to bottom or bottom to top).

OPAQUE/TRANSPARENT   Check to make the underside of the curled page opaque or transparent. Choose the Opaque option if you want the curl to be filled with a blend of gray and white to simulate a highlight. Choose the Transparent option if you want the underlying image to be displayed through the curled paper.

CURL WIDTH PERCENTAGE SLIDER   The Curl Width slider controls the vertical component of the Page curl regardless of whether it is a vertical or horizontal Page curl.

CURL HEIGHT PERCENTAGE SLIDER   The Curl Height slider controls the horizontal component of the Page curl regardless of whether it is a vertical or horizontal Page curl.

 IP: *To apply the effect to a portion of the image, select an area using a mask before you choose the effect. The page will only curl inside the masked area.*

A Technique for Using the Page Curl Filter

In Figure 23-8 I have taken a photograph of some holly leaves and berries and applied two different page curl effects to it. In the upper right it is an opaque curl, and in the lower right it is a transparent curl. In the area that appears under the curl I used the Magic Wand mask tool to create a mask of the area. I next applied a bitmap fill (they really are cranberries) to fill the area. Then, using the Airbrush tool, I created a mild shadow that ran the length of the curl to give it some depth.

The Pinch/Punch Filter

The Pinch/Punch filter either squeezes the image so that the center appears to come forward (pinch) or depresses the image so that the center appears to be sunken (punch). The results makes the image look as if it has been either pulled out or pushed in from the center.

The Pinch/Punch Dialog Box

This filter reminds me of the house of mirrors in the amusement park near where I grew up. They had all of these mirrors that distorted your features. This filter does the same thing. The Pinch/Punch dialog box, shown here, lets you set the effect attribute. In the dialog box, moving the slider in a positive (+) direction applies a Pinch effect, and moving it in a negative direction (–) produces a Punch effect. While the filter can be applied to the entire image, some of the most dramatic effects are achieved by applying the effect to a smaller area of the image that has been defined by a mask. The effect is more pronounced and effective if the object has horizontal and vertical lines.

23

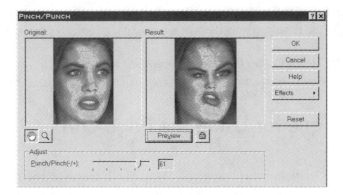

Using the Pinch/Punch Filter

Besides distorting people's faces and bodies beyond recognition, there are actually some productive things that you can do with this filter. The best way to use it is to limit the effects to small manageable areas. Next, make applications in small amounts. In Figure 23-9a, I have made a very loose-fitting mask around the head of the Statue of Liberty. Next I applied a small amount of Punch to it, which gives it a different perspective without the obvious distortion that attracts attention. In the

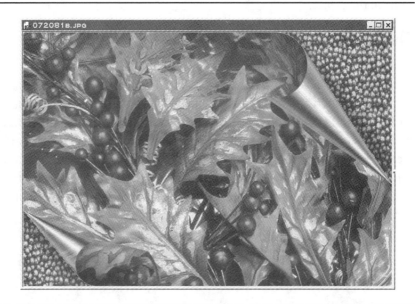

The Page
Curl filter
provides
effects that
are unique
and fun

FIGURE 23-8

"punched" photograph shown in Figure 23-9b, the only indication that the photo has been manipulated is one of the rays protruding from the crown. Even this tell-tale sign could have been eliminated if I had invested the time.

The Boss (Emboss) Filter

The Emboss filter makes the selected area look as if it is pushed out of the image. The effect is achieved by putting what appears to be a slanted bevel around the selected area. The Boss filter is located in the 3D Effects category of the Effect menu. It is called The Boss (to avoid confusion with the original Emboss filter). The Boss filter dialog box is shown in the next illustration. This filter does not have a preview window in Corel PHOTO-PAINT 5, but one has been included in Corel PHOTO-PAINT 6. You must have a mask in place to be able to use this filter.

 IP: *If you are going to apply the filter to the entire image, select All from the Mask menu to quickly mask the image, and then create the mask from it.*

The Boss Dialog Box

The Boss filter and the Glass filter are very similar in their operation. This is because they use the same filter engine (program) internally. This is not an uncommon

a) The original photograph. b) A different look after applying the Pinch/Punch filter

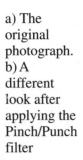

FIGURE 23-9

practice. I only mention it in case you experience a feeling of deja vu. It is the commonality of the programs at work here—you don't need to call the psychic hotline. The controls will be covered in order not of appearance but of use.

DROP-OFF (BEVEL SHAPE) The Drop-off controls of the Emboss dialog box affect the shape of the bevel around the selection. The Height slider controls how far the selection pushes out of the screen toward the viewer. This is the primary way to control the amount of the 3D effect. The Width slider controls how much of the image is taken up by the bevel. Be aware that the bevel grows around the area selected by the mask. Therefore, if it gets too wide or the objects selected are too close together, they will begin to merge into one another. Thin bevels appear steeper than wide ones, so this setting also controls the strength of the 3D effect. Drop-off controls the general shape of the bevel.

SMOOTHNESS The basis of the trade-offs with the Smoothness settings is that if there were no "jaggies," there would also be no sharp lines. So instead of deciding how much The Boss filter would "melt" the bevel, they added a smoothing slider, so you can make the decision yourself. When Smoothness is set low, the edges will be sharper, but little steps in the bevel will be more noticeable. When Smoothness is high, the edges will be more rounded, and it will look like your objects are floating on marshmallows.

BRIGHTNESS/SHARPNESS Brightness is the bright reflection of the light off of the 3D surface. The Brightness slider can make the highlight disappear at the lower settings, or it can wash out part of the image at the higher settings. The Sharpness slider lets you control how small and crisp the highlight is. Sharper highlights tend to make the surface look shinier or even wet. Dull highlights are more spread out and make the surface look chalky.

The shape of the bevel interacts with the highlights. Sharper bevel corners (low width, high height, low smoothing) will make sharper highlights, so you will have to experiment to see how all these parameters combine to make the final 3D effect.

LIGHTING CONTROLS: BRIGHTNESS, SHARPNESS, AND DIRECTION ANGLE You can control the direction that the sun or light source comes from using the Light Direction and Light Angle controls. High light angles light the selection from directly above the surface, which tends to cause bright and even lighting. Low light angles tend to make shadows stronger, thus accentuating the 3D effect. See the previous discussion of this subject under the Glass filter.

Using the Boss Filter

Unlike the Corel PHOTO-PAINT Emboss filter, this filter seems to work best on text, icons, and symbols. In the image shown in Figure 23-10 I have created the text

The Boss
filter
applied to
text
produces a
raised effect

FIGURE 23-10

"BOSS" and applied a fair amount of noise to the image. Then I created a mask from the object and applied The Boss filter using the Wet style.

The Whirlpool Filter

I used to refer to the Whirlpool filter as a poor man's Terrazzo. (I have also called it the "Smear tool on Steroids," which may be a more accurate description.) Since Terrazzo is now part of Corel PHOTO-PAINT 6, one would assume that there is no need for this filter. This is not true. Instead of making tiles, the Whirlpool filter does a blender operation on the selected area and creates some nice textures for use as backgrounds. Jeff Butterworth of Alien Skin Software, the original creator of the filter, states, "We just couldn't resist throwing in something fun. Swirl uses state-of-the-art scientific visualization techniques for examining complex fluid simulations. This technique smears the image along artificial fluid streamlines." This also may be one of the most CPU-intensive filters in the bunch. Be prepared for this filter to take a little time to complete its action. By clicking on Whirlpool, you open the Whirlpool Filter dialog box, as shown here. This filter does not require a mask to operate.

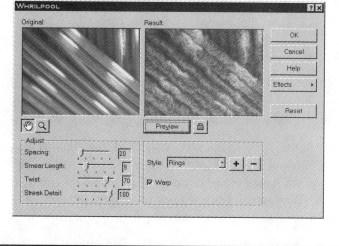

This filter is called Swirl in Corel PHOTO-PAINT 5.

The Whirlpool Filter Dialog Box

The Whirlpool filter has several options that are unique to this type of filter. The controls are described below.

SPACING SLIDER All you really need to understand about spacing (of Whirlpools) is that it randomly places whirlpools in the selection and then smears the selected area with them. The Spacing slider controls approximately how far apart these whirlpools are from one another. A large spacing setting creates more of a "painterly" effect. Smaller settings make the whirlpools close together and create effects that are reminiscent of 1960s design.

SMEAR LENGTH SLIDER Smear Length controls how much the underlying image is blurred. Low values create noisy results, while large settings create smoother results. This is the one setting that has the greatest effect on how long the filter will take to process the image. A longer Smear Length setting results in longer processing time.

TWIST SLIDER   The Twist slider controls whether the flows flow *around* or *out* of the whirlpools. Twist angles near 0 degrees make the whirlpools act more like fountains, because the fluid flows outward in a starlike pattern. Twist angles approaching 90 degrees flow around in rings.

STREAK DETAIL SLIDER   Whirlpool is a form of blurring, so it can remove detail from your image or make your image altogether unrecognizable. To recover some of the image detail, increase the setting of Streak Detail.

WARP   When the Warp check box is checked, the simulated fluid stretches the image "downstream" along the stream lines. Warping makes the Whirlpool effect more striking, but it may not be desirable if you want the original image to remain recognizable. Turning the Warp toggles off causes smearing without moving the underlying image but doesn't affect availability of Smear length.

STYLE   The Style is a drop-down list box listing several whirlpool effect presets. When you choose a preset, dialog box controls change to reflect its settings.

PLUS BUTTON   When you have a particular setting of the Whirlpool that you want to keep, you must click the Plus button to save it. The Save Settings dialog box opens where you type a name to identify the effect.

MINUS BUTTON   To delete a setting from the Style drop-down list, click the minus button to delete a preset from the Style drop-down list box.

Using Filters Together

The sphere shown in Figure 23-11 was created by making a circle mask in the center and applying the Whirlpool filter to it. To make it look like a sphere, I next used the Map To Object filter (sphere). To achieve the shading around the sphere, I inverted the mask and applied The Boss filter.

The Zigzag Filter

The Zigzag filter is a distortion filter. In short, you will get an effect but will, most likely, not be able to recognize the original image when have finished. This filter distorts an image by bending the image lines that run from the center of the image to the edge of the masked area or the circumference. This produces a wavelike action that changes curves to straight lines and creates angles that seem to twist the image from its center outwards. The Zigzag filter is great for simulating ripples and reflections in water. While the effect is slick, its uses are limited.

A combination of 3D filters created the sphere in the center

FIGURE 23-11

The Zigzag Filter Dialog Box

The dialog box for the Zigzag filter, shown here, has three controls that allow you a wide range of control over the effects created by this filter. The preview for this filter doesn't give a very accurate portrayal of the final result, so be prepared to experiment a little.

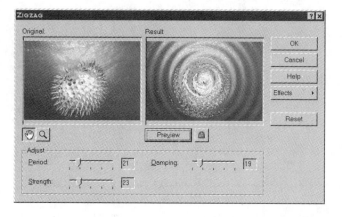

PERIOD SLIDER   The Period slider controls the distance between each cycle in the wave. Using larger values creates greater distances between each wave, resulting in a minimal number of waves. Smaller values create so many waves that it almost looks like a Fresnel lens.

STRENGTH SLIDER   The Strength slider is used to control the intensity of the zigzag distortion.

DAMPING SLIDER   This control is difficult to describe. The Damping slider controls (dampens) the tendency of the zigzag waves to extend beyond the image's edge. The default value is 80, which only allows the waves to go a moderate distance into the image (from the center). Setting the Damping slider to low value will create concentric circles that go to the edge of the image. By applying more damping, you can attenuate the zigzagging effect to only a small distance from the center.

The Render Filters

24

Render filters are used to produce special effects and backgrounds, and make novelty images. Two of the filters, Lens Flare and Lighting Effects, are new with Corel PHOTO-PAINT 6. The Render filters are:

- ► 3D Stereo Noise
- ► Julia Set Explorer
- ► Lens Flare
- ► Lighting Effects

3D Stereo Noise

This filter (originally from the Kai Power Tools 2.0 collection) is my least favorite because it has become such a fad. The 3D Stereo Noise filter takes a perfectly good image and converts it to something akin to a printer failure all over your paper. By staring at the paper, you can see the original image with depth effect. (It is rumored that if you can stare at it for over an hour, just before the onset of a migraine, you can see Elvis.) The 3D Stereo Noise filter, or a program just like it, is what is used to produce those stereogram posters that have gained such popularity at suburban shopping malls in recent seasons. If you stare at them, you can actually see an embedded image with depth perception.

3D Stereo Noise was discovered a long time ago at Bell Laboratories. The researchers observed that when certain points on an image where shifted, it gave the appearance of depth. As used here, the term "stereo" should not be confused with music. Human beings were designed with stereoscopic sight—two eyes that render a single image from two slightly different angles, thus producing depth perception.

The images that produce the best results with the 3D Stereo Noise effect use gray levels, are slightly blurred, and do not have extreme contrast. Don't waste precious system resources by using 24-bit color. The result will be grayscale. The 3D Stereo Noise filter generates a pixelated noise pattern that has horizontal frequencies that correspond to the gray levels of the initial image. This means that white will map to the highest frequency and appear closest to the viewer; black will map to the lowest frequency and appear furthest away.

Making an Image

First, create a grayscale image that uses text and simple objects. Although the filter will apply in all modes, the best images initially use gray levels. The smaller and more detailed the image you choose, the harder it will be to focus the stereo image. Apply a standard Gaussian Blur filter. This will soften the edges of the image for easier viewing. Open the Effects menu and, under the Render subgroup, click on the 3D Stereo Noise filter. This opens the preview dialog box, shown in the next illustration. There are only two options with this dialog box: Depth control, with a relative depth range of 1-9; and a Show Dots check box, which enables the creation of two dots in a box near the bottom of the image to help the user focus on the 3D image. The two dots that appear in the Result window are used to guide you in focusing correctly on the image; adjust your focus so that the dots fuse into one and a three-dimensional effect is achieved.

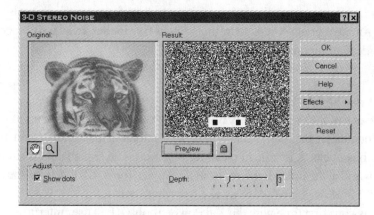

Apply the filter to the entire image. The results will appear to be a random array of black and white noise.

Viewing 3D Stereo Noise Pictures

After you have created a stereo noise picture, it is time to focus your eyes and energies to see the image. I was never able to view the depth onscreen. Maybe you can do better here than I did. Don't feel bad if you don't see the image right away;

it may take a few tries. There are several ways to view the image in-depth. Try enabling the Show Dots check box to produce black dots about a half-inch apart at the bottom of the image. Defocus your eyes and gaze through the image as if you were looking into the distance. The dots you placed at the bottom will separate into four. If you focus so that the middle two dots fuse, depth should pop in or out. Another way is to try crossing your eyes to fuse the four dots into three. You may also try holding the edge of a thin object such as a floppy disk or your hand between your eyes in order to separate each eye's vision.

Controlling Depth in Stereo Images

When you see a 3D object up close, the object seems to be in a slightly different place depending on which eye looks at it. For instance, hold your finger about five inches from your computer monitor and look at it with one eye, then the other. Observe how it seems to move left and right with respect to objects on the screen. This discrepancy gives your brain information on how far away the object is. Against the background of your screen, your finger that is five inches away is displaced about one inch, depending on which eye views it.

Julia Set Explorer 2.0

This is the one of the original filters from Metatools (formally HSC). Just to eliminate a point of confusion, the filter is called Julia Set Explorer in the Render menu, but when the dialog box opens, it is called Fractal Explorer 2.0. The explanation is simple. This filter is a hybrid of the Julia I Explorer from Kai Power Tools (KPT) 1.0 and the interface from KPT 2.0. Now you won't lie awake worrying about it.

If this is your first time with the Kai Power Tools (KPT) user interface, welcome to the jungle! Just kidding. I have heard this User Interface (UI), shown in the next illustration, described as everything from the best UI on the planet to a Klingon Control Panel. I personally opt for the latter. A friend of mine who is a big fan of KPT insists that it is really easy to learn to use. On the other hand, he believes that Neil Armstrong's moonwalk was a fake and that professional wrestling is real, so judge accordingly. Whether you hate it or love it, you have to use it. So, to get the most out of this very powerful fractal generator, you need to spend some time learning your way around.

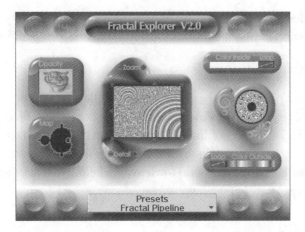

Fractal Explorer Basics

The Fractal Explorer UI, you may have already noticed, doesn't look like your average Windows dialog box.

IP: *The Fractal Explorer UI requires the monitor be in 16.7 million (24-bit) color to display properly. If your UI looks horrible (by that I mean the graphics look muddled), make sure you display is in the proper mode.*

To make the UI less confusing, many of the options, like Help, remain dimmed until you place the cursor over them. The dialog box can be moved around the screen by clicking on the title bar and dragging the dialog box anywhere on the screen. When you exit the filter by clicking on either OK or Cancel, the filter will remember its placement on the screen for the next time it is called up within that session. When you leave Corel PHOTO-PAINT and return, all positioning information is lost and the UI restarts in the center of the screen.

Temporary Resizing

Placing the cursor over the button in the upper-left corner with the Kai circular logo on it brings up the program credits for Kai Power Tools. Double-clicking this button reduces (i.e., minimizes) the Fractal Explorer to its preview window. Clicking once repetitively on the preview window magnifies the image increasingly. Double-click on the preview window and the Explorer is returned to its original happy self.

Help

Clicking on the Help button (to the immediate left of the title bar) brings up the Help menu for Fractal Explorer Kai Power Tools 2.0. Be aware that there may be Help references to things that are not in the Corel version of this product. You can also get help by pressing the F1 key, which turns the cursor into a question mark. Clicking on any part of the UI brings up context-insensitive help. No matter what you click, you are going to get the opening help screen.

Options Menu

In the upper-right corner is the Options button. Clicking on this button brings up menu choices that deal with Apply modes, which are discussed in detail later in this chapter.

Fractal Explorer Controls

Refer to Figure 24-1 for an explanation of the controls on the Fractal Explorer dialog box.

Preview Window

The real-time preview window in the center shows the fractal while it interacts with the underlying image. The initial preview window displays a rough idea of the fractal very quickly, followed by three steps of increasingly refined views. Repeat clicks preempt the preview computation, allowing fast exploration of the fractal space. Color choices are instantly mapped onto the set.

Opacity Selector

The Opacity selector on the UI controls the underlying image view. It is useful when there is a special Apply mode or transparency in the gradient that is part of the fractal. Click on it to sample one of eight preset test images, or to view the underlying image, the current selection, or the contents of the clipboard.

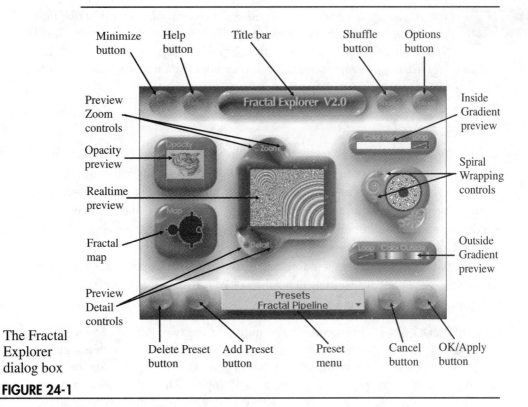

Minimize button
Help button
Title bar
Shuffle button
Options button
Preview Zoom controls
Opacity preview
Realtime preview
Fractal map
Preview Detail controls
Inside Gradient preview
Spiral Wrapping controls
Outside Gradient preview
Delete Preset button
Add Preset button
Preset menu
Cancel button
OK/Apply button

The Fractal Explorer dialog box

FIGURE 24-1

Fractal Map

The fractal map is represented by the shape of a traditional Mandelbrot set. When the cursor is over the fractal map, it changes to a small hand. Click and drag the small circle around the fractal space inside of the fractal map, or simply click and the circle moves to the spot you've clicked to. The real-time preview window displays the changes immediately, without having to manually input any numbers. As you move around the fractal map, you may stop to zoom in or out, using the controls on the preview window, at any time.

24

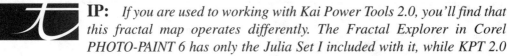

IP: *If you are used to working with Kai Power Tools 2.0, you'll find that this fractal map operates differently. The Fractal Explorer in Corel PHOTO-PAINT 6 has only the Julia Set I included with it, while KPT 2.0 has all of the fractal generators available in a drop-down list that would normally appear in this area.*

Zoom Controls

Zooming within the Fractal Explorer is accomplished in a number of different ways. The easiest method of zooming is to simply place the cursor in the real-time preview window and click to zoom in and H-click to zoom out. The zoom controls on the top of the preview window frame allow centered zooming, and clicking on the preview window enables direct zooming. Whenever the cursor is over the preview window, the arrow changes to a magnifying glass with a plus sign. Click on the spot you wish to magnify inside the preview window, and it zooms in to that spot and makes it the new center of the preview. Holding down the ALT key changes the magnifying cursor to "magnify-minus." Clicking with the ALT key held down zooms out from that point.

CENTERED ZOOMING For centered zooming, use the two controls on the upper left of the preview window frame. The plus sign (+) zooms in, the minus sign (–) zooms out, and the center of the window stays constant. If you click on the word "Zoom" on the interface, a pop-up slider will appear. Drag the slider in either direction to zoom in large steps. This is a fast way to zoom all the way in or all the way out.

Panning Control

The Panning control allows 360 degrees of continuous panning of the fractal through the preview window.

HOW TO PAN On the outside edge of the preview window are eight small arrows. Click on any of the arrows to move the main preview window in that direction. Clicking anywhere on the frame surrounding the preview (in between the arrows) moves the fractal in that direction.

DRAG PANNING Holding down the CTRL key turns the cursor into a hand, which allows the fractal to be "dragged" around the preview window for precise positioning. Limitations don't end at the preview window boundaries. Drag as far away as the screen allows.

Detail Settings

Increasing the detail settings on any fractal set adds new elements to the fractal set. Repeated zooms on a fractal set seem to eventually zoom "through" the fractal to nothing. Increasing the detail settings fills the space by increasing the ability to discern small changes, particularly inside the fractal's interior. The higher the detail is set, however, the more computational time is required for rendering. Use the two controls on the lower left of the preview window frame to control the detail in the fractal image. The plus sign (+) increases detail; the minus sign (–) decreases detail. Clicking on the word "Detail" shows a slider for more precise detail settings.

Gradient Preview/Pop-Up Menu

On the right hand side of the Fractal Explorer dialog box are two gradient preview/pop-up menu dialogs. The top gradient dialog governs the interior of the set, and the bottom one governs the exterior of the set (which is most often the dominant area). The pop-up menu for gradients is the same menu that is used by the Gradient Designer, complete with hierarchical categorization of gradient presets. The Triangle/Sawtooth icon shows the looping control and further affects the way that the gradient is mapped to the fractal set.

Gradient Wrapping Control

Also on the right side, between the Gradient Preview controls, is the Gradient Wrapping control. The fractal set may be colored with any gradient you choose. You can obtain more interesting renders with the same gradient by controlling the repetition of the gradient as it applies to the set in two different directions. There are two controls for mapping the gradient frequency to the fractal set.

The Spiral setting, on the upper left, controls how fast the color cycles as it moves from one potential line to the next. The lines are expressing the potential of any point in four-dimensional space to fall toward the attractors, roughly analogous to space around an electric charge with equal attraction to the electrostatic center. Within a ring, the electrostatic pull is the same and there can be many such rings moving toward the center of the charge.

The Spoke setting, on the lower right of the Wrapping control, determines how often the gradient will be repeated over the entire 360-degree circle around the set. This is the Radial control. These two settings interact with each other. Variations in the Spiral setting will result in widely divergent effects.

The Preset Menu

The Preset Menu is where all of the named or saved fractals are stored. When you press the letter A or click on Add, a dialog box will allow options for item names, category names, and preset files.

Shuffle Button

The Shuffle button allows selection of different Fractal Explorer parameters to randomize. You may check All, or None, or select from the list. Each time the Shuffle button is clicked, the selected parameters are shuffled. The parameters that can be shuffled are:

- ► Exterior Colors
- ► Interior Colors
- ► Exterior Looping
- ► Interior Looping
- ► Apply Mode
- ► Test Image
- ► Equipotential Speed
- ► Radial Speed

Options Button

Clicking on the Options button displays a menu with the Apply Mode list and three other options. Those options are as follows.

WRAP IMAGE INSTEAD OF GRADIENT   This option allows the user to grab color data from an Opacity preview mode, which can be the underlying image, the Windows clipboard, or a Selection. The Fractal Explorer uses the color data contained in the selection, image, or clipboard, and wraps that color around the gradient.

NUMERICAL INPUT   Numerical Input enables the experienced "fractologist" to find previously explored spaces or to explore new fractal spaces by "hard-coding" the algorithm variables.

DRAW GRADIENT ACROSS TOP   This feature creates a bar across the top of the fractal image you create to show you the gradient that was used. It is not active in all modes.

IP: *If a bar appears across the top of your image after applying the effect and you are wondering where it came from, it is because the Draw Gradient Across Top option is set.*

A Quick Tour of Fractal Explorer

To do Fractal Explorer justice would take volumes, and it still wouldn't scratch the surface or do you much good. The real secret is to experiment. That said, let's begin exploring.

Making a Background with Fractal Explorer

One of the things that Fractal Explorer does best is make backgrounds. Let's create one.

1. Open a new image with a setting of 400 x 400 pixels, 150 dpi resolution, and 24-bit color.

2. Open the Fractal Explorer by clicking on Julia Set Explorer 2.0 in the Render drop-down menu of the Effects menu. The Fractal Explorer dialog box opens. Now for the tricky part. You need to open one of the presets. The presets on this dialog box are not the same as normal drop-down lists. On the bottom middle is a rectangular area that contains all of the presets. Click and hold the tiny arrow in the lower-right corner until another pop-up menu opens. When this happens, don't let go of the mouse button. You have three choices at this point: Corel Presets, Misc., and Presets. While still holding down the left mouse button, move the cursor over to select Corel Presets.

3. Still holding down the mouse button, move back over to the drop-down list that just appeared and move the cursor down the list to the bottom. As you do this, the list will begin to scroll downward. Keep going down until you get to Totally Tubular. Now let go of the mouse button. After a moment, the center preview window should display the new fill pattern.

4. The UP ARROW and DOWN ARROW keys allow you to move through the list of Presets. Click the DOWN ARROW key and watch the preview window. It says "Tropical Island." The DOWN ARROW key selects the next preset. By using the UP ARROW and DOWN ARROW keys, you can move quickly though all of the presets and see what they look like. The preview window changes almost instantly to a new shape. Keep watching. The first image you see in the preview window is a really rough

24

approximation of what it will look like. If you give it a moment, the preview window will be refreshed two more times, giving it more detail each time.

5. Now click the UP ARROW key and return to the Totally Tubular preset. Now you are going to make a change. You want to use this effect, but the color is wrong. I picked this preset because the Inside Color setting has no effect on it, so you only need to concern yourself with the Outside Color.

6. Place the cursor over the box that says "Color Outside." When the cursor is over where it is supposed to be, it will change into a tiny representation of a drop-down box. Click on the box and a very long drop-down list will appear.

7. Holding down the left mouse button, move down the list until you reach "Metallic." As you pass some of the names on the list, various-sized drop-down lists will appear. When you get to Metallic, the drop-down list associated with that setting will appear. The default setting for Totally Tubular is Blue Green Metal Cone, which is checked at the top of the list.

8. Still holding the left mouse button, move the cursor down the secondary list to "Gentle Gold" and release the mouse button. The lists disappear and Totally Tubular changes from a blue-green to a gold. Click the OK button on the lower right and you have created an excellent gold background for a presentation as shown below.

9. Open the Fractal Explorer again. This time, select the Corel Preset "60s Wallpaper" preset or click the HOME key on your keyboard. A faint rainbow-color fractal is now sitting on top of the golden background in the preview. You are going to use one of the Apply modes to change the look of the golden background.

10. Click on the Options button in the upper-right corner of the dialog box and another drop-down list appears. This time, select Darken Only and view the results after you let go of the mouse button. Now it looks like you have rolls of wrapping paper. Click the OK button to apply the fractal effect to the original. You can save it if you want. It will not be required for another work session.

IP: *A quick way to preview different Apply modes under the Options list is to hold down the CTRL key and use the RIGHT ARROW key to move down the list and the LEFT ARROW key to move up the list. The preview is updated immediately.*

The Julia Explorer Apply Modes

Now that you have played with them a little, it is time to discover what those Apply modes really do. The Apply mode determines how the fractal you create with Fractal Explorer is going to be merged with your existing image, if there is one. It is similar in operation to the way the Object Merge mode works in the Objects/Layers roll-up. The Apply modes appear on a drop-down list when the Options button is clicked. As a group, the Apply mode options take what is already a wide variety of fractal effects and increase that variety exponentially. Since it is easy to experiment with the Apply modes by using the CTRL-UP ARROW or CTRL-DOWN ARROW keys (see the preceding section on keyboard command shortcuts), the Apply modes are well worth investigating while you are working with different fractals. The Apply modes are as follows.

Normal Apply

This is the one that is used most often. What you see in the preview window is applied to the image or to the masked (selected) area of the image. Normal mode applies the fractal without regard to the underlying image. All underlying image data is destroyed by this process. Transparency in general is not available in this mode unless the gradient, texture, or fractal has some level of transparency. Those areas underneath the transparency will show through, while everything else will be covered with the selected gradient, texture, or fractal.

Procedural Blend

This is a killer application that produces stunning effects with a fractal. Each pixel is evaluated and acted upon based on its luminance value. If the original pixel has a luminance value in the medium range (128 +/– on a scale from 0-255), the apply is normal. If the luminance value is brighter (200+/–), the apply effect will be brightened by that amount. If the original pixel is darker, the apply effect will be proportionately darker. The effect is to wrap a fractal around the underlying grayscale image, based upon luminance values. Any areas of pure white or pure black will show through as pure white and pure black, as the luminance values dictate a full brightening or darkening to maximum values, black and white. The Procedural Blend results in the effect "following" the intensity of the original image and appears to be wrapped around.

Reverse Blend

This is applied in the same way as Procedural Blend, except that the image and the effect are reversed (which is probably why they called it Reverse Blend). Wherever the effect is a medium intensity , the image is added normally. Wherever the effect is brighter or darker than the image, the effect will be modified proportionately before it is added. The real-time preview window is necessary if you want to use this filter effectively.

Lighten Only

The Lighten Only mode reads the luminance values of both the original image and the fractal image and compares them. It then adds the fractal only in those areas where the fractal is lighter than the underlying image.

Darken Only

The Darken Only mode reads the luminance values of both the original image and the fractal image and compares them. It then adds the fractal only in those areas where the fractal is darker than the underlying image.

IP: *Unusual effects can be achieved with multiple applications of Lighten Only or Darken Only.*

Add

The Add mode sums the numerical color values of the underlying image and the fractal you wish to apply and clips them when the values reach the maximum (white). Remember that the Add Apply adds the numerical value of colors. Thus, while yellow plus blue will make green on a real palette, the result of adding their numerical values together is white. In many cases, the results of the Add Apply mode may resemble a Blend function, wherein the brighter areas tend to wash out to white, but not always. Add is more difficult to predict than Blend or Multiply, so the best results are achieved with time and experimentation with the real-time preview window.

Subtract

The Subtract Apply mode compares the underlying image and the fractal, and then combines them using subtractive color theory. For instance, if the image is white and a green effect is applied, the Subtract mode will yield a magenta. (Subtracting green from RGB yields red plus blue, or purple.) While it would be nice to say that Subtract gives the opposite results of what you get with the Add Apply, it doesn't work that way. The color theory behind it gets ugly, so you should experiment with this mode.

Multiply

The Multiply Apply mode takes only the dark components of the fractal and adds them to the underlying image. Everything that is white is ignored, and everything that is black is added proportionately according to its luminance values.

Screen

The Screen Apply mode measures the light components in both the underlying image and the fractal. The lighter components are added to the image, and the darker components discarded or ignored. Everything in between appears to be blended. Both Multiply and Screen will give more predictable results than the other Apply modes discussed so far except Normal.

24

Difference

The Difference Apply mode is probably the most dramatic of the Apply modes. Before you start using it, you should be warned that it is also one of the most difficult Apply modes to predict. The Difference Apply mode uses both the underlying image and fractal color ranges to their fullest, and it measures the difference between the two. This difference is what is applied.

For example, if a black-to-white gradient (such as a Fountain fill) is applied over an image, and then you apply the Difference mode, the black areas of the gradient stay the same. Wherever the gradient is white, the image is inverted to negative colors. For colors that are neither black nor white, the effect is somewhere in between the two. The Difference mode can create very abstract and colorful images. The downside of this is the inability to predict the results ahead of time. This means that a lot of time is needed for experimenting with various combinations in order to get an effect you want.

Tie Me Up/Tie Me Down

If there was ever any question that KPT comes out of California, I think the names of these two Apply modes should erase any doubts. Tie Me Up and Tie Me Down use "modulo arithmetic" for color manipulation. (You are probably wondering what modulo arithmetic is. So am I.) Their function is similar to Add and Subtract, with the distinction that instead of clipping to black or white, the result which would have been clipped is retained and used as color data. When dealing with a lot of black or white within either the underlying image or selection, or within the gradient itself, Tie Me Up/Tie Me Down will not yield anything surprising. On the other hand, some results will be astonishing, with polarized sheens and kaleidoscopic effects.

Keyboard Shortcuts

Knowing several of the following keyboard shortcuts will save you time when exploring images. When Launching Julia Set Explorer from the Effects/Special Drop-Down List, keep this in mind: Holding down the CTRL key while clicking on the word *Julia Set* prevents the image from being loaded into the preview window. This can be a real time saver with very large image files.

Shortcuts within the Fractal Explorer UI

Once you have opened the dialog box (UI), there are several keyboard shortcuts to make life easier when working and navigating your way around as shown on the following list.

UP ARROW	Previous preset (in current category)
DOWN ARROW	Next preset (in current category)
PAGE UP/PAGE DOWN	Moves between lists of Presets
HOME	Top of Corel Presets list
END	Top of the Presets list

Lens Flare

The Lens Flare effect, whose dialog box is shown in the following illustration, produces a spot of light that resembles a reflection within an optical system. In photography, lenses of different focal lengths produce different lens flare effects. Photographers work very hard to make sure the effects added by this filter do not occur. With this filter you can add what they try to get out of a photograph.

When you first open the dialog box, it will immediately render and provide a preview of the selected image. Choose from three lens types to produce the type of lens flare you want. You can also adjust the brightness (1-200 percent) of the lens flare with the slider bar. To change the position of the "flare," click on the preview window at the point where you want the flare to be. Be aware that the preview function is automatic. This means that changing the lens type will start a preview cycle. An example of a photograph that has had the Lens Flare applied to it is shown in Figure 24-2.

IP: *The Lens Flare filter only works with 24-bit color images. To apply this effect to a grayscale, convert the grayscale to a 24-bit color image, apply the Lens Flare filter, and then convert it back to grayscale.*

The Lens Flare filter can also be used to create reflections and highlights. The sphere in Figure 24-3 was made with the Map To Object filter and then the highlight was created by applying the Lens Flare filter.

Lighting Effects filter

The Lighting Effects filter lets you add one or more light sources to your image. Choose from a list of presets or create your own customized lights using the dialog

The Lens Flare filter was used to add the bright spot in the curl of the wave

FIGURE 24-2

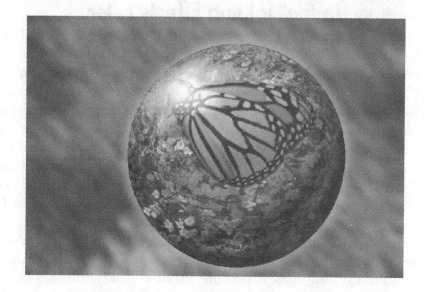

The glare
on the glass
sphere was
also
produced
by the Lens
Flare filter

FIGURE 24-3

box options. You can add multiple lights and individually control the attributes of
each light. The rather intimidating dialog box for the lighting effects is shown in the
following illustration. Using this dialog box is a little less than intuitive. After
opening the filter, the preview window displays what the lighting effect looks like
with the default setting, which is a green light. What were they thinking about?

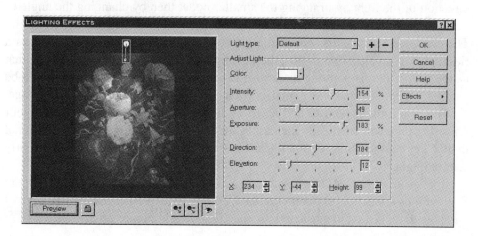

Setting Up the Lighting Effects Filter

The first step in using this filter is to choose a Light Type from the list box. The list box contains a drop-down box with several preset light types available—for example, Spotlight, Narrow Spotlight. You can also add and remove your own styles. Each light source has been assigned appropriate settings to achieve a unique effect. Use the controls to modify existing presets to create exactly the lighting you want. Next, choose a color for the light; white is probably a better starting point than green. Adjust the Intensity slider (used for spotlights) to set the brightness of the light (range of 1-200 percent), but be careful not to set it too high as this can wash out colors. The Aperture slider (1-180°) is used to set the range (width) of the light. The greater the aperture percentage, the greater the area affected by the light. The Exposure slider (1-200 percent) controls the intensity of the light. Positive values add light, while negative values subtract light. This setting works much like the Intensity setting, but is used with ambient and wide-angle lights. By default, when the button with the Eye icon is depressed, the preview window displays all the icons representing light sources currently active in the image.

In the preview window, there are initially two icons. The rectangular icon representing the light consists of a large node that indicates the focus of the light, and a smaller node that indicates the direction and height of the light. The small dot icon is Ambient light. It controls the color and other settings control the "room light." The initial settings are a bright light with a dark color. Click the large node and drag the light source to a desired position. As you adjust the position of the light, the X and Y settings indicate the horizontal and vertical positions. You can adjust the direction of the light by dragging the smaller node, thereby changing the angle of the line. As you adjust the line, the Directional setting indicates the angle of light. The elevation slider is the one that confused me at first. Think of the light as a flashlight. At an elevation of 90°, the flashlight is perpendicular to the image; that is, the actual light is pointing directly at the image. At 0°, the flashlight would be parallel to the image and only a small portion of the light would be striking the image.

This filter allows you to add up to 19 lights. Of course, with 19 lights, your rendering time will drastically increase. Clicking the Plus button adds an additional light. Clicking the Minus button under the Preview window removes the currently selected light.

Shown in Figure 24-4 is a scene at a dock from Corel World's Best Digital Photographs collection. By applying the Lighting Effects filter using three lights I was able to make that image a night scene, as shown in Figure 24-5.

Here is a
daylight
photograph
of a man
mending
a net

FIGURE 24-4

By applying
the Lighting
Effects
filter, we
are able to
make it into
a night scene

FIGURE 24-5

Advanced Fill Topics

25

Before we get too far into this topic, we need to clarify some changes that occurred with the release of Corel PHOTO-PAINT 6. In Corel PHOTO-PAINT 5, there is a separate roll-up called the Fill roll-up. In Corel PHOTO-PAINT 6, the functionality of the Fill roll-up has been incorporated into the Tool Settings roll-up. I wasn't too fond of the new arrangement when I first began to work with it. But now that I have had several months to get used to it, I like it. The Fill roll-up function is now accessed through either the Tool Settings roll-up or the onscreen palette. The Tool Settings roll-up in Corel PHOTO-PAINT 6, like a chameleon, takes on the characteristics of the mode that is selected. When the Fill Tool, Rectangle, Ellipse, or Polygon tool is selected, the Tool Settings roll-up becomes what is called the Fill roll-up under Corel PHOTO-PAINT 5. To access it through the onscreen palette, just right-click on the palette. To cut down the verbiage in this chapter, when the Fill roll-up is referenced, I am talking about the Tool Settings roll-up, truly a rose by another name.

Until now we have looked at fill tools only as far as necessary. In this chapter we will learn everything there is to know about the subject. All of the technical details are here, so if you are having trouble sleeping at night, start reading the definition of Pantone colors. That should put you out pretty quick.

In CorelDRAW, the Fill roll-up is a supporting player; in Corel PHOTO-PAINT, it is a star. As you work with Corel PHOTO-PAINT, you will discover that the Fill roll-up is one of the roll-ups that you use the most. The Fill roll-up controls what fill is applied when you use the Fill tool, or the Rectangle, Ellipse, and Polygon tool. It provides access to a wide variety of preset and custom fills, ranging from simple spot colors to complex custom bitmap fills.

The Fill roll-up, shown next, can be accessed many ways, as follows.

▶ Double-clicking the Fill tool in the Toolbox.

▶ Double-clicking the Rectangle, Ellipse, or Polygon tool in the Toolbox.

▶ If either of the Tools mentioned above is selected, you can also access the Fill roll-up by using CTRL-F8 or selecting the Tool Settings roll-up from the View menu.

When you open the Fill roll-up, you will notice that there are four buttons near the top of the roll-up. Each button switches the Fill roll-up into a different mode of operation. The icon on the buttons indicates the operational mode they activate. Figure 25-1 identifies each of the functions.

 OTE: *If you open the Fill roll-up feature of the Tool Settings roll-up by double-clicking either the Rectangle, Ellipse, or Polygon tool, there will be five buttons at the top. The fifth button is the No Fill button.*

The Mode Select Buttons

Before going into detailed descriptions, let's summarize the button functions.

The first button selects the Uniform Color fill. From this mode, any solid (non-gradient) color can be selected either from the existing palette or from a custom palette.

25

The four fill buttons in the Fill roll-up. Each button switches the Fill roll-up into a different mode of operation

FIGURE 25-1

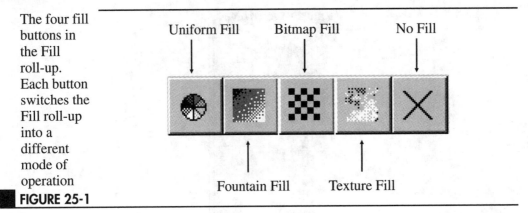

Uniform Fill   Bitmap Fill   No Fill

Fountain Fill   Texture Fill

The second button is the Fountain fill. It operates in the same manner as the Gradient Fill in CorelDRAW 5 to produce Linear, Radial, Conical, and Square fills. This fill comes with a large selection of presets. All of the fountain fills can be customized.

The third button is the Full-Color Bitmap fill, indicated by the checkerboard icon on the middle button. Like its CorelDRAW 5 counterpart, it can provide bitmap fills either from its existing library of fills or from custom fills that are created with Corel PHOTO-PAINT or other graphics programs. This is a powerful tiling engine. Any bitmap file can be used for Bitmap fill patterns (tiles).

The fourth button is the Texture fill, the most unique in the Fill roll-up. This mode does not use existing tiles or patterns. Instead, it creates them at the time of use through a powerful fractal generator. You can produce some unusual and exotic textures (or patterns) with this fill.

The No Fill button is only available when the Rectangle, Ellipse, or Polygon tool is selected. This button prevents fills from being applied.

Fill Status Line

You can see the currently selected fill color/pattern by viewing the status bar. You will notice that there are three small rectangles located on the middle of the status line. They are, from left to right, Paint color (foreground color), Paper color (background color), and the Fill tool color/pattern. Because the area is small, it is sometimes difficult to accurately determine the selected type of fill.

The Uniform Color Fill Mode

Uniform Color Fill is the simplest fill mode and is used to select and apply solid (uniform) colors to an image. When Uniform Color fill is selected, the Fill Color Swatch in the Status Bar reflects the current fill color that is selected.

Selecting a Uniform Color

The currently selected color is shown as a color swatch on the roll-up. To change the color, click the Edit button. This action opens the Uniform Fill dialog box, as shown here. You can select a color from the color palette in the lower-right of the dialog box. There are more colors in this palette that can be accessed by moving the scroll bars. Once you find the desired color, click on the color in the palette. The name of the color appears in the Name box above the palette. Other actions occur and other information is displayed, but we will be discussing these later in the chapter.

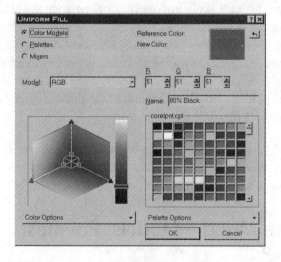

The Uniform Fill Dialog Box

The Uniform Fill dialog box is where you can literally pick any color in the universe. The operation of this dialog box can intimidate the faint of heart. The dialog box is an essential tool for defining and correcting colors for those doing pre-press work.

25

If you only want to make a simple modification to a color so it will look better in an image, you can do that as well.

Just so you know, the Uniform Fill dialog box is common throughout Corel PHOTO-PAINT as well as all of the CorelDRAW 6 suite of applications. Changes made to the palette in this dialog box are global. That means that they apply to all of the CorelDRAW suite of applications. The Uniform Fill dialog box allows you to choose colors from various color models and custom palettes, including CorelDRAW 4 and CorelDRAW 5 (.PAL) palettes.

You can also import and select individual colors from existing .BMP files.

How to Approach the Uniform Fill Dialog Box

There are two general approaches to using the Uniform Fill dialog box. The simplest is to pick the color closest to the desired color from the short palette, modify the color in the Uniform Fill dialog box, and then return to the Fill roll-up. The advantage is speed. The disadvantage of this method is that you will be using an undefined color that may be difficult, if not impossible, for someone at a different location (like a service bureau) to duplicate.

The second approach is to create one or several colors, name them, and save them on a custom palette. This way you can use the colors in another image because the colors have been named and saved. Another site can duplicate your work since you can send the palette along with the image. The disadvantage is that it takes longer to do. That said, let's examine this cornucopia.

 IP: *If you just need to lighten or darken the color you selected in the short palette, use the slider to the right of the color model. Moving it down makes the color darker and moving it up makes the color lighter.*

Setting the Mood—Models, Palettes, or Mixers?

The operation of the dialog box is controlled by which of the three buttons in the upper-left corner is selected. These affect not only the operation but also the appearance of the dialog box. You have three choices, as follows.

▶ **Color Models.** This method of choosing a color allows you to select one of nine color models to establish the color you want. The reason for selecting a specific color model to use when choosing colors is based on the type of work you are doing. For example, if you are color-correcting a photograph that will be printed using the four-color printing process (CMYK), you should choose the CMYK or CMYK 255 color model.

► **Palettes.** Selecting this button changes the color selection to one based not on color models but on a series of predefined palettes. Use Palettes to pick a system of predefined colors such as Pantone or Trumatch. These are the choices if you are using spot colors.

► **Mixers.** The first two choices only offer about 30 million or so colors. There are always those who just cannot find that special color they want with only 30 million to choose from, so Corel provided mixers that provide two different ways to make their own colors.

Color Models

Color models are a method for representing the color of colored items, usually by their components as specified along at least three dimensions. The first button allows you to select one of ten color models. As you change color models, the numerical value system on the right and the 3D color model displayed below the model name change.

The color model options available are as follows.

Color Model Options

► **CMY.** This color model contains only Cyan, Magenta, and Yellow. You should only select this if the final output will be done on a CMY device, such as a three-ink printer. The C, M, and Y values range between 0 and 255.

► **CMYK.** This shows the CMYK model and list value boxes for each of the components in percentages. Cyan, Magenta, Yellow, and Black (CMYK) is the model used for the four-color printing process. *A note about CMYK:* When this model is selected, there may be some display irregularities if you are using blended colors. When blended colors are displayed on the monitor, they show up as banding. The printed output itself is unaffected, but the display may be banded.

► **CMYK 255.** This is like the previous CMYK model, except the values are listed according to a computer-based scale (0 to 255) rather than percentages. As in the previous model, the letters represent Cyan, Magenta, Yellow, and Black ("K" is used to indicate black). This color model is based on the printer's primary colors.

▶ **RGB.** This is the standard of monitor color models. All computer displays are RGB (Red, Green, and Blue)—the same as your eyes. The RGB model is the default color model of Corel PHOTO-PAINT. This is the ground zero of all color models.

▶ **HSB.** The popularity of HSB isn't what it used to be, although components of this model are still used when working with the filters. Hue, Saturation, and Brightness (HSB) is an alternate to the RGB model.

▶ **HLS.** HLS (Hue, Lightness, Saturation) is a variation on HSB and an alternative to RGB. Hue determines color (yellow, orange, red, etc.), lightness determines perceived intensity (lighter or darker color), and saturation determines color depth (from dull to intense). The circular visual selector defines the H value (0 to 360) and the S value (0 to 100); the vertical visual selector defines the L value (0 to 100).

▶ **L*A*B*.** This color model is becoming more and more popular. It was developed by Commission Internationale de l'Eclairage (CIE) based on three parameters: lightness (L*), green to red chromaticity (a*), and blue to yellow chromaticity (b*). The square two-dimensional visual selector defines the a* and b* coordinates from –60 to 60; the vertical visual selector defines the L* value from 0 to 100. This model is device-independent, meaning that it does not need to have information about the devices it is working with to operate correctly. For the prepress industry, it encompasses the color gamuts of both the CMYK and the RGB color models. There are slick tricks you can use to sharpen a PCD file if it is converted into the L*A*B* model. Unfortunately, Corel PHOTO-PAINT 6 does not have that ability. The ability to convert an image into L*A*B* will be in Corel PHOTO-PAINT 7.

▶ **YIQ.** The preferred model when working with video is YIQ, which is used in television broadcast systems (North American video standard: NTSC). Colors are split into a luminance value (Y) and two chromaticity values (I and Q). On a color monitor, all three components are visible; on a monochrome monitor, only the Y component is visible. The square two-dimensional visual selector defines the I and Q values, and the vertical visual selector defines the Y value. All values are scaled from 0 to 255. In Corel PHOTO-PAINT, the Y component of the splitting process produces a grayscale image that is often superior to results obtained with a grayscale conversion using the Convert To command from the Image menu.

▶ **Grayscale.** This is your basic plain vanilla 256 shades of gray color model. No, that's not a typo—gray is a color. By using the arrows on the Gray Level list box, it is possible to select any of 255 levels of grayscale, with 0 being the lightest and 255 the darkest.

▶ **Registration color.** The Registration color model consists of a single color in the CMYK color space, for which C, M, Y, and K are at 100 percent. You can use this color on any object that you want to appear on all separation plates. It is ideal for company logos, job numbers, or any other identifying marks that you may need for the job. This color cannot be added to the custom palette.

 IP: *If the project you are working on is not going to an offset printer, select the RGB or Grayscale color model.*

How to Select or Create a Color Using Color Models Mode

▶ The first step is to remember what color it was that you were working on to begin with. That is found in the upper-right corner. It is labeled **Reference color**. This was the color originally selected on the short palette in the Fill roll-up.

▶ Select a color model. This step is easy: use RGB unless you have good reason to use another model. If you are working with 32-bit color, use CMYK or CMYK-255.

▶ If the only change you want is to make the Reference color darker or lighter, move the slider located between the color model and the palette either up or down watching the color swatch labeled **New Color** under the Reference Color in the upper-right corner of the dialog box.

▶ If you want to create a completely different color you can click on any point in the color model and the color value of the point will appear in the New Color swatch. You can also enter values numerically. For example, with the RGB model, entering a value of 0,0,0 will produce Black and 255,255,255 will produce White.

Using the Printable Color Swatch

As you adjust the slider up and down, a swatch of color will appear (and sometimes disappear) below the New Color swatch called Printable Color. This is an ingenious device that warns you of colors that cannot be printed using SWOP (Standard Web Offset Press). If you are not having it printed on an offset press, don't be too concerned about this feature.

If you are new to color printing, you may not be aware that there are ranges of colors that cannot be reproduced by your printer. The Printable Color warns you when the color you are selecting is outside of the capability of your printer. The swatch of color that appears displayed as Printable Color represents the closest approximation to the desired color that can be printed. To use the color that appears in Printable Color, click the arrow button to the right of the New Color swatch. The color in the Printable Color will replace the New Color.

Once you are satisfied with the color displayed in the New Color swatch, click the OK button and you will return to the Fill roll-up with the New Color selected.

Color Options Button

Clicking this button opens the Color Options menu. There are three choices on this menu: Add Color to Palette, which adds the selected color to the custom palette; Swap Colors, which, when selected, will swap the New Color and the Reference color; and Use Printer Circuits, which, when enabled (a check mark appears by the name), uses the output printer settings in the Corel Color Wizard to make accurate conversions between RGB and CMYK. This feature is either On or Off. If you are doing any conversions between these two color models, it should be left on.

Saving a New Color on a Palette

Now that you have created that special color you wanted, you need to save it. Colors are saved on palettes. Before I show you how to save a color to a palette, you need to understand a few things about palettes. Palettes, like the original artist's palette, are files that store colors. Palette files have a .CPL extension. The palette in the dialog box is the short palette that was originally shown in the Fill roll-up. The palette is displayed regardless of the color model selected. The only way to display another palette is to load a different one. This will be dealt with in more detail in the next section, which concerns Palettes mode.

The Custom palette is the default Corel PHOTO-PAINT palette. The palettes discussed in this chapter store a large selection of colors. You can use a special palette to keep all of the colors used in a particular project or painting. Some people like to keep a palette that contains all of their favorite colors. The choice is yours. Here is how to save a color you have created.

IP: *When creating new colors, especially for company logos, be sure to give the new color a specific name. This can be critical when the job needs to be modified and you are trying to guess which color you used out of a possible ten billion combinations.*

1. After you are satisfied with the new color, enter a name for the color.

2. Click the Color Options button below the color model, and a drop-down list appears. Choose Add Color to Palette and the new color will be added to the bottom of the current palette.

Removing a Color from the Palette

Fair is fair. If I am going to show you how to add a color to a palette, I should also show you how to get rid of it.

1. Click on the color you want to delete.

2. Click on the Palette Options button below the palette and choose Delete Color from the drop-down list.

3. A confirmation box appears, giving you one last chance before deleting the color. Click the Yes button and the color is history.

Renaming a Color in the Palette

Sometimes you don't want to remove the color, just rename it. Renaming colors is simple as well.

1. Click on the color you want to rename.

2. Type in the new name in the Name: box.

3. Click on the Palette Options button below the palette and choose Rename Color from the drop-down list.

OTE: *Don't rename existing industry-standard colors. For example, if you are using Pantone 1615V, don't call it Flaming Neon Ties. While you may find the nomenclature entertaining, it will not be understood by the service bureau or your printer. Another reason for sane color names is that human memory is frail, and if you give a color a cute name, there is a strong chance that when it comes time to look for it again, you may not be able to remember that specific* *shade of green that you created was called Aunt Fred's Toenail Clipping. Now that I've spoiled your fun, the good news is that Corel PHOTO-PAINT gives you 20 characters with which to name your new color creation. This is a vast improvement over the terse eight-character restriction of DOS naming conventions.*

Working with the Palettes

Now that you know how to get colors on and off the palettes as well as rename the colors, the only thing left is how to manage the palettes themselves.

The palette management options are listed on a drop-down list that appears when the Palette Options button under the palette is clicked. The drop-down list has the following options.

NEW PALETTE This palette option opens up an empty palette that you can fill with any combination of colors. If you attempt to create a new palette without saving the current palette that you have modified, you will receive a warning message. To create a new palette, proceed as follows:

1. Select New Palette.

2. When the New Palette dialog box opens, enter the name for the new palette.

3. After you enter a name, click the Save button.

IP: *Sometimes when you are working on a project that requires a number of exact reference colors (e.g., Pantone), you may find it is easier to create a palette specifically for the project with the required colors.*

OPENING AN EXISTING PALETTE The Open Palette option opens the Open Palette dialog box. The default palette is CORELPNT.CPL, an RGB color model palette. When opening an existing palette, you have the choice of opening one of three different types of palettes from the File of Type list:

▶ Custom palette (.CPL)

▶ Spot palette (.IPL)

▶ Process palette (.PAL)

SAVING A PALETTE Selecting this option opens the Save Palette dialog box, which saves the current palette under the same name. This is used to save any changes made to a palette. If you do not save a palette, any change made to it will be lost when Corel PHOTO-PAINT is closed or a new palette is selected.

SAVE AS A NEW PALETTE   Use this option when you have modified an existing palette but do not want to apply the change to the original palette. This is the best way to build a custom palette of favorite colors. The basic palette has 99 colors. By adding colors to the existing palette and saving it under a unique name, you have all of the basic colors plus your personal favorites or specific colors made for a project or client.

IP: *Use the Save As command when you have made changes to the default palette. Many times, image files that you can get from various sources expect to find the default palette. If you have changed it, you may get unpredictable results.*

DELETING A PALETTE   To quote the caterpillar in *Alice Through the Looking Glass,* "You can't get there from here." Well, you actually can; it's just not obvious. OK, watch carefully. Click the Palette Options button and select Open Palette option. When the dialog box opens, right-click the palette you want to delete. A pop-up menu appears and one of the choices is Delete. Like I said, not a direct route.

Palettes Mode

Enabling the second button down in the upper-left corner of the Uniform Fill dialog box opens the Palette mode. This offers a collection of different color-matching-system palettes available to the Corel PHOTO-PAINT user. The number of colors or shades available in each palette is dependent on the color mode of the image. The different palettes are provided when you have projects that work with Spot or color process systems like Pantone, TOYO, and Trumatch. The palettes contain industry-standard colors that are essential for color-matching accuracy when the project is to be output to offset printing.

OTE: *When using the Pantone color-matching system in Palettes mode, be aware that the colors cannot be changed. Only the percentage of Tint can be modified. This is because the ability of a system like Pantone to match the colors printed on the swatch (which you must buy from them) is based on the combination of inks that make up the color and do not change.*

Viewing Palette Selections by Name

Clicking the Color Options button and selecting Show Color Names will cause the currently selected palette to change to an alphabetical listing of all of the color names for the color system selected. Each name is preceded by a color rectangle displaying a sample of the named color. Regarding the displayed colors, please remember that what you see is only a good approximation of what that actual color looks like, even when you are using a very expensive monitor and graphics card and even when you have done all of the calibration voodoo. When using color samples from a color-matching system, always trust the swatches provided by the manufacturer over the screen.

Searching for Colors by Name

The Search provides a quick way to locate a specific, named color in a color system. As each character is typed in, the computer begins its search. As subsequent characters are entered, the search field is narrowed. Here is a quick exercise to find the spot color blue.

1. In the Type: area, click the down arrow button and select Pantone® Spot Colors.

2. Type **BL** in the area labeled Search:. As the letters "BL" are entered under the Pantone spot system, the computer goes to the first BL in the system, which is "black."

3. Then type in **U**, and the search produces Pantone Blue 072 CV.

4. Since many times clients will specify colors by number, enter 273 in the search area. As you type in each character, the list narrows the search until you have Pantone 273. The search system accepts both alphabetic and numeric characters, since many names of colors in color-matching systems have numeric designations.

Exploring the Palettes

When the Palette mode is enabled, a new option is made available in the Color Options menu. It is the Show Color Names option, and when it is enabled, the Name of the palette appears alongside a small swatch of the color. The eight palette choices available when you click the arrow in the Type box are as follows.

UNIFORM COLORS PALETTE   This is the default palette for Corel PHOTO-PAINT. The Uniform Color palette offers 255 standard RGB colors for quick selection. Colors are expressed as RGB values for all images and drawings. Use the scroll bar on the right to display other areas of the palette. Colors can be displayed by name through the Show Color Names option in the flyout menu (the color names correspond to the R, G, and B values). It is a sampling of the entire visible spectrum at 100 percent saturation.

FOCOLTONE PALETTE   This palette offers colors that are available through the FOCOLTONE color system. Because the colors are based on CMYK, there is no need to add additional color separation plates. When FOCOLTONE is selected, the dialog box shows the FOCOLTONE model and a Search For box. The Search For box, located under the Color Options button, is used to search for specific FOCOLTONE color names. FOCOLTONE is a color-matching system. Like all color-matching systems, FOCOLTONE provides a specimen swatch to printers and designers so there is a point of agreement as to what the color specified is supposed to look like.

PANTONE SPOT PALETTE   This is one of two available Pantone palettes. This palette offers colors that are available through the Pantone Spot Colors system (also known as Pantone Matching System). In this system, you define tint through the Tint Number Box, ranging from 0 (lightest) to 100 (darkest) to control saturation. This system also allows you to define PostScript options. Since spot colors correspond to solid inks and are not CMYK-based, each unique color applied to an object results in an additional color separation plate. In Corel PHOTO-PAINT, you can use spot colors only in CMYK images to affect duotones. Colors can be displayed by name or swatch through the Color Options menu.

Selecting the Pantone Spot Colors opens the palette and also opens the Search For box. The Search For box, located under the Color Options button in the lower-left portion of the dialog box, is used to search for specific Pantone Spot Color names. Spot colors are specific colors that are applied to an area and are not the result of multiple applications of inks. Pantone is one of the more popular color-matching systems. As with FOCOLTONE, when using Pantone, you pick out a specific color from a sample and then pick out the color name or number from the Pantone list. When it goes to the service bureau to be made into film, the computer then knows what particular Pantone color was specified.

25

PANTONE PROCESS PALETTE   This operates like the Pantone Spot Colors model except that it shows Process colors. Process colors are colors created by multiple applications of ink. Pantone specifies all the information that is necessary for the printer to be able to duplicate the color. When Pantone Process is selected, it shows the Process Color model and the Search For box. Tint is not an option with Pantone Process. The Search For box, located under the Color Options button, is used to search for specific Pantone Process Color names. The list offers a search capability for colors that are available through the Pantone Process Color system, which is based on the CMYK color model. The first 2,000 colors are two-color combinations; the remainder are three- and four-color combinations. Colors are based on CMYK and therefore do not add additional color separation plates. Use the scroll bar on the right to display other areas of the palette. Colors can be displayed by name or swatch through the Color Options menu.

TRUMATCH PALETTE   This is a competing color-matching system for Pantone. Like Pantone, the Trumatch palette allows specification of colors according to specific samples, but it offers colors that are available through the Trumatch color system. This system is based on the CMYK color model and therefore colors do not add additional color separation plates. Colors are organized by hue (red to violet), saturation (deep to pastel), and brightness (adding or removing black). Use the scroll bar on the right to display other areas of the palette. Colors can be displayed by name or swatch through the Color Options menu.

SPECTRAMASTER PALETTE   This is a specialized color-matching system. The palette offers colors that are available through the DuPont Spectramaster solid color library. This library was developed to provide a paint color selection and matching tool for industrial coatings and colorants. Colors are based on L*A*B* and are converted to RGB for display and CMYK for printing. Colors can be displayed by name or swatch through the Color Options menu.

TOYO PALETTE   If you have a printer who uses only TOYO inks, this is the palette that you will need to use. The TOYO palette offers colors that are available through the TOYO 88 Color Finder system. The range of colors offered here includes those created using TOYO process inks and those that are reproduced using TOYO standard inks. Colors can be displayed by name or swatch through the Color Options menu.

DIC COLOR PALETTE   This palette offers colors that are available through the DIC Color Guide, DIC Color Guide Part II, and DIC Traditional Colors of Japan. Colors in these palettes are created by mixing DIC brand inks. Reproduction through Corel applications is achieved through the CMYK color space. Colors can be displayed by name or swatch through the Color Options menu. Swatches are identified by palette and color ID code:

DIC id# for DIC Color Guide
DIC Part II id# for DIC Color Guide Part II
DIC Traditional id# for DIC Traditional Colors of Japan

The Custom Palette Area

The custom palette to the right of the displayed color-matching system acts the same in this mode as it did in the previous Color Models mode.

 OTE: *The custom palette in the Palettes mode displays the contents of the currently selected custom palette and does not reflect the colors of the color-matching system in use.*

The Mixers Mode

The last of the three modes in the Uniform Fill dialog box allows creation of colors by mixing one or more colors together. There are two modes available in Mixers: Color Blend (default setting) and Mixing Area. The mode is selected with the Mode setting.

Color Blend

Color Blend is new in Corel PHOTO-PAINT 6. The Color Blend box provides a method of picking four colors, and the computer automatically generates all of the intermediate colors. It is from these intermediate colors that you can pick the color you want.

USING THE COLOR BLEND MODE   The operation is simple enough. There are four colors at the four corners of a color square. Each of the four colors is selected by clicking on the color square in the corner, which opens a palette. From the palette, select a color. If the Auto-Blend switch is enabled (depressed), every change in the corner changes all of the colors in the square appropriately. Clicking the Color Options button below the color blend model gives a great degree of control over the operation of Color Blend with the following options.

▶ **Grid Size.** This allows selection of one of ten different grid sizes ranging from 3X3 to 25X25.

▶ **Color Model.** This allows selection of one of three different color models. The choices are CMYK, RGB, and HSB. Another selection added to the drop-down list is Add All Grid Colors to Palette. This option applies all of the colors in the Color Blend area to the custom palette, which is very handy when you want to place a large range of colors in a palette.

The Mixing Area

The Mixing Area is a unique feature of Corel PHOTO-PAINT. The principle behind it is the equivalent to an artist's palette. Lucian Mustatea, who headed up the Corel PHOTO-PAINT 5 team, came up with the idea of allowing the Corel PHOTO-PAINT user to actually mix various colors together to make new custom colors. While I think the idea is neat, I personally do not have the necessary experience to use it effectively. That said, I can still show you how it works.

The Mixing Area contains two buttons: a brush and an eyedropper (color picker). The Color Options button opens additional choices, as follows.

THE BLEND SLIDER   The Blend slider is used to increase or decrease the amount of color blending when you apply color to the mixing area. A large value increases the blending effect (the color is more transparent); a low value decreases the blending effect (the color is more opaque).

USING THE MIXING AREA   By clicking on the Brush button, you can select colors from the colors displayed in the mixing area as well as the Custom Palette. Once the color is selected, it can be applied to the Mixing Area. Additional colors can then be selected with the brush and mixed in the Mixing Area by painting over the previous colors. All colors applied in the Mixing Area are additive. Once you have achieved the desired color, select the color picker (eyedropper) and click on the color. The newly created color will appear in the New color swatch. The colors made in the Mixing Area can be saved.

The Color Options button displays the following commands:

▶ **Brush Size.** This allows selection of one of three sizes of brushes (Small, Medium, and Large); Brush types (Hard, Medium, and Soft); and Color Model (HSB, RGB, and CMYK).

▶ **Load Bitmap…** This command opens the Load Mixing Area File dialog box. You can load any .BMP file into the Mixing area and use it for selecting individual colors from an existing image. The default Mixing Area file is PNTAREA.BMP, located in the COREL\CUSTOM folder.

IP: *This is an excellent way to get and keep colors from an existing image. For example, if you found a file that had a remarkable shade of ruby red, you could bring it into the paint area with the Load command and then select*

the color and save it to a palette. If the file you want is not a .BMP file, load it into Corel PHOTO-PAINT and save it as a .BMP file.

- ► **Save Bitmap**… This opens the Save Paint Area File As dialog box for saving paint areas for later use.
- ► **Clear Bitmap**… This clears the existing paint area.

Well, that does it for Uniform fills. The next section is less complicated and a lot more fun.

The Fountain Fill Tool

Next to the Effect filters, the Fountain fill tools represent the greatest tools for creating stunning backgrounds and fills. A fountain fill is a fill that fades gradually from one color to another. This type of fill is also called a "gradient" or "graduated" fill. Corel PHOTO-PAINT lets you create linear, radial, conical, and square fountains using the Fountain Fill icon in the Fill roll-up window. To open the Fountain Fill tool, click on the second button from the left on the Fill roll-up. The only change in the Tool Settings roll-up (Fill roll-up) at this point is the contents of the swatch. To access the Fountain Fill dialog box, shown here, click the Edit button.

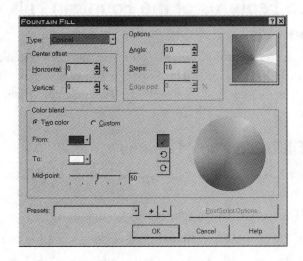

From this dialog box, it is easy to select and configure one of four types of fountain fills.

Using the Fountain Fill Dialog Box

Operation of the fountain fills from this menu uses system defaults and is very simple. It involves the following three steps:

1. Select one of the four fills at the upper-left of the roll-up: Linear, Radial, Conical, or Square.

2. Select From and To colors for the fill using the Two Color # selection button located in the Color Blend section of the roll-up. When either the From or To color button is depressed, a short color palette with less than 99 colors opens to choose from. Selecting the Custom button changes the dialog box, offering different ways to add more than two colors to the Fountain fill.

3. You can change the angle of a Linear fill by clicking on the inside of the preview menu and dragging the point of gradient origin or direction with the mouse. You can change the offset of a Radial, Conical, or Square fill the same way. Use the right mouse button to change the angle of a Conical fill. Use the CTRL key to limit rotation to 15 degree increments and offsets to 10 percent increments.

Advanced Features of the Fountain Fill Dialog Box

If you require greater control of the fills, there are more advanced control features in the Fountain Fill dialog box. The Fountain Fill dialog box edits and creates fountain fills. It is laid out into four sections: Type, Center Offset Options, Color Blend, and Presets.

Fountain Fill Dialog Box Options

▶ **Preview Box.** This shows you how the fountain fill will look with the colors you have chosen.

▶ **Type.** This selects one of four types of fountain fills.

▶ **Linear.** This selects a fountain fill that changes color in one direction.

▶ **Radial.** This selects a fountain fill that changes color in concentric circles from the center of the object outwards.

▶ **Conical.** This selects a fountain fill that radiates from the center of the object like rays of light.

▶ **Square.** This selects a fountain fill that changes color in concentric squares from the center of the object outwards.

The Center Offset Section of the Fountain Fill Roll-Up

The Center Offset repositions the center of a Radial or Conical fountain fill so that it no longer coincides with the center of the object. Negative values shift the center down and to the left; positive values shift the center up and to the right.

At first appearance this seems pointless. Why would anyone in their right mind waste the time to use a value system to determine where the offset is when you can move the cursor to the desired offset position? However, the Center Offset is necessary when you need to make several fills with exactly the same offset values.

The Options Section of the Fountain Fill Roll-up

The Options section of the Fountain Fill dialog box allows you to adjust any of the settings to customize the appearance of the fountain. The choices are described in the following paragraphs.

THE ANGLE BOX   The Angle box determines the angle of gradation in a Linear, Conical, or Square fountain fill. The preview box shows the effect of changing the angle. If you rotate the object, the fountain angle shown in the preview box adjusts automatically after a one-second delay. This delay prevents Corel PHOTO-PAINT from acting on a new setting before the entire value has been entered. You can also change the angle by dragging the line that appears when you click in the preview box. Use the right mouse button (or the left mouse button and SHIFT) to change the angle for Conical and Square fountains. Holding down the CTRL key while dragging constrains the angle to multiples of 15 degrees.

THE STEPS BOX   The Steps box displays the number of bands used to display and print the fountain.

IP: *When increasing the value of the Steps, be aware that a large number increases the smoothness of the transitions. The negative side of the increase is that the fountain fill becomes very complex and takes longer to display. In CorelDRAW, complex fountain fills take a long time to print. In Corel PHOTO-PAINT, they take no longer than anything else because it is all bitmaps.*

25

IP: *Beware of producing too narrow a range of colors over a large area, which produces banding. For example, if a range of six shades of colors is spread over an 11" x 17" area, banding will result.*

THE EDGE PAD   The Edge Pad increases the amount of start and end color in the fountain fill. It is used primarily with circles and irregularly-shaped objects in which the first and/or last few bands of color lie between the object and its highlighting box. The effect is to take away from the smooth transition between the starting and ending colors. The Edge Pad can be used when applying shading to an object such as text. Entering a large number into the Edge Pad box will cause a wide band to separate the top and bottom of a Linear fill. The Edge Pad option is not available for Conical fountain fills and therefore is grayed out.

The Color Blend Section of the Fountain Fill Roll-up

The Color Blend section of the Fountain Fill dialog box is where you select the colors you want to use in your fill. There are two modes of operation in the Color Blend area: Two Color (default) and Custom.

TWO COLOR BLEND   Two Color Blend is the system default. It takes the intermediate colors along a straight line beginning at the From color and continuing across the color wheel to the To color. This is best for appearances of shading and highlights. The operation of the Two Color Blend is controlled by one of the four controls (three buttons and a slider) to the right of the From and To colors. They are:

- ▶ **Direct.** When selected, it determines the intermediate fill colors from a straight line beginning at the From color and continuing across the color wheel to the To color. This option produces a color series composed of blends of the From and To colors.

- ▶ **Mid-Point Slider.** New to Corel PHOTO-PAINT 6, this is only available with Direct selected. It adjusts the midpoint between the From and To colors. The Mid-Point slider allows the user to control the distribution of color/shading of the fountain fills.

- ▶ **Rainbow (counterclockwise).** When selected, this option determines the intermediate colors from a counterclockwise path around the color wheel. The rainbow pattern is displayed in the preview area of the fill. Enabling the Rainbow button allows you to make multicolored effects. It utilizes the spectrum of colors within a specified path around the color wheel. The From and To colors coincide with endpoints of the path.

▶ **Rainbow (clockwise).** This is the same as above except the direction is reversed.

IP: *It is very easy to have part of the area you are filling blend into the background at the points where the background and the Rainbow fill are similar. This can result in the object being filled disappearing at those points. To avoid this, determine the colors that "blend" and make the rainbow exclude them. This is achieved by selecting a color near the "blend" color and making the rainbow fill get to the end color by avoiding the "blend" color. (It is at a time such as this that you will appreciate the rotation buttons.)*

CUSTOM BLEND   The Custom Blend allows you to add more than two colors to a fill and in specific locations on the fill. In the Custom feature, even more incredible effects and backgrounds come to life. When the Custom button is clicked, the dialog box changes as shown in the following illustration. The Custom option allows you to select up to 99 intermediate colors from the palette at the right of the dialog box. Specify where you want the color to appear by adding markers above the preview box. The markers look a lot like the tab markers on my word-processing program.

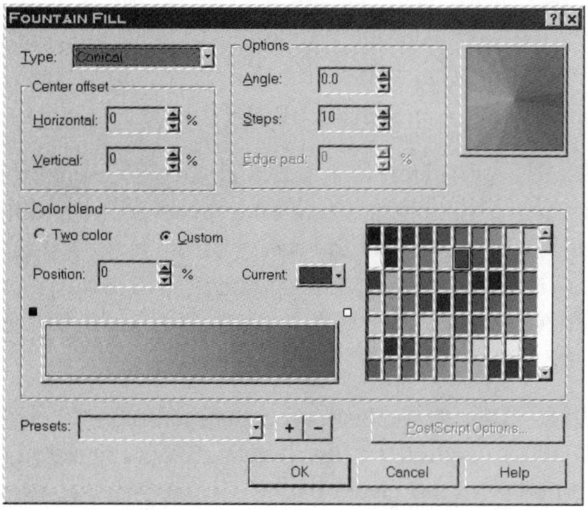

25

ADDING MARKERS   There are two ways to add markers, as follows. Double-click just above the preview box in the color blend area. The marker will appear, and the preview box in the color blend area and in the upper-right corner of the Fountain Fill dialog box will reflect the change after a one-second delay. (If you have a slower machine, it may take longer.)

Select the To or From color square at either end of the preview ribbon and specify a new value in the Position box. (The first works the best.)

IP: *Use the position box to enter precise positions for the markers. An easy way to do this is by double-clicking where you want the marker and then putting the exact position for it in the Position box. For example, by double-clicking near the middle of the fill you can get an approximate center position. To be exact, enter 50 percent in the Position box. The half-way point between the middle and each end is 25 and 75 percent, and so on.*

After adding a marker, choose a color from the palette. To reposition a color, select its marker and drag it to the desired spot, or edit the value in the Position box. The preview box in the color blend area and in the upper-right corner of the Fountain Fill dialog box will reflect the change after a one-second delay. To delete a color, double-click on the marker. *Note:* More than one color marker can be selected at a time by holding down the SHIFT key when selecting or deselecting.

The Presets Area

The Presets area lets you save the fountain settings you specified so that you can apply them to other objects at a later time. It also contains over 100 predesigned fills that were installed with Corel PHOTO-PAINT.

SELECTING A PRESET   To select a preset, click on the down arrow to the right of the preset text box and a list appears. Click on a preset name and the preset appears in the preview window. If you want to browse through the list, just click on the first one you wish to view, and then each time you press the down or up arrow, the next preset will be selected and previewed. You might enjoy doing this if your cable TV is out and you are really bored.

SAVING A PRESET   To save a preset, type a name (up to 20 characters in length) in the Presets box, and then click the plus button. (Clicking the minus button removes the selected settings from the Preset list.)

The Full-Color Bitmap Fill

The Full-Color Bitmap fill is enabled by selecting the Bitmap Fill button on the Fill roll-up. It is the one in the center that looks like a checkerboard. The Bitmap fill allows you to fill a selected area with a bitmap image. There are a large number of images in the Corel library (located in the COREL\CUSTOM\TILES folder). In addition to the bitmap images provided, you can import almost any bitmap that can be read by your PC.

 OTE: *Corel PHOTO-PAINT 6 can import vector-based images for use as bitmap fills. With Corel PHOTO-PAINT 5, if you have a vector-based image, you have to load it into Corel PHOTO-PAINT and save it as a bitmap image before you can use it.*

Loading a Different Bitmap Image

When you invoke the Bitmap fill in the Fill roll-up, you will be able to see the currently selected image in the preview window.

To change the image, you must click the Edit button. This will open the Full-Color Bitmap Pattern dialog box, new to Corel PHOTO-PAINT 6, as shown here.

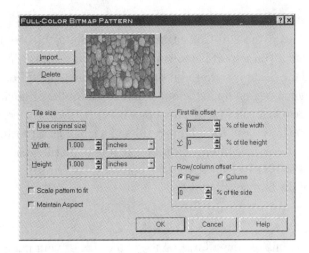

How the Bitmap Fill Operates

Here is a brief summary of how the Bitmap fill works. You have so much versatility when using bitmaps for fills that it is sometimes difficult to get a grip on all of it. Here are some pointers about using files for bitmap fills:

▶ Remember that if you use the Fill tool (the bucket), the fill will be calculated to the boundaries of the mask or the edges of the image. If the bitmap image is larger than the mask or the image, Corel PHOTO-PAINT will fill as much as will fit, beginning with the lower-left corner of the original image.

▶ You can control what appears in a flood-filled area by using the many tile size/placement controls in the Full-Color Bitmap Pattern Dialog box.

▶ The Rectangle, Ellipse, and Polygon tools, on the other hand, will fill to the perimeter of the defined area. If there is a mask, the masked area that falls within the area will be filled.

 IP: *When using Corel Photo-CDs as bitmap fills, make sure to crop them in the Import dialog box to get rid of any black film border. If you don't, the results can be really ugly.*

Controlling the Size and Position of the Bitmap Tiles

With the settings in the Full-Color Bitmap Pattern dialog box set to their defaults, if the bitmap that you import is too small to fill the area, it is tiled. If the image is too large and the Scale Pattern to Fit option is disabled, the fill does not resize the bitmap but rather, beginning in the upper-left corner of the original bitmap, it takes all of the bitmap that can fit in the area that is being filled. As a result, if you have a large file you have used for a bitmap fill and a small area to fill, you might find that a large portion of the bitmap didn't make it into the fill area.

In Corel PHOTO-PAINT 6, you can control the size, offset, and several other parameters of the bitmap fill.

Tile Size

The controls in this section allow you to set the size of your pattern tiles. You can choose one of the preset sizes or enter custom dimensions. By selecting Use original size, the bitmap file will not be scaled to a new size. If it is not checked, the bitmap will be scaled to the size set in the Width and Height settings. These settings are grayed-out if the Use original size option is enabled.

Scale Pattern to Fit

When enabled, it scales the tile pattern to fit entirely within the tile preview window. It also disables the entire Tile size section of the dialog box when enabled.

Maintain Aspect

The Maintain Aspect feature, if selected, maintains identical tile width and height values. When enabled, any value entered in one number box will cause the other box to change automatically.

First Tile Offset

Controls in this section set the offset of the first tile (and therefore the rest of the pattern) relative to the top left-hand corner of the object. If you want the pattern to start flush with the corner, set the X and Y values to zero percent.

Row/Column Offset

These controls shift either the rows or columns of tiles so that the pattern is staggered rather than continuous. The percentage of tile side setting shifts alternating rows or columns by the amount specified. This feature helps break up the repeating patterns, which would normally not allow many types of bitmap fills to be used.

Selecting Between Currently Loaded Bitmap Images

On the right side of the preview window in the Full-Color Bitmap Pattern dialog box is a tall down arrow button. Clicking the button or anywhere in the preview window opens a color preview of the first nine bitmaps that have been imported into Corel PHOTO-PAINT. If there are more bitmaps than can be displayed, scroll bars appear on the right side of the preview window that allow the user to see the remainder of the bitmap fills in Corel PHOTO-PAINT.

25

Importing Bitmaps

Clicking the Import button opens the Import dialog box, where you can import a graphic to use as your bitmap pattern. The Import dialog box is the same one used to open a graphic file. The only exception is that none of the options like Crop and Resample are available. There is a large selection of bitmap fills available on the CD-ROM containing the \TILES folder. There is also a selection of small bitmap fills available on the CorelDRAW 6 and Corel PHOTO-PAINT 6 CD-ROM buried in the CLIPART_BITMAP folder.

Now on to the next section of the Fill roll-up: Texture fills.

The Texture Fills

This is the feature that makes Corel PHOTO-PAINT unique. I do not know of another package that can do the things that can be done with Texture fills. There are some tricks to using the fills effectively, but you will learn them here. The Texture Fill dialog box is used to select one of the 100-plus bitmap texture fills included in Corel PHOTO-PAINT. Each texture has a unique set of parameters that you can modify to create millions of variations. Although most of the textures look fine on color monitors, if you are using a monochrome monitor, you may not get a very good representation of the texture's appearance. If you are printing on a monochrome printer, you may get good results with some of the fills and poor results with others. The results depend on your printer, your taste, and your willingness to experiment.

What's in a Name?

As with the filters, don't let the names of the fills confuse your thinking. As an example, using the Rain Drops, Hard Texture fill, I was able to obtain the effect of a cut metal edge.

I came across this cut metal effect when I was writing the Corel PHOTO-PAINT 5 Plus manual for Corel. I found by filling each character individually, the size of the "raindrop" doesn't get too large. Too large? This leads to our first general rule regarding the texture fills. As in Boyle's law of expanding gases (gas expands to fit the volume of the container):

Rule of bitmap textures: A texture fill expands to fit the volume of the available area.

In the following illustration I have created squares of various sizes and filled them with the same texture fill. As you can see, as the squares increase in area, the size of the fill increases proportionally. While this can be used to create some unusual effects, it can also catch you by surprise, especially when working with a large image only to find that when it is applied, it looks nothing like the thumbnail preview.

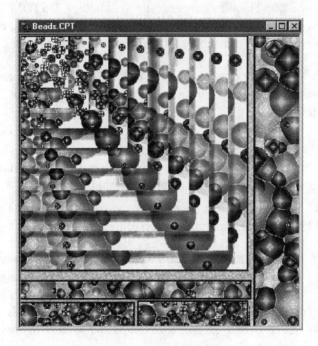

Also note the very narrow rectangle on the right side. I put it in there so you would realize that the fill size is calculated by creating a square that is determined by the greatest dimension of the mask. For example, if you made a mask that was 50 x 500 pixels, the resulting fill would be as if it was a 500 x 500-pixel square. So how do you get around this? Not as tough as you may think. While there are several possibilities, I will cover a few basic methods.

25

Controlling Texture Fill Size by Making a Custom Bitmap Fill

This is the method that I use most often. The bitmap-fill engine does excellent tiling, and it is very simple to use. Here is all you need to do:

1. Create a new image. Size is not critical, but I recommend about 80 x 80 pixels at a resolution of 300 dpi.

2. Pick the texture fill that you want to use. After making whatever adjustments you deem necessary, click on the Fill tool (the bucket) and click in the new image.

3. Save the file. The tiles are generally kept in the CUSTOM\TILES folder, but you can put them anywhere you wish. Even though all of the Corel tiles are in CPT format, any bitmap format will work.

IP: *Save your custom tiles in Corel PHOTO-PAINT format. This way it is easy to locate them in a sea of tiles that have .BMP or .PCX extensions by selecting the CPT filter.*

4. Click on the Bitmap Fill button in the Fountain Fill dialog box. Click the Edit button and then click the Import button. In the Import dialog box, select and load your newly created custom bitmap tile.

5. Using the Fill tool (bucket), click on the area to be filled. The area will flood with a nonexpanding version of the texture fill.

IP: *Be aware that some textures don't work this way very well. They can show up as unwanted patterns. For example, I tried using this technique with the Planets fill from the Sample 5 library. The result was that the patterning of the fill showed up as a pattern in the background. This would still work if I had many objects over it, such as spaceships and planets, to break up the image.*

Exploring the Bitmap Texture Fill Dialog Box

When the Texture Bitmap mode of the fill roll-up is selected, the currently selected fill is displayed in the preview window. The Edit button opens the Texture Fill dialog box. This dialog box allows you to edit and create an unlimited number of new texture fills from existing fills. Unlike bitmap fills, you cannot import files for use as texture fills. The texture fills are actually fractals that are created as they are applied. This goes a long way to explain why some textures can take a long time to apply.

If you cannot find the exact file that you want in the 160+ preset textures that were shipped with Corel PHOTO-PAINT, you can edit the existing textures by clicking on the Edit button. The Edit button below the preview of the fill opens the dialog box, shown next, that contains all of the controls for the fill.

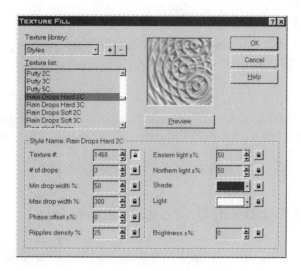

Texture Library

This list box displays the names of the texture libraries. Corel PHOTO-PAINT ships with four libraries described in the following paragraphs: Samples, Samples 5, Samples 6, and Styles.

SAMPLES   This is the original set of samples that were made with the Texture generator in the Styles library. For example, Clouds, Midday was created with Sky, 2 Colors. It is a quick way to get a texture without having to wade through all of the texture parameters to make it. The Samples library shipped with the original version of Corel 5.

SAMPLES 5/6   These libraries are like Samples except that there are more variations. Some of my personal favorites are in this library. I find that I use the Night Sky and Planets textures in the Samples 5 library more than almost any other texture. The Sample 5 library first shipped with the maintenance release of Corel PHOTO-PAINT 5. The Sample 6 shipped with Corel PHOTO-PAINT 6.

STYLES   These are the building blocks of the bitmap texture fills. It is from the textures in this library that all of the other samples in the other three libraries are made. This library is a read-only library. If you modify a texture and want to save it, you will not be allowed to save it in this library. You must either create a new library or save it in one of the Samples libraries.

25

Texture List

This lists the texture fills available in the currently selected library. Clicking on a texture in the Textures list will select it, and the default setting for the texture will display in the preview window.

 IP: *Each time a library is selected, the texture list returns to the default texture for that library. For example, if you were in Samples 5 and had been working with Night Sky and then you switched over to look at something in Styles, when you returned to Samples 5, it would have returned to the default texture.*

Preview and Locked/Unlocked Parameters

Each time the Preview button is depressed, Corel PHOTO-PAINT varies the appearance of the selected texture by randomly changing all unlocked parameters. This button does more than is apparent at first. There are over 15,000 textures with several million possible combinations for each one. Rather than requiring you to wade through a sea of permutations, Corel PHOTO-PAINT textures have certain variables that are either locked or unlocked by default.

The unlocked parameters are the ones that the graphic engineers at Corel thought provided the best way to modify the textures. Every time the Preview button is depressed, the unlocked parameters change randomly. This is especially important for the texture pattern settings.

You can lock and unlock a parameter by clicking the Lock button next to it. You can also use the Preview button to update a texture after changing the parameters yourself.

 IP: *Until you get used to using a texture, I recommend using the default settings for the locks. They generally provide the best, quickest results.*

Save As (Plus Button)

After changing the parameters of a texture in the library (or a new library you created), click the Plus button in the upper-right corner to overwrite the original. This opens a dialog box for naming (or renaming) a texture you have created. The texture name can be up to 32 characters (including spaces). The Library Name option allows you to create a new library in which to store the textures. You can type up to 32 characters (including spaces). The Library List displays libraries where you can store the modified texture. (*Note:* You must save any modified Style textures in a library other than the Styles library, because Styles is a read-only library.)

Delete (Minus Button)

This deletes the selected texture. You can only delete textures from libraries you created and added.

Style Name and Parameter Section

This part of the Texture Fill dialog box shows the name of the selected textures. Because each texture has different value assignments, methods, colors, and lights, it would take a separate book to list even a few of the combinations provided by the parameters. The value boxes in this area list parameters for the selected texture. Changing one or more of these parameters alters the appearance of the texture. The changes are displayed in the preview box whenever the Preview button is depressed. The Style Name fields list numeric parameters. All textures have a texture number, which ranges from 0 to 32,768. The names of the other parameters vary with the texture selected and have ranges from 0 to 100 or –100 to 100.

To change a numeric parameter, enter a value in the text box or use the cursor and click on either the up or down arrow.

IP: *If you are going to ascend or descend very far on the numeric list referenced above, you can use a speedup feature of the up and down arrows. Place the cursor between the up and down arrows. The cursor will change into a two-headed arrow cursor with a line between the two arrowheads. After the cursor changes, click and drag either up or down, and the selection list will move rapidly up or down the list (depending on which way you choose). To see the change entered, click the Preview button.*

25

The right side of the field lists up to six color parameters, depending on the texture selected. To change a color, click on the color button and select a new color from the pop-up palette. If you desire a specific color or named color that is not on the color palette, click on the Others button. The Others button opens the same dialog box (but it is called Select Color) as the Uniform Fill dialog box. (See the Uniform Fill section for specific details regarding the use of this dialog box.) After you have made the desired changes, click the Preview button to see the effect the new color has on the selected texture.

The No Fill Button (Rectangle, Ellipse, and Polygon Tools)

The only difference between the Tool Settings roll-ups using the previous tools and the Rectangle, Ellipse, and Polygon tools is the addition of one button. It is the No Fill button. This isn't a joke; it really is a No Fill fill. It is rarely used, but there are times when it is necessary. Using it in combination with the Rectangle, Ellipse, or Polygon Draw tools provides a way to make empty rectangles, circles, or polygons. To use it, select one of the aforementioned drawing tools, open the Tool Settings roll-up, and select the No Fill Fill button or "button X".

Width and Roundness of Borders

With the Tool Settings roll-up, you can control the size and shape a border made by the Rectangle, Ellipse, or Polygon tool.

Width

This determines the thickness of the border in points (remember, a point is 1/72 of an inch).

Transparency

The Transparency setting determines how transparent the fill will be when applied to the image. This setting can be of great benefit when you need to apply a fill for an effect. It can also be a real pain. You must understand that when you change the transparency, it remains, and it is very easy to forget that you now have a transparency setting. What happens to me is that I will apply a color like red and I observe that it looks washed out. I sit there puzzled, wondering if I have left some sort of mask on the image, and then after a few moments I remember that I have a transparency setting. This transparency setting only works for the Rectangle, Ellipse, or Polygon tool. It does not affect the transparency setting for the Fill tool.

Roundness (Rectangle Tool Only)

The "roundness" of the corners is determined by the Roundness settings. A rough representation of the rounded curve is continuously updated as the value of roundness is increased or decreased. Make sure the Width value box is set to a value other than "0," or you will end up making nothing. (Think about it: What does a rectangle with a border width of 0 points and no fill look like? That's reserved for the Zen masters.)

Paint Mode

The Paint mode drop-down box lets you control the way paint colors and paper colors combine to create new colors and effects. With most paint tools, the paint color simply replaces the paper color (just as you would use a colored paint to paint a white wall). However, with the paint modes, it is the combination of paint colors and paper colors that produces the new color.

Anti-Aliasing

Anti-aliasing removes jagged edges from a mask, object, or image by adding duplicated pixels where the mask, object, or image edge contacts the background image.

Joints (Polygon Tool Only)

This setting gives you four choices for how Paint is to treat the joints of multiple line figures. Use the drop-down list to select the type of joint. Choices are Butt, Filled, Round, and Point.

- ▶ **Butt.** The Joints are the squared ends of the lines where they meet and overlap.
- ▶ **Filled.** The open areas caused by the overlap are filled.
- ▶ **Round.** The corners are rounded.
- ▶ **Point.** The corners end in points.

Using the Rectangle Tool

The Rectangle tool is used to draw hollow or filled rectangles and rounded rectangles. Without the tools in this flyout, we wouldn't be able to control the fill of masked areas as well as we do.

Here are the Rectangle drawing tool facts:

- ▶ If the CTRL key is held down while defining the shape, the rectangle is constrained to a square.

▶ Holding down the SHIFT key while creating a rectangle will cause the rectangle to shrink or grow (depending on the direction of the mouse movement) from the center.

▶ When the Rectangle is produced, it is filled with the current fill setting in the Fill roll-up.

▶ If the No Fill setting is selected, a hollow rectangle is created. It doesn't consume system resources; it doesn't do anything. Sounds Zen. Very good, Grasshopper.

To Draw a Rectangle or Rounded Rectangle

▶ With the Width value greater then zero, select the Rectangle tool and choose the border color by left-clicking the desired color on the onscreen preview and the Fill color by right-clicking on the desired color. The paint (background) color determines border color.

▶ The rectangle is filled with the current Fill color when the left mouse button is released.

▶ The rectangle is hollow if No Fill is selected in the Fill roll-up.

▶ Specify the width and roundness of the border in the Tool Settings roll-up.

▶ Press the left mouse button to anchor the rectangle and drag until you have achieved the desired size.

▶ If the rectangle is not what you desire, it can be erased by pressing the ESC key *before* releasing the mouse button.

The Ellipse Tool

The Ellipse tool draws hollow or filled ellipses. If the CTRL key is held down while defining the shape, the ellipse is constrained to a circle. Holding down the SHIFT key will shrink or grow the ellipse/circle from the center.

To Draw an Ellipse

▶ Click the Ellipse tool and choose the border color by clicking on the desired color in the onscreen preview with the right mouse button.

► The paint (background) color determines border color. The ellipse is filled with the current fill color unless the No Fill is selected in the Fill roll-up.

► Specify the width of the border in the Tool Settings roll-up.

► Press the left mouse button to anchor the ellipse, and drag until you have achieved the desired size.

► If the circle is not what you desire, it can be erased by pressing the ESC key *before* releasing the mouse button. Holding down the SHIFT key produces a circle.

The Polygon Tool

The Polygon tool produces closed multisided figures. By selecting different Joint settings in the Tools Settings roll-up, the Polygon tool can provide a wide variety of images.

To Draw a Polygon

► Select the Polygon tool.

► Choose Color, Width, type of joints, and Transparency of the border and fill.

► Click where the polygon is to begin in order to anchor the starting point. Move the cursor where the first side of the polygon is to end. As the cursor is moved, the closed shape of the polygon is continually redrawn on the screen to assist the user in what the final shape will look like.

► Click the left mouse button again to complete the first side. Continue moving the cursor to define the remaining sides.

► Double-clicking the end of the last line completes the polygon.

► Holding the CTRL key down while moving the cursor constrains the sides of the polygon vertically, horizontally, or at 45 degree angles.

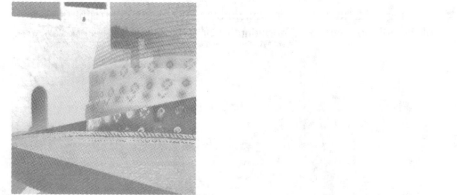

Advanced Color Topics
and Other Matters

26

In this chapter we are going to expand on some topics that were only briefly mentioned earlier in the book. The topics include how to perform color correction on Photo-CDs, using Corel PHOTO-PAINT 6's new Duotone® feature, and a few others.

Loading Photo-CDs

In Chapter 5 we explained how to open and load a Photo-CD. In this section we will explain how to use the tools provided in Corel PHOTO-PAINT 6 to apply color correction to them. To review, when a photo-CD is initially opened, the dialog box displays the Image tab as shown in Figure 26-1. If color correction is not desired, the only choices that must be made are the size of the image and the color selection. The size choices and their size in pixels are Wallet (128 x 192), Snapshot (256 x 384), Standard (512 x 768), Large (1024 x 1536), and Poster (2048 x 3072). The available color selections are 16.7 million (24-bit), 256 colors (8-bit), and 256 grayscale. After you have the size and color, click the OK button and the image will load. After the file loads, Corel PHOTO-PAINT issues a warning that the Photo-CD is a read-only file that cannot be modified. I am still hoping that Corel will offer some sort of preference setting to disable the warning message in the next release. When you load a lot of Photo-CD images, you get a little weary of the message box that continually states the obvious.

If you want to apply color correction, click on the Enhancement tab, which opens the color-correction page of the dialog box. This is a great color-correction system that makes some of the not-so-great Photo-CDs on the market look much better. Either of the color-correction systems provided will correct the color of the image before you import it into Corel PHOTO-PAINT. Any correction applied at this stage of the process is superior to any correction that might be applied after the image is in Corel PHOTO-PAINT.

IP: *Larger file sizes require large amounts of system memory, take longer to load and to apply effects, and require more disk space for storage. Therefore, always try to pick a size and color depth that is sufficient for your application.*

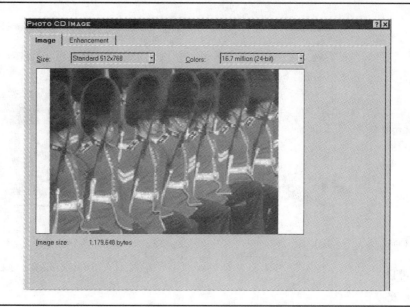

The
Photo-CD
dialog box

FIGURE 26-1

Color-Correcting Photo-CD Images

Selecting the Enhancement tab on the Photo-CD dialog box initially opens the Photo-CD Enhancement dialog box for the Gamut CD color-correction system, as shown in Figure 26-2. This dialog box allows you to correct the color of the image before you import it into Corel PHOTO-PAINT. The way it works is that it allows you to select neutral colors (black, white, and grays) in the image, and then the software maps these neutral colors to adjust the dynamic range of the image. This color correction is within the gamut system, so it doesn't go beyond the capability of color printing. If you are unaware of gamut, in short, it is a system that knows what colors can or cannot be printed by Standard Web Offset Process (SWOP). Colors that cannot be printed are referred to as being "outside of gamut." The Gamut CD correction system ensures that all of the colors in the Photo-CD are within gamut. The best part is that the Gamut CD color correction almost always improves the overall appearance of the image, even if you don't need the color correction for

26

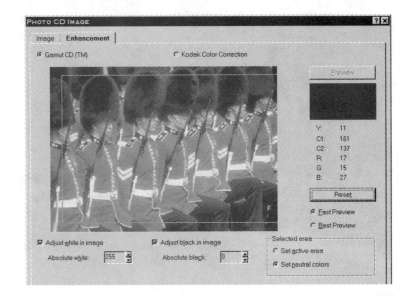

The Gamut CD Color correction system provides automatic color correction for Photo-CDs

FIGURE 26-2

printing purposes. Although this dialog box is anything but intuitive, it has been improved over the one in Corel PHOTO-PAINT 5.

Nevertheless, after you learn how to use it, if you apply it every time you bring in an older or poor-quality Photo-CD, your Photo-CD image will look better. Most of the newer Photo-CDs from the good digital stock agencies have already applied color correction, making this enhancement unnecessary. I have several old Photo-CD images that had black backgrounds until I applied correction, and they turned out not to be black backgrounds after all. In one, a night shot of a wolf, the "black background" turned out to contain a forest that had turned into mud before the correction was applied.

Photo-CD Enhancement Dialog Box Options

The following options are available using the GamutCD™ Color Correction system.

Color-Correction Methods

▶ **GamutCD** This color-correction method uses gamut mapping to enhance the color fidelity and tonal ranges of the CD image. Gamut mapping is a system that ensures that colors in a computer image are reproducible by a printer. Of the two methods, I have had the greatest success with this one.

▶ **Kodak color correction** The Kodak color-correction method allows you to alter color tints, adjust Brightness and Color Saturation, as well as make adjustments to the level of contrast. The Kodak system, while excellent, is not automatic, making it more complicated to use.

Set Active Area Using GamutCD

Generally, the default area should be used. If you need to change the active area, select the Set Active Area option and click and drag the mouse to specify an active area within the image in the view field. This ensures GamutCD will base its color correction on the area of the photo that you are going to use and helps cut out any black borders left over from the original scan that would interfere with accurate correction.

Set Neutral Colors

Define neutral colors by clicking on pure whites, blacks, and grays within the active area, which leaves a small "x" on the preview image in most displays. The more samples that are selected, the better the color correction.

Adjust White in Image

Choose this option if you have good white elements in the photo. If you do not have a white, disable this option, as the gamut mapping will over-brighten your picture as it maps the lightest elements of your picture to white. This option will assist GamutCD in enhancing the tonal range of your image and removing color cast. If your white is not pure white, you may wish to lower the 255 setting in the number box to the right.

Adjust Black in Image

Choose this option if you have good black elements in the photo. If the image does not have blacks, disable this option, as the gamut mapping will darken your picture as it maps the darkest elements of your picture to black. This option will assist GamutCD in enhancing the tonal range of your image and removing color cast. If your black is not pure black, you may wish to raise the setting in the number box to the right from 0.

Color Swatch and Values

This option displays the YCC and RGB color value of the currently selected color from the image as the cursor is moved around the image in the preview window. The color swatch displays the color that is being assessed.

YCC The YCC color system is the heart of the Photo-CD. The Y represents the luminance or grayscale values of the image, and the C values are the color chrominance values. The YCC color space is similar to the way television broadcast color is transmitted. The YCC values are of little help in setting up the GamutCD system.

RGB RGB represents the values of the Red, Green, and Blue color components in the image. It is the RGB information that is of the greatest help in establishing the neutral colors of the image.

Fast Preview option

This option displays the effect the GamutCD settings you have chosen will have on the image. The first time you preview, you may wonder why it is called "Fast Preview." Click the Preview button to find out, and click "Best Preview" the next time. Bring a book.

Best Preview

This option displays the effect the GamutCD settings you have chosen will have on the image. This method will be more accurate than Fast Preview but will take longer to build. Actually, several of the people who wrote the Corel PHOTO-PAINT program think it is faster to just click the OK button to see the color correction. If you do that, you will lose your sample settings. Use the Fast Preview instead. If you are paid by the hour and need to milk the job for some more time, you will love Best Preview.

Using GamutCD Color Correction

This is all great, but how do I use it? That was my question to the people at Corel when I was writing the Corel PHOTO-PAINT 5 manual. Their answer surprised me: they hadn't used it that much themselves. I shouldn't have been surprised that these folks work their brains out writing code for Corel PHOTO-PAINT and have little time for loading and correcting their favorite Photo-CDs. Since that time, they and

I have learned a lot about using GamutCD. So here is Dave's handy-dandy method for using the GamutCD Color Correction System, based on lots of practice and a little too much coffee.

The principle of this system is that you select the neutral colors (white, black, and gray) in an image. The GamutCD system uses those colors for its gamut mapping to enhance the color fidelity and tonal ranges of the image, ensuring that the colors in a computer image can be reproduced by a printer.

1. Open the Photo-CD image. The Photo-CD dialog box opens. Pick the size and color desired.

2. Click the Enhancement tab. Ensure that the GamutCD button is enabled. I highly recommend using the default Active area, which is shown by the light-colored rectangle on the image in the preview window. If you needed to change the Active area, click the Set Active Area button and drag a rectangle in the preview window that includes the portion of the image you wish to be included in the color-correction calculations.

3. Click on the whitest white spot you can find. Don't trust your eyes on this one. Watch the Color swatch on the right side of the dialog box as you move the cursor over the white area. Specifically, watch the numbers by R, G, and B (which stand for Red, Green, and Blue). The whitest white will produce the highest numbers in RGB. This is basic color theory. Pure white reads 256 on each of the RGB channels. Make several of these white samples. The more you make, the more accurate the color correction will be. Don't lose your mind here—three or four samples are sufficient.

4. Click on the blackest black you can locate in the active area. "Active area" is the key phrase here—do not click on the black border. The idea with these samples is to establish the dynamic color range of the image, so shooting some of the black off of the negative border will throw the correction off. You pick the black the same way you pick the white, by the numbers. In this case, you are looking for the lowest numbers in the RGB values.

5. Find a good middle-of-the-road gray if there is one (optional). This is used to set the midtones, and finding a gray can be very subjective. Use the numbers again. In this case you are looking for RGB numbers around the 128 value (blue will be a little higher). Most grays are in the 180-185 region. If you use a gray, the result will be shifted toward the warmer colors.

26

6. Select the Fast Preview option and click the Preview button. On a good 24-bit color monitor, the difference can be very impressive. If you like the results, click the OK button. If not, reset the color correction by clicking the Reset button and start over again.

Notes on the GamutCD Color-Correction System

Here are some pointers about using GamutCD.

► There isn't a specific order to enter the neutral colors. The computer sorts it all out.

► If there isn't a good black (RGB less than 90) or a good white (RGB greater than 220), don't use them, and uncheck the respective Adjust White In Image or Adjust Black In Image check box.

► If you don't like the results of the preview, click Reset and choose the color samples again. The image will appear the same, but the color values will be correct.

► If the preview is too dark, try increasing the value in the Black In Image value box. If the preview is too light, try decreasing the value in the White In Image value box.

The Kodak Color-Correction System

This color-correction method, which is selected by enabling the Kodak Color Correction button in the Enhancement page, opens the dialog box shown in Figure 26-3. The Kodak system allows you to alter color tints, and adjust brightness and color saturation, as well as make adjustments to the level of contrast.

This is not an automatic system like the Gamut Image Enhancement System. You can control the tints of the three primary colors, red, blue, and green (RGB); Brightness; and Saturation (the amount of color in the image). There are several adjustments in the dialog box that are unique to Photo-CD images. The effects of changing any of these settings do not appear in the preview window until the Preview button is clicked. There is no automatic preview. The controls for this dialog box are as follows.

The Kodak
color-
correction
system
offers a
wide
assortment
of manual
color
correction
tools

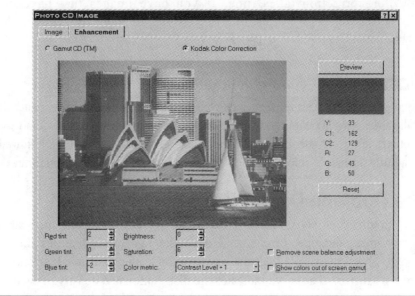

FIGURE 26-3

Color Metric

This allows you to adjust contrast by selecting preset amounts from a drop-down list.

Remove Scene Balance Adjustment

Enabling this button removes the Scene Balance Adjustment, which is made by the photo-finisher at the time the original image was scanned and preserved on the Photo-CD disc. You should remove this if the image looks lifeless or dull. It may result in some areas of the image blowing out (bright spots becoming large white areas).

Show Colors Out of Screen Gamut

If the changes you've made are too extreme, the preview will display out-of-gamut pixels as pure red or pure blue. Colors that are out of gamut cannot be printed accurately, and it is important for critical prepress work for all colors to be within gamut boundaries.

26

Color correction takes time. If you have images that have not been color-corrected, it is worth the time spent trying to apply correction at this stage rather than in Corel PHOTO-PAINT.

Duotones

A duotone is a grayscale image printed with two inks. This technique expands the depth of the image by allowing additional shades for highlights, shadows, and midtones. Duotones are great attention-getters and take less ink. The duotone feature is ideal for adding an accent color to a photograph or for extending the tonal ranges of inks.

The Duotone Dialog Box

The Duotone dialog box, shown in Figure 26-4, lets you convert grayscale images to monotone, duotone, tritone, and quadtone images. It features three tabbed property sheets that display a grid area with a single, diagonal, unedited curve cutting across its surface. The curve indicates the distribution and density of each ink from the shadow, through the midtone, to the highlight areas of the image.

By manipulating curves on the Inks tab, you control how each ink is used in the highlights, midtones, and shadows. The highlights and shadows run from left to right across the horizontal plane of the grid. The ink density runs vertically from bottom to top. Each ink curve is edited separately by clicking the desired ink icon located to the right of the grid. By default, each curve is straight; they run diagonally across

The
Duotone
dialog box
is complex,
but offers
complete
control over
the process
of making
Duotones

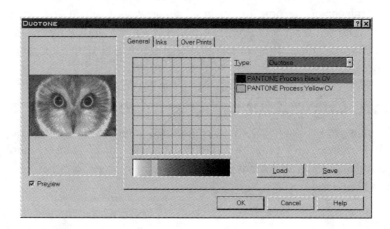

FIGURE 26-4

the grid from bottom left to top right, indicating that the grayscale value of each pixel comprising the image is presently identical to the value of the selected ink. To adjust the curve, click on a point along the curve and drag the node to the desired position. You can also click on an area of the grid; a node is instantly created and positioned.

The major options for the dialog box are described in the following sections. Not all of the options are described due to their complex nature relating to the duotone printing process. For information on options not described in this chapter, click on the option in question with the right mouse button. A message bar appears that says "What's this?" Click on the message box with the left mouse button and a very detailed explanation of the option will appear.

Type

This displays a drop-down list from which you can choose from one of four types of images, as follows.

MONOTONE   A monotone is a grayscale image that is printed with a single ink, which produces all the shadows, midtones, and highlights in the image. A monotone is like a conventional grayscale image.

DUOTONE   A duotone is a grayscale image that is printed with two inks, typically a black ink and a colored ink. The black ink is applied to shadow areas and the colored ink (usually a Pantone color, and sometimes CMYK process inks) to midtone and highlight areas. This produces a colored tint on the black and white image, which is effective in establishing a warm or cool effect, depending on the colored ink.

TRITONE   A tritone is a grayscale image that is printed with three inks. The advantage of either Tritones or Quadtones for general printing is limited.

QUADTONE   A quadtone is a grayscale image that is printed with four inks.

Ink Display

The display to the right of the grid displays the currently selected ink colors. The default ink used in a duotone is a Pantone Process color. To select a different color than the one shown, double-click the ink and the Select Color dialog box opens where you can select a new color.

When creating duotones, tritones, and quadtones, prioritize your inks in order from the darkest at the top to the lightest at the bottom of this display. Because Corel

26

PHOTO-PAINT prints inks in the order they appear in the dialog box, the inks will print from the darkest to the lightest. This ensures rich highlights and shadows and a uniform color range.

Load/Save Buttons

The functionality of the Load and Save buttons depends on the duotone property sheet currently selected. When the General Tab is selected, the Load button opens the Load Duotone File dialog box, where you access duotone (CPD) files. The Save button allows you to save custom CPD files. When the Inks Tab is selected, the Load button opens the Load Ink File dialog box, where you access ink (CIK) files; the Save button allows you to save custom settings.

 IP: *To convert an image to a duotone, it must first be in grayscale format.*

Converting an Image into a Duotone

Here are the basic steps involved in converting an image into a duotone. The same procedure applies to converting them to tritones and quadtones.

1. Click Image, Convert To, Duotone.

2. In the Type list box, click Duotone.

3. To choose different colors for the duotone than those displayed, double-click on a color's icon and select a different color from the dialog box.

4. Repeat Step 3 to choose a second color if desired.

5. Click the Inks tab and adjust the duotone curve for each ink. By moving the curve, you can adjust how much color is applied to the highlights, midtones, and shadows in the image. Having the Preview option checked displays the changes immediately.

6. If you want to specify how the overprint colors display onscreen, click the Over Prints tab, click Edit, and adjust the settings.

7. Enable the Preview check box to see what the image will look like.

8. Click OK. The image displays as a duotone.

Let's get on to another Corel PHOTO-PAINT color feature—the Color Mask roll-up.

The Color Mask

The Color Mask operates in a manner similar to the Magic Wand Mask tool. The Color Mask that is applied to the image is created by Corel PHOTO-PAINT based on user-selected colors. The colors are selected using the color picker (eyedropper) in the Color Mask roll-up. The selected colors can be either modified or protected. Doesn't sound like a tool that would serve much purpose, right? However, once you get comfortable with using the Color Mask, you will save yourself literally hours of time in retouching and re-creating photographic images.

Simply put, the Color Mask creates a mask based on the colors in an image. For example, if the color red is selected, any pixel in the image that contains red will be masked. Unlike the Magic Wand Mask tool, the Color Mask affects all colors within an image, not just those that are attached to it. The Color Mask is independent of the regular mask and both masks can exist on the image simultaneously. The Color Mask roll-up can also be used to create regular masks.

The strength of the Color Mask is its ability to either protect or allow modification of groups of colors that define an area. Below is a photograph from the Corel PHOTO-PAINT 6 CD. The tree branch and fruit look great, but the background is lacking.

We could use the Magic Wand Mask tool and make a mask to isolate the sky from the rest of the image. The problem with this approach is that the sky is visible in many spots throughout the leaves. The Magic Wand tool, if you recall, works with similar colors that are contiguous (connected to each other). To make a mask for the fruit and branches with the Magic Wand would require individually selecting a lot of little spots and including them in a mask. It would take a long time. With the Color Mask roll-up, I was able to quickly mask all of the background in only a few minutes. After creating a regular mask with the roll-up, I then used the Paste from File command to place a different photograph to use as a new background on the image. All that remained was to select Clip Object to Mask from the Object menu. The result is shown below. Just as a note: although the finished image looks cluttered in grayscale, it looks fine in color.

This is only one use of the Color Mask. There are several other uses, which we will discuss and learn later in this chapter.

The Color Mask Roll-Up

The Color Mask roll-up is opened by depressing CTRL-F5 or selecting Roll-ups in the View menu and picking the Color Mask roll-up from the drop-down list. I will be honest with you—when I first opened the Color Mask roll-up, my first instinct was to close it again. I would have never used it again if it hadn't been for the encouragement of the Corel PHOTO-PAINT development team, who assured me that once I got the hang of the thing, I would use it all the time. They were right. While it looks like a numerical nightmare, once you understand it, it won't be nearly as intimidating. The Color Mask roll-up is shown on the next page.

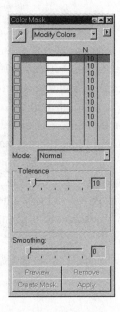

Modify/Protect Color Mode Selection

The Color Mask roll-up is divided into several sections. On the top is the mode selection area. There are two modes: Modify Selected Colors and Protect Selected Colors. The name of the first mode, Modify Selected Colors, might be misunderstood. The Color Mask is just that, a mask. A mask does not modify anything. Its function is to allow the modification of selected colors. Anything selected by the mask in this mode can be modified; anything not selected cannot have any effects applied to it. Clear?

Modify Selected Colors isolates the selected color(s) so that any changes applied affect only the selected color(s).

The Protect Selected Colors mode is the inverse of Modify Selected Colors. It protects the selected color(s) so that the changes affect only the colors that are not selected.

The Eyedropper Button

To the left of the mode selection area is an Eyedropper button. Clicking this button turns the cursor into an eyedropper which is used to select colors from an image or color palette and to fill the color swatches with the selected color. The colors selected are the ones that will be included in the Color Mask.

26

Color Controls

Below the Mode drop-down list are several columns (how many columns depends on the color mode that is selected) and 10 rows. Each row of selected color or range of colors has three parts: On, Color Swatch, and a Tolerance value. The check boxes (left) turn the protection mode or modification mode for specific colors on or off. When color protection or modification is enabled, there is a check mark in the box. The color swatches in the middle display each color selected from the image or a color palette that will be masked in the image. The numeric value(s) on the right represents the color value(s) for each color according to the color mode selected in the Mode drop-down list box. The numbers entered in the boxes control the range. Higher values create a greater range of color; lower values create a smaller range of color.

Now, let's discuss Tolerance.

The Tolerance Slider

At this point we could go into a long-winded explanation of color models, which would leave you more confused than ever. Instead, let me oversimplify a few concepts for the sake of clarity. (So if you are a color expert, don't send me letters. OK?)

The Color Tolerance values represent color ranges using the selected color as a starting point. This works as follows:

The maximum number of shades of a selected color that can exist is 256. This means the largest value that can be entered is 255. (In the computer world, 0 is a number, so 0 through 255 represents a total of 256.) If we select a color and enter 255 in the Tolerance column, we will have selected every pixel in the image. A small Tolerance number indicates a narrow range of colors centered around the selected color. A large Tolerance number indicates a wide range of colors centered around the selected color. A maximum of 10 color ranges can be masked. A Color Mask can be used in conjunction with other masks to allow even further fine-tuning of the color ranges.

This last point is important. If you are selecting a range of colors, many times you will find that some of the colors that you want to include also exist in an area you want excluded. To accomplish this, make the Color Mask as specific as possible (many colors/narrow range, i.e., small numbers). After you have applied the Color Mask, use the masking tools to isolate further the areas of the image you want modified or protected.

The Smoothing Slider

The Smoothing slider evens out differences in adjacent pixels by forming a smooth edge transition between a newly created mask and the background image. Higher values produce more pronounced smoothing. A large Smoothing value will cause the Color Mask not to follow the selected color pixels at the points where they form ragged edges.

The Mode Selector

The Mode Selector displays a drop-down list of tolerance modes. Each mode lets you choose a method for defining the range of colors that will be used in a color mask. There are five options:

▶ **Normal**   This is the default mode and its election values are determined by the composite color value of each pixel.

▶ **Hue**   Selecting Hue causes Corel PHOTO-PAINT to only examine the Hue (color) component of each pixel when determining whether or not to include it in a Color Mask. The other values (Saturation and Brightness) are ignored.

▶ **Saturation**   Like Hue mode except Corel PHOTO-PAINT only evaluates Saturation (the amount of color in a pixel). The other values (Hue and Brightness) are ignored.

▶ **Brightness**   Same as above except only Brightness is evaluated and Hue and Saturation values are ignored.

▶ **HSB**   Similar to Normal mode except the Tolerance of each component—Hue, Saturation, and Brightness—can be set individually.

The ability to use different color evaluation modes offers a great deal of flexibility to the Color Mask roll-up.

Color Mask Flyout Menu

Located in the upper-right corner of the roll-up is the Color Mask flyout. Clicking the right-arrow button opens the flyout menu, which provides the following options:

▶ **Open Color Masks**   Selecting this option displays the Open dialog box. From this dialog box you can select an existing Color Mask, which will have a CMK extension.

26

▶ **Save Color Masks**   This is used to save an existing color mask. Selecting it opens the Save As dialog box where you can save the mask. This is a very important feature as it allows you to modify a color mask without having to rebuild what could be a very complex color setting each time.

▶ **Reset Color Mask**   Selecting this option clears all of the colors and resets the Color Mask to its default mode.

▶ **Edit Color**   This opens the Select Color dialog box. From here you can specify the exact color that you want to replace. From a practical standpoint, it serves very little purpose unless you are looking for a specific color, like Pantone 1166.

Preview Mask Button

The Preview Mask button displays a preview of the mask. Colors that are protected or modified are displayed. The color of the preview mask is selected in the Advanced section of the Option dialog box located in the Tools menu. When the Preview Mask is on the screen, any keyboard or mouse action clears it. However, the action that clears it is lost. Remember this if you can't figure out why the mask did not apply or why something didn't happen when you clicked it. (I mention this because it has taken me some time to get used to it.)

The Apply Button

Clicking the Apply button applies the Color Mask, covering the entire image. Because it is a mask, you cannot see any change in the image after it is applied. When a Color Mask has been applied, an icon appears in the lower-right portion of the status bar of the Main screen. Masks are not additive. When the Apply button is depressed, any existing Color Mask is wiped out.

The Create Mask Button

When the Create Mask button is clicked the area currently selected by the Color Mask is made into a regular mask. Once it is a regular mask, it can be modified with the mask tools or commands under the Mask menu.

The Remove Button

This button removes a currently applied Color Mask. It is not available if a Color Mask has not been applied. This is the only way to remove a color mask from an image.

Using the Color Mask Roll-Up

Finally, right? Here is the general procedure, plus commentary, for using the Color Mask roll-up.

▶ Choose Color Mask roll-up from the mask menu or press CTRL-F5.

▶ Choose either Modify Selected Colors (to mask the colors) or Protect Colors (to mask everything but the selected colors) mode from the drop-down list box.

▶ Click the Eyedropper button. The cursor changes to the Eyedropper tool. Select the desired color to be masked in the image by clicking on it with the eyedropper cursor. The point at the tip of the eyedropper is where the color pixel is selected. As the cursor is moved around, the color under the cursor is displayed within the first color swatch in the column. When you click the left mouse button on the color in the image the Color box is checked and the next row is highlighted. Each time you click on a color in the image, that color is added to the current row and the next row is highlighted. When you reach the bottom it automatically jumps to the top row.

▶ Either accept the default Tolerance settings or enter a number or drag the Tolerance slider to set the tolerance. Higher values allow for greater range (more shades) of the selected color; lower values narrow the range (the number of shades).

▶ Click Preview Mask to view the mask. The mask color appears red (by default) wherever the colors fall within the ranges of all the selected colors. If you have a lot of the Preview color in the image, go into the Advance Preferences section of the Options dialog box under the Tools menu and change the Preview color (called Mask tint) to one that does not blend easily into the image.

26

IP: *When you see the Preview Mask on the screen, make note of where the mask does not cover the desired area. There are two methods to increase the coverage. Either increase the range of the color(s) near the area, or select an additional color (if you have another color button available). The disadvantage of increasing the range is that the color may spread into parts of the image you did not want included. If some of your Preview Mask is covering a part of your image that you do not want masked, you can reduce the Tolerance value of the color nearest to the area. If that does not work, then turn off the color and select several similar colors with narrow ranges. This should do the trick. If not, you can always use the mask tools and place a mask over the area (although this is the least desirable solution).*

► To apply the Color Mask, click on the Apply button. The only visual indication you have that the mask has been applied is that the Color Mask icon appears in the status bar of the Main screen. The Color Mask will remain until one of the following occurs: 1) the Remove button is clicked, obviously; 2) the Create Mask button is clicked; 3) the Color Mask is converted to a regular mask and the original Color Mask is lost; or 4) the File is closed. Unlike regular masks the Color Masks cannot be saved with an image.

Exploring the
Painting and Drawing
Tools

27

Here you will explore Corel PHOTO-PAINT's drawing and painting tools, some of which you have seen in other chapters. Corel PHOTO-PAINT 6 is not classified as a "natural-media" paint program—one designed to faithfully reproduce the effect of charcoal, oils, and so on. Programs that are natural media include Fractal Design's Painter and Fauve Matisse. Although Corel PHOTO-PAINT is not a natural-media program, it does have excellent drawing and painting tools that provide the user with the ability to enhance existing images or create original images and effects. The brushes in Corel PHOTO-PAINT 6 have been improved in both their selection and their effect.

Two Different Worlds

Painting and drawing tools are used to accomplish different tasks. The brush (painting) tools are used most often to:

- ► Enhance images by adding shadows and highlights.
- ► Create masks using the Brush Mask tool.
- ► Touch up mistakes.
- ► They can also be used to create images or add special effects to existing images. The Tool Settings roll-up is used to control the large selection of settings available with each brush tool.

The drawing tools enable you to create lines, curves, ellipses, rectangles, and polygons.

Painting Tools

One of the first surprises I had when I first opened Corel PHOTO-PAINT 6 was that the flyout for the brushes had disappeared. Next, I had to jump between the Brush Settings roll-up and the Tool Settings roll-up to control the brushes. Fortunately for all of us, about midway through the beta cycle our friends in Ottawa consolidated all of the brush functions into the Tool Settings roll-up.

One of the first changes you will notice is that the brush flyout is gone. Brush selection is now made from the Tool Settings roll-up.

The Brush tools paint an area characteristic of the type of brush selected using the current Paint color. Remember that all brushes replace (not cover) pixels with the currently selected Paint (foreground) color. To select a brush tool, you must double-click the Paint Tool button in the Toolbox. This action opens the Tool Settings roll-up. Select the desired brush tool from the buttons near the top of the roll-up. The following descriptions apply to all of the brush tools unless otherwise noted.

Exploring the Tool Setting Roll-Up for Brushes

Double-click the Brush tool in the Toolbox and you will open the Tool Settings roll-up as shown in the illustration below. The roll-up is divided into three Tabs:

► Brush Selection and Control

► Brush Texture, Watercolors, and Brush stroke

► Dab and Color variation

These three tabs contain different brush settings that relate to the way the brush operates. While the great number of settings might seem a little intimidating at first sight, it isn't difficult once you understand how they affect the brushes.

 IP: *Don't jump right into the Tool Settings roll-up and start changing the settings. Most of the time you do not need to modify brush texture or brush variation settings. The preset styles are sufficient to satisfy most requirements.*

27

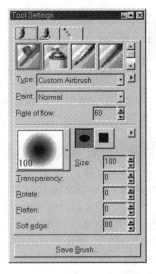

Brush Selection

Across the top of the roll-up is a row of four icons revealing the four brushes of the 15 that can be selected. The arrows on the right side of the brush selection icons can be a little confusing. There are up-down arrows, but the brush selection icons move left to right. Each icon represents a group of brush styles. For example, the Chalk icon, when selected, can be used as either Custom Chalk, Big Soft Chalk, Square Chalk, or Custom, depending on the style chosen. To select a brush, simply click on the icon. The brush attributes reflect the brush selection.

Selecting brushes is a two-step process. First, click on the brush icon that you want. Second, click the down arrow to the right of the Name box and pick the style of brush you want from the list of names that appears. Some brushes have many styles to choose from, while others only have a few. The styles are really presets. The difference between Chalk and Big Soft Chalk is found in the different settings that are saved as Styles with each one. More on Styles later when you learn how to save a brush setting.

Brush Tool Control

All of the brushes are referred to as brush tools or just brushes. This can get confusing since one of the brush tools is called a spray can. Another term that is used is the

Nib. In Corel PHOTO-PAINT, the nib is the end of the brush that applies color to images. In this section we will be describing the controls that are common to all of the brush tools.

The first tab of the roll-up, Brush Control Tab, provides control over the brush shape, size, and transparency of the paint. Here is how the settings work.

Type

This setting contains all of the saved styles for the selected brush. Many of these preset styles have names that indicate their function. Examples include Power Sprayer, Chalk, Custom, and so on.

Reset Selection

The arrow (pointing outward) to the right of the Name box opens a menu that allows you to reset the brushes to their default values. You can reset a single brush, the brush Type, or all the brush Types. This is really handy when you have been making all kinds of changes to the brushes and need to return them to their original values.

Paint

This setting determines the way the paint pixels are applied to the image. The Merge modes first appeared at the bottom of the Objects/Layers roll-up in the first maintenance release of Corel PHOTO-PAINT 5. For all of the unique photographic effects that are possible with Corel PHOTO-PAINT, the potential of Merge modes goes generally untapped. The Merge mode is the method by which the paint combines with the colors in another image. Normally, when you apply color to an object or the background, the applied color(s) simply replaces the original colors in the image. Corel PHOTO-PAINT Merge modes give you an alternative to just replacing colors. Each of the 17 modes (20 in color) provide different ways to merge the two color components mathematically, the description of which would be confusing. The names of the Merge modes actually define what actions are. For example, choosing the Subtract Merge mode takes the color value of the Paint color and subtracts it from the color value of each pixel to which it is being applied to produce a darker resultant color. So how can you determine what the result will be of each mode? Practice. After using them for a while, you can more or less predict what the Merge modes will do.

Rate of Flow

The adjustment below the Paint is only active when the Airbrush or Spraycan tool is active. The Rate of Flow setting controls the paint repetition rate. For example, the Air Brush paint tool will apply more paint as the rate of flow increases. A low value will produce a faint brush stroke; a high value will produce a heavy, dark brush stroke.

Shape Buttons

The Shape buttons are used to select the shape of the brush. The two available shapes are Round and Square. When you change the shape of the nib from square to round or vice versa, the values of the nib size, nib transparency, and so on do not change.

Nib Preview and Brush Selection

In addition to the two shape buttons, clicking on the preview window opens a partial visual display of a number of nib types, which are variations on the settings of the general tool. In Corel PHOTO-PAINT 5, these are called Custom Brushes. The preview window to the left of the Shape selection buttons also displays a thumbnail of the current nib. As you make changes to the nib attributes using the roll-up options (size, flatness, rotate, and so on), the nib also changes in the preview window. If the Preview Window is chosen by clicking on it, an additional screen appears, showing a large selection of brush presets. Any custom nibs that are created by the user and saved will appear at the bottom of this display.

Create from Mask button

Located to the right of the two shape buttons, this button opens the Create From Mask flyout menu. With a mask in your image, clicking Create From Mask opens the Create a Custom Brush dialog box where you create a new, custom nib using the shape of any mask made with a mask tool.

Size

This allows adjustment of Round or Square paintbrush sizes from 1 to 100 pixels. The actual size of brush nib selected is shown in the preview box. If the nib is too large to appear at its actual size in the preview window, it is assigned a numeric value as an indication of its exact size. The Preview Window shows the size and shape of the selected nib. The red text in the corner indicates the size of the nib in pixels.

Transparency

This sets the level of transparency of the brush stroke. It is similar to adjusting the amount of water mixed with watercolors. The higher the setting, the more transparent the brush stroke. At a very high setting, the color acts more like a tint. A setting of 0 has no transparency, whereas a setting of 99 makes the brush stroke invisible regardless of any other settings.

Rotate

This rotates the Round or Square brush nib by the amount entered. You can see the effect of the rotating in the Preview Window as the change is being applied. Value is in degrees, up to a maximum of 360. Obviously, rotating a Round nib serves no purpose, but rotating a flattened Round nib does.

Flatten

The Flatten slider controls the height of the Round and Square brush nibs. Values are in percentage of height. You can see the effect of the flattening in the Preview Window as the change is being applied.

Soft Edge

This sets the edges of the brush nib to either soft, hard, or in between. Soft edges make the brush stroke the least dense at the edges; hard edges are dense up to the edge, with little to no softening, depending on the nib size and other brush settings. The Preview Window displays the edge selected. The higher the value, the greater the softness of the edges. I have shown several settings in Figure 27-1.

Save Brush

This saves a brush setting using a style name in the Name box. Clicking this button opens the Save Type As dialog box, where you can assign a name for the new, custom brush type. Click OK. The new brush type is immediately displayed in the Name drop-down list box.

That covers the most used portion of the Tool Settings roll-up. Now, before we look at the rest of the brushes, we need to explore the other two tabs of the Tool Settings roll-up.

27

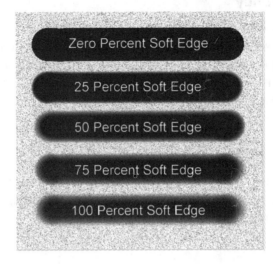

The effects of different settings of the Soft Edge value

FIGURE 27-1

Brush Tool Dab and Color Variation Tab

This part of the roll-up is the tab on the far right—not the middle tab. Because it is the second most important part of the roll-up, we are looking at it next. It is divided into two parts, Dab Variation and Color Variation, as shown in the following illustration.

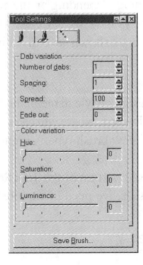

Dab Variation

This section contains the controls for spacing, spread, fade-out, and number of dabs applied when any of the brush tools are applied. These value settings can have a significant effect on the speed with which the brush stroke is applied. If the settings are not adjusted for optimum performance the brush tool will not move on the image in real time, but rather will drag behind the cursor.

Number of Dabs

This sets the number of dabs created in brush strokes. For example, if the value is set to 25 (the maximum) and I click the cursor on the image once, the currently selected brush stroke will be applied (dabbed) 25 times. It is recommended that you keep the number of dabs low unless you are working to achieve a special effect.

Spacing (1-999)

This setting determines the distance, in pixels, between applications of the brush. To create a brush stroke, the pointing device draws a line across the image. At a frequency determined by the Spacing setting, the brush is applied to the line. For example, if a brush stroke is made with a setting of 5 (pixels), Corel PHOTO-PAINT will produce the selected brush on the image area at a spacing of every 5 pixels. While it may seem that a setting of 1 would be desired, a lower setting slows down the generation of the brush stroke considerably. It can be really slow on some systems. When a large brush is being used, the setting can be larger (and this is recommended) because of the overlap caused by the larger brush.

Spread (1-999)

This sets the distance between individual brush strokes. Higher values make the distance between brush strokes greater. The Paint Brush style Light Turin is a good example of the use of the Spread setting. Light Turin is set with a Spread setting of 100 (maximum) and a Spacing of 1. This means that when a brush stroke is applied, the brush pattern is repeated at 1-pixel intervals (Spacing) and the center of each repeating brush stroke can be up to a maximum of 100 (pixels) offset from the center of the brush stroke. In the following example I applied the first brush stroke at the intersection of the 0,0 and the ending brush stroke at the 0,275 point. Notice that the Spread setting of 100 caused the brush to be applied in a 50-pixel radius (half of 100). The application actually went outside of the 50-pixel radius because the Spread setting is applied to the center of the brush.

27

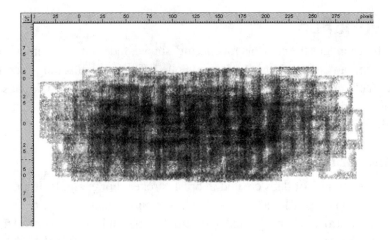

Fade Out

By adjusting the rate, this setting determines the length of the brush stroke before it fades entirely. This is similar to adjusting the pressure of the brush against the canvas as the paint is applied. The greater the Fade Out value, the more fade-out is applied and the quicker the fade-out of the brush stroke occurs. As the Fade Out value decreases, the amount of fade-out applied to the brush stroke diminishes; a value of 0 turns off the Fade Out function completely, as shown in Figure 27-2.

Fade Out works by counting the number of brush applications to determine when to begin applying the gradual fade-out function. This is important for the following reason: Spacing, the next parameter, controls the distance between brush applications. Increasing spacing between brush applications increases the distance that the brush stroke will go before Fade Out begins.

The Color Variation section of the roll-up is mainly used with the Artistic Brush tools. Therefore, we will discuss them in the section "The Artistic Brush Tools" later in this chapter. Now, let's look at the middle tab of the Tool Settings roll-up.

Exploring Brush Texture, Watercolors, and Brush Stroke

Up until now we have been looking at controls that determine the size and stroke attributes of the brush tools. The middle tab, shown in the following illustration, contains the settings that control how the pixels are laid down in the image.

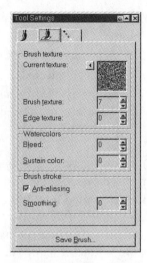

The Brush Texture Section

The Brush Texture section contains the controls that can be used to load different textures and adjust the amount of texture applied by the brush. In Corel PHOTO-PAINT, texture is the grainy surface quality produced by a brush. In the

The effects of different fade settings on one of the brush tools

FIGURE 27-2

27

upper-right corner is a thumbnail representation of the currently selected texture. To its left is a small left-arrow button. Clicking the button opens the Texture Flyout menu, where you can load different textures or reset textures to their default settings as determined by the Brush tool and type selected.

The Brush Texture (0-100) setting is used to increase the amount of texture applied to the brush stroke. Making it a larger value will make the effect more coarse. The coarser textures simulate natural-media brushes. This natural-media quality is also referred to as painterly effects.

The Edge texture (0-100) setting controls the amount of texturing along the edges of a brush. As the setting increases, the edge of the brush stroke becomes more ragged.

In the following image I have painted four different brush strokes to show the effect of different Brush texture and Edge Texture settings. Letter A is the Medium Rub type. It has a Brush texture/Edge texture setting of 30/5. Letter B is the Dry Blend Pastel type with a texture setting of 82/0. The next type shown as line C is Big Soft Chalk style. Its texture setting is 75/10. The last example shown as stroke D is Light Rub, which has the highest Brush Texture value of 95 and Edge texture setting of zero.

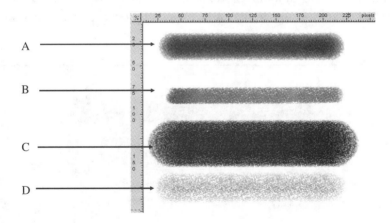

Watercolors Section

This section contains two controls that operate synergistically.

Bleed (0-100)

The Bleed setting controls the amount of color diffusion when two or more colors are combined (as when red paint, for example, contacts blue). Bleed is especially useful when working with watercolors, where interesting effects may be achieved by blending two or more colors together.

Sustain color (0-100)

The Sustain Color control works in tandem with the Bleed control. The Bleed control works in tandem with the Transparency control on the first tab of the Tool Settings roll-up. Consequently, you must enter a Bleed and Transparency value in the respective boxes before entering a Sustain Color value and beginning painting.

Sustain Color retains brush paint color when painting over a colored background while applying bleed to the brush. Typically, using Bleed, the brush will eventually (during the course of an extended brush stroke) run out of paint and simply smear the background/image color with the brush. With Sustain Color set to any value except zero, traces of the paint color remain throughout the brush stroke.

Brush Stroke Section

This section contains one adjustable and one nonadjustable setting.

Anti-aliasing

The Anti-aliasing check box, when enabled, removes jagged edges from the brush stroke by adding duplicated pixels where the brush stroke contacts the background image.

Smoothing (0-25)

The smoothing setting controls the amount of brush stroke smoothing. Smoothing helps to create a more flowing and fluid paint stroke by smoothing out the jagged and/or sharp angles while you paint. Increasing this setting tends to slow down the brush tools noticeably.

Next you will learn about selecting colors and controlling where the brush goes.

The Paint Brush Tool

This is the original brush tool. The Paint Brush tool is selected by clicking on its icon button. There are 18 different styles of brushes available for the Paint brush tool. In Figure 27-3, I have shown a sampling of the different Paint Brush styles that are available. The Paint Brush tool paints an area in the current paint color. Remember that the Paint Brush works by replacing (not covering) the pixels with

27

A sampling
of the
different
Paint Brush
styles

FIGURE 27-3

the currently selected Paint (foreground) color. Before looking at the other brushes, let's explore several areas pertaining to Brush tool operation—which leads to the next topic, selecting brush colors.

Selecting Brush Tool Color

There are so many ways to pick out a color for the Brush tools, it gets confusing. Basically, you can pick a color from the onscreen palette, use the eyedropper and select a color from an existing image, or make your own color with the Color roll-up.

The Quick Way to Get a Different Color

Brush tool color can be quickly selected by placing the brush over the desired color well in the onscreen palette and clicking the left mouse button.

Getting a Color from an Image

Many times you need to select a color from an existing image. It doesn't even have to be the image you are working on, just an open image. To get color from an existing image, use the eyedropper tool. To pick a color:

► Select the Eyedropper tool from the Toolbox. The cursor changes to an eyedropper.

► Place the eyedropper over the desired color.

▶ Click the left mouse button to make the color under the cursor the brush color.

 IP: *A quick way to pick a color from the image is to hold down the E key. This action opens the Eyedropper tool for as long as the E key is held down.*

When All Else Fails...

Sometimes the color you want is not on the short onscreen palette or in an open image. At that point you need to "roll your own" color through the Color roll-up or the Paint Color. This is like going from Los Angeles to Dallas via Honolulu—in other words, a very roundabout approach. The Color roll-up is opened by double-clicking the Eyedropper tool in the Toolbox or by using the keyboard combination CTRL-F2. You can also open the Paint Color dialog box, by double-clicking the square displaying the paint (foreground) color in the status bar. The operation of the Color roll-up and the Paint Color dialog box is identical to the Uniform Fill dialog box that is explored in Chapter 25.

Controlling Where the Brush Goes

There are several built-in controls for use with the Brush tools that govern how and where they operate.

Controlling Vertical and Horizontal Movement

Using the CTRL key constrains the application of the brush tools to a vertical or horizontal direction. The constraint methodology used by Corel PHOTO-PAINT is unique—so much so that you may not think at first that it is working. In other programs, most horizontal or vertical constraint keys keep the cursor from moving outside of a fixed line. In those programs you can move the mouse anywhere you want, but the cursor is going to stay right on that line. With Corel PHOTO-PAINT, the constrain key does not constrain cursor movement—it only controls where the effect is applied. For example, if the brush width is set to 5 pixels, and we begin to draw a line with the CTRL key held down, Corel PHOTO-PAINT internally makes a 5-point-wide horizontal mask (invisible) across the page at the point where the line was started. As long as you hold down the CTRL key, the cursor can be moved anywhere around the image area, but the paint color will only be applied in that

27

5-point-wide horizontal line. The constraint applied with the CTRL key does not prevent the brush from moving outside of either the vertical or horizontal direction—it only prevents it from having an effect outside of the chosen direction.

Changing Direction

Many times when applying a brush stroke on a straight line, you need to change directions. Pressing the SHIFT key changes the direction of constraint. This means if you begin a horizontal line with the CTRL key depressed and then at some point hold down the SHIFT key, you will begin to apply an effect to a vertical line as long as the SHIFT key is held down. Release the SHIFT key and you will return to a horizontal line at the point you released it. If you hold down more than 11 keys at the same time, you have too many fingers. See a doctor.

IP: *When using the CTRL-activated constrain key multiple times, remember to first click the left mouse button on the place you wish to begin. If you hold down the CTRL key first, the brush will constrain in the direction of the last constrained line.*

Automatic Brushstroke Application

Here is my favorite. It is new with the Corel PHOTO-PAINT 6 release. I can make Corel PHOTO-PAINT automatically apply the currently selected brush tool by clicking it at a starting point on the image and then, while holding down the ALT key, clicking at the point where I want the stroke to finish. The result is a straight brush stroke between the two points. If you click at a third point while still holding down the ALT key, another brush stroke will be laid down connecting the second to the third. These point-to-point brush strokes will continue as long as you hold down the ALT key when you click the next point.

This is a great feature for placing shadows on the edges of objects or making highlights. You can also use it to create borders using unique brushes.

Constraining the Stars ... by Example

Selecting a custom brush and using the constrain key, it was possible to create the illustration shown next in just a few minutes. The texture on the stars comes from using a high brush texture setting (explained later in this chapter). I started by placing a star in the upper-left corner, and then holding down the CTRL key, dragging the brush to the right. By using a value of spacing that equaled the size of the brush, all of the stars are equidistant from each other. When I reached the upper-right side of the image, I depressed the SHIFT key (while continuing to hold down the CTRL key) and dragged the brush down. Upon reaching the lower-right corner, I released the SHIFT key and dragged the brush left. You get the idea. Selecting a different custom brush, I repeated the same procedure inside of the first row of stars. By doing the entire row in a single pass, if I didn't like the results, I could quickly Undo it with a single command.

Spacing and Fading Revisited

Figure 27-4 was created to demonstrate the relationship between values of Spacing and Fade Out. Notice that even though the Fade Out setting remained constant, the fade changed with the different Spacing settings. Remember that the fade "counts" the number of times a brush is applied and begins to fade based on that count. When the Spacing setting is smaller, there is a greater number of brush applications in the stroke; therefore, the fade appears more quickly.

You may have thought that Spacing was one of those settings that a graphics engineer came up with on a cold Ottawa winter evening with nothing else to do. Now you know that there are a lot of things that can be done with this control. Almost all of it has to do with custom brushes, which happens to be the next subject.

IP: *Spacing values affect the Fade Out. Increases in Spacing increase the distance before Fade Out occurs.*

27

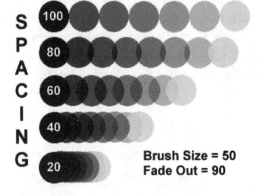

The
relationship
between
different
Fade Out
and Spacing
values

FIGURE 27-4

Creating Your Own Brushes

With Corel PHOTO-PAINT, you can create your own brushes. The procedure to make a brush is very simple. Mask the portion of the image that you want to use for a brush nib. Click the button to the right of the two shape buttons on the first tab in the Tool Settings roll-up, which opens the Create From Mask flyout. Click Create From Mask to open the Create a Custom Brush dialog box as shown here.

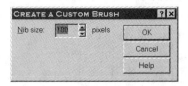

The initial Nib size in the Create a Custom Brush dialog box will either be the longest of the two dimensions (height or width) or 100 pixels, whichever is greater. If the area being masked is larger than 100 pixels, it will be scaled proportionately so that the longest dimension is 100 pixels. The value of the nib can be made smaller in the dialog box as well. Reducing the Nib size will cause the brush to be scaled proportionately to the smaller size. All color images being used for brush nibs are converted to grayscale. Any feathering on the mask is translated into the grayscale portion of the brush. Clicking the OK button will cause the new brush to appear in the preview window of the Tool Settings roll-up. It is not saved at this point.

Saving New Brushes

To save a custom brush, click on the Save Brush button at the bottom of the Tool Settings roll-up. This opens the Save Type As dialog box, where you assign a name for the new, custom brush type. Click OK. The new type is immediately displayed in the Type drop-down list box.

Deleting Brushes

To delete a brush type, choose the brush type to be deleted by selecting its Name in the drop-down list and click on the right-arrow button to the right of the Type list. Choose Delete Brush from the flyout menu that appears. When you click the Delete Brush button, you receive a warning message asking if you want to delete the brush type.

Now let's look at a few of the other brushes that are available in Corel PHOTO-PAINT 6. This will not be a detailed description of each Brush tool, but rather a discussion of the features of a few specific Brushes.

The Airbrush and the Spray Can Brush Tools

The Airbrush and the Spray Can Brush tools are nearly identical in Corel PHOTO-PAINT 5. In Corel PHOTO-PAINT 6, there is a substantial difference between the two. Unlike the smooth pattern that comes out of an airbrush, the Spray Can pattern more closely resembles the uneven pattern from a can of spray paint. The Airbrush and Spray Can Brush tools spray the current Paint (foreground) color like an airbrush/spray can—the center of the spray has more concentrated color, and the color lessens in intensity as it gets near the edge of the tool shape. The size, shape, and qualities of the Airbrush and Spray Can tools are set from the Tool Settings roll-up as discussed earlier. The one additional setting these Brush tools have is Rate of Flow.

Rate of Flow

This is the one unique setting for these two Brush tools. This setting determines the speed at which the color is placed. In effect, these tools act like real air brushes and spray cans. With the rate of flow set to 1, the color flows slowly; therefore, the tool must be held at the same position for a longer period of time to achieve a denser pattern. At a rate of 100 (maximum), the effect is applied so fast it almost acts like the Paintbrush tool.

Using the Airbrush and Spray Can Tools

The Airbrush tool is one of the best tools for applying minor color touch-up to an image. You also can't beat it for making shadows behind an image.

There are a few tricks to using these tools effectively. First, be patient. Start off using a low setting for Rate of Flow. It will seem like the paint doesn't go on fast enough at first, but remember that you can go back over an area several times and apply more. And unlike the real thing, this paint will not run if you put on too much of it.

 IP: *Remember that these brushes work like real airbrushes and spray cans; that is, the longer you remain over a spot, the denser the paint applied under the cursor becomes. This is unlike any of the other brushes.*

The Artistic Brush Tools

The Artistic Brush tools produce brush strokes that appear like those used in several art styles such as Impressionist and Pointillist. At times, I think the real purpose of the Artistic Brush tools is to place a serious load on your CPU, giving you extra time to write friends, catch up on your reading, and feed the goldfish while the CPU is sweating its brains out.

The brush stroke incorporates a selected number of lines in colors that are similar to each other. For example, it turns a single shade of red into eight shades of red. The size, shape, and qualities of the Artistic Brush tools are set in the Tool Settings roll-up. In the previous discussion of the settings for the Tool Settings roll-up, the principal controls for these brushes, which are found in the Color Variance section on the third tab of the roll-up, were not mentioned. Let's look at them now.

Color Variation

This section controls how the various parts of the HSB color model will vary when applying Artistic brush strokes. This does not prevent the use of these controls with other brushes, it just means that they are used most often with the Artistic Brushes. The section has three variance controls, described in the following sections.

The Hue Slider (0-100)

This slider determines the variation of color in the brush based on the paint color. It controls the variation of color in the brush, or the Hue. Each Artistic brush style incorporates several colors. The H Variance determines the colors of the lines. For example, with a higher number, the colors can range from yellow, magenta, cyan, to violet. With a lower number, the color variation is reduced and ranges from pink, magenta, to violet. If you are working on a grayscale image, H Variance varies the shades of gray. (Don't forget that gray is a color.)

 IP: *Use this setting with caution. The default setting is 15, and when you take it to the maximum setting, you will have samples from just about every color in the rainbow.*

Saturation (0-100)

This sets the variation for the purity of the color. Purity is the number of colors used to mix a specific color. Lower values decrease the number of colors used in the mix; higher values increase the number of colors used to produce the selected colors. The greater the number of colors used to mix a color, the duller the final color looks.

 IP: *The default value of this setting is 15. That is a great setting. I recommend you leave it alone.*

Luminance (0-100)

This sets the variation of light colors to dark colors that are used in the brush. Higher values make the variation of light greater, giving a greater range of light-to-dark variation in the brush strokes. Confused? What it means in practice is that the greater the amount of light variance (which, in the HSL model, this brush is built on), the greater the differences in the colors themselves.

Applications for the Artistic Brush Tools

If you were expecting me to use this tool to paint a portrait, you were wrong. I have said this many times before, but I am going to repeat it: Don't be limited by the name of the brush or filter; just ask yourself what the brush or filter actually does. You might say that the Impressionism brush tool produces brush strokes that look like those used in impressionist art, and that would be technically correct. But what does this brush actually do to make the brush strokes? It creates duplicates of the original brush in random colors and locations. This answer suggests that there are other things that can be done with it besides imitating impressionist art. The following are several examples.

Making Wallpaper with the Impressionism Brush

This is simple.

1. Select the Artistic Brush by scrolling to and clicking its button.

2. From the Type drop-down list, select Pointillism.

3. Next, click in the Nib preview window and scroll down the selection of brush nibs until you see a nib that looks like a star. Don't select the sheriff's star in the center, pick the seven-pointed one that looks like a starfish. Click on it. Notice that the Type name changed to Custom Artistic.

4. Change the Paint color to a bright primary color like red or blue by clicking on the onscreen palette with the left mouse button.

5. Create a new image that is 24-bit color, 300 pixels by 300 pixels at 150 dpi. After the new image opens, hold down the left mouse button and drag the brush across the image. The brush is painting multicolored stars. Continue painting the stars until they look something like the following image. Yours will look better because they are in color.

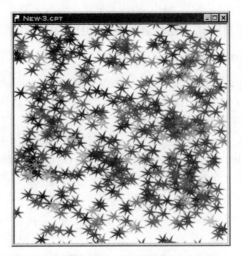

6. You're not done yet. Select 3D Effects in the Effect menu and choose Whirlpool. In the Whirlpool filter dialog box, choose the Super Warpo setting and click the OK button. It will take a few moments for this filter to process. When it is finished, you have a nice multicolored feathered background as shown below.

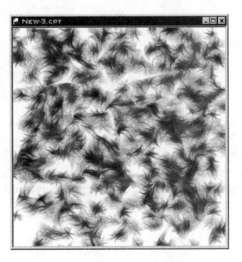

27

Another Artistic Brush Application

This exercise is even simpler. Let's first remove what we just made.

1. From the Mask menu, select All. When the image is masked, click the DEL key to remove the contents of the image area. From the Mask menu, select None to remove the mask.

2. Change the Brush nib again by clicking on the Brush nib preview window and selecting the five-petal flower. It is on the right side of the preview palette under the airplane.

3. Select the Circle Mask tool from the Toolbox and make a circle mask like the one shown below.

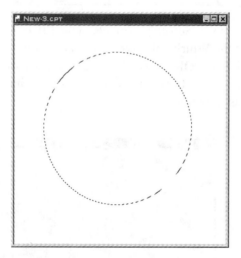

4. From the Mask menu, select Stroke Mask. When the Stroke Mask dialog box opens, select the Artistic Brush from the palette of Brushes and click the OK button. There you have it—an instant floral wreath as shown next.

Well, now you have an idea of what the brushes do and how they work. The best way to learn about them is to use them.

How to Set Up a Pressure-Sensitive Stylus

Until now we have been doing all of these operations with a mouse. The past few years have seen many new models of digitizer pads with pressure-sensitive styluses appear on the market. These new pads have small footprints (meaning they are small) and offer a variety of options. If you are not familiar with the stylus, it looks and handles like a pen. In most cases it is cordless. You move the stylus on a digitizer pad, which moves your cursor on the screen as if you were writing with a pen. The feature that has become so popular over the last few years is the pressure-sensitive aspect. As you increase pressure on the tip of the stylus by pressing it harder onto the pad, this pressure information is sent to Corel PHOTO-PAINT, where it controls one or more parameters of the selected brush.

While all of the features and exercises are designed for and have been done with a mouse, the stylus and pad offer advantages, especially when working with the brush tools.

Corel has incorporated a large number of options for setting up and using a stylus, which Corel calls a Pen. The Pen page of the Options dialog box, shown here, is found in the Tools menu. It is used to customize Corel PHOTO-PAINT to suit your working environment.

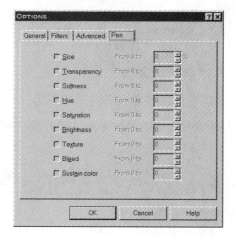

The Pen page lets you control the relationship between pen and tablet pressure/sensitivity and the effect caused when using different paint options. As you press down on a drawing tablet with a pen and cause the pressure to change, the paint effect changes. For example, if you set the Size option to From 0 to 10, as you apply pressure to the tablet, the nib widens (just as a paintbrush does if you apply more pressure to the stroke) by a maximum of 10 percent.

To set the pen up, you only need check all the options that you want to have affected by pressure information. You can get an explanation of what each option does by right-clicking on it. When the What's This message appears, click on it with the left mouse button and a brief description of the option and its action with the pen appears in a message box.

While experimentation is required here to properly adjust the stylus to suit your drawing style, I recommend starting with a basic setting of 40 for the Size option and seeing how you like it. I strongly suggest that you don't have more than one or two options selected simultaneously unless you are trying to achieve a specific painterly effect.

A

B

INDEX